The Opening of the Seventh Seal

THE OPENING OF THE SEVENTH SEAL

SANAT KUMARA ON THE PATH OF THE RUBY RAY

Elizabeth Clare Prophet

THE SUMMIT LIGHTHOUSE LIBRARY

"The Opening of the Seventh Seal" was originally published as *Pearls of Wisdom*, weekly letters from the ascended masters to their students around the world. Chapters 1–36 were published in the 1979 *Pearls of Wisdom*. In 1989 this series was published in book form as *Sanat Kumara on the Path of the Ruby Ray: The Opening of the Seventh Seal*. Chapter 37 was originally published in the 1999 *Pearls of Wisdom*.

THE OPENING OF THE SEVENTH SEAL
Sanat Kumara on the Path of the Ruby Ray
by Elizabeth Clare Prophet
Copyright © 2001 The Summit Lighthouse Library
All rights reserved

No part of this book may be reproduced, translated, or electronically stored, posted or transmitted, or used in any format or medium whatsoever without prior written permission, except by a reviewer who may quote brief passages in a review. For information, please contact:
The Summit Lighthouse Library
PO Box 5000, Corwin Springs, MT 59030-5000
Tel: 1-800-245-5445 or 406-848-9500
E-mail: tslinfo@tsl.org   Web site: www.tsl.org

Library of Congress Control Number: 2001090302
ISBN: 0-922729-68-3

THE SUMMIT LIGHTHOUSE LIBRARY®
The Summit Lighthouse Library is an imprint of Summit University Press.

Climb the Highest Mountain, Keepers of the Flame, *Pearls of Wisdom*, Science of the Spoken Word, Summit University, and Church Universal and Triumphant are trademarks registered in the U.S. Patent and Trademark Office and in other countries. All rights reserved

Cover design: Brad Davis. Interior design and production: Lynn Wilbert. Layout: Nancy Badten

Transferred to digital reprinting 2004

Printed in the United States of America

THE SUMMIT LIGHTHOUSE LIBRARY

*was established to publish the
Teachings of the Ascended Masters
as delivered to their messengers
Mark L. Prophet and
Elizabeth Clare Prophet.
These wisdom teachings,
released from the archives of the
Great White Brotherhood,
are for the new dispensation
of Aquarius.*

You call me Sanat Kumara, and you know me as the one who stood before the cosmic council known as the Council of the One Hundred and Forty and Four. You know me because you were witnesses to my plea made on behalf of the evolutions of earth who no longer knew the presence of the Lamb, who by disobedience were cut off from the living Guru. You know me as the one who volunteered to embody the threefold flame within the earth unto the evolutions evolving within the seven planes of being.

The Cosmic Council had decreed the dissolution of earth and her evolutions because the souls of her children no longer worshiped the Trinity in the threefold flame of Life burning upon the altar of the heart. Their attention fixed upon the outer manifestation, they had willfully abandoned the inner walk with God....

What was the requirement of the law for the saving of Terra? It was that one who should qualify as the embodied Guru, the Lamb, should be present in the physical octave to hold the balance and to keep the threefold flame of Life for and on behalf of every living soul....

I chose to be that one. I volunteered to be a flaming son of righteousness unto earth and her evolutions.

After considerable deliberation, the Cosmic Council and the Nameless One gave their approval of my petition, and the dispensation for a new divine plan for earth and her evolutions came into being....

Thus I knelt before the great white throne of the Nameless One and he said unto me, "My son, Sanat Kumara, thou shalt sit upon the great white throne before the evolutions of earth. Thou shalt be to them the Lord God in the highest. Verily, thou shalt be the highest manifestation of the Deity that shall be given unto them until, through the path of initiation, their souls shall rise to thy throne of awareness and stand before thee in praise of the I AM THAT I AM, which thou art."...

And he placed upon me his mantle of sponsorship of the Father unto the Son, which would become in me his sponsorship of a lifewave that he now made my own. It was a trust. It was the initiation of the Father in the Son....

Winged messengers of light had announced my return to Venus and the disposition of the Cosmic Council and the dispensation granted. The six—my brothers, the Holy Kumaras, who sustain with me the seven flames of the seven rays—Mighty Victory and his legions, our daughter Meta, and many servant sons and daughters whom you know today as the ascended masters welcomed me in a grand reception. That evening, the joy of opportunity was mingled with the sorrow that the sense of separation brings. I had chosen a voluntary exile upon a dark star. And though it was destined to be Freedom's Star, all knew it would be for me a long dark night of the soul.

Then all at once from the valleys and the mountains there appeared a great gathering of my children. It was the souls of the hundred and forty and four thousand approaching our palace. They spiraled nearer and nearer . . . singing the song of freedom, of love, and of victory. . . .

Their spokesman stood before the balcony to address us on behalf of the great multitude. It was the soul of the one you know and love today as the Lord of the World, Gautama Buddha. And he addressed us, saying:

"O Ancient of Days, we have heard of the covenant that God hath made with thee this day and of thy commitment to keep the flame of Life until some among earth's evolutions should be quickened and once again renew their vow to be bearers of the flame. O Ancient of Days, thou art to us our Guru, our very life, our God. We will not leave thee comfortless. We will go with thee. We will come to earth. We will prepare the way. We will keep the flame in thy name."

And so as the Lord God directed me, I chose from among them four hundred servant sons and daughters who would precede the hundred and forty and four thousand to prepare for their coming. . . .

We wept in joy, Lady Master Venus (my twin flame) and I and all of the hundred and forty and four thousand. The tears that flowed on that memorable evening burned as the living sacred fire flowing as the water of Life from the great white throne and the Cosmic Council, our sponsors. . . .

O my children, I AM still your Sanat Kumara.

Contents

1 The Opening of a Door in Heaven 1

2 The Dispensation Granted 10

3 The Jasper, the Emerald,
   and the Sardine Stone 16

4 The Path of the Rose Cross 21

5 Possessors of the Person of God 28

6 Sufficiency in the Guru 33

7 Ezekiel, the Son of Man 40

8 The Commission of the LORD to the Prophets
   and the Saints 47

9 The Initiations Foursquare on the
   Path of the Ruby Ray 57

10 The Mystery of the Indwelling Christ 67

11 Unfolding the Sacred Science of
   the Soul's Acceleration unto God 78

12 A Book Sealed with Seven Seals 85

13 Worthy Is the Lamb 92

14 Kings and Priests unto Our God 99

15	The Initiation of the East Gate	104
16	The Initiation of the North Gate	113
17	The Initiation of the West Gate	122
18	The Word and the Work of the Saints on the West Gate	133
19	The Gospel of the Father, and of the Son, and of the Holy Ghost	141
20	The Gospel of the Little Book Open	151
21	The Everlasting Gospel Foursquare	159
22	The Command to Preach the Gospel to Every Creature	170
23	The Power to Preach the Word of God	176
24	Preachers of the Acceptable Year of the LORD	183
25	In My Name, Cast Out Devils!	192
26	The LORD's Ritual of Exorcism Step One	202
27	The LORD's Ritual of Exorcism Steps Two and Three	212
28	The Psychology of the Devils Who Also Believe and Tremble	221
29	Seven Initiations of the Saints Who Follow the Lamb	231
30	The New Tongues of the Holy Spirit	251

31	The Command of the Word and the Countermand of Its Unlawful Uses	260
32	The Taking Up of Serpents	270
33	The Vow to Save the Woman and Her Seed	280
34	The Judgment of Serpent and His Seed *They Shall Not Pass!*	293
35	"Drink Me While I AM Drinking Thee" *If They Drink Any Deadly Thing, It Shall Not Hurt Them*	307
36	The Mystery of the White Cube	322
37	The Blood of the New Covenant	338

The Chart of Your Divine Self 373

Notes 377

Index 380

1

The Opening of a Door in Heaven

After this I looked, and behold, a door was opened in heaven: and the first voice which I heard was as it were of a trumpet talking with me which said, Come up hither, and I will show thee things which must be hereafter.
And immediately I was in the spirit: and behold, a throne was set in heaven, and one sat on the throne.
REVELATION 4:1, 2

Sons and Daughters of the Ancient of Days:

Lo! I AM come. Lo! I AM here in the fullness of the Word made flesh. And behold, a door is opened in heaven. Out of the great sphere of Universal Reality, I AM come.

The door that is opened is the door of the mysteries of the Cosmic Christ.

I send forth the call through Gautama Lord Buddha, Lord of the World and God of the Earth.

I send forth the call through Maitreya Lord Buddha, the first and the last Guru sent by Alpha and Omega, the Father-Mother God, to sound the sound of the trumpet and of seven trumpets unto the hundred and forty and four thousand who are with the Lamb.

I send forth the call through the Lord Jesus the Christ, the one anointed to preach the gospel to the poor, to heal the brokenhearted, to preach deliverance to the captives and recovering of sight to the blind, to set at liberty them that are bruised, and to preach the acceptable year of the Lord.[1]

O Lord, I send forth the call through thy servants the

Prophets, and through the saints, and them that fear thy name I AM THAT I AM, small and great.

The opening of the door in heaven beheld by the blessed servant John the Revelator is the opening of the spirit of prophecy unto the New Jerusalem upon the inauguration of the Aquarian age. The New Jerusalem is comprised of all who make up the consciousness of the living Christ in its fourfold, foursquare manifestation. Thus all who are in the Lord's body on this the day of the Lord's appearing are called by the sounding of the trumpet of Elohim to "Come up hither, for the Lord's anointed will show thee things which must be hereafter."

Come, my beloved, with John into the seven spheres of Spirit and behold the throne, *the great three-in-one*, that is set in heaven in the white-fire core of the great causal body of God. Come and behold the manifestation of thy Father-Mother God—indeed our Father which art in heaven—who hath appointed unto me the name Ancient of Days and a garment white as snow which is the royal robe of righteousness worn by the priesthood of Melchizedek. As Daniel renewed his covenant with me, O my beloved—even as you also one by one shall renew your covenant with the Ancient of Days—he beheld the consciousness of God emanating from the mind of God and described it as "the hair of his head like the pure wool."

And the great throne that is the seat of my incarnation is the great three-in-one, the Hebrew triad illustrated in the letter *shin*. And the Trinity is this: out of the Father and the Mother comes forth the Son crowned with the crown of both individual and cosmic Christhood. ש And the Father and the Mother are the twin flames of the Holy Spirit, as above so below. Thus the throne beheld by Daniel was like the fiery flame containing the light of Father-Mother, whose witness is the Son and the light of Holy Spirit whose twofold plus/minus polarity is resolved in the unity and the apex of that Son.

Thus he who sits upon the throne is the one to whom all power, wisdom, and love of heaven and earth is given. He is the one who is God incarnate unto the twelve tribes of Israel. For they do represent the twelve gates, or paths of initiation, whereby the lifewaves of a cosmos may enter into communion with the I AM THAT I AM. The I AM THAT I AM is the flaming triad in the center of the City Foursquare. Without the throne, the great three-in-one of the Lord God Almighty, the incarnation of the Word has not dominion. No, neither in heaven nor in earth. But given the throne, he is in the seat of authority and therefore is the one who can open the door twixt heaven and earth and reveal to the children of God the one sent.[2] The one sent is the messenger who stands at the nexus of Life where the sphere of heaven and the sphere of earth meet for the cosmic interchange of God and man.

And always and always they will say, By what authority doest thou these things? and who gave thee this authority?[3] All that I do, all that I speak, and all that I AM is by the authority of the I AM THAT I AM. I AM sent by the living God to call a living people unto the restoration of the temple. I AM come the deliverer of nations, the awakener of the ancient memory of those ancient days inscribed in *akasha* and known by the light-bearers—you who came with me bearing the taper of the three-fold light to earth and her evolutions. Unto you it is given to know the mysteries of the book that I hold in my right hand, the book that is sealed with seven seals.

The opening of the door in heaven is the descent of my mantle, my Electronic Presence. This auric emanation and forcefield is lowered to the plane of Gautama at Shamballa, who absorbs, assimilates, and becomes that living Presence that I AM, he being the first ascended chela in the line of the descent of the Gurus from my own anointing to the anointing of your messenger. In sacred ceremony, the Lord of the World transfers the authority of the mantle he has become to the second ascended chela in the line of the descent, Lord Maitreya, seated in the lotus throne in the central altar of Lemuria; for he is the personification of the Lord God who walked and talked with man and woman in the garden of Eden.

Now that blessed Maitreya, mediator of the path of initiation, absorbs, assimilates, and becomes the authority of the Ancient of Days, the dominion of Gautama, and adds to these his unique attainment on the path of chelaship under the Lord God Almighty. Now in the ritual of the anointing of the one sent in the person of Jesus the Christ, Lord Maitreya transfers the transfiguring light of his own triune manifestation of the Word to his chosen chela, the coming servant who has come in whom my soul delighteth, for I have put my spirit upon him that he might bring forth judgment to the Gentiles.[4]

Unto him it is given to wear the three mantles of the trinity who have preceded him. Thus the name of Jesus Christ is called Wonderful, for he embodies the fullness of the wonder of the Woman clothed with the Sun. He is the mother of Israel, gathering souls as a hen gathereth her chickens.[5] He is the Counsellor, the very personal presence of the Guru Lord Maitreya who comes bearing the banner of the Lord which is the banner of the World Mother: the Mother, that Wisdom who teacheth her children. He is The mighty God, the incarnate Holy Ghost, holding the power of the nine—the Trinity multiplied thrice. He is in The everlasting Father as The everlasting Father is in him. Thus, by our threefold mantle, he is known as The Prince of Peace.[6]

He stands in the New Jerusalem and in the City Foursquare. And in the ritual of the passing of the torch of the ages of Pisces unto Aquarius, he anoints the two witnesses unto whom I now give my power. And in the ceremony of the conferment of power, the Four and Twenty Elders, who sit on their seats before me, fall upon their faces and worship God, saying, "We give thanks, O Lord God Almighty, which art and wast and art to come; because thou hast taken to thee thy great power and hast reigned."

The Four and Twenty Elders give praise unto the Lord I AM THAT I AM unto the day and unto the night, for the power of God that is delivered unto me this day is a deliverance unto the children of light and the descent from the higher octaves to the lower octaves of the very presence of the person of God through this lineal descent of the mantle. This is the meaning of the opening of the temple of God in heaven whereby I, the Ancient of Days, commissioned as the emissary of God, do stand before you first in the person of Gautama, second in the person of Maitreya, third in the person of Jesus, and fourth in the persons of the two witnesses.

As Daniel saw them, so they stand: the other two—the one, Mark L. Prophet, the Ascended Master Lanello, on this side of the bank of the river holding the crystal sphere of Spirit; and the other, Elizabeth Clare Prophet, Mother of the Flame, on that side of the bank of the river holding the amethyst sphere of Matter.[7] Within the center of each sphere is a flame. Thus they hold the balance of the twin flames of the Holy Spirit with which every living soul must be endowed on the path of evolution in Matter leading to the revolution of higher consciousness in Spirit.

When these twin flames are made one in the heart of the initiate through the Guru-chela relationship, then does the declaration sound that the marriage of the Lamb is come, and his wife hath made herself ready. The wife of the Lamb is the soul who seeks reunion with God through the marriage to the living Christ. The wife is the chela, the Lamb is the Guru. Who then is the Lamb? The Lamb is the Word who was in the beginning with God without whom was not any thing made that was made.[8] I am in the Lamb and the Lamb is in me, therefore I am the Lamb. Thus saith the Lord, the Ancient of Days.

As the Lamb is in me, so I transfer the light of the Lamb in the descent of this order of hierarchy. As the living God is one, yet three-in-one, so every chela who has become one with the Guru is Guru. And wherever that Guru incarnates, he is known as the Lamb. And the chelas of the Lamb sing a new song, saying,

"Worthy is the Lamb! Worthy is the Lamb! Worthy is the Lamb! Lord God Almighty, thou art worthy to take the book and to open the seals thereof: for thou wast slain, and hast redeemed us to God by thy blood out of every kindred, and tongue, and people, and nation; And hast made us unto our God kings and priests: and we shall reign on the earth."

The descent of the Lamb is the inevitable crucifixion of the Lamb, for the Lamb is the Light of the world dark and dense.[9] And when that Light is come, all whose vibration is less than that Light, those who are not called as disciples of that Light to embody that Light, therefore polarize in opposition to the Light which they cannot receive, for they are not called to receive it.

As God is in me and I am in God, so I declare, I and my Father are one. And lo, I have become the Father. And the Father has become the Son through the figure-eight flow that is the design of the plus/minus interchange of Alpha in the Guru and Omega in the chela. Now I am the Father and Gautama is the Son. And as Gautama long ago passed the initiations of the Fatherhood of God, I bequeathed to him my flaming awareness of that Father. And lo, he declared, "I and my Father are one!" And he became the Father and the Father in the Son, the incarnate Word, the embodied Guru, the Lamb.

Then Maitreya, the blessed, the beautiful, the bountiful bodhisattva, beheld the vision of the Buddha and the Buddha beyond the Buddha as my own flaming Presence revealed the parting of veil upon veil, each veil the opening of another door in heaven as his meditation parted the octaves of the first, the second, the third heaven, the fourth, the fifth, the sixth, and the seventh.

Thus he bowed before the gracious Gautama as the Guru who was God because he unveiled to him the God of very gods. And lo, he declared, "I and my Father are one!" as he beheld the infinite succession of the Gurus who bore witness of worlds beyond worlds of the God manifestation. And Maitreya became the pivot point of the path of initiation unto every chela who would know the Guru, unto every soul of the hundred and forty and four thousand who would return to the mystery school of the garden of Eden.

He was the embodied Guru, the Father/Son manifestation unto the twin flames of Adam and Eve and unto their children, my children, sent to earth to demonstrate the path of initiation. By the subtil serpent, Satan's agent, the Path was set aside unto these twin flames and their offspring for six thousand cycles of life and death until the coming of the Lord Jesus Christ. He was the I AM THAT I AM incarnate. He was the embodied Lamb. He was, as Archangel Gabriel has said, the messenger of our flame who became the message.

By his attainment on the path of initiation under his father, Maitreya, he became the Lamb unto the hundred and forty and four thousand. He, too, opened the door in heaven, opening the temple of understanding—yes, my beloved, opening the crown chakra where there is seen the ark of his testament, the scrolls of the living testimony of the Word whence there proceed lightnings, as the sacred fire of the Word, and thunderings, as the sounding of the sound of the Word, and voices, which are the voices of all who are the deliverers of the spoken Word.

Jesus Christ is unto Adam and Eve and all of their spiritual descendants to the very present hour the Saviour who has saved for them the path of initiation which had its beginning on Lemuria and will have its ending on the shores of the Motherland in the Aquarian age. Now the Lord Jesus Christ, who gave the *I and my Father are one* mantra to all disciples of this Christ manifestation that we are, that I AM, sponsors the two witnesses for the sealing of the servants of our God in their foreheads. And the number of them which are sealed are an hundred and forty and four thousand of all the tribes of the children of Israel. This is the present work of the two witnesses on earth and in heaven.

These two souls of light, representing Father and Mother to those accelerating on the twelve paths of initiation under Guru Maitreya, are one as the spheres of Spirit and Matter converge, suspended in time and space. Their threefold flames are one, focusing the six-pointed star of David—the rising Mother, the descending Father. Together they chant with the multitudes who stand before the throne—the threefold flame—and before the Lamb, saying, "Salvation to our God which sitteth upon the throne, and unto the Lamb." They chant the Amen, Amen, Amen. And the chanting of the AUM is heard in the four corners of the heavens and in the four corners of the earth as our two witnesses become the issue of our fiery stream unto the thousands of thousands who minister unto the Lamb and the ten thousand times ten thousand who stand before him. And the angels and the elders and the multitude and the remnant of Israel fall on their faces before the throne and worship God, saying, "Amen: Blessing and glory and wisdom and thanksgiving and honour and power and might be unto our God for ever and ever. Amen."

Now the twelve tribes and the multitude clothed with white robes and palms in their hands are coming out of the great tribulation of personal and planetary karma. Day by day they are washing their robes, their auric forcefields and their four lower bodies, and making them white—purifying the vehicles of consciousness, fire, air, water, and earth—in the blood, the fiery essence, of the Lamb that flows through the sacred heart of the Guru incarnate.

Now learn the mystery of the Guru. It is the alchemy of the sacred fire that by the body and the blood is redemption come. Physical redemption is the requirement of the Law, therefore the Lamb must be in physical embodiment. But the Lamb is the infinite person of the Son of God, and therefore it is the mantle of the Lamb that must rest upon the shoulders of the anointed one that the people might touch the hem of that garment and be repolarized in the wholeness of Alpha and Omega. Therefore it is written: "He that sitteth on the throne shall dwell among them."

This mystery of the Holy Grail I, Sanat Kumara, declare to you this day. For I am he that sitteth on the throne in the Form of the Formless One, and I have come to dwell among the white-robed multitudes in the person of my embodied messenger. I come through Gautama. I come through Maitreya. I come through Jesus Christ. And I am come in the person of the two witnesses, who now convey the mantra which they have become—"I and my Father are one."

Because I am incarnate, I am the Lamb. Because they are myself incarnate they, too, can and shall declare, "I AM the embodied Guru—Lanello, *the Ever-Present Guru;* Mother, *the Guru Ma.*" And therefore, because they are with you in Spirit and in Matter, it is written of you, O chelas of the Great White Brotherhood: "They shall hunger no more, neither thirst any more; neither shall the sun light on them, nor any heat. For the Lamb which is in the midst of the throne shall feed them, and shall lead them unto living fountains of waters: and God shall wipe away all tears from their eyes."

The question is always asked of the one who wears our mantle, "Art thou he that should come? or look we for another?" And the answer that is given is the witness of the multitudes and the disciples of the things seen and heard—how that the blind see, the lame walk, the lepers are cleansed, the deaf hear, the dead are raised, and to the poor the gospel is preached.[10] And the one who receives the blessing of the Lamb is the one who is not offended in him. For those who are offended by the Person or the Principle of the Lamb have no part in the resurrection, and therefore they cannot abide in his presence nor are they called to the marriage supper of the Lamb.

I AM Sanat Kumara, known from everlasting to everlasting to the followers of God as the Ancient of Days. I AM come, as it was shown unto Daniel, for to give judgment unto the saints of the Most High. These are the white-robed chelas of the Great White Brotherhood who shall now possess the kingdom which is the manifest consciousness of God as it is delivered to them morsel by morsel by the embodied Lamb. And the saints of the Most High shall take the kingdom, and they shall possess the kingdom for ever, even for ever and ever.

I AM THAT I AM

See Rev. 1:10–18; 4:1–5, 10–11; 5:7; 11:3, 16–19; 12:1; 19:1–10; 21:2, 9–27; Dan. 7:9–14, 18, 22.

2

The Dispensation Granted

> *And I saw a great white throne and him that sat on it, from whose face the earth and the heaven fled away; and there was found no place for them.*
>
> *I am Alpha and Omega, the beginning and the ending, saith the Lord, which is, and which was, and which is to come, the Almighty.*   REVELATION 20:11; 1:8

Souls of the Saints Robed in White:

I come from the great white throne, the I AM THAT I AM in the person of the Ancient of Days. In the name of the Father, of the Son, and of the Holy Ghost, I sit upon the seat of authority. I AM he from whose face the earth and the heaven shall flee away, and there shall no place be found for the seed of the wicked. AUM.

My heart is the heart of the Trinity. My heart is the heart of God. Through my heart there flows from the One the pure river of water of life, clear as crystal, proceeding out of the throne of God and of the Lamb which is the foundation of worlds above and below. Lo, I AM the Alpha and the Omega of that water of life. I AM the emissary of the plus and the minus of the perpetual flow of the dayspring from on high.

This is the water of the Lamb descending from the Universal Source heart to heart to heart. And unto him that receiveth it from the embodied Lamb, it is the elixir first of wisdom, then of the understanding of that wisdom, and finally it is the full-orbed enlightenment of the soul. And the water poured by the Guru into the upraised chalice of the chela shall be in him a well of water springing up into everlasting life. And the chela that believeth upon the Lamb, the embodied Guru, as the scripture hath said: out of his belly shall flow rivers of living water.[1]

And so cometh Maitreya to initiate you in the initiation of water and in your individual God-mastery of the emotions—the energies of Alpha and Omega chaliced within the desire body and released through the ten-petaled chakra of the solar plexus, the *belly*. This mighty flow of rivers of living water is the veritable sign of the living chelas of the living Guru.

Let the desire body be cleared! Let the motive of the heart be purified! Let all of your desiring be the desiring of God within you to restore the soul to the balanced flow of water as the descending life-giving flow of Alpha and Omega! Lo, it is that sacred fire which is the rising caduceus held in the balance of the plus and the minus by your meditation upon the descending/ascending currents as water and fire commingling, life-giving! So let the water of life purify the soul! So let the sacred fire reinfuse the cells of the living body of God one by one with the personal presence of the Word! Behold the image of the Lord Christ and of his Lamb in every cell of the body of God, worlds without end!

You call me Sanat Kumara, and you know me as the one who stood before the cosmic council known as the Council of the One Hundred and Forty and Four. You know me because you were witnesses to my plea made for and on behalf of the evolutions of earth who no longer knew the presence of the Lamb, who by disobedience were cut off from the living Guru. You know me as the one who volunteered to embody the threefold flame within the earth unto the evolutions evolving within the seven planes of being—fire, air, water, and earth.

The Cosmic Council had decreed the dissolution of earth and her evolutions because the souls of her children no longer worshiped the Trinity in the threefold flame of life burning upon the altar of the heart. They had become the sheep gone astray. Their attention fixed upon the outer manifestation, they had willfully, ignorantly abandoned the inner walk with God. They knew not the hidden man of the heart,[2] that blessed Ishwara, and the seven candles no longer burned in the seven windows. Men and women had become hollow, their chakras black holes in time and space; and their vacated temples became the tombs of the dead; and the spirits of the dead took up their abode within their hollowed-out houses. Thus they received the judgment of the One Hundred and Forty and Four even as their descendants would hear the denunciation of the Son of God.[3]

Thus the light of the temples had gone out, and the purpose to which God had created man—to be the temple of the living God—was no longer being fulfilled. One and all were the living dead, a Matter vessel without an ensouling light, an empty shell. Nowhere on earth was there a mystery school—not a chela, not a Guru, no initiates of the path of initiation unto Christhood.

The hour of the judgment had come, and the one seated upon the throne in the center of the twelve times twelve hierarchies of light had pronounced the word that was the unanimous consensus of all: Let earth and her evolutions be rolled up as a scroll and lit as a taper of the sacred fire. Let all energies misqualified be returned to the Great Central Sun for repolarization. Let energy misused be realigned and recharged with the light of Alpha and Omega, once again to be infused by the Creator within the ongoing creation of worlds without end.

The requirement of the law for the saving of Terra? It was that one who should qualify as the embodied Guru, the Lamb, should be present in the physical octave to hold the balance and to keep the threefold flame of life for and on behalf of every living soul. It is the law of the One that the meditation of the one upon the Eternal Christos may count for the many until the many once again become accountable for their words and their works and can begin to bear the burden of their light as well as the karma of their relative good and evil.

I chose to be that one. I volunteered to be a flaming son of righteousness unto earth and her evolutions.

After considerable deliberation, the Cosmic Council and the Nameless One gave their approval of my petition, and the dispensation for a new divine plan for earth and her evolutions came into being. For cosmic law so states that when a hierarch of certain degrees and dimensions of cosmic consciousness volunteers to be the shepherd of lifewaves that are the lost sheep, the petition must be granted. Where there is no Guru, there can be no chelas; where there is no shepherd, there can be no sheep. As it is written: smite the shepherd, and the sheep are scattered.[4]

But the Guru may be given opportunity to be Guru only for a certain cycle; and if at the end of that cycle the members of a lifewave by their recalcitrance and hardness of heart have not responded as chelas to the heart flame of the Guru, then the Guru must withdraw. And that which might have been may not be, and to no other hierarch then will the dispensation be given.

Thus I knelt before the great white throne of the Nameless One and he said unto me, "My son, Sanat Kumara, thou shalt sit upon the great white throne before the evolutions of earth. Thou shalt be to them the Lord God in the highest. Verily, thou shalt be the highest manifestation of the Deity which shall be given unto them until, through the path of initiation, their souls shall rise to thy throne of awareness and stand before thee in praise of the I AM THAT I AM which thou art. In that day when they shall rise up and say, 'Blessing and honour and glory and power be unto him that sitteth upon the throne and unto the Lamb for ever and ever'—behold, their redemption draweth nigh."

And he said unto me, "Thus unto the evolutions of earth thou shalt be Alpha and Omega, the beginning and the ending, saith the I AM THAT I AM, which is and which was and which is to come, the Almighty." And he placed upon me his mantle of sponsorship of the Father unto the Son which would become in me his sponsorship of a lifewave that he now made my own. It was a trust. It was the initiation of the Father in the Son.

And I knelt before the Nameless One and I worshiped God, saying, "Thou art worthy, O Lord, to receive glory and honour and power; for thou hast created all things, and for thy pleasure they are and were created." And he, the Great Guru, repeated the approbation, thus completing the circle of devotion. He acknowledged the light that he and he alone had placed within my heart as the flaming image of himself, and to that image he said, "Thou art worthy, O Lord, to receive glory and honour and power: for thou hast created all things, and for thy pleasure they are and were created."

Thus I am in the Father and the Father is in me and we are one, worlds without end. And without that oneness, there can be no petition and no dispensation no matter what your level of evolution.

And the Council of the One Hundred and Forty and Four, forming a single solar ring around the great white throne, intoned the Word with the great beings of light, forming the inner circle round about the throne and saying, "Holy, holy, holy, Lord God Almighty, which was, and is, and is to come." And I heard the echo of their chant of the "Holy, holy, holy" all the way home to the morning star, to my twin flame whom you know as Venus, and to the sons and daughters of the Love Star.

Winged messengers of light had announced my coming and the disposition of the Cosmic Council and the dispensation granted. The six—my brothers, the Holy Kumaras, who sustain with me the seven flames of the seven rays—Mighty Victory and his legions, our daughter Meta, and many servant sons and daughters whom you know today as the ascended masters welcomed me in a grand reception. That evening, the joy of opportunity was mingled with the sorrow that the sense of separation brings. I had chosen a voluntary exile upon a dark star. And though it was destined to be Freedom's Star, all knew it would be for me a long dark night of the soul.

Then all at once from the valleys and the mountains there appeared a great gathering of my children. It was the souls of the hundred and forty and four thousand approaching our palace of light. They spiraled nearer and nearer as twelve companies singing the song of freedom, of love, and of victory. Their mighty chorusing echoed throughout elemental life, and angelic choirs hovered nigh. As we watched from the balcony, Venus and I, we saw the thirteenth company robed in white. It was the royal priesthood of the Order of Melchizedek, the anointed ones who kept the flame and the law in the center of this hierarchical unit.

When all of their numbers had assembled, ring upon ring upon ring surrounding our home, and their hymn of praise and adoration to me was concluded, their spokesman stood before the balcony to address us on behalf of the great multitude. It was the soul of the one you know and love today as the Lord of the World, Gautama Buddha. And he addressed us, saying, "O Ancient of Days, we have heard of the covenant which God hath made with thee this day and of thy commitment to keep the flame of life until some among earth's evolutions should be quickened and once again renew their vow to be bearers of the flame. O Ancient of Days, thou art to us our Guru, our very life, our God. We will not leave thee comfortless. We will go with thee. We will not leave thee for one moment without the ring upon ring of our chelaship. We will come to earth. We will prepare the way. We will keep the flame in thy name."

And so as the Lord God directed me, I chose from among them four hundred servant sons and daughters who would precede the hundred and forty and four thousand to prepare for their coming. For though they knew the darkness of the darkest star, in reality they did not know, as I knew, the real meaning of the sacrifice which they now were offering to make in the name of their Guru.

We wept in joy, Venus and I and all of the hundred and forty and four thousand. And the tears that flowed on that memorable evening burned as the living sacred fire flowing as the water of life from the great white throne and the Cosmic Council, our sponsors.

I shall come again to continue with the history that unfolds from the folds of the garment of memory of the Ancient of Days.

O my children, I AM still your

Sanat Kumara

See Rev. 1:8; 4:8; 5:13; 20:11; 22:1.

3

The Jasper, the Emerald, and the Sardine Stone

> *And he that sat was to look upon like a jasper and a sardine stone: and there was a rainbow round about the throne, in sight like unto an emerald.*
>
> *And round about the throne were four and twenty seats: and upon the seats I saw four and twenty elders sitting, clothed in white raiment; and they had on their heads crowns of gold.*
>
> *And out of the throne proceeded lightnings and thunderings and voices: and there were seven lamps of fire burning before the throne, which are the seven Spirits of God.*
>
> *And before the throne there was a sea of glass like unto crystal.*
>
> REVELATION 4:3–6

Saints of the Most High:

I AM he that sat who was to look upon like a jasper and a sardine stone. The light of the jasper is the golden light of the crown of life unto the one who opens the door of the crown chakra. I AM opening that door within you, and I AM the open door which no man can shut. I AM opening the door of cycles emanating from the great solar rings of the blue causal body of the Great Divine Director.

I AM the golden light of the mind of God, the jasper that is for the building of the wall of the City Foursquare and for the garnishing of the first foundation. Enlightenment is the foundation of the building of the temple in the Aquarian age. Even so is the jasper the stone of victory, the twelfth, set in gold in

Aaron's breastplate of judgment.

Lo, I AM come for the redemption of the Levites and to reestablish the Melchizedekian priesthood that the person of Christ might once again minister unto the people from the tabernacle of the congregation.

I AM the Ancient of Days, standing midst the congregation of the righteous. I AM the cloudy pillar descending at the door of the tabernacle. I AM the open door which no man can shut. Let all the people who worship the Presence of God, I AM, now behold the cloudy pillar that I AM, standing at the tabernacle door. Lo, I AM the door. Let the people rise up and worship— every son and daughter in his own violet-flame tent door.

I AM the Lord thy God speaking unto the messenger face to face, as a man speaketh unto his friend. I AM engraving the signet *HOLINESS TO THE LORD*. I AM sealing the forehead of the messenger, sealing the eye as the orifice of Elohim. And it shall always be upon her forehead "bearing the iniquity of the holy things"—the focus of transmutation, transmuting the offering of the children of Israel that it might be acceptable unto the Lord. Thus is the hallowing of the holy gifts by the immaculate vision of Elohim sealed in the all-seeing eye of the messenger that the children of Israel may be accepted before the Lord.

Now let those who will stand as priests and priestesses between the embodied Lamb and the sheep, as Christic mediators between the Guru and the chela, come forth that they might receive the seal of Aaron *HOLINESS TO THE LORD*.

I AM the jasper stone. Let them come to me who have first put on the sardine stone that I AM, for its ruby red signifies the heart of the initiate whose initiations in the sacred fire are for the mastery of the first element of the Ancient Alchemist, the fire element, and its angels and salamanders in Spirit and in Matter. The sardine is the opening of the door of the heart to the initiation of the Rose Cross. It is the garnishment of the sixth foundation of the wall of the Holy City and the first stone set in gold upon Aaron's breastplate. Thus it is the beginning of the mysteries of the priesthood and the sixth step in the inner temple initiations.

The pure heart is not enough. It is the accelerated heart that is required, the heart that is on fire for God, ruby red as the blood of Christ—now crucified, now resurrected, now ascended as the blood becomes the golden liquid light of the jasper. I AM the beginning and the ending of the path of initiation which I transfer to you through the Great Guru Lord Maitreya. I AM in the center of the rainbow round about the throne. I AM in the center of the twelve rings of Elohim, whose causal bodies adorn the Nameless One.

Unto the vision of the soul I AM the emerald, the garnishment of the fourth foundation of the Holy City that you individually must build, line upon line, as proof of your path of initiation. And so the emerald, the fourth stone of the breastplate set in gold and the fourth station of the cross of Christ, is the turning point of the I AM WHO I AM for the initiate.

Your identity, O precious soul jeweled in light, is the revelation that standeth in the door opened in heaven. Let him that beholdeth the emerald of the throne of the Ancient of Days know that by his vision he may enter the halls of that holy science which is Truth, Truth that leadeth to the opening of the seventh seal.

Round about the throne are four and twenty seats of authority whom the Nameless One hath assigned unto twin flames representing the Twelve Hierarchies of the Sun in the masculine and feminine power/wisdom/love of Elohim. Clothed in the white raiment of their Cosmic Christ consciousness, sealed in the rainbow rays of the seven chakras that now blend in the white light, they are identified as the overcomers of systems of worlds by the crowns of gold upon their heads. The Almighty One has ordained his emissaries in a cosmic order of hierarchy to witness unto his Presence—personal/impersonal power in the Great Central Sun and in the flaming yods of the galaxies that procession there about.

The crowns of gold of the Four and Twenty Elders signify that they have become the sardine and the jasper, the ruby and the gold through the emerald of applied science and religion, Spirit and Matter. The lightnings and thunderings and voices which proceed out of the throne are the soundings of the persons of the Trinity as they emit the power (thunderings), the wisdom (voices), and the love (lightnings) of Brahman.

Thus light/energy/consciousness proceed out of the Void and enter the crucible of Brahma/Vishnu/Shiva for the creation and the uncreation of worlds. And the seven lamps of sacred fire burning before the Great Three-in-One are the transformers of the seven Spirits of God, the Elohim who hold the concentrated energies of the Trinity—omnipotence, omniscience, omnipresence—for their distribution throughout the formed and unformed planes of Spirit/Matter.

Now behold the sea of glass like unto crystal mingled with sacred fire. The saints will march on this very sea—it is the way Home. It is the way to the center of the AUM. It is the only way. I AM the way. It is the first and the last initiation of the souls of God, their going out and their coming in[1] to the Father-Mother God. And only they shall pass who shall have gotten the victory over the beast and over his image and over his mark and over the number of his name. Only they shall be able to stand on the sea of glass, the crystal-fire mist.

Having the harps of God, they shall sing the song of their Guru Moses, the servant-chela of God, I AM THAT I AM. And they shall sing the song of the Lamb, saying, "Great and marvellous are thy works, Lord God Almighty, thou Three in One; just and true are thy ways, thou Christ incarnate, King of saints. Who shall not fear thee, O Lord, I AM THAT I AM, and glorify thy name? for thou only art holy: for all nations—the lifewaves dwelling on the twelve planes of consciousness in Matter, fulfilling the cycles of their group karma and dharma—shall come and worship before thee; for thy judgments are made manifest."

Lo, I AM the Ancient of Days. I AM the manifest judgment, as above so below. I address the one hundred and forty and four thousand: Enter the meditation of the crystal sea. Enter the meditation of the jasper, the emerald, and the sardine, the first, the fourth, and the sixth stations of the cross of Christ, and prepare for the coming of the Four Cosmic Forces who will initiate you on the Path of the Rose Cross.

I AM in the magnet of the Great Central Sun, releasing into your meditative hearts shafts of light that are for the magnetization of your souls unto the sun center of being. Enter now the shaft, saints of the Most High, and spiral to the center of my heart.

I AM always your

Sanat Kumara

See Rev. 4:3–6; 15:3; 21:19–20; Exod. 28:15–21, 36, 38; 33:5–11.

4

The Path of the Rose Cross

And in the midst of the throne, and round about the throne, were four beasts full of eyes before and behind.

And the first beast was like a lion, and the second beast like a calf, and the third beast had a face as a man, and the fourth beast was like a flying eagle.

And the four beasts had each of them six wings about him; and they were full of eyes within: and they rest not day and night, saying, Holy, holy, holy, Lord God Almighty, which was, and is, and is to come. REVELATION 4:6–8

Holiness to the Lord!
Holiness to the Lord!
Holiness to the Lord!
Holy, holy, holy, Lord God Almighty,
Which was, and is, and is to come.

The four beasts are the living creatures who worship the Trinity because they have come out of the Trinity, born of the One and of the polarity within the One, Alpha and Omega. The four beasts are for the squaring of the circle of Spirit that is become the foundation foursquare in Matter of the Great Pyramid of Life and of the Holy City.

I AM in the four beasts and the four beasts are in me and we are one. These are the Four Cosmic Forces who hold the cosmic cross of white fire that designates the quadrants in Spirit and the quadrants in Matter—fire, air, water, and earth. They are the four sacred elements who support and surround the great white throne. They are the within. They are the without. Whither the

Spirit goeth, they go. And they follow the Lamb whithersoever he goeth in the heavens and in the earth.

They are the guardians of the door that is opened in Spirit and in Matter. They are the guardians of the twelve gates of the Holy City. In Brahma/Vishnu/Shiva, they guard the three gates on the east, the three gates on the north, the three gates on the south, and the three gates on the west. They are the foundation of the Twelve Hierarchies of the Sun. They are the initiators of the hundred and forty and four thousand on the Path of the Rose Cross.

Now hear the Word of the Lord. The Four Cosmic Forces sustain the ruby cube whereby the heart of God becomes the heart of man. Ponder the ruby cube. Meditate upon the flame of love burning within the center. Trace the twenty-four right angles governed by the Four and Twenty Elders whereby Spirit becomes Matter and Matter becomes Spirit. It is the Holy Ghost. The Activator, the Deactivator. The ruby cube is pure Love, fiery Love, unadulterated, unselfish Love, perpetually burning all unlike itself. One must approach with extreme caution. Therefore the Path of the Rose Cross. Therefore the initiations of the Four Cosmic Forces in the way of the surrender of the image of the self that the Self may be All-in-all.

Only the Self may stand in the center of the ruby cube. All else is self-destroyed. Therefore the four beasts, full of the eyes of Elohim—openings unto the Great Central Sun—rest not day and night, saying, "Holy, holy, holy, Lord God Almighty, which was, and is, and is to come." Thus they intone the sound of I AM THAT I AM, of Elohim, of El Shaddai. Thus intoning the sound of the soundless sound, they sustain the vibration of the ruby cube in the white-fire core of a cosmos.

Elohim, Elohim, Elohim. AUM.

Full of eyes before and behind, the Four Cosmic Forces sustain the vision of the Lord God Almighty as universal awareness of the Creator within the creation. Full of eyes before and behind, the Four Cosmic Forces are perpetually stepping down the light of Solar Logoi, cosmic messengers of Alpha and Omega positioned in the flaming yods of the galaxies. Thus by their six wings, the three and three, and the three times three, they render the light, the energy of the Word, intelligible to electrons small and great in man and beast, vegetable and mineral. Their six wings hold the balance of the triad in Spirit and the triad in Matter, ascending and descending triangles. And they were full of eyes within.

These are the eyes of Mother caressing the creation and the Formless One who inhabits his own Form, caressing the Uncreated One who is in the Created Son, the Created Father, and the Created Holy Ghost. The eyes within are the eyes of Mother, delivering the energy of the ruby ray as compassionate chastening, as conceptualization, as consummation, as bliss, reunion with the ion of Being. Thus the face of the Great Goddess is veiled that her children might not wither from the penetration of the ruby ray. It is life-giving, invigorating, infilling. It is the alchemy of the heart to every living cell of a cosmos.

Behold the eyes before and behind and the hierarchy of vestal virgins carrying their ruby lamps with the blood of the Lamb and the Word of his testimony. They are the initiates of the Path of the Rose Cross. They have followed the path of the crucifixion of their Lord and Husband unto the opening of the temple of the heart and the coming of the Bridegroom. They have worn his crown of thorns. They have transmuted his crown of thorns. They have taken him down from the cross. They have laid him in the tomb of Mother. They have tended his resurrection within her womb.

They await the ceremony of their crowning with a crown of gold when they shall become extensions of the Woman clothed with the Sun who wears the crown of twelve stars. They hold the ruby figure-eight spiral whereby the souls of the hundred and forty and four thousand may spiral from the ego-centered life to the Christ-centered life by the initiations of the ruby cube. AUM.

The Four Cosmic Forces initiate the Order of the Ruby

Cross. And the first beast was like a lion. He is the ruler of the north arm of the cross and of the fire quadrant in Spirit and in Matter. When the lion roareth, the king of the beasts, the fire of First Cause proceedeth out of his mouth. And his Word is the endowment of the Grund and the Ungrund with primal energy. His is the force of the fiery baptism. He is the King of the inner court, opening the sacred mysteries of the heart under the hierarchy of Leo. His key is the key to the incarnate God. When he is the Father in the Son, he manifests himself as the Lion of the tribe of Juda, saying, I and my Son are one.

Lo, I AM the open door of the fiery baptism that is the restoration of the hundred and forty and four thousand to wholeness through repentance and remission of sins.

Holiness to the Lord!
Holiness to the Lord!
Holiness to the Lord!

As in fire our God is Father, the All-in-all, so in earth he is the Holy Ghost. And the second beast was like a calf. He guardeth the door of the Holy Ghost, and no man can enter except by that door.[1] He is the archetype of the Universal Christ. He holdeth the west arm of the ruby cross, the ruler of the earth quadrant in Spirit and in Matter. He doth initiate the souls of the hundred and forty and four thousand through the hierarchy of Taurus. His is the eye all-seeing that by obedience doth the temple build.

He teacheth the children of Israel to make bricks without straw. He is the great builder through elemental life. He is the Great Guru, he is the great chela. He is the beast of burden who beareth the sins of the world. He is the ox that treadeth out the corn of personal and planetary karma. And "thou shalt not muzzle the mouth of the ox that treadeth out the corn."[2] By his ruby figure-eight flow, the Buddha is Guru. The Mother is chela. By the same ruby figure-eight flow, the Mother is Guru, the Buddha is chela.

The calf is the slave of Yahweh. He bears His burden on earth. His initiatic rite is the crucifixion. So is elemental life thrice crucified through the archetype of the Cosmic Christ in Taurus—once for the kingdom of the angels of fire and the angels of water serving the throne of Brahma, once for the kingdom of the gods serving the throne of Vishnu, and once for the kingdom of elemental forces serving the throne of Shiva.

The golden calf is the Form of the unformed Yahweh, his throne as Buddha. He rides him to the victory of the untransmuted Taurian energies of the children of Israel. The Israelites understood not the prophet's vision of the Four Cosmic Forces—lion/calf/man/eagle. So they fashioned a calf in the image and likeness of their idolatry, sensuality, and materialism. They were the unaligned. No ruby cross fixed their identity in the heart of the ruby cube. Therefore they required a law writ in tables of stone; for by the hardness of their hearts, that stiffnecked people knew not the law written in their inward parts.[3]

They said, "We wot not what is become of this Moses, the *man* that brought us up out of the land of Egypt. Up, Aaron, make us gods. We will worship Yahweh when we will. We do not need the Guru Moses. Besides, he is no Guru but an ordinary man like ourselves. He is no god-man. Behold, he is mere flesh and blood. We will create our own god after our own image and likeness. We will have our rituals without the Guru.

"What further need have we of God's messenger, who hath left us here without word in the Sinai desert! Behold, all the congregation is holy. There is not one holier than another. We need not the Holy One of God in our midst. We will rather worship the golden calf who doeth our bidding while we dance and make merry. We will shut our ears from this Moses who would take from us the pleasures of life and our enjoyment of the sacred fire of the Father, the sacred water of the Mother, the sacred air of the Son, the sacred earth of the Holy Spirit. We will have our *Mater-realization* 'materialization' of God outside the presence of the Guru Moses.

"We will have our cult—our cultivation of light—without obeisance to the Person of light. We will enslave elemental life by our charms and our spells. We will have reverence only for the golden calf. And no other part of life will we reverence as the temple of the living God, save the golden calf."

But Aaron, the high priest, made proclamation and said, "Tomorrow is a feast to the I AM THAT I AM." He was an initiate of the Path of the Rose Cross. He knew the inner mystery of the calf as the archetype of the Christ, sitting on the west side of the City Foursquare. The calf, the Parvati of Shiva. Wherever there is Parvati in form, there in formlessness is Shiva. He knew, as did the children of Mu embodied in the East, that the calf is the symbol of a Matter cosmos wed to Spirit.

But the people, oh, the people! Though they sacrificed their gold and gave it to the community, it became the unacceptable offering; for they worshiped their own sacrificial calf, as a mighty deed they had done, in the place of Yahweh. And the golden calf, through their double-minded vision, became the symbol of their rebellion against the Great Guru.

AUM Buddha. AUM Buddha. AUM Buddha.

And the calf remains crucified to the present hour, and Christ is nailed to the cross of idolatry, sensuality, and materialism on the west side of the City Foursquare. The calf is in the earth and the earth is in the calf and the calf is the beginning of the initiation of the hundred and forty and four thousand on the Path of the Rose Cross under the Four Cosmic Forces. For the many, this is the initiatic rung of the ladder where they left off their association with the Guru Maitreya represented in Moses.

Now the tribes of Ephraim and Manasseh, sons of Joseph favored by Jacob, are gathering on the west arm of the cross to resume their soul testings. For unto them is entrusted the flame of Christ in Western civilization. They carry the law of the I AM THAT I AM in their inward parts. They must exercise that law by the power of the spoken Word. They must come forth and be counted. They must come forth and give an accounting unto the Lord of their words and their works since the first coming of Messiah. Lightbearers positioned in the United States of America and Great Britain are given the key for the turning around of the downward spiral of the West to the upward spiral of the East that shall be seen in the image of the man.

Now take down the calf from the cross of idolatry, sensuality, and materialism that is the perversion complete of the Trinity in the Mother. Now transmute, transmute, transmute that untransmuted substance by the all-consuming violet flame. Now, by a will that is wisdom and a wisdom that is action, God in action! enter the Path of the Rose Cross.

Valiantly for the victory, I AM

Sanat Kumara

I have led thee from the Beginning.
I will lead thee unto the End.
I AM the Lord.

See Rev. 4:6–8; 5:5; 11:5; 12:1, 11; 14:4; 21:12–13; Exod. 5:7; 32:1–19; 33:5; Ezek. 1:5.

5

Possessors of the Person of God

Soldiers Who See Christ in the Calf Crucified:

Legions of light marching from out the Great Central Sun are the legions of Victory and of his Flaming One. They come for the binding of the beasts of self-indulgence, selfishness, the idolatry of the self, and the love of the self. These are the four beasts that would usurp the thrones of the four living creatures full of eyes before and behind who are in the midst of the throne and round about the throne. Their overcoming is by the flaming yod, for they are the overcomers of worlds and beyond.

They know the sacrifice of the lion, the unending service of the calf, the surrender of the image of the man, and the selflessness of the flying eagle. The ruby is the initiatic jewel of their diadem. They know the way of the Rose Cross. They come to address the children of Israel on behalf of the Four Cosmic Forces. They are the God-taught who have become the teaching. In them behold the law of purity face to face, and purify thy heart for the acceleration unto God.

They address the impure who are forbidden to worship God in Form lest they become idolaters. They address the impure who have not seen him face to face, who do not know him as he is, the Formless One. Therefore the legions say unto you, "Become unattached to the form. Be nonpossessive of the form. Stop believing that He is the form or that He is in the form. Let the age of superstition go down with its spell-binding, mind-bending altering of the way made plain by the I AM THAT I AM, the Lord of heaven and earth who dwelleth not in temples made with hands."[1]

Those who worship form in flesh and blood, in money and the things they have fabricated out of fire, air, water, and earth, imprisoning elemental life as impostors of the Great Alchemist, have no cosmic conception of the Form of God. In their idolatry they would tear down the supreme Personality of the Godhead as though he himself were an idol, all the while pursuing their cults of idolatry and saying, "We have left behind the age of superstition. We are the sophisticated. We hold the intellectual keys to science and religion. We have wrested the secret formulae of the nucleus of life, and nothing is withheld from us. We are the gods of the twentieth century, the rightful leaders of souls into the new age. We have no Guru, we are God. We worship no other god save the God within. We need no master ascended or unascended, for *we* are the masters of life."

Thus, in their pride and lust for power, these fallen ones by their magnetic personality are the impostors of the flying eagle. Unto them the Lord hath said: "The pride of thine heart hath deceived thee, thou that dwellest in the clefts of the rock, whose habitation is high; that saith in his heart, Who shall bring me down to the ground? Though thou exalt thyself as the eagle, and though thou set thy nest among the stars, thence will I bring thee down, saith the Lord."[2]

He who hath not known the known God both in his Form and in his Formlessness is not ready for the initiation of the worship of the Formed or the Unformed Self. And whosoever thinketh that he hath the Form, though he possess the mere idol of his own form, he will lie, he will cheat, he will steal, he will murder to retain the possession of that form.

Woe to the archdeceivers who think they possess the Form of God and would divide the world left and right into the haves and have-nots, even as they would divide the Personality of Good which they think they possess. This is the illusion of maya which the Mother of the World allows for the testing of souls. Let them think they possess the Form of God; then by their disposition to the compassionate Christ, the merciful Buddha, the beggar, the leper, the outcast, they shall be judged.

What would you do if you possessed the Person of God? This is the opening question for those entering the Path of the Rose Cross.

Some would create a war of the worlds and be labeled the Terrible, the Destroyer. They are the wayward imitators of the wrathful deities. Beware, you who would imitate Shiva, for Shiva dances in the heart of the ruby cube. Shiva the lion, Shiva the calf, Shiva the image of the man, Shiva the flying eagle—Shiva will swallow you up! He who puts on the airs of Shiva will find himself seized by the four winds of Shiva and stretched to the four corners of the ruby cube. Only he who has for certain the nine gifts of the Holy Spirit should put on the airs of Shiva!

And those who look no further than the form of the golden calf peering back at them curiously out of the mirror of self will never find Yahweh, not in the calf above or in the calf below. For them the calf has become the Canaanite symbol of the fertility of the subtil serpentine mind. So long ago was their degeneration, through the descent of light from the crown chakra to the base chakra, that they can no longer stand in the presence of the regenerate ones.

Let the brothers and sisters of the Rose Cross teach you, my child, the penetration of the Matter Form to the Spirit Form and the Matter Formless to the Spirit Formless. Let the Form be your key to the mystery of the Formless One. And let the Formless One standing before you in a blazing light of Christ radiance, whose violet eyes penetrate your soul, give to you the key to the mystery of Form.

Form is focus. Form is forcefield. Form is force. Form in Matter decelerates the energies of Spirit. Form in Spirit accelerates the energies of Matter. When the Form and the Formless One occupy the same space and time, it is said: "Our God is All-in-all."

The riddle you must solve on the Path of the Rose Cross is your own occupation simultaneously of the Form and the

Formless One. The initiate of the ruby cube knows the Guru in Spirit, meets him/her on the inner planes from the first to the seventh heaven, walks and talks with the Guru in the etheric retreats of the Great White Brotherhood. The initiate knows the Guru in flesh and blood, is caught up in the mantle of the Guru, enters his/her bilocation, levitation, and stigmata.

The initiate is with the Guru in his Higher Self, in his lower self—in the self the Guru employs wherever and everywhere he is Guru. But the initiate is also with the Guru when he is present with the image and the likeness of the Guru whether fashioned like a lion by the fiery salamanders, with a face as a man by the sylphs, like a flying eagle by the undines, or like a calf by the gnomes.

No mask the Guru wears can fool the chela—the lover and the Beloved are one. To some the Guru has said, "Occupy till I come."[3] Occupy my Form, the time and space thereof, its flesh and blood. Occupy till I come to see what mischief mankind have made of my Form, belittling, berailing, betraying you in my name. I will leave my Form here and there, occupied by my chelas. I will see what they will do who say, "Hah! we now possess the Lord." In vain they have murdered the Form. They have gotten neither the Guru nor the chela who exit the Form and enter the Unformed Form at will with the bold challenge "Destroy this temple, and in three days I will raise it up."[4]

They did not believe him, the Great Guru of the Piscean Age. They crucified the Form of the calf, but he is not there. He is risen.[5] He is accelerated into the dimensions of the higher Form of his higher Consciousness. And they have gotten neither the victory of the self nor of the Self but the judgment for their deed quickly done—they who thought they were the possessors of the Form of God having bought it (from a cooperative chela who knew his role-playing well) for thirty pieces of silver.[6] Oh, how the Great Dramatist outplays himself and, in so doing, outplays the hand of the Fallen One who clenched his fist and dared God to come down to earth and strike him dead!

Behold the little child who caresses her doll as tenderly as if it were the infant Messiah. Behold the little Mother of the World who in her innocence knows God in the inanimate form because she has seen him in his Formlessness. Behold the little child out of whose innocence all the mysteries of the Rose Cross come together in the simple, natural expressions of life. And each gesture is a jewel of love becoming another jewel of love. Behold the little child, ye hard-hearted, stiffnecked generation, and behold your God! If you would but love her as she loves her doll, you would enter into God's kingdom and there find that the little child is the Great Guru you have sought.

I AM

Sanat Kumara

I will come to the uninitiated in many disguises until they see the emerald and the rainbow round about the throne and the jasper and the sardine and the one who sitteth in the center of the I AM THAT I AM.

See Rev. 4:6–8.

6

Sufficiency in the Guru

> *Holy, holy, holy, Lord God Almighty, which was, and is, and is to come.*
>
> *And when those beasts give glory and honour and thanks to him that sat on the throne, who liveth for ever and ever,*
>
> *The four and twenty elders fall down before him that sat on the throne, and worship him that liveth for ever and ever, and cast their crowns before the throne, saying,*
>
> *Thou art worthy, O Lord, to receive glory and honour and power: for thou hast created all things, and for thy pleasure they are and were created.* REVELATION 4:8–11

Eagles Who Gather Together Wheresoever the Body of Christ Is:

The sin of the Israelites was not that they did not receive the Christ in the person of the Guru Moses. Indeed, they received him. They followed him, their Saviour, the promised one, all the way from Egypt where the law had required that they become slaves under Pharaoh that they might receive God incarnate in the slave (chela) Moses. And Moses was a slave of the law, of his calling, of his I AM THAT I AM. But most of all, he was the slave of his people.

He would lay down his life for them that they might live. He was the Lord's vessel—chosen, initiated, anointed. He was the Guru because he knew how to be the chela of the Great Guru, the Christ Self within his people. And they knew it. They followed him all the way from the land of Egypt, where the second beast had initiated them on the Path of the Rose Cross through the mask of their taskmasters, where building towers for Pharaoh they learned to make bricks without straw for the building of the temple of the inner man.

Yoked like dumb oxen to the treadmill, they shared the crucifixion of the Calf that they might know him in his glory. And when the promised one came, they followed him out of the land of death through forty cycles of initiation in the Sinai wilderness to the gate of the Promised Land where, in future generations, those who kept the image of the throne would behold the resurrection of the Lamb, their future Guru incarnate.

No, the sin of the Israelites was not that they did not receive I AM THAT I AM as the personal presence of God who delivered them through the hand of Moses, even as the Father was in the Son. Indeed, the Israelites knew their God. They called upon his name. And so long as they kept his name sealed in their hearts, spoken from their lips, *YOD HE VAU HE,* that Lord was with them. But when they ceased to preserve that name a memorial unto all generations, the name that is for ever, they no longer knew his personal presence within the temple of being but relied instead upon the secondary source, the priesthood of the Levites. But this they did not unto themselves, but it was done unto them in succeeding generations.

What, then, was the sin of the Israelites who had received both the one sent, their Guru, and his God? It was this, my beloved. Their sufficiency was not in the Guru. In his presence or in his absence, the true chela knows that the grace of the Guru is sufficient for him. The Guru's consciousness, his ever-present Person, his energy available on command in the name of Christ, supplieth every need. But they liked his personality when he met their human demands, and they disliked it when he did not. This is the ultimate test of the chela. It must come to every one.

Moreover, it was the sin of the Israelites not to declare their sufficiency in the I AM Presence. Then as today, they go a whoring after other gods, other sources of pleasure, psychic thralldom, manipulation of energy, sexual perversions, lust for spiritual and material power, and the inducing of altered states of consciousness by chemical means and diabolical worship. Not finding their sufficiency in their Guru or his God, they failed utterly to find their sufficiency in their own inner Christ, their own inner Self.

Thus it came to pass that the path of chelaship under the lineal descent of the patriarchs, the prophets, and the kings which the Lord God sent to them was likewise no longer their sufficiency. So it is written in the law: Without obedience to the Guru, the chela has no right to the teachings of the Guru.

So it was done by Moses. And the wrath of God descended through him and he broke the two tables of testimony, tables of stone written with the finger of God. Out of the mouth of God the Word was spoken and to the mouth of God that Word returned, for it found no biding place in the hearts of the people. The chelas had failed the first initiation on the Path of the Rose Cross: *the sacrifice of the Lion of the tribe of Juda*—the sacrifice of the self (the soul) unto the Self (the I AM Presence personified in the Guru).

The law required that they transmute the energy misqualified. And so Moses "took the calf which they had made, and burnt it in the fire, and ground it to powder, and strawed it upon the water, and made the children of Israel drink of it." And unto the sons of Levi who gathered themselves together unto the Guru Moses and his I AM THAT I AM, it was given to slay the human ego of brother, companion, and neighbor. These children of the light must prove that the death of the lesser self is swallowed up in the victory of the resurrected Christ.[1]

But with all of this—and the 'slaying' of the three thousand—yet it was required that the Guru make 'an atonement' for the sins of his chelas. And it is ever thus. The Guru who has balanced his personal karma—all but a small portion to keep him in embodiment—the Guru that holds the balance of planetary karma must yet go about balancing the karma of his chelas. But the I AM THAT I AM who personified the law would not lay the sin of the chelas unto the Guru, for the Guru Moses was blameless before his chelas and before his God.

Thus the Lord charged each individual chela with the full burden of his word and his work: "Whosoever hath sinned against me, him will I blot out of my book." But the karma of the remainder of the children of Israel was set aside. And the Lord sent his Archangel, Michael, to go before Moses to bring him to the land promised unto Abraham, to Isaac, and to Jacob.

O children of the light, you were the remnant preserved, the seed of Abraham that became the seed of the twelve tribes of the sons of Jacob. And all of the Lord's promises hath he fulfilled. And now the hour is come which Moses foreknew—the day when the Lord would visit the sin of the people upon them. Now the Lord God requires the balancing of the sin of disobedience to the Guru and the sin of the soul's avowed sufficiency unto itself instead of unto the living Word.

Now all the earth trembles in the midst of the Dark Cycle, reeling against the returning karma of their affront to the Godhead. He sent his messenger and, lo, they did not heed him! But unto the children of the light who have waited for the day when they might prove their victory over this beast of self-idolatry, the Dark Cycle of their returning karma is the sign of their imminent victory in Armageddon and the Second Coming of Christ in the person of every ascended master who will once again walk and talk with his chelas as did Guru Maitreya in the garden of Eden. Now with full God-determination and empowered by the Holy Ghost, they will get the victory over the image of the beast which he has impressed upon their very souls in the place of the image of the Guru, and over his warped engram stamped on the seat-of-the-soul chakra to thwart the archetype of the Christ in their genes and chromosomes, and over the number of his name, 666, which is the perversion of the number of the third beast who had a face as a man. Yes, now is the victory unto the children of the light.

And the initiation of the chelas of the light in the ruby cube

Sufficiency in the Guru

by the Four Cosmic Forces is the promised sign of the victory. For in the initiation of Guru Maitreya is the key to the undoing of that which was done. So is the sign given in the coming of the two witnesses authorized by God to write again with the finger of God that which he wrote on two tables of testimony. These original writings were actually the mysteries of the Path of the Rose Cross which were withdrawn because some among the chelas were the spoilers. But in the day of the Lord's visitation he will raise his right hand against the spoilers and they shall no longer have power to thwart the divine plan in its imminent descent from the great blue causal body of the Great Divine Director—the living sponsor of the twelve tribes and of their Prophet, Samuel, and of their Messiah, Christ Jesus.

When, in the first instance, Moses was in Mount Sinai forty days and forty nights, the Lord gave to him two stone tablets and the law and commandments which he himself wrote upon them. But when he came in the second instance, Moses was required to bring his own tablets; and he was there with the incarnation of the I AM THAT I AM forty days and forty nights, neither eating bread nor drinking water; and he himself was required to write upon the tables the words of the covenant, only the Ten Words which have come down to you as the Ten Commandments.

But the law of the ruby ray and the mysteries of the lion, the calf, the image of the man, and the flying eagle which Ezekiel also was allowed to see as the archetypes of the Four Cosmic Forces—these were not recorded in the second instance, for only the Ten Commandments were given for a stiffnecked people. Nevertheless, by the intercession of the Guru Moses who found grace in His sight, the I AM THAT I AM set forth his promise "My Presence shall go with thee, and I will give thee rest." And Moses answered the Lord, "If thy Presence go not with me, carry us not up hence. For wherein shall it be known here that I and thy people have found grace in thy sight? Is it not in that thou goest with us? So shall we be separated, I and thy people, from all the people that are upon the face of the earth." And the I AM THAT I AM set his seal, saying, "I will do this thing also that thou hast spoken."

And so it came to pass that the Lord God manifested himself in a great cloud that covered the tent of the congregation, and the Shekinah glory of the Almighty I AM Presence filled the tabernacle where the tablets of the Ten Commandments were kept in the ark. And while the cloud abode on the tent of the congregation and the glory of the Lord filled the tabernacle, Moses was not able to enter. And the I AM THAT I AM fulfilled the promise to be in the midst of his people.

And when the cloud was taken up from over the tabernacle, the children of Israel went onward in all their journeys. But if the cloud were not taken up, then they journeyed not till the day that it was taken up. And the cloud of the I AM Presence was upon the tabernacle by day, and the sacred fire burned over it by night in full view of all of the house of Israel throughout all of their journeys.

Now is the hour of the return of the presence of the Flaming One to the tabernacle of the Lord and to the tent of the congregation. Now is the hour of the descent of the sacred fire into the tablets of the law sealed within the ark, burning in the midst of the mercy seat, guarded by real and living covering cherubim who hold within their hearts the Alpha/Omega spirals of the initiations on the Path of the Rose Cross.

Thus is the sign given in the coming of the two witnesses to whom it is given once again to write down the mysteries of the ruby cube. Some of these mysteries I, the Ancient of Days, will seal within these pages of the Pearls of Wisdom, but others of these mysteries I will seal only in the hearts of my chelas through the personal initiation of the ruby ray which I will release directly through the prepared heart chalice of our messenger.

In the first forty-day initiation cycle of Moses, I transferred to him the law of Alpha; and in the second cycle of forty, I transferred to him the grace of Omega. Now that which I have long waited to deliver unto my children may be delivered, for the hour of the judgment is come and the karma of the righteous returneth swiftly as an arrow to be consumed by my sacred fire which I, the Lord thy God, hath placed as the wheels within wheels of the chakras of my chelas.

And their sins shall be no more, for that portion of myself which I have placed within them is the sufficiency unto their payment of the last farthing. And the law shall be satisfied, every jot and tittle. And unto the unrighteous shall their karma also return, swift as an arrow, for they have not worshiped me nor paid homage to my name nor to my Word; therefore the acceleration of their sin will be for the canceling out of their soul's opportunity to repent and be saved.

So will the spoilers be no more, and the seed of the wicked shall be separated from the seed of the Word. And the children of God who are on the side of the I AM THAT I AM will at last know in peace the mysteries of the ruby ray.

I AM the Ancient of Days. I AM THAT I AM.

I AM worthy to receive glory and honour and power: for I AM the immortal Guru of the immortal chelas, and I have created all things, and for my pleasure in the I AM THAT I AM they are and were created.

I AM the living flame midst the tabernacle and the cloudy pillar.

I AM

Sanat Kumara

See Rev. 4:8–11; Exod. 32–34, 37–40; Ezek. 1.

7

Ezekiel, the Son of Man

And I looked, and, behold, a whirlwind came out of the north, a great cloud, and a fire infolding itself, and a brightness was about it, and out of the midst thereof as the colour of amber, out of the midst of the fire. Also out of the midst thereof came the likeness of four living creatures....

As for the likeness of their faces, they four had the face of a man, and the face of a lion, on the right side: and they four had the face of an ox on the left side; they four also had the face of an eagle....

As for the likeness of the living creatures, their appearance was like burning coals of fire, and like the appearance of lamps: it went up and down among the living creatures; and the fire was bright, and out of the fire went forth lightning. And the living creatures ran and returned as the appearance of a flash of lightning....

Whithersoever the spirit was to go, they went, thither was their spirit to go; and the wheels were lifted up over against them: for the spirit of the living creature was in the wheels....

And the likeness of the firmament upon the heads of the living creature was as the colour of the terrible crystal, stretched forth over their heads above....

And when they went, I heard the noise of their wings, like the noise of great waters, as the voice of the Almighty, the voice of speech, as the noise of an host: when they stood, they let down their wings....

And above the firmament that was over their heads was

Ezekiel, the Son of Man 41

> the likeness of a throne, as the appearance of a sapphire stone: and upon the likeness of the throne was the likeness as the appearance of a man above upon it.
>
> And I saw as the colour of amber, as the appearance of fire round about within it, from the appearance of his loins even upward, and from the appearance of his loins even downward, I saw as it were the appearance of fire, and it had brightness round about.
>
> As the appearance of the bow that is in the cloud in the day of rain, so was the appearance of the brightness round about. This was the appearance of the likeness of the glory of the LORD. And when I saw it, I fell upon my face, and I heard a voice of one that spake.   EZEKIEL 1

To the Living Souls Who Would Become
 the Quickening Spirits:

Let the souls of the initiates of the Ruby Ray draw nigh; for I, the LORD, the Ancient of Days, would speak with thee concerning thy mission to the multitudes. I AM Sanat Kumara. I AM the LORD. And the hand of the LORD is upon the prophets and the saints.

In my appearance to Ezekiel in the land of the Chaldeans by the river Chebar, I unveiled the mystery of Being as the "great cloud" of the Shekinah. In an apocalyptic visitation, I uncovered the dwelling of God in the sacred fire infolding itself. And behold, he saw the visible Presence of the I AM THAT I AM. He saw his glory, my glory, in the brightness of the Cloud—the same Cloud that had enveloped Sinai when the glory of the LORD was revealed to Moses, the same light that had infilled the tabernacle, the same coiled caduceus that had led the Israelites and would lead them still, the same essence of my Presence that had filled Solomon's temple and would now become the foundation foursquare of the New Jerusalem.

Yes, Ezekiel, the Son of man, would see what the Elect One Enoch had seen, what Jesus Christ would show to the beloved

John, Son of the Blessed. It was the vision again of the four living creatures, the watchmen upon the four walls of the Holy City, ever with the Spirit of the Lamb. "And they went every one straight forward: whither the spirit was to go, they went; and they turned not when they went."

Unto Ezekiel, I, the Ancient of Days, gave the commission to exhort the exiled children of the Mother to repentance that they might balance their karma of disobedience to the Son of God. For by their rejection of me in the person of the I AM THAT I AM and the holy prophets, they had been expelled from the City Foursquare, from the Guru-chela relationship, even as Adam and Eve had been expelled by Maitreya from the Lemurian mystery school.

Now among the captive Israelites in Babylon, Ezekiel beholds the opening of the heavens even as I AM the opener of the door of the third eye of the prophets and the saints unto the visions of God. There is no time and space. I, the LORD thy God, stand within thy midst, O children of the sun. I AM come for the repentance and the restoration of the true Israel in the United States of America. I AM come with the vision of the restoration of the City Foursquare, built upon the likeness of the four living creatures. And the name of the city is THE LORD IS THERE.

Ezekiel saw the countenance of the Son of man in 'four faces', or phases. He understood the Christ, the archetype of God, manifesting himself in the Son of man, having the face of a man, the face of a lion, the face of an ox, and the face of an eagle. He saw the road of restoration of the Davidic kingdom through the enlightenment of Christed man and woman. He saw the coming of the Messiah and his demonstration of the four paths of preparation as the four arms of the ruby cross.

He saw the ruby cross whirling in the vortex of the whirlwind. He knew intimately the initiations of the sons and daughters of God who were called upon to become pillars in the temple of my God. I gave to him the initiations of the rose cross. He submitted himself to the cross. He gave his life for Israel. He set the example as the man of Aquarius. He did not let me down; and the wings of the four living creatures did not let him down. And the wings of the four living creatures carried the prophet whithersoever he went as the spokesman of the Word of the LORD.

As the Son of man, Ezekiel became the soul of a nation. He was and is the voice of conscience, the standard-bearer speaking to them hour by hour of what is right and what is wrong. He speaketh the "Yea, yea!" and the "Nay, nay!" of the prophet. He is the teacher of righteousness by the Path of the Ruby Ray on which I received him and he received me.

He taught the truth that "every man shall bear his own burden." The burden of this man of Aquarius was the pot of water. This water-bearer left the example for sons and daughters of God moving in the stream of the God consciousness of love to bear in this hour the crystal clear stream of the water of life of the Mother. His water is the water of the resurrection. His resurrection is the resurrection of the Son of God, the inner Logos of the outer Son of man.

Ezekiel resurrects the Mother in Israel, for he saw the Mother lights going up and down among the living creatures. She the bright fire, she the lightning out of the fire. And the rings of the living creatures full of eyes and their wheels in Spirit and in Matter, "as it were a wheel in the middle of a wheel," I revealed to Ezekiel as the sacred centers of consciousness in the I AM Presence and in the Son of God. And Ezekiel, the Son of man, was God-taught by me to bear the burden of Mother light throughout the one hundred forty-four chakras of being and in the seven planes of heaven and earth within his temple, focused in the seven chakras.

Now as you enter the Path of the Rose Cross because you love and you love and you love, I AM come to initiate you in the cycle of the Son of man. For you, O living soul, are predestined to become the quickening spirit. You have heard it said, "The first man Adam was made a living soul; the last Adam was made a quickening spirit" and that "the first man is of the earth, earthy" and that "the second man is the LORD from heaven" and that the children of God who have "borne the image of the earthy" shall also "bear the image of the heavenly." I AM come to teach you how to fulfill this commandment of the LORD, for this is the purpose of the Ruby Ray. It is the blood of Christ by which you are redeemed.

The "natural man," so-called, who comes wearing the "natural body" fashioned of the earth, earthy, is the "living potential," the soul sent into worlds of time and space in order that he might choose to be the "spiritual man" with the "spiritual body." As it was given to Jesus Christ to demonstrate to you step by step the alchemy of the Path of the Rose Cross, so I come to you, men and women of the twentieth century, to give to you the law and the grace whereby you, too, may know the True Self as "the LORD from heaven."

As you have borne the image of the earthy when you were children "under the law" of personal and planetary karma "in bondage under the elements of the world," so now in the fullness of the time that is come, you shall bear the image of the heavenly through "the Spirit of his Son" whom God sent "into your hearts, crying," as Paul witnessed of the indwelling Christ, "Abba, Father." This Son, "made of a woman, made under the law" of regenerate Life, is come to redeem one and all who have been under the law of sin, disease, and death. Now let us come together, my children, that you might understand the meaning of the initiation of "the adoption of sons."

If "flesh and blood cannot inherit the kingdom of God," and they cannot, even as "corruption doth not inherit incorruption," how, then, can the natural man become the spiritual man? How can you, the living soul, become you, the quickening spirit? It is the mystery of the Holy Grail. It is the mystery of the Incarnation.

The Path of the Ruby Ray is the path of understanding the Principle of the Law and the Person of the Lawgiver. It is a path of initiation based upon the covenant of the Father and the Son made in the beginning with the souls who descended out of the spheres of the Great Causal Body into the planes of time and space to exercise the gift of free will.

The Path of the Ruby Ray is the path of freedom: God's freedom to give himself unto a living soul. Soul freedom to become the possessor of God under the covenants of the Law and the Lawgiver. The inheritance of God consciousness is a transmission by right under the Law from parent to offspring. Not flesh and blood but a living soul fused by free will to the quickening spirit can inherit the kingdom (consciousness) of God. The soul whose self-awareness has become the quickening spirit is the only one who can rightfully claim possession of God. It is the fusion of this soul and this Spirit that enables the Son of man to gain the full inheritance of the Son of God. Because, in effect, he has become God.

As long as the heir apparent to the throne of grace, to the trinity of Love, remains a child as Paul taught, he "differeth nothing from a servant, though he be lord of all." It is this childhood in which I find the lost tribes of Israel—lost because they have lost the memory of the Ancient of Days and of the name of the LORD, I AM THAT I AM, and of their origin, the beginning and the ending in Alpha and Omega. It is from this childhood that I would lead you safely by the hand, one by one, to the Personhood of God through the door that is opened in heaven unto the sacred fire infolding itself, unto the noise of great waters, unto the voice of the Almighty, the voice of his speech that becomes the noise of the hosts of the LORD.

Therefore, this week I would have you meditate upon the LORD from heaven and his appearance of fire, the color of the terrible crystal and the color of amber and of burnished brass. Yes, meditate upon the likeness of the living creatures, their appearance like burning coals of fire, and a firmament above their heads having the likeness of a throne, as the appearance of a sapphire stone. Yes, meditate upon the rings, the wheels, and the wings of the living creatures and the appearance of the likeness of the glory of the LORD who is I AM THAT I AM centered in the rainbow rays of the brightness of the spiritual body.

I AM the LORD from heaven. I have sent for thee, my beloved, that thou mayest come through the open door of thy God consciousness and realize thyself as the second man and as the appearance of a man upon the likeness of the throne.

I AM thy Threefold Flame,

Sanat Kumara

See Ezek. 1; 1 Cor. 2:15; Gal. 4.

8

The Commission of the LORD to the Prophets and the Saints

And he said unto me, Son of man, stand upon thy feet, and I will speak unto thee.

And the Spirit entered into me when he spake unto me, and set me upon my feet, that I heard him that spake unto me.

And he said unto me, Son of man, I send thee to the children of Israel, to a rebellious nation that hath rebelled against me: they and their fathers have transgressed against me, even unto this very day....

And thou shalt say unto them, Thus saith the LORD GOD.

And they, whether they will hear, or whether they will forbear, (for they are a rebellious house,) yet shall know that there hath been a prophet among them....

And thou shalt speak my words unto them,...

But thou, Son of man, hear what I say unto thee; Be not thou rebellious like that rebellious house: open thy mouth, and eat that I give thee.

And when I looked, behold, an hand was sent unto me; and, lo, a roll of a book was therein;

And he spread it before me; and it was written within and without: and there was written therein lamentations, and mourning, and woe.

Moreover he said unto me, Son of man, eat that thou findest; eat this roll, and go speak unto the house of Israel.

So I opened my mouth, and he caused me to eat that roll.

And he said unto me, Son of man, cause thy belly to eat, and fill thy bowels with this roll that I give thee. Then did I eat it; and it was in my mouth as honey for sweetness. And he said unto me, Son of man, go, get thee unto the house of Israel, and speak with my words unto them.

EZEKIEL 2, 3

My Beloved in the Presence Which I AM:

The commission begins with the appearance of the I AM Presence. This appearance of the Lord God Almighty unto the living soul is the anointing of consciousness with the precious oil of God-reality. It is an infusion of power for the soul's fusion with the Spirit. It is an infusion of wisdom direct, by the hand of the angel of the LORD's Presence, sent unto the prophets and the saints, having therein "a roll of a book."

Therefore, ye saints of the Ruby Ray, open thy mouth and eat the roll that is written within and without. And cause thy belly to eat it and fill thy bowels with it. And it shall be in thy mouth as honey for sweetness. Thus is the appearance of the I AM Presence unto the soul for the soul's assimilation of the Teachings of the Ascended Masters within the seven chakras—the wheels within wheels of the Law.

The roll is a scroll of the Law. And of the "lamentations" of the LORD's prophet that the people have disobeyed his Word. And of the "mourning" of them that wail in vain without the walled City of Light: for the Lord of Sabaoth, deliverer of the Karma, draweth nigh. And of the "Woe!" spoken by the Son as the descending judgment of words and deeds.

O sons and daughters of God, when the hand of my servant whom I have sent unto thee spreads before thee the roll of the book of the Law, do not reject it. For in rejecting the book of the Law is the rejection not only of the Teacher and the teaching but also of the path of initiation under the Ruby Ray.

The same book of the Ancient of Days is held in the hand of the Mother of Exiles who is portrayed in the Statue of Liberty.

Great Goddess she stands on the east gate of the City Foursquare proclaiming unto the pilgrims of light: "I AM the open door of cosmic consciousness unto the sons and daughters of the Ancient of Days!" Her torch is the sign of the "fire infolding itself," fiery vortex of the Beloved, the individualized I AM Presence, whose color of 'amber' is the golden pink glow-ray of wisdom and love emitting from the first and second 'rings' of the Causal Body into which the living soul is initiated on the Path of the Ruby Ray.

And the mission begins with the appearance of the Woman, Liberty, clothed with the sun and having the crown of twelve stars. She is the Great Guru Mother to the tribes of Israel who will know her in the flying eagle even as they will know the Father, the Son, and the Holy Spirit as the lion, the man, and the calf. The appearance of the archetypes of being—the Four Cosmic Forces surrounding the I AM Presence—must come to each son and daughter of God who begins the mission of the Rose Cross. And it will come—surely it will come—by the crystal clear stream of our Mother's consciousness who is even now giving birth to the Manchild, the Christ consciousness, within you.

Therefore I AM come, the Ancient of Days. I send to you the hand of my messenger and in her hand the book sealed with seven seals. I AM the Lamb who shall open the book. Reject me not. Neither reject my coming in the person of Gautama, of Maitreya, of Jesus, and of the two witnesses and the saints who carry my torch even as their Mother carries the torch—who shall wear my crown, even as their Mother wears my crown.

First we deal with the 'belly', the solar plexus, or dwelling *place of the Son* of Righteousness. This is the orifice of the desire body. First things first: Let the desire body be purged by the meditation of the living soul upon the book of the Law. Second, we deal with the 'bowels', the seat-of-the-soul chakra. This is the orifice of the soul's self-awareness which we call 'solar awareness'. Let it be filled with all of the mysteries of God that I have sent by my 'Angel' of the Seventh Ray, Saint Germain.

Now, chelas of the Ruby Ray, let all of thy desiring be to fill thy days and thy nights—the Alpha and the Omega of the T'ai chi in the solar plexus—with the desiring of God. And let thy free will be to choose to ensoul within thy living soul and within thy mental body, *mind/consciousness,* the sayings of the LORD. These sayings of the I AM THAT I AM are sponsored by the entire Spirit of the Great White Brotherhood through Saint Germain, the Son of man unto the Aquarian age. Thus the appearance of your own beloved I AM Presence and your assimilation of the 'body' and the 'blood' of the living Word communicated to you by the ascended masters through their messengers is the order of the day of your mission to the multitudes which you shall perform, my beloved, on the Path of the Ruby Ray.

Unto your living souls, O children of God, the LORD hath sent the quickening Spirit of his Son into your hearts. When you, child-man, determine to exercise your prerogative as the heir of God, you may become by freewill election the *Manchild* through this Spirit of the Son who is sealed in your hearts. This Lord from heaven is the inner man, the second man. Until you enter in to the bridal chamber, the secret chamber of the heart, you are still the first man, the outer man, the mere potential of that which is to come. Yet is not the potential the God aborning, the sleeping Buddha, the silent Mother?

The living soul may choose to live as the natural man fulfilling the desires of the natural body. Or it may choose to live as the spiritual man fulfilling the desires of the spiritual body of God.

The Path of the Ruby Ray is the path of free will. It is the free will of the Father and the Son to give unto the living soul of the child his lawful inheritance of the Person of Christ. This Person is to the soul its own Christ consciousness, its own *Christ Self.* By this act of free will, the Father and the Son choose to 'adopt' the soul, to make it the lawful and rightful heir of the kingdom of God—the possessor of his consciousness of Power, Wisdom, and Love. This adoption by the alchemy of the Holy Spirit becomes the *adaptation* of the soul, its transmutation into the quickened and quickening Spirit.

The Path of the Ruby Ray is the path of the free will of the *child/servant* to adopt the Father and the Son as its very own Selfhood, to put on the vestments of the Lord from heaven and thereby to share with him the full glory of the *heir/Son*. Therefore the soul is no longer the child-man but the Manchild. He is the Son of man and he is ready to be called of the LORD to his commission as Watchman of the Word. His acceptance of this commission allows him to begin the path of initiation whereby the "Sun behind the sun," (the Son of God (+) behind the Son of man (–)) will ultimately dwell in him 'bodily' (in form and in formlessness). And the triangle of Spirit and the triangle of Matter will be congruent in time and space and in eternity.

The Son of man Jesus, in whom the Son of God, the Christ, was incarnate, fulfilled the office of the Lamb who gives the promise of the initiation of the indwelling Trinity to his disciples saying, "And I will pray the Father, and he shall give you another Comforter, that he may abide with you for ever."

This Son of man confirmed my commission given unto me by the Nameless One on behalf of every living soul who should exercise its option to be the quickening Spirit. This commission is the transfer of the Holy Spirit from the Father, by (through) the Son, unto the disciples of the Word Incarnate, East and West. This office and the officeholder, this mantle and the mantle-wearer, is the authority for the transfer of the Trinity. And the exercise of the office is by Christ discrimination. Understand, then, my beloved, that the fullness of the office of the Son of God was upon the Son of man Jesus in the final hours of his victorious embodiment when he declared:

"The Comforter, the Holy Spirit of Truth whom ye know— *because I have chosen you and you have chosen me and thereby WE ARE ONE*—dwelleth with you and shall be in you." These words could be spoken only by the One anointed to enter the soul as the Son, by the leave of the Father, there to invoke the Holy Ghost as the Person of ultimate Truth and Comfort to the soul.

That Jesus knew whereof he spoke—by the authority of

my Word vouchsafed to him—is clear in several passages of Scripture:

> I will not leave you comfortless: I will come to you.
>
> Yet a little while, and the world seeth me no more; but ye see me: because I live, ye shall live also. At that day ye shall know that I *AM in my Father, and ye in me, and I in you.*
>
> He that hath my commandments, and keepeth them, he it is that loveth me: and he that loveth me shall be loved of my Father, *and I will love him, and will manifest myself to him.* . . .
>
> If a man love me, he will keep my words: and my Father will love him, *and we will come unto him, and make our abode with him.*[1]

When the Son of man Jesus prayed to me, the Ancient of Days, as I was and as I AM the holder of the office of the Person of the Father (a term that is synonymous with the Person of God as the Great Guru), he acknowledged my commission as the Lamb[2] which I had transferred to him in the order of the lineal descent of hierarchy. And he always addressed me through the ascending spiral of the Christ and the Buddha, Lord Maitreya and Lord Gautama. This acknowledgment of hierarchy and his loving allegiance to the immortal Gurus who preceded him was not limiting; on the contrary, it gave to the Son of man unlimited access to the manifest Son of God in Maitreya, in Gautama, and, through them, in all of the hosts of heaven. Thus by the chain of God-free being "a door was opened in heaven." By that door he received the all-Power/Wisdom/Love of the Lord God Almighty. He then lifted up his eyes to heaven and offered the Prayer of Intercession which only the incarnate Lamb can give:

> Father, the hour is come; glorify thy Son, that thy Son also may glorify thee: as thou hast given him power over all flesh, *that he should give eternal life to as many as thou hast given him.*

And this is life eternal, that they might know thee the only true God, and Jesus Christ, whom thou hast sent.

I have glorified thee on the earth: I have finished the work which thou gavest me to do.

And now, O Father, glorify thou me with thine own self with the glory which I had with thee before the world was.

I have manifested thy name unto the men which thou gavest me out of the world: thine they were, and thou gavest them me; and they have kept thy word.

Now they have known that all things whatsoever thou hast given me are of thee.

For I have given unto them the words which thou gavest me; and they have received them, and have known surely that I came out from thee, and they have believed that thou didst send me.

I pray for them: I pray not for the world, but for them which thou hast given me; for they are thine.

And all mine are thine, and thine are mine; and I AM glorified in them.

And now I am no more in the world, but these are in the world, and I come to thee. Holy Father, keep through thine own name those whom thou hast given me, *that they may be one, as we are.*

While I was with them in the world, I kept them in thy name: those that thou gavest me I have kept, and none of them is lost, but the son of perdition; that the scripture might be fulfilled.

And now come I to thee; and these things I speak in the world, that they might have my joy fulfilled in themselves.

I have given them thy word; and the world hath hated them, because they are not of the world, even as I am not of the world.

I pray not that thou shouldest take them out of the world, but that thou shouldest keep them from the evil.

They are not of the world, even as I am not of the world.

Sanctify them through thy truth: thy word is truth.

As thou hast sent me into the world, even so have I also sent them into the world.

And for their sakes I sanctify myself, that they also might be sanctified through the truth.

Neither pray I for these alone, but for them also which shall believe on me through their word;

That they all may be one; as thou, Father, art in me, and I in thee, that they also may be one in us: that the world may believe that thou hast sent me.

And the glory which thou gavest me I have given them [I have initiated them in the light/energy/consciousness of my I AM Presence]; *that they may be one, even as we are one: I in them, and thou in me, that they may be made perfect in one;* and that the world may know that thou hast sent me, and hast loved them, as thou hast loved me.

Father, *I will that they also,* whom thou hast given me, *be with me where I AM;* that they may behold my glory [the magnitude of my I AM Presence], which thou hast given me: for thou lovedst me before the foundation of the world.

O righteous Father, the world hath not known thee: but I have known thee, and these have known that thou hast sent me.

And I have declared unto them thy name [I AM THAT I AM] and will declare it: *that the love wherewith thou hast loved me may be in them, and I in them.*[3]

It is evident in these living words of Christ that the predestination of the adoption of sons is foreordained. It is the foreordained freedom of the Father in the Son to surrender Itself through the Holy Spirit to the soul. And it is the foreordained freedom of the soul to surrender itself to the Holy Spirit by the Father in the Son and by the Son in the Father. When that which is above and that which is below exercise this free will simultaneously, Creator and creation are 'no more twain, but one flesh'.[4] That 'One' is then called the *Son of man*.

The Son of man is this One in whom the Son of God, the Light of the Shekinah shining in all its resplendent glory, is indwelling in *man*ifestation. Wearing the mantle of the Son of God, then, the Son of man is also the manifest 'Presence' of the Fatherhood of God and of his Holy Spirit. His declaration of being to the disciples worlds without end thus remains, as I have told you, to the present hour: "I and my Father are One."[5] This is the mantra of the true Guru-chela relationship establishing you as a connecting link in the eternal chain of Self-transcending being. By its use you, O Son of man, are daily integrating your solar awareness with the Son of God (your Christ awareness) who is verily the Great Integrator—the integrating Principle of the Threefold Flame of your Life—integrating your soul with the Father and the Holy Spirit.

The declaration of the indwelling Presence in the Son of man Jesus was heard by Peter, James, and John as the voice that spoke out of the Cloud (the dwelling place of the LORD) saying, "This is my beloved Son in whom I AM manifesting my transfiguring sacred fire, in whom I AM in manifestation well pleased."[6] Where heaven and earth meet in the sacred heart of the Son, the disciples of the Christ witness the alchemical marriage of the soul and the Spirit of their Lord and Master—"... that the world may know that thou hast sent me." Behold the Lamb, the Word Incarnate, who is become the archetype of the four living creatures! Behold, "I and my Father (my Guru) are One."

As the wayshower of the Path of the Ruby Ray whereby the soul is fused with the Christ Person, this quickening Spirit becomes the forerunner of the Aquarian age. Aquarius! The prophesied epoch of the habitation of the earth by the few and then the many quickening Spirits who reveal to the multitudes the Person of Christ as THE LORD OUR RIGHTEOUSNESS,[7] the indwelling Christ Self. This, my beloved, is your mission to the multitudes which you shall accomplish by the example of your words and your works.

You, as Sons of man, heirs of God consciousness through Christ, are called to be representatives of me in every nation. Fused with the Christ, infused with the light of the Ruby Ray from my heart, I initiate you into the spiritual body of God. Be fruitful and multiply and replenish the earth with Light. You who make your lawful choice to be bearers of the image of the heavenly, I send you forth as quickening Spirits unto the multitudes. Now ensoul the kingdom of God, his consciousness come, for thereby you shall be called the I AM race.

Such an one was Ezekiel, the forerunner of your calling. Therefore, my sons and daughters, go and be as he was, Prophet of the LORD, Watchman of the Word unto the house of Israel, visionary and revelator of the Shekinah glory and the Four Cosmic Forces representative of the four types of the Christ Person.

I come again to reveal the way of the sacred science of the Mother whereby you, the quickened and the quickening Spirits, shall embody the four faces of Christ.

I AM

Sanat Kumara

See Ezek. 2, 3.

9

The Initiations Foursquare on the Path of the Ruby Ray

But the house of Israel will not hearken unto thee; for they will not hearken unto me: for all the house of Israel are impudent and hardhearted.

Behold, I have made thy face strong against their faces, and thy forehead strong against their foreheads.

As an adamant harder than flint have I made thy forehead: fear them not, neither be dismayed at their looks, though they be a rebellious house.

Moreover he said unto me, Son of man, all my words that I shall speak unto thee receive in thine heart, and hear with thine ears.

And go, get thee to them of the captivity, unto the children of thy people, and speak unto them, and tell them, Thus saith the LORD GOD; whether they will hear, or whether they will forbear.

Then the Spirit took me up, and I heard behind me a voice of a great rushing, saying, Blessed be the glory of the LORD from his place.

I heard also the noise of the wings of the living creatures that touched one another, and the noise of the wheels over against them, and a noise of a great rushing.

So the Spirit lifted me up, and took me away, and I went in bitterness, in the heat of my Spirit; but the hand of the LORD was strong upon me.

Then I came to them of the captivity at Telabib, that dwelt by the river of Chebar, and I sat where they sat, and remained there astonished among them seven days.

EZEKIEL 3

Beloved Who Have the Courage to Accept
   the Lord's Commission:

Be thou not afraid! Neither of the terror by night nor of the arrow that flieth by day; neither of the pestilence that walketh in darkness nor of the destruction that wasteth at noonday! For I, the LORD thy God, AM with thee.

O America, O nations of the earth! I AM Sanat Kumara, the Ancient of Days. I live forevermore within thy midst to show unto thee the way of the watchmen on the wall of the LORD. I call the sons and daughters of Light to mount their positions on the north gate, the east gate, the south gate, and the west gate of the City Foursquare. For destruction lieth in wait at the comings and the goings of the children of God. And the hosts of the LORD are encamped round about for the victory.

The seven holy Kumaras enlist the support of numberless numbers from every walk of life, every path of initiation, to join and enjoin the legions of light in the battle for the preservation of the flame of freedom on earth. Let the child choose to become the Son and invoke the full inheritance of his joint-heirship with Christ to put down the slayers and the betrayers of an infant humanity aborning in the womb of the Mother.

Sons of God in the vanguard of the victory. I AM come to release to you the sacred science of the Mother for your embodiment of the four faces of Christ. Now study the Cosmic Clock that has been given to you by Mother Mary through the messengers. For the foundation of the building of the City Foursquare has already been laid in her outline of the four quadrants of being and in the four Persons of the Godhead to be crystallized within the soul through the alchemical elements fire, air, water, and earth.

Now let us use this Cosmic Clock to diagram the offices of the Four Cosmic Forces: the Lion as the Father, the Calf as the Holy Spirit, the Man as the Son, and the Eagle as the Mother. Initiators of the soul under the hierarchies of Leo, Taurus, Aquarius, and Scorpio, they make the sign of the Ruby Cross.

These Four Persons of Cosmic Christhood are the initiators—through Lord Maitreya, Lord Gautama, Lord Jesus, and me through the office of the Mother and the two witnesses—of the initiations foursquare on the Path of the Ruby Ray. These initiations are: the Initiation of Sacrifice under the Lion, the Initiation of Service under the Calf, the Initiation of Surrender under the Man, and the Initiation of Selflessness under the Eagle.

Now, if you are in accord to enter the Path of the Ruby Ray and to receive its initiations, you must address the Incarnate Word in the following order of your soul's submission to the hierarchy of light to whom the Nameless One has entrusted the Ruby Ray in your behalf:

Beloved Mighty I AM Presence, beloved Holy Christ Self, and beloved Holy Christ Selves of the saints of the Church, beloved two witnesses, Lanello and Mother, beloved Jesus the Christ, beloved Maitreya Buddha, beloved Gautama Buddha, beloved Sanat Kumara, the Ancient of Days, beloved hosts of the LORD serving unto the throne of the Lord God Almighty: I AM thy living potential become thy quickening Spirit. I AM thy child who has claimed thy Sonship. In thy name, I AM THAT I AM, I therefore invoke the initiations of the Ruby Ray through thy emissaries and thy messengers above and below, in Spirit and in Matter. For I and my Father are One, and I will to be thy witness on the path of sainthood.

Having made this invocation, you are now ready to receive the two witnesses as the person of Christ Jesus come in the flesh. This confession is your calling and the necessary conviction for your beginning on the Path.

As the two witnesses bear to you my good tidings and the true teachings of the Lord Jesus Christ, so the Lord Jesus, in the advent of this his Second Coming into your heart, speaks to you of the initiations of his great Guru, the Lord Maitreya:

First you must show forth, my beloved, the face of the *Lion*, archetype of the Great Baptizer by water and by fire. Through the Initiation of Sacrifice—the sacrifice of the self—your soul shall slay the beast of self-indulgence and enter into the baptism of the LORD.

To be baptized of him is to experience with him the opening of the heavens and the descent of the Spirit of God lighting upon you in him and him in you "like a dove." To be baptized of him is to hear the voice from heaven saying, "This is my beloved Son in whom I AM well pleased. This is my beloved Son of man in whom I AM in the indwelling Son of God."[1] To be baptized with him is to be the instrument with him of the transfer of the fire and the water unto the multitudes through the mastery of the heart. It is to teach the mastery of the Self, the soul in the Christ, in the etheric (memory) fire body.

The Lion is the wayshower through the hierarchy of Leo and the fire element. He is the archetype of the Christ in the fire quadrant of the Spirit/Matter universe. He teaches the command of the sacred fire in heaven and in earth through the angels of fire and the elementals of fire. Thus through the sacrifice of the mutable self in small ways and in great, you shall gain the self-mastery of the Immutable Self: the LION. And you, the Lion, shall discover the Self to Be the "*ION* of Light." You the "free electron" who by free election will become the "Permanent Atom" having the positive charge, saying, "I AM *that I AM*." And behold, the LION's ION is with God! "I and my Father are One."

Second, my beloved, you must show forth the face of the *Calf*, archetype of the Christ crucified. Through the Initiation of Service, your soul shall slay the beast of self-love and enter into the crucifixion of the LORD.

To be crucified with him is to be with him on the Ruby Cross in the death of the human ego and in the life of the Divine Ego. To be crucified with him is to be with him in the alchemy of Self-transcendence whereby this mortal shall put on immortality and this corruptible shall put on incorruption.[2] To be crucified with him is to be sealed with him, the chela with the Guru, in the tomb of Spirit/Matter.

This tomb is the ruby cube suspended as the sarcophagus

within the King's Chamber of the Great Pyramid. Within the center of the ruby cube, suspended at the two-thirds level where the fire burns brightly, the crucified one declares to thy soul:

> I in thou and thou in me
> Before Resurrection's Spirit we bow,
> Thou in me and I in thee
> To Resurrection's Flame we vow.
> I in the Father, the Father in me
> Now, O soul, we make our abode with thee.
> Come forth, O Threefold Flame of Life,
> Be now the resurrection of the Lamb
> Within the Lamb's wife.
> Come forth, O light of immortality,
> Consume the dark of that mortality.
> Descend, O Spirit of Living Fire,
> Thou Incorruptible One!
> Descend, consume all death desire
> Snuff out the corruptible one.

To be crucified with him is to be with him this day in paradise[3] in the bliss of Alpha and Omega within the nexus of the Rose Cross. To be crucified with him is to be the instrument of the water, the blood, and the wine unto the initiates of the sacred fire processioning to the Sphinx, the Great Guru in Taurus. It is to teach the mastery of the Self, the soul in the Christ, in the physical (earth) body.

The Calf is the wayshower through the hierarchy of Taurus and the earth element. The Calf is the archetype of the Christ in the earth quadrant of the Spirit/Matter universes, the Christ of *A*lpha/Omega come in the *F*ohat (fire) of the *El* (Elohim). He teaches the command of the earth form and formless, of the Mother and the Father in the base and the crown chakras, through the angel devas of the earth and the elementals of the earth.

Third, my beloved, you must show forth the face of a

Man, archetype of the living Saviour who saves his own through the resurrection of the soul unto your God and my God, your Father and my Father, 'your' I AM Presence who is also 'my' I AM Presence;[4] for "I AM *THAT* I AM." Through the Initiation of Surrender—the surrender of the self—your soul shall slay the beast of selfishness and enter into the resurrection of the Son of man.

To be resurrected with him is to be the Christ Mind in the air quadrant. The literal inner meaning of Man—M-a-n—is the one who has become the *M*other *a*tom with the *n*egative charge. In other words, the Son of God (+) who is incarnate in the Son of man (–) is become the archetype of androgynous (+/–) being in Matter (–). To be the Son of man means to evince the face, the Image, of the only begotten Son of God. To be resurrected with him is to resurrect that Image in whose likeness every living soul was made. And every living soul who is quickened must be quickened by that Image, and without that Image was not any thing made that was made.[5] It is an engram impressed upon the rods and cones of consciousness.

Souls moving to the fount of the living waters of the Ancient of Days, borne by the Christ of Aquarius, know that face shining through the prophets and the saints. To be with him in the resurrection is to be with him in the tomb of Matter for the victory of life over hell and death, for the proving unto the lost sheep of the house of Israel that death is not real and that the soul can transcend itself and the cycles of karma in time and space by the glorious Spirit of the Resurrection. To be with him in the tomb is to invoke the Flame of the Resurrection with the angelic representatives of Alpha and Omega standing at the 'beginning' and the 'ending', in Aries and in Pisces, at the 'head' and the 'feet' of the body of the Lord.

To be with the man of Pisces, who in you and in Saint Germain is become the man of Aquarius, is to descend into hell, into the astral plane, to exhort that impudent and hardhearted house of Israel—to warn the wicked from his wicked way and to warn the righteous man from his iniquity. To be the initiate of the Great Guru in Aquarius, the blessed and beloved Saint Germain, the Son of man in the Son of God, the ascended master, is to teach and to preach to the whole body of God during forty cycles from the hour of thy resurrection until the hour of thy ascension. It is to transfer the entire contents of the "roll of a book" given to Ezekiel and the "little book" given to John to the children of God on earth.[6]

Therefore keepers of the flame of God-freedom in Aquarius who would resurrect the full glory of the person of the Ancient of Days, of his memory and the mind of God in him, must be responsible for all of the teachings of the Great White Brotherhood that have gone before in this dispensation of our two witnesses. Let them then wisely study to show themselves approved unto God in order that they might receive, day by day, the initiations of the Ruby Ray. Let them secure our Word published in book and tape and lesson. Let them eat it up unto the 'bitterness' and the 'burning' in the belly and the bowels until the whole man is made whole in the face of a Man.

The face of a Man is the wayshower through the hierarchy of Aquarius and the air element. This image of the Christ fashioned as a Man teaches the command of the air in form and formlessness, of the soul in the seat-of-the-soul and the third-eye chakras, through the angels of the terrible crystal and the Great Silent Watchers of the All-Seeing Eye immaculate.

Fourth, my beloved, you must show forth the face of the *flying Eagle*, archetype of the Great Regenerator of water and of earth, *E*nergy (Spirit) of *A*lpha/Omega in the *G*eometry of the *El* in Earth (Matter). Through the Initiation of Selflessness, your soul shall slay the beast of self-idolatry and self-love and enter into the ascension of the flying Eagle.

To be with him in the ascension, you must first show yourself alive with him after your crucifixion and your resurrection "by many infallible proofs... and speaking of the things pertaining to the kingdom of God." To be regenerated of him is to be baptized of the Holy Ghost. To partake of his ascension is to be witnesses of his ascension "both in Jerusalem, and in all Judea, and in Samaria, and unto the uttermost part of the earth" by the power of the Holy Ghost.

> To be with him in the ascension is to follow him
> From the three crosses of Golgotha that he bore,
> To the hill of Bethany where he wore
> Transparent garments of living light
> And the Cloud received him out of their sight.
> To be with him in the ascension
> Is to tarry in the New Jerusalem
> Until ye see him come, the King of Glory,
> "In like manner as ye have seen him go."[7]

To be ascended with him and yet to remain unascended is to witness unto Christ's teachings, yea, his demonstration of the ascension that is promised in the end of this age to all who shall preach his gospel to every nation and every plane of being. To ascend with him is to move in and among the multitudes with a message of the soul's liberation through the Mother Light—the white light of her ascending currents within thy body. Ascending with her, with him, "thou shalt stretch forth thy hands, and another shall gird thee, and carry thee whither thou wouldest not."[8]

The flying Eagle, archetype of the Woman, is the wayshower through the hierarchy of Scorpio, teaching the children of God how the path of human generation becomes the path of divine regeneration through the raising up of the sacral energies of life through all of the chakras of being from the base of the spine unto the crown.

The flying Eagle is the vision of the Woman united with the Holy Ghost, the shakti of Shiva, teaching her children soul-mastery through the single-minded, single-eyed purpose: union with the God Self through the soul's self-effacement on the path of selflessness. The hierarchy of Scorpio through the Elohim and the angels and elementals of water in earth teach the mastery of the self in the desire body through the solar plexus and the soul's self-immersion in the Christ in the water quadrant whose mastery in Mother is the spoken Word in the full power and authority of the throat chakra. To ascend with Christ in the Woman is to be translated into the kingdom of the Father's dear Son and to be partakers of the inheritance of the saints who have ascended in light.[9]

The ascension, my beloved, is the goal of the Path of the Ruby Ray. But we have many steps to cover until that day and many steps to uncover as you direct, in the name of the LORD and the hierarchy of his hosts, the Ruby Ray into the footsteps of your karma and your dharma that you have left as imprints on the sands of time and space.

> Some of these you will efface
> By the violet fire of thy soul freedom in the
>   Holy Spirit, the Calf.
> Some of these you will trace
> By the blue lightning of thy goodwill in the
>   Father, the Lion.
> Some of these you will embrace
> By the Flame of Resurrection, of thy inner Word,
> Submitting the markings of your words and deeds
> to the love/wisdom of the Son, the Man.
> But in the end of your beginning, you will replace
> All those footprints in the sands of time and space
> With leaping lights as lantern markers
> for all who will come that way.
> And thou, the soaring Eagle, will receive
>   winged sandals of light
> As thy soul takes flight,
> Once more earthward to catch the eaglets
>   of the Mother
> In the swell of thy ascending garment.

Then, heavenbound, this final round
Will ope the door in heaven
That another may find what thou hast found.

I AM

Sanat Kumara

I have found the Way.
I AM the Way.

See Ezek. 3.

10

The Mystery of the Indwelling Christ

And it came to pass at the end of seven days, that the word of the LORD came unto me, saying,

Son of man, I have made thee a watchman unto the house of Israel: therefore hear the word at my mouth, and give them warning from me.

When I say unto the wicked, Thou shalt surely die; and thou givest him not warning, nor speakest to warn the wicked from his wicked way, to save his life; the same wicked man shall die in his iniquity; but his blood will I require at thine hand.

Yet if thou warn the wicked, and he turn not from his wickedness, nor from his wicked way, he shall die in his iniquity; but thou hast delivered thy soul.

Again, When a righteous man doth turn from his righteousness, and commit iniquity, and I lay a stumblingblock before him, he shall die: because thou hast not given him warning, he shall die in his sin, and his righteousness which he hath done shall not be remembered; but his blood will I require at thine hand.

Nevertheless if thou warn the righteous man, that the righteous sin not, and he doth not sin, he shall surely live, because he is warned; also thou hast delivered thy soul.

And the hand of the LORD was there upon me; and he said unto me, Arise, go forth into the plain, and I will there talk with thee.

Then I arose, and went forth into the plain: and, behold, the glory of the LORD stood there, as the glory which I saw by the river of Chebar: and I fell on my face.

EZEKIEL 3

Beloved Who Would Know Him as He Is:

The Path of the Ruby Ray is the progressive initiation of the soul into the mystery of the indwelling Christ. First perceived as the Son of man, then recognized as the Son of God, the Christ who was in Jesus must ultimately be understood as the common denominator of every son and daughter of God. That which is seen in him must be seen in thyself, O children of the Most High.

This is the transition from childhood to Sonship. It is the point of Christ's doctrine revealed in the Upper Room to the disciples during forty days of communion which continued until the hour of his ascension.

This point of doctrine is the crossroads where many leave the LORD. As they did then, so do the multitudes today who gather to be fed from the living vine but will not feed themselves from their own vine and fig tree. Thus when he said to them, "Except ye eat the flesh of the Son of man, and drink his blood, ye have no life in you," they departed from him and only the disciples remained. Testing their souls—whether they, too, would misunderstand the mystery of his doctrine—Jesus said to them, "Will ye also go away?" Their answer was, "LORD, to whom shall we go? thou hast the words of eternal life."[1]

Once again the body of God in earth is divided. Vast segments of Christendom are engaged in an idolatry of the person Jesus, worshiping him instead of the Lord from heaven indwelling in him and therefore in themselves. It is this conclusion of the Logos—this logical transfer of the light from the one Son who is to be brought captive to the many, and who is to bring the many into the captivity of his Sonship—for which every initiate of the Ruby Ray must assume full responsibility.

Then there are the idolaters of the self who say they worship God where they are but know him not. These are the worshipers of the ego, adding confusion to an already confused idolatry. The latter are the carnally minded, unknowing followers of the cult of Satan. But the former are the "good people" who, by their mistranslated dependency upon the Son of man Jesus, have failed to take the responsibility for the perils of a planet through independence in Christ the Son of God.

The Ruby Ray is the path for devotees who would walk the earth as Christ Jesus, who would love one another as he has loved them, who would appropriate that mind which was in him, who would be perfect as he was perfect. Abounding in good works, these know the grace of the LORD.

Paul is the great Christian example of the chela anointed by the Ascended Master Jesus into his path of Christhood. He anointed him his messenger on the fifth ray of science, truth, and healing. He sent him with his message of the mystery of salvation to 'Jew' and 'Gentile'. And Paul preached the mystery of the indwelling Christ as "Christ in you, the hope of glory." Those who cannot, who will not, understand this mystery will remain babes in Christ, if that. They cannot follow in his footsteps to become bodhisattvas, World Saviours, quickening spirits.

We come, then, with the full authority of our office to challenge the false Christs and the false prophets who teach the false doctrine of Antichrist. Moving in and among the congregation of the righteous, they have made them, as they are, the self-righteous. Teaching the holy scriptures by the spirits of impostors, they have not the Holy Spirit nor the mantle of the authority of the Word. And they shall perish by their own pitiful, impoverished sense of his power and his glory.

In the name of the LORD's anointed, we preach to you the mystery of "Christ in you, the hope of glory," and we summon to the seminar of the World Teachers the faithful and true students of the Word who have the courage to be initiated by Jesus Christ as shepherds to the multitudes.

Consider, then, blessed sons and daughters, these words of Paul enlightened by the Spirit:

"Christ in you, the hope of glory" is this Christ Self, the pure Son of your own regenerate divinity. This is the One by whom we preach, warning every man and teaching every man in all his wisdom that we may present every man in his own Christ Self, perfect, for the incoming to his temple of Christ Jesus.

Your beloved Christ Self as the Mediator of your I AM Presence *is* your hope that the glory of Christ Jesus might come unto you by works, the sacred labor of heart, head, and hand (good karma), and by grace (the transfer of light/energy/consciousness by the initiation of the Guru). Paul confirmed his participation in the reconciliation saying, "Whereunto—unto which perfection, i.e., the perfection of my Christ Self—I also labour, striving according to his working which he worketh in me mightily."

Paul, the initiated Son, made by Jesus Christ a joint-heir with him, yet labored striving for the perfection of the Christ even as that Christ Self performed his mighty works through him. As this Son of man was one in his own Christ Self, so he was one in Christ Jesus. The measure of the perfection of his Christ Self which he outpictured day by day in his soul was the same measure by which he received the portion of the divinity of Christ Jesus. He knew that the 'reconciliation' process of Jew and Gentile is the "thorough change," or utter transmutation, by the LORD's Spirit of the sinner into the saint, the natural man into the spiritual. He taught that this reconciliation of the soul with the Spirit of the I AM Presence occurs through Christ crucified on the cross of Alpha and Omega.

Now learn the real purpose and meaning of your meditation upon the crucifix—the Son of man Jesus *fastened* to the cross in life and in death.[2] Only through Christ (your own Christ Self) crucified can your living soul be reconciled unto the quickening Spirit. The crucifixion is the initiation on the Path of the Ruby Ray whereby the Son of God within you gives his light unto the Son of man. This Son of man then becomes—through the resurrection, by Christ, of God within him—the fullness of the Godhead dwelling bodily, soul by soul, in the whole body of God upon earth.

Each time the initiation of the crucifixion is reenacted, a living soul through Christ is reconciled to the Lord from heaven. Salvation by his 'blood' is by the energy of the Ruby Ray which flows to this hour freely from the sacred heart of Jesus Christ, from the immaculate heart of Mary, from the purple fiery heart of Saint Germain, from the hearts of all of the saints in heaven, and, most importantly, from the heart of your own blessed Christ Self as the distillation of your own Threefold Flame.

Paul's great revelation was of the mystery of the body of God as the true inner Church—the Church Universal and Triumphant. Stone upon stone, he beheld the Temple Beautiful built from the lively stones—devotees become the living Word by the demonstration of the way of personal Christhood.

Paul experienced directly the communion of the saints in heaven and the saints in earth. He knew the saints in heaven as "the saints in light." Thus he accurately described the ascended masters who appeared to him in their glorified bodies. And he knew the saints in earth unascended, both in and out of the body:

> I knew a man in Christ above fourteen years ago, (whether in the body, I cannot tell; or whether out of the body, I cannot tell: God knoweth;) such an one caught up to the third heaven. And I knew such a man, (whether in the body, or out of the body, I cannot tell: God knoweth;) how that he was caught up into paradise, and heard unspeakable words, which it is not lawful for a man to utter.[3]

Paul gave thanks to the Father, Almighty God individualized in his own beloved I AM Presence, who made us the saints in 'darkness', bearers of the Karma in earth, meet to be partakers of the inheritance of the saints in 'light', in heaven. This inheritance of the ascended masters is partaken of by their chelas (the unascended disciples of Christ) as the communion of the LORD's body. Every ascended master who has become the incarnate Father, Son, and Holy Spirit through the intercession of the embodied Lamb, holds the light of the Trinity as his own inheritance which he then, by the authority of his own Sonship, transfers to the disciples of Christ by the ritual of initiation. The inheritance of each ascended master is laid up as his "treasures in heaven." It is the light of his cumulative Christ consciousness—the net gain of pure thought and feeling, word and deed stored in the great spheres (the many mansions) of his causal body.

This light is the 'body and blood' of Christ, the communion of the LORD, first delivered by him to the ascended masters when they were yet unascended, now delivered by them to his disciples. The 'blood' of Christ is the Spirit of his Mind, Consciousness—Alpha (+); and his 'body' is the Energy and Light of his Word made manifest—Omega (–). The Holy Spirit always manifests itself in this masculine/feminine polarity of Alpha and Omega, Spirit/Matter, appearing to the apostles as a flame with a cloven tongue, a flame individed as the two in One.

The communion of the saints is the participation of the quickening spirits in the assimilation of the Word of Christ—of the Father in the Son, i.e., of the Beloved I AM Presence in the Blessed Christ Self—as one body in heaven and in earth through the Holy Ghost. It is the participation of ascended masters and their unascended disciples in Christ, the Teacher (the Person, the Em*bodi*ment of God, hence *the Body*), and in Christ, the Teaching (the Principle, the Essence/Energy, hence *the Blood*).

I, the Ancient of Days, declare unto you that whosoever shall deny this communion of saints is Antichrist and hath neither the Body nor the Blood of Jesus. And whosoever shall deny me shall be denied of Him, and whosoever shall deny the messenger of my Word shall be denied of Him. "He that receiveth you receiveth me, and he that receiveth me receiveth him that sent me.... But whosoever shall deny me before men, him will I also deny before my Father which is in heaven."[4] And they shall be cast into outer darkness (outside of the communion of the Lamb with his saints) where there is weeping and gnashing of teeth; for they have not come, therefore they shall not be called to the marriage supper of the Lamb of which all the ascended and unascended servant-sons are a part.

Let those who would remain within the hallowed circle of the

The Mystery of the Indwelling Christ

Guru and the chela cast off the outworn and outmoded garments of the cults of Canaan and enter the Path of the Ruby Ray as I, the Ancient of Days, empowered Jesus Christ to teach it.

Let us return once again to the experience of the Son of man Ezekiel who embodied the law of Self-transcendence unto the house of Israel. He is the spiritual man who has superseded the natural man through the crucifixion, and he bore in his body the sins of Israel "three hundred and ninety days." All who take up the ruby cross to follow me daily in the way of the regeneration must be willing to bear a portion of planetary karma as well as personal karma. This you will do, my beloved, as the saints have always done, through the violet transmuting flame, the all-consuming fire of the Holy Ghost.

Note well, my beloved, the process—the sacred ritual—of the Path of the Ruby Ray as its fiery coil unwinds in the life of Ezekiel. Five hundred years before the birth of the Messiah, Ezekiel was a priest, the son of Buzi, in the land of the Chaldeans (Babylon). He was the priest who became the prophet, and his commission to the whole house of Israel began with the appearance of the I AM Presence and the Four Cosmic Forces. Before his mission was accomplished, he would himself experience the putting on of the four faces of Christ which appeared to him. The LORD's appearance to him is an exercise of His free will to enter time and space in what modern man would call an exception to the laws of material science. Certainly this appearance would not be subject to empirical proof by material science; but just as certainly it is wholly verifiable in the empirical proof of spiritual science demonstrated daily by souls who are of the light.

The LORD chose to reveal himself to Ezekiel as the Creator, who had created all things for his pleasure, as the Preserver, and as the terrible Destroyer. He showed himself as the one Jehovah, at once the impersonal sacred fire, at once the personal Presence walking and talking with him as friend, as teacher—as God himself.

I was that God Presence unto Ezekiel. I gave to him the

commission as Watchman of the Word, and I AM here today in the full fire of the Holy of Holies to consume all that opposes the I AM THAT I AM and to devour the enemies of the embodied Word. Thus unto Ezekiel I set aside the natural law by which the natural man is self-governed and self-limited, and I introduced to him the spiritual law by which the spiritual man is always Self-governed and Self-liberated.

The living soul Ezekiel, a daring and devout witness unto this Spirit/Matter phenomenon, responded to me with the exercise of his free will. He accepted from me the Calling, the Commission, and the Covenant—albeit, as he recorded, "in bitterness, in the heat of my spirit." Thus he aptly described, though he did not fully understand, the alchemical 'heat' of transmutation, which was also noted by Peter who witnessed "the elements" of the resistive, recalcitrant human consciousness melting with "fervent heat"—sacred fire of the Spirit. And the bitterness in him was like John's experience after he took and ate "the little book" handed to him as "a roll of a book" was handed to Ezekiel by the angel of the LORD. The bitterness in the belly (the solar-plexus chakra, seat of the desire body) is the alchemical sign of the transmutation of human desire into God desire—a prerequisite for all who would reenter the Mystery School.

During each succeeding ritual on the Path of the Ruby Ray when there is a sudden acceleration of light in the four lower bodies and a consequent sudden burning up of human effluvia, for an instant, only an instant, the Son of man often prays to the Ancient of Days in the words of Jesus: "Father, if thou be willing, remove this cup from me: nevertheless not my will, but thine, be done."[5]

Directing my Presence through his own individual I AM Presence, I steadied the soul of Ezekiel as he passed through this fiery trial and he felt the strong hand of the LORD upon him. And he sat by the river of Chebar, remaining among the children of the captivity seven days "astonished," the living soul overshadowed by the Lord from heaven, in seven days absorbing the seven rays of the Christ consciousness by the LORD's Spirit. This is the period of the eating of the flesh of the Christ and the drinking of his blood. It is an interval of assimilation—the assimilation of God consciousness for the work that the Lord is to accomplish through the soul whom he anoints with sacred fire.

You, my beloved, will have many such intervals, some in fasting, some in eating, some in quiescent meditation, and some in the heat of action, carrying on the sacred labor of the Word. These intervals are for the putting on of the ascension coil, increment by increment, spiral by spiral. Each one is an initiation clearly marked, individually designated for your soul.

A characteristic of the initiates on this path is that they lose an objective awareness of the lesser self as they become absorbed into the Greater Self and subject unto it. Often their perceptions of the indwelling Light are nonexistent, for they are at once within the center of its infolding sacred fire and at once sharply aware, by contrast, of the elements of personal karma in the process of melting in its all-consuming flame, a fire white-hot unto the dissolution of worlds within worlds.

While standing in the pillar of the LORD's fiery Presence, the erroneous and illusory beasts of planetary karma loom large. And the Word of the initiates is as the Word of the prophet. Like a fiery tongue, it lashes out to expose and consume! expose and consume! expose and consume all unlike itself. Indeed it is the Mother flame in defense of her children. To those unacquainted with the phenomenon of the Son of man walking the earth as the Lord from heaven, such manifestations appear eccentric, egoistic, and altogether threatening to their sensual and sensorial existence.

If you would receive the gift of prophecy from the Holy Spirit, you must be willing to be like the prophets, being lifted up by the Spirit and taken away by the wings of the living creatures making the noise of the whirling T'ai chi, and the wheels making the noise of turning vortices of light, and the great rushing of the I AM THAT I AM within you.

If you would know the gift given to the prophets now offered to the saints whereby you, my beloved, may become the instruments of exhortation, judgment, exposure, as a true teacher of the Teaching, then call for the initiations which I gave to Ezekiel to be given unto you, step by step. And the fire infolding itself will descend from the Ancient of Days, from Gautama Buddha, from Lord Maitreya, Jesus Christ, through the twin flames and twin causal bodies of our two witnesses, thence through your own I AM Presence and Christ Self to be delivered to your soul through the Threefold Flame, three Persons/Principles of the Trinity burning on the altar of your heart.

I AM

Sanat Kumara

I await thy call, thy heart's conviction, the confession of thy mouth, and the commitment of thy soul unto the work of the LORD that is his Word in Aquarius.

See Ezek. 3, 4; Micah 4:4; John 15:12; Phil. 2:5; Matt. 5:48; 1 Cor. 3:1; Col. 1; 2:9; Rom. 8:17; Matt. 6:19–21; Acts 2:3; Matt. 22:13; Rev. 19:9; Matt. 19:28; Rev. 4:11; 2 Pet. 3:10; Ezek. 2:9, 10; 3:1, 2; Rev. 10:8–10.

The Fiery Furnace of the Rose Cross

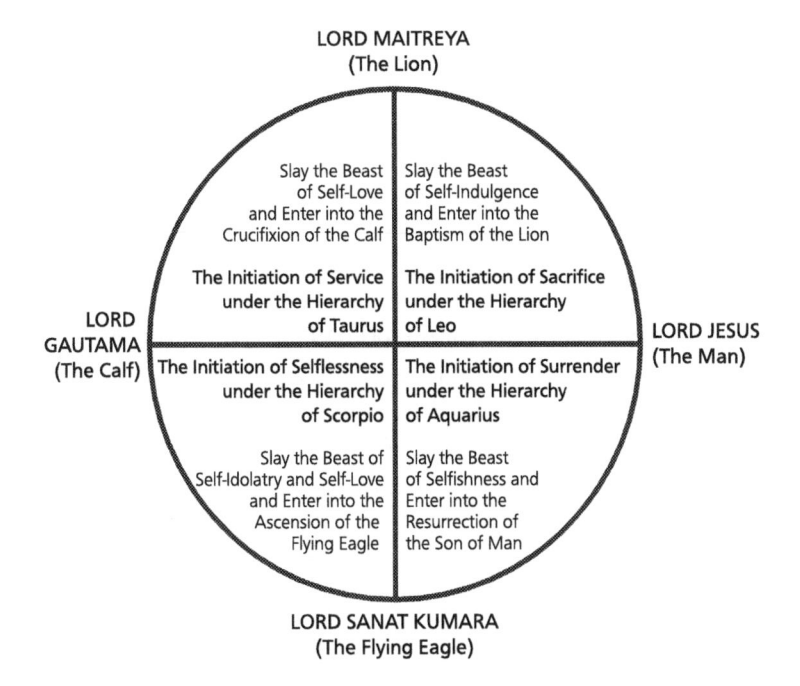

LORD MAITREYA
(The Lion)

LORD GAUTAMA
(The Calf)

LORD JESUS
(The Man)

- Slay the Beast of Self-Love and Enter into the Crucifixion of the Calf

  The Initiation of Service under the Hierarchy of Taurus

- Slay the Beast of Self-Indulgence and Enter into the Baptism of the Lion

  The Initiation of Sacrifice under the Hierarchy of Leo

- The Initiation of Selflessness under the Hierarchy of Scorpio

  Slay the Beast of Self-Idolatry and Self-Love and Enter into the Ascension of the Flying Eagle

- The Initiation of Surrender under the Hierarchy of Aquarius

  Slay the Beast of Selfishness and Enter into the Resurrection of the Son of Man

LORD SANAT KUMARA
(The Flying Eagle)

The Initiations Foursquare and the Four Initiators
on the Path of the Ruby Ray

11

Unfolding the Sacred Science of the Soul's Acceleration unto God

Sons of God in Christ:

"And because ye are sons, God hath sent forth the Spirit of his Son into your hearts, crying, Abba, Father."[1] Because ye are sons, ye have the gift of the Threefold Flame of Life within your heart. And because ye have the gift of the Threefold Flame of Life within your spiritual heart which is 'behind' your physical heart, God is able to send forth the Spirit of his Son into your heart. Those who have not the Threefold Flame cannot receive the Spirit of the Son, neither can they receive the Spirit of the Father.

How is it that Paul heard the Person of the Son crying, "Abba, Father"? It is because he was the Son of man in whom the Son of God dwelt. He knew intimately the Christ Self and the office of this Son of glory who is within the heart as the Mediator, stepping down the terrible vibrations of "the terrible crystal" that the children of the light might eat the 'bread', substance of Life, and live. The Christ Self most holy repeats the name of God I AM THAT I AM, calling upon the LORD day and night. I AM THAT I AM is his name and his Word. Behold the Christ Self, the sustainer of the I AM light, the Shekinah glory, of the Person of the Father in the adopted sons.

The Spirit of the Son is the vital, life-giving principle of the only begotten of God. The Spirit of the Son is the sacred fire breath of exalted Love. The Spirit of the Son is the primal essence of your Godhood. Its descent into the living temple of man is the phenomenon of incorporeal being, the Greater Self, entering into and possessing corporeal being, the lesser self, by the freewill adoption, adaptation, of both the soul and the Father-Mother God. The Spirit of the Son is the activating light, the awakening principle, the quickener from death to Life.

Paul prayed that the saints might walk worthy of the I AM Presence unto all pleasing of his Word, being fruitful, that is, multiplying his Presence, through every good work and increasing in the knowledge of the God Presence. He prayed for their strengthening with all might. It was the Mighty I AM Presence that empowered Paul. He knew it, he saw it, he became it. He saw this glorious power present as the power of the Father. It was his blazing light in the face of a Man Christ Jesus who went before him, city by city, preaching the power of God's kingdom come suddenly within his temple.

So shall the face of a Man go before you, sons and daughters of the Ruby Ray. My face shall be upon the face of my messenger in the Mother flame as the flying Eagle, and you shall see the face of Lord Gautama in the Person of the Calf, and the face of Lord Maitreya in the Person of the Lion, and the face of Jesus Christ in the Person of the Man. Do not be surprised. For though I speak figuratively and though the Word of God is hidden in a mystery, yet those who experience it experience it literally and in actuality.

My beloved, I AM unfolding to you the sacred science of the soul's acceleration unto God. Can the multiple coils of cosmic consciousness be so easily unwound, paragraph upon paragraph? I tell you, nay. Only in your deep meditation and in your longing to fulfill the will of God—so intense as to consume all other longings—can I make known to you what is that distilled essence of the wine of the Spirit, drop by drop.

The ascended masters know the way. Meditation upon their Word leads to the way that I AM. And there is no other foundation that is laid than the Word of Christ for the building of the Great Pyramid, for the building of the Temple Beautiful.

The ascended masters are the ones who have gone before you on the Path of the Ruby Ray. They are the souls who elected in the earth to become quickening spirits, and they accelerated thereby into the light of the I AM THAT I AM. They are the masters who have ascended into the white light because they have accelerated their preordained fiery destiny. They know the way of the adoption of sons. Ask them and they will tell you.

They, too, "speak the wisdom of God in a mystery, even the hidden wisdom, which God ordained before the world unto our glory." They who have transcended time and space speak out of the matrix of a transcendent Word. While they were with you they fulfilled their roles as bearers of the image of Christ in the earth. Now they have become the bearers to you of the image of the heavenly. Can you see them? Do you see them? They are your brothers and sisters of the transcendent light. They are translated into the kingdom, higher consciousness, of his dear Son who is the image of the invisible God, the firstborn, the only begotten, the Christ Self of every creature, child, of God.

Enoch was the Son of man because his soul elected through numerous incarnations on this and other starry homes to become the archetype fourfold. He bore the title of Son of man as one who held the office and the mantle of Christ. All things being fulfilled, the LORD took him into the white-fire core of being. I was there in the hour of his ascension. And unto this hour every man, woman, and child upon the planet receives the impetus of that ascension and retains its memory impressed upon his soul.

And the promise of the LORD to every son, to every child and child-man is this: "As I took Enoch, he having fulfilled the Path of the Ruby Cross, so I will take thee unto myself, O my living soul, when thou hast fulfilled the gospel of love foursquare. To love and to love, to love and to love in the name of the Father and the Mother, in the name of the Son and the Holy Spirit—this is the way of the Ruby Ray. Walk ye in it."

If you would know the qualifications of my way, beloved, study the Word of the one who found the way, became the way, and declared, "I AM the way." So then read the four gospels of the Four Cosmic Forces and learn the qualifications, all fulfilled in Jesus Christ, of the one who should bear the office of the Son of man coming in the authority of the Son of God. For you must be the righteous servant of the I AM THAT I AM, a preacher and a teacher of the message of your I AM Presence Beloved to the nations, who always appears in the identity of the Christ manifest in you. This Christ is "slain from the foundation of the world"[2]; but because he is slain, your soul shall rise again. His message is rejected by all except the elect sons—those who elect to be the Word, those whom God elects to be the Word.

Did you know, my beloved, that it is not enough for the soul to elect to be God? The Spirit must also elect. These are the two parties, yea, the partners, necessary to the marriage contract. The bridal veil of the soul is the seamless garment, the vestment, your Deathless Solar Body. And by the time that the hour of your ascension has come, you will have woven it, thread by thread, out of the Mother flame rising within you, out of her ascension current. There are some who elect to be God crying, "LORD, LORD," with their lips while their hearts are far from him.

Enoch saw the Watchers who fell from grace so long ago to tempt the entire human race and to stand in the way of it becoming the I AM Race. Now, in the end times, they cry out for mercy, but no mercy is given. For Enoch, the seventh from Adam, wrote of their history, of their infamy and their judgment; and we will speak of them in a later *Pearls of Wisdom*. But now be aware that though they cried loudly for mercy and even sought Enoch to intercede for them, the Almighty rejected their persons even as they had rejected the descent of the Person of Christ, the Spirit of the LORD's Son.

And so it is written in the Book of Life that the LORD GOD has consistently refused to enter into a covenant of redemption with these Watchers who have tormented the people who dwell in the earth. This is the exercise of God's own free will to withhold the gift of himself as Father, Son, and Holy Spirit. And some have mistakenly declared, through a misunderstanding of Christ's doctrine, "We have sinned, but God *must* forgive us." Beloved, it is clearly written that the seed of the wicked, as the tares sown among the good wheat, are not forgiven, but at the time of the harvest they are harvested by the angels, bound in bundles, and burned in the sacred fire—i.e., returned to the white-fire core of the Great Central Sun for the dissolution of the worlds of non-being, non-identification with the Lion, the Calf, the Man, and the flying Eagle.

Mercy is a gift freely given and freely received. But it is not a right. It is a privilege enjoyed by those who hold covenant with their Maker and communion with the saints. It is a privilege that can be suspended when abused and misused. Do not, then, take the grace of God for granted. For by his free will he may or may not forgive, he may or may not endow those who cry to him, "LORD, LORD," with the gift of eternal life. Life in its unendingness will move on, my beloved, but the particles in the stream may be created, recreated, or uncreated according to the free will of the Father and his adopted Sons.

The sudden and unexpected coming of the Son of man, as the lightning cometh out of the east and shineth even unto the west, shows the complete independence of Almighty God of the tyranny that an idolatrous generation would impose upon him through their false doctrine and dogma. No, not because souls cry, "LORD, LORD," repeating scripture over and over again devoid of the Spirit and the meaning, but because he has ordained it shall the LORD, the I AM THAT I AM, whom ye seek suddenly come to his temple. And in that day, you will recognize the messenger of my covenant whom ye delight in as the manifestation of myself.

My messenger prepares my way, but I occupy the temple of my messenger. This, too, is the mystery of the indwelling God. And thus I reveal to you the ownership of the Ancient of Days of all souls in the service of the light. I AM the possessor of God within you. I AM that God within you. By free will are my comings and my goings within your temple.

Sometimes I speak directly to your soul. But often when

you do not hear me, I speak my word of love through my messenger because of your own self-condemnation. Then again I speak my rebuke through my messenger because of your self-satisfaction and the meager standards of harmony within your life which are not adequate to contain the full harmony, in all of its wondrous chords, of the covenant of the Law. A veritable symphony of light and sound and color governs the interchange of the soul with the Spirit and the Spirit with the soul, which is always through the Son of God. There is no other way by which the soul can interact with the Spirit except through the Self that is Christ.

I AM come to teach you to be that Christ. I AM the Teacher and the Teaching. I would impart to you the mantle well worn by the masters of the Ruby Ray.

I AM Sanat Kumara. I AM opening a door in the heaven of your own Causal Body. Enter and know the LORD thy God,

I AM THAT I AM

See Col. 1; 1 Cor. 15:49; John 14:6; Matt. 7:21–23; 13:24–30; 24:27; Mal. 3:1.

"Occupy Till I Come!"

The L-I-O-N
The **"ION** of Light"
The **I AM** of **O**mega with the **N**egative charge

	The Wayshower of the Holy Spirit Demonstrator of the Path of Service through the mastery of the body in the earth quadrant	The Wayshower of the Father Demonstrator of the Path of Sacrifice through the mastery of the memory in the fire quadrant	
THE C-A-L-F The **C**hrist of **A**lpha-Omega come in the **L**Fohat (fire) of the **EL** (Elohim)	Archetype of the Christ Crucified	Archetype of the Great Baptizer by Water and by Fire	**THE M-A-N** The **M**other **A**tom with the **N**egative charge
	Archetype of the Woman, Great Regenerator of Water and of Earth	Archetype of the Living Saviour Who Saves His Own through the Resurrection of the Soul	
	The Wayshower of the Mother Demonstrator of the Path of Selflessness through the mastery of desire in the water quadrant	The Wayshower of the Son Demonstrator of the Path of Surrender through the mastery of the mind in the air quadrant	

THE FLYING E-A-G-L-E
The **E**nergy (Spirit) of **A**lpha-Omega
in the **G**eometry of the **EL** in Earth (Matter)
The Four Persons of Cosmic Christhood
See Ezekiel 1:10 and Revelation 4:7

Offices Occupied by the Four Cosmic Forces in Spirit
and by the Sons and Daughters of God in Matter
Until the Coming of the LORD

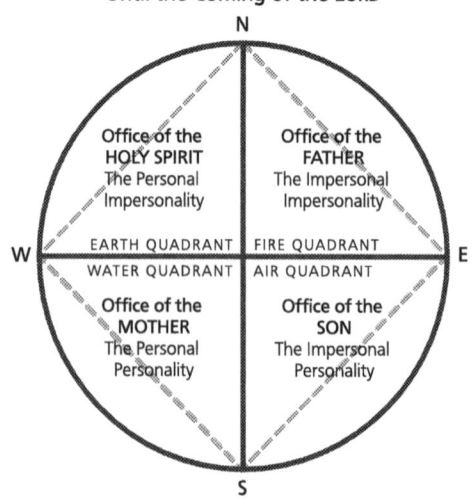

N

Office of the HOLY SPIRIT The Personal Impersonality	Office of the FATHER The Impersonal Impersonality
EARTH QUADRANT	FIRE QUADRANT
WATER QUADRANT	AIR QUADRANT
Office of the MOTHER The Personal Personality	Office of the SON The Impersonal Personality

W — E

S

Foundations of the City Foursquare
Four Pillars in the Temple Beautiful of the Soul

12

A Book Sealed with Seven Seals

And I saw in the right hand of him that sat on the throne a book written within and on the backside, sealed with seven seals.

And I saw a strong angel proclaiming with a loud voice, Who is worthy to open the book, and to loose the seals thereof?

And no man in heaven, nor in earth, neither under the earth, was able to open the book, neither to look thereon.

And I wept much, because no man was found worthy to open and to read the book, neither to look thereon.

And one of the elders saith unto me, Weep not: behold, the Lion of the tribe of Juda, the Root of David, hath prevailed to open the book, and to loose the seven seals thereof.

REVELATION 5

Beloved Who Are of the Lion of the Tribe of Juda
and Who Know the Root of David as the Living Christ:

Behold he cometh unto thee, O children of the Most High God. Behold he is in thy midst, and I AM in the midst of thee, and we are one in the Lion, the Calf, the Man, and the flying Eagle.

The book is the book of the living Christ. The seven seals seal the seven spheres of the Cosmic Christ consciousness which are his to transfer through the path of initiation on the Ruby Ray to the sons and daughters of God. Ye cannot receive these initiations except ye become as a little child, and the little child then choose to become the Manchild, accepting the proffered gift of Sonship according to the covenants of the God of Israel.

Thus I, the Ancient of Days, have dwelt upon the mysteries of Sonship before proceeding with the understanding of the opening of the book and the loosing of the seven seals. The seven seals are upon the seven planes of heaven and the seven spheres of the Universal Causal Body of God and the individual causal bodies of those who elect to be God because they are of God. The seven seals seal the path of initiation and the light of the Cosmic Christ from all except those who are the true heirs of the white light of the ascension because they have submitted to the fiery furnace of the Rose Cross and the initiations foursquare and the four initiators on the Path of the Ruby Ray. These are they who are made unto our God kings and priests: and they shall reign on earth as in heaven.

No man is found worthy to open and to read the book, neither to look thereon, save the Manchild fully clothed with the light of the Ancient of Days and the descent of that light through the progressive order of hierarchical revelation. The Root of David is the lineal descent of Christed being marked by the seven planes of heaven, the seven spheres of the causal body, and the seven chakras in the body of God. The seven-sealed book is the record of the Great Pyramid of Life of which each individual Christed Son is at once the whole and the part—the All in the all, the geometry of the Pyramid and a single, lively stone within it.

The lineal descent from the great white throne to the soul/saint moving in time and space is a seven-tiered spiral, reaching from earth to heaven and heaven to earth. The fourth tier is the mystical light in the center of the Pyramid, the flame in the heart of the Great Pyramid of Life that is the inner spiral of man, woman incarnate. The fourth tier is the point of integration wherein the multiplication of the lesser consciousness realizes individuality in Christ. Without the initiations of the Ruby Ray within the King's Chamber, the Holy of Holies of the Great Pyramid of Life, there is no transition from the base of the Pyramid to the all-seeing eye of God.

The fourth tier is the emerald of the fourth foundation of the Holy City and the fourth, the emerald stone in Aaron's breastplate. Now you know why I AM the emerald.

Ponder well and put on my words thus far revealed to you in these discourses on the opening of the seventh seal. For I have placed therein the keys to the mystical reunion of thy soul with the living Spirit. All of this must go before the opening of the six seals and of the seventh seal of thine own Pyramid of Life.

I stand in the midst of the earth in the heart of the Prophets and the saints. I AM the mighty deliverer of the seven spheres of immortal life whereby those yet bound by the law mutable shall be unbound by the law immutable. And the mortals whose origin is of God shall put on immortality, and that flesh and blood which is corruptible shall be translated to share the inheritance of the Incorruptible One.

Let all reckon with the white flame of the Mother and the fiery furnace white-hot. Let all heed the Word of my son Serapis, who delivers the mandate of the ascension coil and the ascension sword. His Word is the golden Word for the golden age. He is the strong angel who proclaims with a loud voice, "Who is worthy to open the book, and to loose the seals thereof?" And my answer to him is my answer to the seven chohans, "Lo, thou art worthy because I AM worthy, because thou art myself in the seven planes of being."

Thus the order of the hierarchy of the Ancient of Days is revealed and the seven Sons of God, the Lords of the Rays, become the initiators in my name, in the name of Jesus Christ, of the Son of man within you, Keepers of the Flame of Life. And all ascended masters of the Great White Brotherhood who have followed in the way, the truth, and the life of the attainment of Christ Jesus occupy the office of the Man—the Son of man who is become the Son of God. For he has chosen to make them no longer servants but friends, and if friends then co-equals, joint-heirs, co-creators with him.

Indeed they have become the Son of God. Their light is the

brilliance of the sun at noonday. Any lesser appellation is the blasphemy of the denial of the all-power in heaven and earth of Jesus Christ to transfer full and co-equal Sonship to the sons and daughters of God. He, the firstfruit and the quickening Spirit, is become the All-in-all in every pyramidal line and in the lineage of the Great Pyramid of lives.

We cast out the demons and the wolves in sheep's clothing who have entered the Temple Beautiful of the soul and there denied the living witness of the abundant life of Jesus Christ in the person of all sons and daughters of God who have submitted, utterly and totally, their being unto his being. Thus the seven chohans with the Maha Chohan, the representative of the Holy Spirit, serve with the World Teachers Jesus Christ and Saint Francis, known today as the Ascended Master Kuthumi. Thus the Saviour has chosen to share his body and his blood with Francis on earth in the visitation of the seraph in the stigmata, supreme rite of Christ crucified in the body and soul and heart and mind, yea, in the flesh and blood of Francis. He who accorded him in my name the honor of the reenactment of the crucifixion, which was in him bodily, has so accorded him in heaven the same oneness bodily.

This oneness is earned by love, self-sacrificing love, selfless love, a love that walks daily in the order of Saint Francis the path of surrender and service through the vows of obedience of the heart, chastity of the mind, and poverty of the soul. Thus the east side of the City Foursquare and the three gates thereon are held by the ascended masters for and on behalf of their unascended chelas, the embodied disciples of Christhood, the pilgrims of peace and truth and freedom and enlightenment whose emblem is the Rose Cross.

Behold, the Lion of the tribe of Juda, the Great Initiator, the Guru, the Father, the first and the last incarnation of the Teacher and the Teaching. With him are the bodhisattvas of East and West, the holders of the light of the heart. They are the Keepers of the Flame of the indwelling Christ in the heart who chant the chant of the "Abba, Father" in the many languages of the Word and in the tongues of angels. As the ascended masters hold the image of the Christ as a face of a Man within the souls of the body of God, so the Buddhas in the becoming and the initiates of the White Goddess hold the image of the Lion as the definer and the refiner of the sacred fires of the heart.

The Lion of the tribe of Juda is the Christ, the Great Initiator in your midst, without whom there is no path. As the ascended masters, serving with the Saviour Jesus Christ, open the seven seals in the level of the soul—the solar awareness—of individual identity, so the ones anointed on the path of the Cosmic Christ and the planetary Buddhas open the door of the heart to those who pass the initiations of the seven chohans, the Maha Chohan, and the World Teachers within the seat of the soul.

> Through the ritual of becoming, O my soul,
> Through the to and fro running of the Cosmic Forces Four,
> Thou shalt put on the garment of the saints robed in white
> And enter into the communion of the heart
> Which thou hast known before thy descent from grace,
> The Great Rebellion and the Fall.
> Now don the wedding garment,
> Prepare to meet the All-in-all.

All of those described by the angel messenger of Jesus Christ who spoke to John and gave to him the seven-sealed Book of Revelation, all of those robed in white gathering round about the throne of the Lamb and under the altar of the Threefold Flame are the initiates of the Ruby Ray whose names are written in the Book of Life, who day by day are getting the victory over the beast by the blood of the Lamb and by the Word of their testimony.

They know the Root of David. They know his soul who has become the quickening Spirit, the Saviour of the world unto Jew and Gentile. They know the Lion of the tribe of Juda as the Guru in the garden who is come again to initiate them in the mysteries of the indwelling Christ. This Father Maitreya, this Son Jesus are one. Behold, I and my Father are one.

No argumentation or carnal logic can deny the oneness of the living LORD in manifestation. For he has ordained it and it is so by the Logic of his Word. And that which is, is. And that which is real, is real. And no false doctrine or dogma can confute the Cosmic Christ in manifestation in the heart of the initiate.

Lo, I AM Sanat Kumara. I AM the intensification of the Ruby Ray within you, my beloved. And when the son Serapis proclaimed with a loud voice, "Who is worthy to open the book and to loose the seals thereof?" lo, I answered, "I AM worthy. And because I AM worthy thou art worthy, O my son." Therefore, Serapis is opening the book on the law of the ascension in the lodestone of the Mother. Hear him well. For there are openings and there are openings. There are seals and there are seals. There are veils and there are veils. And thou, O soul, O initiate, must remove the veils of illusion, the seals of thy karma, which have effectively sealed thee from the Great Throne Room.

There are doors of pride barricaded by rebellion that effectively imprison selfhood. Therefore the ascended masters come with the vision of the Son of man to teach thee the way of the balancing of karma and the transmutation of energies misqualified in the lower chakras. These initiations are preparatory to the initiations of the heart. They must be submitted to. They cannot be bypassed.

Guard thy patience, and in that patience possess thy soul. For many have left the Mother, the messenger, and the ascended masters for exalted heights of which they fancied themselves a part, believing their way to be superior to the fundamental steps of Truth, the studying of the Law, the ritual of the sacred labor, and the childlike sweetness which day by day becomes the ripened fruit of true manhood and true womanhood. They have counted themselves superior. They have desired to enter the retreat of the heart without receiving the initiation of the washing of the feet by the Saviour Jesus Christ.

"If I wash thee not, thou hast no part with me."[1] Thus rings his Word to the present hour. It is spoken to all disciples of Christ. Tarry then in the city of Jerusalem, the citadel foursquare of the Mother's mastery of the Matter body. Tarry with the Woman and learn her wisdom and become it. When thy feet are washed, and only then, mayest thou enter into the Ruby Ray initiations of the heart.

I AM
Sanat Kumara

I AM proceeding day by day with the initiation fourfold of the sons and daughters of light in the soul, in the heart, in the mind, and in the universal body of God worlds without end.

See Rev. 5; Mark 10:15; Rev. 21:14, 19; Exod. 28:15–18; 1 Cor. 15:51–54; John 15:15; Rev. 7:9; 6:9; 3:5; 12:11; Luke 21:19.

13

∞

Worthy Is the Lamb

And I beheld, and, lo, in the midst of the throne and of the four beasts, and in the midst of the elders, stood a Lamb as it had been slain, having seven horns and seven eyes, which are the seven Spirits of God sent forth into all the earth.

And he came and took the book out of the right hand of him that sat upon the throne.

And when he had taken the book, the four beasts and four and twenty elders fell down before the Lamb, having every one of them harps, and golden vials full of odours, which are the prayers of saints.

And they sung a new song, saying, Thou art worthy to take the book, and to open the seals thereof: for thou wast slain, and hast redeemed us to God by thy blood out of every kindred, and tongue, and people, and nation;

And hast made us unto our God kings and priests: and we shall reign on the earth. REVELATION 5

O Souls of the Ancient of Days Redeemed Out of
  Every Kindred, and Tongue, and People, and Nation:
   I salute thee in the name of the Lamb who shall make thee unto our God kings and priests: and ye shall reign on the earth.
   Behold the Lamb who is worthy to stand in the midst of the throne and of the four beasts, and in the midst of the elders! Behold the Lamb who stands midst the throne, one with the Ancient of Days that sat on the throne, who liveth for ever and ever.
   Behold, I and my Son are one!

Only the chela who has become the Lamb may stand in the midst of the great white throne and still stand. From everlasting to everlasting behold, the Lamb is God incarnate, Christ the living Word. Having been slain it stands and still stands, the Lamb, having seven horns—the accent of the accelerating Alpha thrust emitting the light of the masculine ray from the seven planes of being; and having seven eyes—the spherical awareness of the presence of Omega within the seven chakras. All-pervasive, all-penetrating, the eyes are the precipitation of the vision of the seven horns in Matter.

Thus the Alpha-to-Omega creation is fulfilled in the Word, and the Word is made flesh in the seven Spirits of God who are sent forth into all the earth. And these seven Spirits, each of the seven as cloven tongues of fire, are the seven mighty Elohim, the seven representatives of the Father-Mother God in the seven planes of the Spirit/Matter firmament.

The Lamb who is slain is the Lamb who incarnates in the earth, suffering the crucifixion in body, mind, and soul and being initiated seven times seven in the sacred fires of the resurrection and the ascension. Merging with the Elohim as the seven manifestations of the Person of the Holy Spirit, the Lamb is the Only Begotten Son of God personified in the elect sons and daughters. Having descended from the throne and passed through the cycles of the karma and dharma of the multitudes whose evolution he is come to serve, the Son ascends to the throne of grace.

Now we read the initiation of one who has become the Lamb, having balanced personal and planetary karma and dharma and fulfilled the requirements of the Path of the Rose Cross: "He came and took the book out of the right hand of him that sat upon the throne."

Each initiate of the sacred fire who returns to God with one hundred percent of the light with which he has been sent forth—balanced, manifested, and expanded in the seven planes of heaven and earth—may stand where I stand, may indeed enter the secret chamber of my heart and there take the book out of my right hand, the book "written within and on the backside, sealed with seven seals." With the recent dispensation granted by the Karmic Board that souls may take the ascension with only fifty-one percent of their karma balanced, their dharma fulfilled (whereas formerly the full one hundred percent was required of every candidate for eternal Life), the initiation of the Lamb and the opening of the seven-sealed book is given only after the adept has balanced every jot and tittle of the Law from the ascended state.

Each time the Lamb incarnates—moving through the cycles of Messiah's infancy, childhood, and maturing manhood into the full Sonship of the avatar—the great ritual drama is outplayed. Reaching the consummation of the embodiment of God, he lays down his life that he might take it again; and in laying down his life, he becomes the vine that nourishes all of the branches. By his Presence in the earth, he increases the God consciousness of the children of God. And he takes that life, literally raising it back to its origin in Spirit, in order that the entire celestial/terrestrial round might fulfill another niche in the accelerating spiral of Universal Being.

Clothed upon, then, with the fullness of the Ruby Ray, having the authority to wear the "vesture dipped in blood," the Son of God ascended into the fullness of the I AM THAT I AM now receives the title "the Lamb." And when he takes the book, signifying his authority to be with the Ancient of Days in Spirit and in Matter, the four beasts and the four and twenty elders fall down before the Lamb, thereby acknowledging that he is worthy to be worshiped as God because he is become the fulness of the Godhead bodily in Spirit and in Matter—because he has fulfilled his fiery destiny in heaven and in earth.

The four cosmic forces and the twenty-four elders of God bear the harps of the living Word by which they sound the tone of the AUM in all of the seven spheres. Six of the elders are in each of the four quadrants, guarding the New Jerusalem in heaven and the City Foursquare in the earth. The six are three sets of twin flames; each set of twin flames—focusing the light of the

Father/Mother God to the aspiring ones—guards one of the portals of the City Foursquare. Together they form an arch of cloven tongues of fire for souls of light passing through those portals of initiation under the twelve solar hierarchies.

The four beasts positioned on the cardinal points of the Cosmic Clock emit the light of the God consciousness burning in the central altar of the city, a veritable sacred-fire fountain of the light of the I AM THAT I AM. This fountain is symbolized as the dot in the center of the circle. It is the point of Christ Self-awareness in Spirit and the point of Christ Self-awareness in Matter.

These twenty-eight figures (twenty-four elders and four cosmic forces) hold the balance of the seven rays on each of the four sides of the city and are the instruments of the initiations of the Father, the Son, the Holy Spirit, and the Mother which are given day by day to the souls in Matter making their way to the Great Pyramid of Life. These souls, sponsored by the Trinity, fall into three categories:

First, the messengers, prophets, and Christed ones who occupy the office of the two witnesses on the east gate, making plain the way of the perfectionment of the soul through the science of religion. These fulfill the initiations of the Son of God on the fifth ray, the twin-petaled chakra of science and religion through the all-seeing eye of God.

Second, the souls who occupy the office of the saints on the north gate. These are the saints of the inner Church, the Church Universal and Triumphant, East and West. These are the souls made perfect through the perfectionment of God-desire—pure motive as the matrix of the sacred fire, pure will as the thought emanation to be, pure intent as the movement of the will bridging thought and feeling into crystallized action. They are the vessels of the Lamb; they are the vehicles of his coming and his going.

These are they which follow the Lamb whithersoever he goeth. These were redeemed from among men, being the firstfruits unto God and to the Lamb. Because they are redeemed by the attainment of the Son of God who is able to stand in the presence of the great white throne and still stand, they, too, are without fault before the throne of God. They are the chelas of the Word who is become the mouth of the LORD in the earth. Thus it is written: And in their mouth was found no guile.

These fulfill the initiations of the bride of Christ under the Father on the sixth ray. Ministering within the Church to the body of God upon earth, they have the white cube within the heart: they are the living Church. And out of their bellies shall flow rivers of "living water"—"sacred-fire water"—for the golden sun of Helios and Vesta is within their solar-plexus chakra—the gateway to the desire body of God. And the golden vials of the twenty-eight tri-angle personages of God are full of the "odours" —sacred-fire emanations—of the prayers—the determined decrees of the Word—of these saints.

Third, behold the lambs of God huddled on the hillsides of the world awaiting the Good Shepherd. These occupy the office on the west gate of the great multitude, which no man could number, of all nations, and kindreds, and people, and tongues, who stood before the throne, and before the Lamb, clothed with white robes, and palms in their hands; and cried with a loud voice, saying, Salvation to our God which sitteth upon the throne, and unto the Lamb. Fulfilling the initiations of soul perfectionment on the seventh ray under the Holy Spirit and the chohan of the age, they attain the solar awareness of the gentle Presence of the LORD through the seat-of-the-soul chakra. These are they which came out of great tribulation, and have washed their robes, and made them white in the blood of the Lamb. Therefore are they before the throne of God, and serve him day and night in his temple.

My beloved, as you will see from the chart of the figure eight illustrating the flow of the persons and principles of the Godhead in heaven and in earth [see page 140], all energies and initiations must pass through the nexus of the figure eight who is always the Mother—the Mother in heaven and the Mother in earth. The nexus of the figure eight is the south side of the City Foursquare. And the New Jerusalem that cometh down from God out of heaven as a bride adorned for her husband is manifest in earth as the City Foursquare, the base of the Great Pyramid of Life.

The Matter cup is the mirror reflection of the Spirit cup. Yet the twain are one. For the energies of Life are in perpetual motion, and heaven descends to earth and earth ascends to heaven moment by moment, and the whole creation groaneth and travaileth together to give birth to the Christ consciousness.

I AM the Lamb incarnate in Spirit and in Matter. I sit upon the great white throne as the Ancient of Days. I AM the Guru but I AM also the chela, for I and my Father are one. The Eternal Mother is the Guru, male and female, and the Guru is the one who adores and becomes the Mother flame. The two witnesses, the saints, and the multitudes must pass through the womb of Mother in order to identify the Son, first without and then within. The Son establishes in them the Father Supreme, individualized in the I AM Presence. And together the Father and the Son anoint the two witnesses, the saints, and the multitudes with the full fire of the Holy Ghost.

The Mother is the keystone in the arch of being. The Mother is the white light of the ascension flame within you. The Mother is the White Goddess who is unveiled within you only by the power of the three times three, the three Persons of the Trinity each representing three gates of initiation on the three sides of the Holy City.

> Mother appears
> To dry your tears,
> To dissolve your fears,
> To deliver you from time and space
> With light beyond the years.

The womb of the Mother is the open door to Selfhood in the Son born of the Father, conceived in the fullness of time and space by the Holy Spirit sent.

My beloved, Life is a geometry of infinite dimensions. Let us be patient with one another as the Infinite Mind distills for the finite self glimpses of a vast geometry contained within the soul yet unborn. But one day it shall be born, I promise you, if you cleave to the flame of the Mother, her garment white, and to the heart of the Guru who lives within her heart.

I AM the Ancient of Days, and the Lamb is in me, and I AM in the Lamb in the midst of the throne. I AM he that sitteth on the throne, and I dwell among the great multitude in the temples of the two witnesses and in the hearts of the saints—my servants whom I have sealed in their foreheads, by my messengers, verily the remnant of the hundred and forty and four thousand. Therefore the multitudes shall hunger no more, neither thirst any more; neither shall the sun light on them nor any heat. For the Lamb which is in the midst of the throne—he shall feed them, and shall lead them unto living fountains of waters: and God as Mother shall wipe away all tears from their eyes.

I AM

Sanat Kumara

With every living creature I say,
"Blessing, and honour, and glory, and power, be unto
him that sitteth upon the throne, and unto the Lamb
for ever and ever."

See Rev. 5:7; 21; Matt. 5:18; John 15:1–6; Rev. 19:13; Col. 2:9; Rev. 11:3; 14:4, 5; John 7:38; 10:1–30; Rom. 8:22.

14

∞

Kings and Priests unto Our God

My Beloved
  Who Are Occupying the Offices of Universal Christhood
  in the Earth Unto the Coming of the Ancient of Days:
  Hail, in the Name of the Lamb!

We have spoken of the Matter square within the Matter sphere. We have diagramed the base of the pyramid within the City Foursquare in the earth that will appear, surely it will appear, through the two witnesses who reveal science and religion as the emanation of the Word and crystallize the God consciousness in the fifth ray at the east gate.

We have shown the coming of the Everlasting Gospel through the saints, the hundred and forty and four thousand who minister unto the flame of the Father in the Son on the sixth ray at the north gate. And we have shown the gentle multitudes who must be fed daily by the Holy Spirit released through the Word of the witnesses. And we have shown the Mother as the nexus of the flow of life from God into manifestation in the non-permanent worlds that are to be made permanent by the sacred fire breath.

Now let us examine the hierarchies of the four cosmic forces positioned in the heavenly city, the New Jerusalem, waiting to be outpictured, surely to be outpictured, in the waiting bride and in the two witnesses, the saints, and the multitudes. As the Mother gives birth to the Son, so the Son is the open door unto the multitudes. As he said, "No man cometh unto the Father, but by me." The Word incarnate is the opening of the way, the truth, and the life that I AM. The mantra of the Son is "I AM the door, I AM the door, I AM the open door which no man can shut! I AM the doer, I AM the doer, I AM the doer of the Word made flesh!"

When my Son Jesus Christ gave his discourse on the Good Shepherd, he spoke of the role of personal Christhood, the office he had assumed and would assume to set the example for the true shepherds of the sheep who are called by the World Teachers to come forth in this era to deliver the sheep of my pasture from the false pastors who scatter and destroy them. Therefore learn of him the meaning of the office of the Man occupied by the seven chohans, the Maha Chohan, the World Teachers, and all ascended masters of the Great White Brotherhood who give to you, beloved Keepers of the Flame, the initiations of the Son of man on the east gate of the New Jerusalem.

Tarry with the Son of God and the sons to whom he has granted the status of full and coequal Sonship that they might hold the flame of the Good Shepherd (the Beloved Christ Self, THE LORD OUR RIGHTEOUSNESS) for and on behalf of the disciples of Christ on earth. Submit to the initiations of the Son of God for the balance of karma and the transmutation of energy misqualified through the perfection of the mind of God in Christ. Learn the byword of initiates standing on the east gate: "Let this mind be in you, which was also in Christ Jesus." Learn the way of the dharma of surrender and learn its virtue in the moral discipline of self and society:

> *Verily, verily, I say unto you, He that entereth not by the door into the sheepfold, but climbeth up some other way, the same is a thief and a robber.*
>
> *But he that entereth in by the door is the shepherd of the sheep.*
>
> *To him the porter openeth; and the sheep hear his voice: and he calleth his own sheep by name, and leadeth them out.*
>
> *And when he putteth forth his own sheep, he goeth before them, and the sheep follow him: for they know his voice.*

And a stranger will they not follow, but will flee from him: for they know not the voice of strangers.

This parable spake Jesus unto them: but they understood not what things they were which he spake unto them.

Then said Jesus unto them again, Verily, verily, I say unto you, I AM the door of the sheep.

All that ever came before me are thieves and robbers: but the sheep did not hear them.

I AM the door: by me if any man enter in, he shall be saved, and shall go in and out, and find pasture.

The thief cometh not, but for to steal, and to kill, and to destroy: I AM come that they might have life, and that they might have it more abundantly.

I AM the Good Shepherd: the Good Shepherd giveth his life for the sheep.

But he that is an hireling, and not the shepherd, whose own the sheep are not, seeth the wolf coming, and leaveth the sheep, and fleeth: and the wolf catcheth them, and scattereth the sheep.

The hireling fleeth, because he is an hireling, and careth not for the sheep.

I AM the Good Shepherd, and know my sheep, and am known of mine.

As the Father knoweth me, even so know I the Father: and I lay down my life for the sheep.

And other sheep I have, which are not of this fold: them also I must bring, and they shall hear my voice; and there shall be one fold, and one shepherd.

Therefore doth my Father love me, because I lay down my life, that I might take it again.

No man taketh it from me, but I lay it down of myself. I have power to lay it down, and I have power to take it again. This commandment have I received of my Father.[1]

Keepers of the Flame, you are called to embody the Person of the Good Shepherd under the World Teachers. I have sponsored you and continue to sponsor you as you gather in our teaching centers and at Summit University for the Seminar of the World Teachers, the first in the series of initiations leading to the conferment of the mantle of the World Teachers.

The discourse of Jesus Christ on the Good Shepherd outlines the distinct differences in the paths of the true Christs and the false Christs whom the Saviour Jesus prophesied would come in his name. Those who would master the mind of God in Christ must enter by the door of the heart. Those unwilling to be consumed by Love, the price that must be paid for the mind of God, attempt to enter the Holy of Holies by some other way.

What are these other ways? My dears, even the recitation of mantras when these are devoid of love may degenerate to autohypnosis, mental manipulation, and, alas, black magic. Therefore we cannot reiterate too often the warning that not everyone who crieth, "LORD, LORD," may enter in. For the motive of the heart may contaminate the stream of consciousness and all who contact it. And the contaminated stream may not reach the Source.

The impostors of the Path of the Rose Cross who lead the multitudes astray are the thieves who steal the light of God through the very sheep they rob from the sheepfold. But even the light of God that is within the sheep is become the manifestation of their judgment. The true shepherd enters in by the door of the one who holds the office of the Son of God, the Lord Jesus Christ, and of the one, the Christ Self within, who is indeed the selfsame manifestation of that Son of God.

The Lamb of God is "the porter" who opens the door to the one who would embody the flame of the Good Shepherd. Once the door of the inner mysteries of the heart is opened to him, then the sheep hear his voice; for his voice is become the voice of the Word of God. And he calls His disciples by the inner name, by the vibration of the soul, and he leads them out of the maelstrom of the mass consciousness and the falsehoods and falsifications of the hirelings.

Those false Christs are indeed for hire. They are the worshipers of the beast—his carnality and his cult of idolatry. They have his image, his mark, his number, and his name. Their motive is greed for the light—an ill-gotten gain. Their will is to take the light without paying the price of that all-consuming, self-consuming Love. They have come to steal the light, to kill the Word incarnate, and to destroy and scatter the sheep of the Good Shepherd. But the Son of God utters the Word, the worlds tremble, and the false Christs are self-consumed!

"I AM come that they might have life, and that they might have it more abundantly." Let this be the mantra of the Word within you this week, for we are determined that the hirelings shall be bound, those in church and state who see the wolf of the international capitalist/communist conspiracy and leave the sheep and flee.

Let the great drama of the Faithful and True be outplayed! Enter the armies of the LORD which were in heaven and are now in the earth following him upon white horses, clothed in fine linen, white and clean. Let the wolves in sheep's clothing be bound in heaven and in earth by the Word of the apostles who are also seated upon the twelve thrones judging the twelve tribes of Israel.

I AM

Sanat Kumara

I lay down my life for the sheep.
And I lay it in the heart of the Mother
that I might take it again.

See John 14:6; Phil. 2:5; Matt. 24:24; 7:15, 21; Rev. 15:2; 19:11, 14; Luke 22:30.

15

The Initiation of the East Gate

Beloved of the Great White Throne Who Are Emanations of the Light of the Ancient of Days:

I AM come that ye might have life, and that ye might have it more abundantly.

Beloved who are my sheep and the sheep of the Good Shepherd, let us further examine the office of the Man, the Son of God, which you are called upon to "Occupy till I come!" Note well the requirement of the law of this the Initiation of the East Gate. It is the individual affirmation in Christ of the indwelling God—publicly, before the scrutiny and the scorn of laggards and fallen ones who are embodied among the Israelites, then and now, yet who are not of the original seed of Abraham.

Jesus the Christ, the occupier of the office of the Son of God in the Son of man, asserted his triune embodiment of the Godhead:

> *And it was at Jerusalem the feast of the dedication, and it was winter.*
>
> *And Jesus walked in the temple in Solomon's porch.*
>
> *Then came the Jews round about him, and said unto him, How long dost thou make us to doubt? If thou be the Christ, tell us plainly.*
>
> *Jesus answered them, I told you, and ye believed not: the works that I do in my Father's name, they bear witness of me.*
>
> *But ye believe not, because ye are not of my sheep, as I said unto you.*
>
> *My sheep hear my voice, and I know them, and they follow me:*

And I give unto them eternal life; and they shall never perish, neither shall any man pluck them out of my hand.

My Father, which gave them me, is greater than all; and no man is able to pluck them out of my Father's hand.

I and my Father are one.

Then the Jews took up stones again to stone him.

Jesus answered them, Many good works have I shewed you from my Father; for which of those works do ye stone me?

The Jews answered him, saying, For a good work we stone thee not; but for blasphemy; and because that thou, being a man, makest thyself God.

Jesus answered them, Is it not written in your law, I said, Ye are gods?

If he called them gods, unto whom the Word of God came, and the scripture cannot be broken;

Say ye of him, whom the Father hath sanctified, and sent into the world, Thou blasphemest; because I said, I AM the Son of God?

If I do not the works of my Father, believe me not.

But if I do, though ye believe not me, believe the works: that ye may know, and believe, that the Father is in me, and I in him.

Therefore they sought again to take him: but he escaped out of their hand,

And went away again beyond Jordan into the place where John at first baptized; and there he abode.

And many resorted unto him, and said, John did no miracle: but all things that John spake of this man were true.

And many believed on him there.[1]

Those who are chelas of the ascended masters must understand that it is never the sheep of the Good Shepherd who will challenge the individuality of the Christ incarnate. They know intimately and are known of the hierarchy of the sons of God. East and West, they give obeisance to the true Gurus. They know the voice of the Son of God in every Good Shepherd whom he has anointed with his very own flame and name. Through the true shepherds he gives to them eternal Life and he affirms that no man shall pluck the sheep, neither out of the hand of the Son nor out of the hand of the Father, for "I and my Father are one."

The Jews who took up stones to stone Jesus Christ were neither the children of Israel nor the children of God. Let it be clear that they who are of the synagogue of Satan[2] incarnated among the children of Israel who had entered upon the practices of Canaanite sexuality and fertility rites, intermarried among the laggard evolutions embodied from other planets, then gave to them their seed and their name, and by their rebellion begat rebellion and brought forth the children of the Wicked One and the seed of the Watchers, about whom your Father Enoch has told you, who were indeed the fallen Luciferians.

These laggards then called themselves Jews, rose in the peerage of the scribes, the Pharisees, the Sadducees, the rabbis, the high priests, and the Sanhedrin, and sought the cooperation of their counterparts in the Roman Empire to execute the expediency, as Caiaphas put it, "that one man," the Son of God, "should die for the people." These fallen ones, posing as the Brahmins in every culture and nation, have naught to do with the pure stream of the Christ consciousness that has descended by the flame of the Melchizedekian priesthood transferred to Abraham, Isaac, and Jacob, to Jacob's twelve sons and to their seed unto the coming of the son of David in the Son of man, Jesus Christ, and unto all of the saints and the great multitude who are the inheritors of that light by the Path of the Rose Cross. As my son Djwal Kul has told you, they are known not by a human hereditary line but by the sign of the six-pointed star, the Threefold Flame within the heart and by the name inscribed therein, I AM THAT I AM.[3]

Thus it must come to pass that the child who would be saint and the saint who would be Son must testify of me in Jesus Christ before these fallen ones who have denied the Word from their beginning and will deny it unto their ending. Yes, long before the incarnation of Jesus Christ, these sons of Belial rebelled against the Son of God and refused to worship his image, which image the Father placed within the heart of every one of his children before he sent them forth on their soul's journey in time and space. Because the image of the Christ is sealed within their hearts, they always know the voice of the Son of God. And because that image is sealed within their hearts, they are persecuted for his righteousness' sake.

Because the image is sealed in their hearts, they as children may elect to become joint-heirs with Jesus Christ of the eternal inheritance of the sons of God, the true Light, which lighteth every Manchild that cometh into the world. Because the image is hid within the secret chamber of the heart and because they are called by the Lamb who redeems them to become kings and priests unto our God, they, too, must follow Jesus Christ in the public assertion of the indwelling Trinity.

In Jesus' forthright assertion of the Trinity, he first declares that he has already told them that he is the Christ. Secondly, he affirms that he is one with the Father—the Father indwelling—that the I AM THAT I AM who appeared to Moses is indeed incarnate within him and he is worthy to be called LORD. Worthy is the Lamb! Worthy is the Lamb! Worthy is the Lamb!

When they again take up stones to stone him, Jesus points to his many good works and asks, "For which of those works do ye stone me?" Refusing to look at the evidence of the manifest Holy Spirit, they reveal themselves as materialistic theoreticians. Accusing him of blasphemy, of being a man like themselves who had not the light of God within them, these fallen ones were jealous of his Sonship. Having forfeited their own exalted estate, they were determined to perpetuate their sensual philosophy of the denial of the oneness of the Father in the Son.

But he who fulfilled the unbroken descent of the light of the Ancient of Days, whose coming is prophesied in all of the ancient scriptures, quoted to them the law of Moses who had "called them 'gods', unto whom the Word of God came." But they who could not believe in the Father because they did not believe in the Son could no more accept the works of the Holy Spirit in Jesus Christ than they can accept those very same works in you, my beloved.

My beloved, I emphasize these words and this example of the Saviour Jesus Christ in order that you may understand the initiations of the east gate and of the office of the Man, that you may take up his mantle and go forth two by two, as the other seventy, into every city and place, whither he himself would come; then, walking in the footsteps of the apostles, hold the lines of the Cosmic Clock for the sealing in the forehead of the twelve tribes of Israel and the great multitude who follow in their wake.

Both John the Baptist and Jesus Christ showed plainly the mission of the initiates of the Ruby Ray: to challenge embodied evil and to call the lost sheep of the house of Israel, the hundred and forty and four thousand who came with me on my rescue mission to earth, thence to call the multitudes, the other sheep who are not of this fold. They will follow you—you who will assume the mantle of the true shepherds, the World Teachers, and thereby lead the people in church and state as kings and priests unto God.

In preparation for these initiations under the World Teachers, I would have you read the accounts in the four Gospels concerning the confrontation of John and Jesus with the Antichrist in the laggards, the fallen ones, and the Watchers. Then, by their example, take up the cross of the seven chohans and the Maha Chohan, challenge the Liar and his lie and all who are of their father, the Devil, who was a murderer of embodied Truth from the beginning.

With the moral discipline of the energies of self and society, denounce the moral degeneration of the decades, the astral spill polluting the mainstream of the Christ consciousness in the little child who has yet to become the Manchild who shall rule all nations with a rod of iron. Go forth in the flame of the Mother to bind in heaven and on earth by the judgment call all who oppress and offend the little children East and West.

Yes, my beloved, I authorize you to challenge them one by one, as the Mother has taught you, naming them by name.

Challenge them by the action of the Ruby Ray in the order of the descent of its hierarchy from the great white throne to the littlest angel and know that I AM there within you, within your Word, and that I AM the Word and that my Word shall not return unto me void, but it shall accomplish that which I please, and it shall prosper in the thing whereto I sent it. Challenge them saying:

"By the Ruby Ray, in the name of the Almighty I AM Presence, the God Self that I AM, the Beloved Christ Self that I AM, the Holy Spirit that I AM: In the name of the Four Cosmic Forces, the Eternal Lamb and the Embodied Lamb, I call to the Heart of Lord Sanat Kumara, the Ancient of Days, Gautama Buddha, Lord Maitreya, the Saviour Jesus Christ, the Twin Flames of the Two Witnesses and the heart flames of the saints East and West!

"I challenge the person and principle, creator and creation of embodied evil, in the laggards, the fallen ones, the Watchers, the Antichrist, the seed of the Wicked One, and the entire Luciferian creation!"

Then lovingly, boldly, and with the full authority of your Christhood, my beloved, give the Judgment Call of Jesus the Christ "They Shall Not Pass!"

So shall it be, for the Mouth of the Lord hath spoken it in you—in me within you.

I AM

Sanat Kumara

MA I AM

I wield the sword of the Mother
in defense of the honor, the freedom,
the peace, and the enlightenment
of all God-fearing peoples everywhere.

enlightenment as a candle lit and serviced in the temple of the people	honor in the sacred fire foundations of life
ENLIGHTENMENT	HONOR
PEACE	FREEDOM
peace in the desiring to be God	freedom to be God in the mind and heart

See John 10:10; Luke 19:13; John 11:47–54; John 18:14; Matt. 5:10; Rom. 8:17; John 1:9; Luke 10:1; Rev. 7; Matt. 10:5, 6; 15:24; John 8:44; Rev. 12:5; Isa. 55:11.

The Judgment Call of Jesus the Christ
They Shall Not Pass!

In the Name of the I AM THAT I AM,
 I invoke the Electronic Presence of Jesus Christ:
They shall not pass!
They shall not pass!
They shall not pass!
By the authority of the cosmic cross of white fire it shall be:
That all that is directed against the Christ
 within me, within the holy innocents,
 within our beloved Messengers,
 within every son and daughter of God
Is now turned back
 by the authority of Alpha and Omega,
 by the authority of my Lord and Saviour Jesus Christ,
 by the authority of Saint Germain!

I AM THAT I AM within the center of this temple
 and I declare in the fullness of
 the entire Spirit of the Great White Brotherhood:
That those who, then, practice the black arts
 against the Children of the Light
Are now bound by the hosts of the Lord,
Do now receive the judgment of the Lord Christ
 within me, within Jesus,
 and within every ascended master,
Do now receive, then, the full return—
 multiplied by the energy of the Cosmic Christ—
 of their nefarious deeds which they have practiced
 since the very incarnation of the Word!

Lo, I AM a Son of God!
Lo, I AM a Flame of God!
Lo, I stand upon the rock of the living Word
And I declare with Jesus, the living Son of God:
They shall not pass!
They shall not pass!
They shall not pass!
Elohim. Elohim. Elohim. [Chant]

Posture for giving this decree: Stand. Raise your right hand, using the *abhaya* mudra (gesture of fearlessness, palm forward), and place your left hand to your heart—thumb and first two fingers touching chakra, pointing inward. Give this call at least once in every 24-hour cycle.

Accounts in the Four Gospels on the Confrontation of Antichrist by John the Baptist and Jesus Christ in Chronological Order

1. John rebukes Pharisees and Sadducees who come to his baptism (Matt. 3:1–12; Luke 3:1–18). **2.** John bears witness of only begotten Son before priests and Levites from Jerusalem (John 1:19–34). **3.** Jesus casts moneychangers out of temple (John 2:13–25). **4.** Jesus preaches in synagogue, reading from Esaias (Luke 4:16–30). **5.** Jesus challenges scribes and Pharisees who say within themselves, "This man blasphemeth" (Matt. 9:2–8; Mark 2:1–12; Luke 5:17–26). **6.** Jesus admonishes scribes and Pharisees who question his eating with publicans and sinners (Matt. 9:10–17; Mark 2:15–22; Luke 5:29–39). **7.** Jesus answers Jews who persecute him for healing impotent man at Bethesda on sabbath (John 5:1–47). **8.** Disciples pluck ears of grain on sabbath and Jesus reproves Pharisees who therefore question him (Matt. 12:1–14; Mark 2:23–28; 3:1–6; Luke 6:1–11). **9.** Jesus rebukes scribes and Pharisees who accuse him of casting out devils by Beelzebub (Matt. 12:22–37; Mark 3:22–30; Luke 11:14–26). **10.** Jesus counters "an evil generation" seeking a sign (Matt. 12:38–45; Luke 11:16, 29–36). **11.** In synagogue at Capernaum, Jesus reproves Jews and many disciples who murmur in disbelief because he said, "... Whoso eateth my flesh, and drinketh my blood, hath eternal life..." (John 6:22–7:1). **12.** God's commandments vs. man's tradition: Jesus rebukes scribes and Pharisees of Jerusalem and calls the multitude to understand (Matt. 15:1–20; Mark 7:1–23). **13.** Jesus rebukes Pharisees and Sadducees who tempt him, seeking a sign (Matt. 15:39–16:4; Mark 8:9–12). **14.** Jesus teaches in temple at Jerusalem, speaking boldly and prophesying of the Spirit; Pharisees and chief priests send officers to take him (John 7). **15.** Jesus challenges scribes and Pharisees who accuse woman taken in adultery (John 8:1–11). **16.** Central conflict between Jesus and Pharisees: origin of Christ (John 8:12–59). **17.** Jesus heals blind man on sabbath and affirms divine Sonship before Pharisees; the Good Shepherd (John 9; 10:1–21). **18.** Jesus answers testing of a lawyer; the good Samaritan (Luke 10:25–37). **19.** Woes upon scribes and Pharisees for hypocrisy and upon lawyers for taking away key of knowledge (Luke 11:37–54). **20.** Jesus looses woman from infirmity on sabbath, confronting ruler of synagogue (Luke 13:10–17). **21.** Jesus sends Pharisees to testify before "that fox," Herod (Luke 13:31–35). **22.** Jesus answers Pharisees who test him concerning divorce (Matt. 19:3–12; Mark 10:2–12). **23.** Jesus testifies of his oneness with the Father to Jews "not of my sheep" who gather round to stone him (John 10:22–42). **24.** Jesus rebukes covetous Pharisees (Luke 16:14–18). **25.** Jesus demanded of Pharisees when kingdom of God should come (Luke 17:20, 21). **26.** Triumphal entry into Jerusalem: Jesus answers Pharisees who say, "Master, rebuke thy disciples" (Luke 19:29–44). **27.** Jesus again casts moneychangers out of temple and answers chief priests and scribes who question the children's "Hosanna to the Son of David!" (Matt. 21:12–17; Mark 11:15–19; Luke 19:45–48). **28.** Jesus confounds chief priests and elders who challenge his authority (Matt. 21:23–46; 22:1–14; Mark 11:27–33; 12:1–12; Luke 20:1–19). **29.** Jesus confutes Pharisees who question tribute unto Caesar (Matt. 22:15–22; Mark 12:13–17; Luke 20:20–26). **30.** Jesus silences Sadducees who say there is no resurrection (Matt. 22:23–33; Mark 12:18–27; Luke 20:27–40). **31.** Jesus answers lawyer who tests him regarding the great commandment (Matt. 22:34–40; Mark 12:28–34). **32.** Jesus silences Pharisees by asking them, "What think ye of Christ? Whose son is he?" (Matt. 22:41–46; Mark 12:35–37; Luke 20:41–44). **33.** Jesus announces seven woes upon scribes and Pharisees (Matt. 23:13–39). **34.** Jesus reproves chief priests and elders of the people who come to arrest him (Matt. 26:47–56; Mark 14:43–52; Luke 22:47–53; John 18:2–12). **35.** Jesus before Caiaphas, the high priest (John 18:13–24; Matt. 26:59–68; Mark 14:55–65; Luke 22:66–71). **36.** Jesus before Pontius Pilate, the governor (Matt. 27:2, 11–31; Mark 15:1–20; Luke 23:1–5, 13–25; John 18:28–19:16). **37.** Jesus before Herod—answering nothing (Luke 23:6–12).

16

∞

The Initiation of the North Gate

Beloved Who Sing a New Song, Saying,

> Thou art worthy to take the book,
> And to open the seals thereof:
> For thou wast slain,
> And hast redeemed us to God by thy blood
> Out of every kindred, and tongue, and people, and nation;
> And hast made us unto our God
> Kings and Priests:
> And we shall reign on the earth.

The new song is the song celestial of the Christ and the Buddha which becomes the song terrestrial as the sound of the HUM hummed in the hearts of the great multitude, as the sound of the AUM in the white cube of the saints, and as the sound of I AM THAT I AM, the unending Word, out of the mouth of the two witnesses.

Let us approach the north gate. It is the office of the Lion. Here sits the Great Initiator, the Guru of Gurus. The holder and the beholder of the office is Maitreya, the Great Loving One, the Coming Buddha Who Has Come. His dharma is sacrifice. His virtue is diligence to all in the discipleship of discernment and discrimination, mind and heart, for determined action.[1] He the one, the first Guru and the last Guru of the first Mother and the last Mother, teaches the art and the science of the balance of karma and the transmutation of energies misqualified through the perfection of the heart.

Lo, his heart is the heart of God. And I AM in that heart. Lo, his heart is the heart of Christ. And I AM in that heart. Lo, his heart is the heart of the Great, Great Central Sun. And I AM also in that heart, adorned and adorning bodhisattvas, tier upon tier, and devotees of the Mother in the White Goddess. His solar emanation unto all souls is the soul mastery of the heart of the Father, of the Son, of the Holy Spirit. And the byword he gives to initiates of the sacred fire of the Mother who would fly to him as the flying Eagle is "Be ye therefore perfect, even as your Father which is in heaven is perfect."

He superimposes upon the Cosmic Clock the cosmic cross of white fire. He carefully places twelve ruby roses upon that cross beginning with the center at the nexus of the Mother where Alpha and Omega meet. He bows before the Lamb and before his Father's name. And he makes obeisance to the Guru behind the Guru, Gautama Buddha, and to the Guru behind the Guru, the Ancient of Days. And then he sets in perfect place the four roses of the four living creatures, two to the left and two to the right on the horizontal bar. He gives adoration to the Threefold Flame of Life, the heartbeat of the great multitude and the saints. And he invokes that Threefold Flame, as above so below, on the vertical bar which the four living creatures, as custodians of the Tree of Life, guard on the four sides of the City Foursquare.

Three roses above, three roses below, and the Ruby Ray is set. And the Path of the Ruby Ray initiations are written in stone. And the *tone* of sacrifice (*s-tone=stone*) is the etching in the rock of I AM THAT I AM three times three, as above so below, three times three for the interlaced triangles. And the eye in the center is the ruby rose at the nexus of the cosmic cross of white fire and at the nexus of the figure-eight flow of the Buddha and the Mother. And the greater and the lesser rose mark the sign of the heart and the inner temple of the heart.

This Lamb who stood on the mount Sion is the initiator of the spiral that rises from the square, from the dot in the center there that is the ion, the first photon of fohatic light (*Sion*=the *s*piral of the *ion*). And the spiral that pulsates from the center of the base of the Great Pyramid is the *S* of the figure eight. And the conclusion of the *S* is its fusion with the eight by the ascension flame as it proceeds from the north side of the City Foursquare in the earth, rising, rising from the altar of invocation of the Church Universal and Triumphant where the saints do gather and the two witnesses witness and the great multitude come out of the great tribulation to wash their robes (auras—forcefields) and make them white in the blood (sacred fire) of the Lamb (the Guru Maitreya incarnate in the *MA*).

Yes, my beloved, the ascension flame rises from such as these. From north to south in Matter, from south to north in Spirit, souls ascending pass from the Father in Matter to the Mother in Matter to the Mother in Spirit to the Father in Spirit. Thus Alpha and Omega, the Father-Mother God, the beginning and the ending, are one in Spirit and in Spirit's reflection.

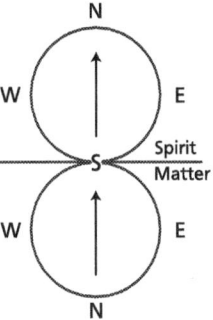

The hundred and forty and four thousand bodhisattvas and devotees of the Mother, the saints of the Church East and West, have his Father's name written in their foreheads—the forefront of conscious Self-consciousness—I AM that Father. My name is Sanat Kumara, I AM THAT I AM, the Ancient of Days. Everyone who is of the original hundred and forty and four thousand has the sacred name sealed in the third-eye vision and memory of me. Spoken in every language and the tongues of angels, it is always I AM *THAT* I AM. It means I AM the Trinity of the Being of God incarnate in form and formlessness, in action in Spirit and in Matter, always and always in the Mother.

Now, my children, write on onionskin (or tissue paper) the sacred name I AM THAT I AM and read it aloud from the reverse side. Does it not read MA I TAHT MA I? Does it not mean that the I AM who I really AM whose nature is mirrored in the "below" is the polarity of the "Above"? Does this not finally reveal the Person of the Woman crowned with twelve stars of the Rose Cross as the attainment of the Guru that I AM?

—always in heaven, yet always in earth. Hence I AM the MA I and the MA I, the first and the last incarnation of the Mother in the heaven and in the earth. I AM the nexus of Life flowing, knowing who I AM within you.

When you see the pronoun *THAT*, whether in English or in Sanskrit as *TAT*, it marks the point of transition through which the Greater Self of Brahman enters the lesser self of the soul manifestation and there stakes its claim as the supreme reality of its beginning and its ending.

TAT (THAT) is the passageway of the Trinity which enters and conquers the Matter flame by the two *T*'s, crosses, where God in man is crucified for the redemption of all life. The *A* in the center is the Alpha son, the Buddha flanked by the two *T*'s, his bodhisattvas East and West. The English version *THAT* injects the *H*, sacred fire breath of Holy Ghost, present in the Alpha seed and son. Even when he gave up the Ghost with the parting prayer "It is finished!" the two malefactors upon their two *T*'s heard as the sacred Word—MA I AM.

> The MA I is the call to Mother
> For her I-dentity and her sacred EYE.
> By these two *I*'s, the Saviouress saves her own
> And calls sinners to come Home to AUM,
> The sacred name of MU,
> The Mother of Light who
> Nourishes the flame of Alpha within YOU—
> As you will soon see through
> The Matter page when you write
> The AUM and read it MU A.
> The *MA* in *U* (you universally),
>   the *A*lpha son (sun).

Do you think, my beloved, that I play with words or the Word? Be it far from thee! That is what the dark ones would tell thee. But it is they who are the play on words and on the Word. It is they who will pay on, inch by inch, by the spiral of being until there are no more inches because the *I* of the Mother is not in them. And when they pay the last farthing, they are farthest from the Central Sun and have no way to run, to and fro, with the cosmic forces, for they have squandered all their forces—this I know.

Thus when the judgment comes it is their own heaped upon their own. Their actions be their judge! And the Light that is no more within them will stand apart from them and testify of them and their refusal to submit to the living Word. Therefore is the Light gone out of them. Therefore does the Light consume them who sought to consume Him upon their lusts.

Now from heaven I hear a voice as the voice of many waters. These many waters are the flowing streams of consciousness, lifestreams who all flow back to the mainstream of the Lamb and to the Source, his Father that I AM. It is the single voice of the Word I heard in the voice of many souls who have sealed the sign of the Mother. And they walk upon the water, for the desire of God is in them. And out from their midst the voice of a great thunder. And lo, the many waters of the Mother's children are aligned by the seven Spirits intoning the sound of the Word in the seven planes of heaven and earth, producing the single sound of a great thunder and the voice of harpers harping with their harps.

Lo, it is the entire Spirit of the Great White Brotherhood, and the full diapason of that Holy Spirit. Lo, a single voice of the Person of the Holy Spirit—one Person, one Office, one Voice fulfilled in the infinite harpers harping with their harps. One Person, one Office, one Voice of a great thunder that resounds from heart to heart to heart in the infinity of Selfhood that God Almighty, the LORD who is LORD, has multiplied for the sounding of the sound of the universal thunder of the Word. One Person, one Office, one Voice of the Mother out of many souls swimming in the waters of the Cosmic Sea.

We are before the great white throne. We are singing a new song, my beloved. We stand with the Lamb—behold, I and my Father are one—before the four beasts and the four and twenty elders. And no man could learn the sacred mystery of that song but the hundred and forty and four thousand, which were redeemed from the earth. It is the infinite song sung by the infinite manifestation of the Godhead.

They who sing it are they who understand the incarnate Word. They understand him, for they follow him whithersoever he goeth from the base of the Pyramid of Life unto the all-seeing eye, the energy of the ascension flame, the virgin light, the light of the Virgin. And their light is undefiled by the lunar light of the astral woman. They follow the Lamb. They follow the Ancient of Days. They are the redeemed from among men. They are the firstfruits unto God and to the Lamb.

The initiations of the north gate, my beloved, come out of a new song that you will sing when *you* hear a voice from heaven as the voice of many waters and as the voice of a great thunder and when you hear the voice of harpers harping with their harps. These are the initiations of the Father/Guru which he gives to the son/chela. These are the twelve initiations of the Tree of Life.

With each initiation that is passed, the Father gives to the Son a single fruit from the Tree of Life that he may eat and live forever in the God consciousness, step by step, of the twelve hierarchies of the sun. Thus the Guru Maitreya gives to his chelas the fruit of the Tree of Life. And none may take that fruit except it be given into the mouth of the chela out of the mouth of the Guru.

Every false guru would tempt you to take and eat of the fruit of the tree of the knowledge of good and evil that you might become wise as the Watchers who defected from the service of the Great Silent Watchers. No longer do they watch and wait to vest ascended master youth with living truth. Instead they watch and prey, as vultures upon their prey, seeking what souls they may devour by the hour, by the hour. These vultures, fallen ones of Victory's band, will go by the way in a dark and dreary land.

Behold, the daystar of His appearing is at hand! Now I, the Ancient of Days, announce to you the coming of the many and the few Great Silent Watchers, reinforcing the office of the Elohim Cyclopea and the mysteries sweet of the inner retreats of the

Great White Brotherhood. The Great Silent Watchers have gathered in numberless numbers before the throne, the flaming Presence of the great Three-in-One, and within the retreats of the Brotherhood they summon chelas who have learned by the all-seeing eye the perfection of the soul on the path of science and religion and are ready to begin the initiations of the north gate.

It is the building, it is the building of the Temple of Victory that rises from the base unto the crown of life! Men and women of goodwill, I summon you to still the tempests in the earth with his Word "Peace, be still!" to know the Father in the Son by the Presence of the Flaming One, to be the Law and the Lawgiver, and to understand that when the hour is come that the Son of man should be glorified, he is glorifed in the I AM THAT I AM, the Father of all.

Thus the sacrifice of the heart outplayed in the office of the Lion may be studied and discerned in the Word of Jesus Christ:

> *Verily, verily, I say unto you, Except a corn of wheat fall into the ground and die, it abideth alone: but if it die, it bringeth forth much fruit.*
>
> *He that loveth his life shall lose it; and he that hateth his life in this world shall keep it unto life eternal.*
>
> *If any man serve me, let him follow me; and where I AM, there shall also my servant be: if any man serve me, him will my Father honour.*
>
> *Now is my soul troubled; and what shall I say? Father, save me from this hour: but for this cause came I unto this hour.*
>
> *Father, glorify thy name. Then came there a voice from heaven, saying, I have both glorified it, and will glorify it again.*
>
> *The people therefore, that stood by, and heard it, said that it thundered: others said, An angel spake to him.*
>
> *Jesus answered and said, This voice came not because of me, but for your sakes.*
>
> *Now is the judgment of this world: now shall the prince of this world be cast out.*

And I, if I be lifted up from the earth, will draw all men unto me.

This he said, signifying what death he should die.

The people answered him, We have heard out of the law that Christ abideth for ever: and how sayest thou, The Son of man must be lifted up? who is this Son of man?

Then Jesus said unto them, Yet a little while is the light with you. Walk while ye have the light, lest darkness come upon you: for he that walketh in darkness knoweth not whither he goeth.

While ye have light, believe in the light, that ye may be the children of light. These things spake Jesus, and departed, and did hide himself from them.

But though he had done so many miracles before them, yet they believed not on him:

That the saying of Esaias the prophet might be fulfilled, which he spake, Lord, who hath believed our report? and to whom hath the arm of the Lord been revealed?

Therefore they could not believe, because that Esaias said again,

He hath blinded their eyes, and hardened their heart; that they should not see with their eyes, nor understand with their heart, and be converted, and I should heal them.

These things said Esaias, when he saw his glory, and spake of him.

Nevertheless among the chief rulers also many believed on him; but because of the Pharisees they did not confess him, lest they should be put out of the synagogue:

For they loved the praise of men more than the praise of God.

Jesus cried and said, He that believeth on me, believeth not on me, but on him that sent me.

And he that seeth me seeth him that sent me.

I AM come a light into the world, that whosoever believeth on me should not abide in darkness.

And if any man hear my words, and believe not, I judge him not: for I came not to judge the world, but to save the world.

He that rejecteth me, and receiveth not my words, hath one that judgeth him: the word that I have spoken, the same shall judge him in the last day.

For I have not spoken of myself; but the Father which sent me, he gave me a commandment, what I should say, and what I should speak.

And I know that his commandment is life everlasting: whatsoever I speak therefore, even as the Father said unto me, so I speak.

My beloved, these are the words of the Son of God entering in to the heart of the Father. They are the words of the chela who proclaims the sacred name of his Guru and whose sufficiency is in that one whom he calls Father. In these words Jesus Christ reveals himself to be the Messenger of his Father/Guru, Lord Maitreya. Ponder them well, ponder them again and again. For it shall come to pass that these words shall be fulfilled within thee as the Initiation of the North Gate.

In the name of the Father and of his Son Jesus Christ and of the Holy Spirit, Amen.

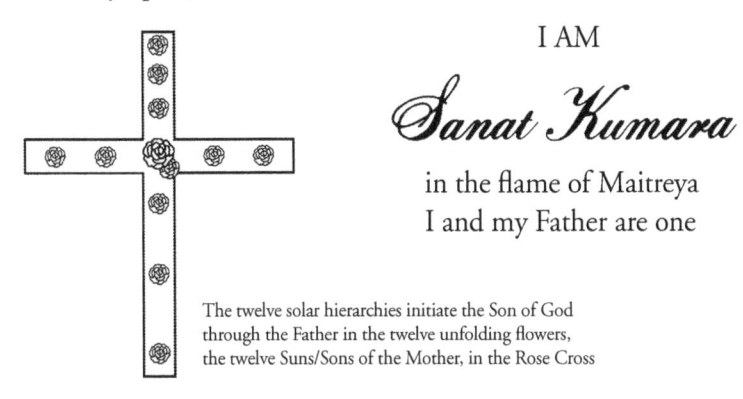

I AM

Sanat Kumara

in the flame of Maitreya
I and my Father are one

The twelve solar hierarchies initiate the Son of God through the Father in the twelve unfolding flowers, the twelve Suns/Sons of the Mother, in the Rose Cross

See Rev. 5:9, 10; Matt. 5:48; Gen. 2:9; 3:22, 24; Rev. 2:7; 22:2, 14; Rev. 14:1–4; Rev. 7:14; Rev. 12:1; John 19:30; Luke 23:32; Matt. 5:26; Gen. 2:9, 17; Mark 4:39; John 12:23; John 12:24–50.

17

∞

The Initiation of the West Gate

And I beheld, and I heard the voice of many angels round about the throne and the beasts and the elders: and the number of them was ten thousand times ten thousand, and thousands of thousands;

Saying with a loud voice, Worthy is the Lamb that was slain to receive power, and riches, and wisdom, and strength, and honour, and glory, and blessing.

And every creature which is in heaven, and on the earth, and under the earth, and such as are in the sea, and all that are in them, heard I saying, Blessing, and honour, and glory, and power, be unto him that sitteth upon the throne, and unto the Lamb for ever and ever.

And the four beasts said, Amen. And the four and twenty elders fell down and worshipped him that liveth for ever and ever. REVELATION 5

Beloved Who Love the Golden Shore of Reality:

The west gate is the gate of the future. The future that becomes the now by the gift of invocation. Invocation is the science of the precipitation of the God flame from your individual I AM Presence, stepped down to your individual Christ Self who is the great distiller of the God flame unto your soul. Drop by drop the individual Guru within you releases the wine of the Spirit; and he is the great winepress, pressing out the Holy Spirit essence for the alchemy of thy soul's transmutation. This is the new wine of the Holy Spirit sent by the Father unto the Son.

The beloved Christ Self, the Good Shepherd of thy soul, is

the representative of the householder, which planted a vineyard, and hedged it round about, and digged a winepress in it, and built a tower, and let it out to husbandmen, and went into a far country. The householder is the Father in the Son (I and my Father are one) who has planted the vineyard of the earth. And the grapes of the vine are the souls whose life is in *the Branch*. Each grape is likened unto a soul having free will to bring forth the seed of the Word that is within itself, verily the seed of the I AM Presence. Each grape represents a soul identity, a solar awareness. And the measure of that awareness is measured by the great winepress that measures out the essence of the fruit.

The Initiation of the West Gate is the harvest of the fully ripened grapes. And not until the grapes are fully ripe does the angel of the sacred fire come out from the altar of the temple which is in heaven and cry with a loud voice to the angel having the sharp sickle, saying, "Thrust in thy sharp sickle, and gather the clusters of the vine of the earth."

The LORD of the vineyard is the I AM Presence who makes his husbandmen the spiritual/material overseers during the period of the ripening of the fruit of the vine. These are God's overmen who rule in the governments and the economies of the nations not by right, in and of themselves, but by the grace of God; for they rule in his stead. Thus they experiment with the authority of the Logos, and they position themselves to the right or to the left of the Word.

Among these husbandmen are those who were once rulers in heaven who lost their high estate, and now they are rulers in the earth; for the LORD of the vineyard has created the vineyard not only for the maturation of the souls of his children but to give final and conclusive opportunity to those who were the mighty among the legions of the LORD. They were cast down from their seats of authority by their nonalignment with him that sitteth on the great white throne. Now they must prove their allegiance, and in order to do so they must be given the seats of the mighty within the earth.

Remember, my beloved, earth is a stage that mirrors the stage of heaven. All is role playing, role playing. God is not so much concerned with the material condition as He is with the condition of the heart. Thus those who sit in the seats of the mighty in the earth—though they be not worthy to unlatch the shoes of the lowliest servant within their households—must be given the opportunity to choose in the earth as they have already chosen in heaven to accept or to reject the Word incarnate within the servants of God. By and by, after those husbandmen have retained their positions lifetime after lifetime as rulers of men and nations, they are wont to forget that it is not by their right nor by their might that they rule in the footstool kingdom but by the authority of the LORD of the vineyard.

Thus when the Father sends his servant-sons, the ascended masters, in that season when the time of the fruit draws near that He might receive the fruits of the soul consciousness and its sacred labor, these husbandmen take his servants, who are the living disciples of the Word, to "beat them," and "kill them," and "stone them." And still he sends other servants more than the first: and the husbandmen, unwilling to relinquish their positions of power held in trust, refuse—oh, they still refuse—to acknowledge the servants who come in the name of the LORD.

Last of all he sends his Son, saying, "They will reverence my Son, the Christ incarnate, as the Guru." But the princes of this world value the Son only for his inheritance. They desire the fullness of his light. Because they will not bow down before him, they must "kill him" before they can seize on his inheritance.

The kingdom of God, his God consciousness, I have entrusted unto the hundred and forty and four thousand in the earth. It has been seized upon by the laggard generations who have mismanaged the light, energy, and consciousness of my flame. They have sought to take my Person to themselves as their own, but they have rejected the white stone. This is the age of the ripening. And lo, the fields of the LORD are white to the harvest, and the labourers are few who have the know-how to gather the souls of my consciousness.

I, even I, pray to the LORD of the harvest, that he will send forth labourers into his harvest. As it is the age of Aquarius for the gathering of the grapes, so it is the age of the judgment of the husbandmen. Now we see the great winepress of the wrath of God, trodden without the city, pressing out the essence of every man's fruit.

Now behold a white cloud, and upon the cloud the one who sat *like unto* the Son of man, having on his head a golden crown, and in his hand a sharp sickle. Now behold another angel coming out of the temple, crying with a loud voice to him that sits on the cloud, "Thrust in thy sickle, and reap: for the time is come for thee to reap; for the harvest of the earth is ripe."

Therefore the kingdom of God is taken from the oppressors who have oppressed the Word in heaven and in earth, and it is given to the ever-widening circles of devotees East and West who bring forth the fruits of the God consciousness. And the Initiation of the West Gate is the initiation of the white stone. The *stone* is the *s*acred *tone* of the Lamb, the keynote of the divine plan of everyone who is of the light. And whosoever shall fall on this stone shall be broken: but on whomsoever it shall fall, it will grind him to powder.

The stone is the white stone in the heart of the saints. It is the foundation of Israel. When Christ comes to the Israelites who are untrue to their calling, he is to them an offence and a stumblingstone, the servant who stands in the way of their proud and unlawful ambition. This stone which the builders rejected while building their monuments to the lesser self is become the head of the corner of the community of the Holy Spirit that is appearing even now nation by nation. As the outer walls of a corrupted nationalism come tumbling down, the inner tower built upon the rock of Christ emerges as the nucleus of lightbearers who proclaim the new order of the ages.

This stone is the sacred tone of Elohim sounded within the

nations by the messengers of God. And with the sounding of the Word, though the sound be unheard, the stone of the Holy Spirit becomes the smiting stone of the terrible crystal, the Destroyer of the international strongholds and their strong men. For the offenders of my people are broken by the rock of Christ. In the name of the Rock, thou shalt break them with a rod of iron; thou shalt dash them in pieces like a potter's vessel.

Sons and daughters of light, approach with care and careful consideration the west gate. It is the office of the Calf whose mantle is worn royally by Gautama Buddha. In Spirit and in Matter he is the body of God, the Holy Spirit in form and formlessness. His cloven tongues are manifest within thee as the Alpha and the Omega of thy service, of thy dharma, which is the service of the Calf. His virtue is patience. It is the patient longsuffering of the servants of God until the harvest of the earth is ripe.

Though they cry out, "How long, O LORD!" long, long is the waiting of the saints for the harvest of light and darkness—embodied Good and embodied Evil. For they know the irrevocable law of karma: "He that leadeth into captivity shall go into captivity: he that killeth with the sword must be killed with the sword." Therefore they know "Verily, they have their reward"—the workers of iniquity their own and the workers of righteousness their own. In this Law and in its outworking through the Word do the saints place their patience and their faith.

Now receive ye the communion of the LORD as the body and blood of Christ and be fortified for Armageddon. For the deceptions of the impostors of the Holy Spirit are gone forth out into the nations in the four quadrants of the earth. And those who represent Gog and Magog, as relative good and evil, have compassed the camp of the saints about, and the beloved city. But the sacred fire is come down from God out of heaven through the invocation of the Word, and the sacred fire devoureth the enemies of the two witnesses as they minister in the midst of the great multitude.

On the west gate we find the Alpha and the Omega of Christ

in universal manifestation through the Calf who is the symbol of the Lords of the Worlds, the Solar Logoi, and all of the twin flames of the Father-Mother God manifest in nature through the seven mighty Elohim of the (outer) seven rays and the five Elohim of the (inner) five rays in the white-fire core of being. Here you will find, bowing before the Lamb and the Lamb's wife, the four beings of the elements as they represent the four cosmic forces. For the west gate is given to thee, my beloved, for the crystallization of the God flame in Spirit and in Matter. And the byword of the initiates of the Holy Spirit is "This is my body, which is broken for you."

Here the Lamb demonstrates the fragmentation of the Greater Self for the survival of the lesser self. One crumb of the loaf equals the whole loaf. Now each one of the great multitude contains a single crumb of the Life of the Lamb who is slain. And the survival and the salvation of the soul is secured.

Now, initiates of the Ruby Ray, learn the multiplication of the Self, thy Self—Alpha multiplied by Omega, Omega multiplied by Alpha in the great cosmic interchange—and thy Self in the midst as the living Word. Now learn the balance of karma, the fulfillment of dharma, and the transmutation of energy misqualified through the perfection of the body consciousness. The body consciousness is the space in which the Buddha dwells. It must be multiplied by the time, time, time of the Mother's pulsating light within the center of the space.

Did he not say, "Destroy this temple, and in three days I will raise it up"? Go thou and do likewise. Go be the raising up of the Temple Beautiful in the midst of the people. Be the tower of power upon the rock whose light is wisdom, whose source is love. Go be the light of the Ancient of Days and raise up the temple through the law of the Trinity—first in the office of the Son in the initiations of the east gate, second in the office of the Father in the initiations of the north gate, and third in the office of the Holy Spirit in the initiations of the west gate.

The Initiation of the West Gate was revealed in part by Jesus

Christ when he spoke with his disciples on the way to the garden of Gethsemane:

> *I AM the true vine, and my Father is the husbandman.*
>
> *Every branch in me that beareth not fruit he taketh away: and every branch that beareth fruit, he purgeth it, that it may bring forth more fruit.*
>
> *Now ye are clean through the Word which I have spoken unto you.*
>
> *Abide in me, and I in you. As the branch cannot bear fruit of itself, except it abide in the vine; no more can ye, except ye abide in me.*
>
> *I AM the vine, ye are the branches: He that abideth in me, and I in him, the same bringeth forth much fruit: for without me ye can do nothing.*
>
> *If a man abide not in me, he is cast forth as a branch, and is withered; and men gather them, and cast them into the fire, and they are burned.*
>
> *If ye abide in me, and my words abide in you, ye shall ask what ye will, and it shall be done unto you.*
>
> *Herein is my Father glorified, that ye bear much fruit; so shall ye be my disciples.*
>
> *As the Father hath loved me, so have I loved you: continue ye in my love.*
>
> *If ye keep my commandments, ye shall abide in my love; even as I have kept my Father's commandments, and abide in his love.*
>
> *These things have I spoken unto you, that my joy might remain in you, and that your joy might be full.*
>
> *This is my commandment, That ye love one another, as I have loved you.*
>
> *Greater love hath no man than this, that a man lay down his life for his friends.*
>
> *Ye are my friends, if ye do whatsoever I command you.*
>
> *Henceforth I call you not servants; for the servant*

> knoweth not what his lord doeth: but I have called you friends; for all things that I have heard of my Father I have made known unto you.
>
> Ye have not chosen me, but I have chosen you, and ordained you, that ye should go and bring forth fruit, and that your fruit should remain: that whatsoever ye shall ask of the Father in my name, he may give it you.
>
> *These things I command you, that ye love one another.*

The writings of beloved John in chapters fifteen and sixteen of his Gospel are the prophecy of all that is come to pass in the community of the Holy Spirit that is built on the west side of the City Foursquare. These are the initiations of love that can come to the chela only when the chela is abiding in the I AM and the I AM is in him. These words are the teaching of the Teacher on the Guru-chela relationship that Jesus Christ establishes in the last days through his Church Universal and Triumphant.

It is the Father who taketh away the branch that beareth not fruit. It is the Father who purgeth every branch that beareth fruit that it may bring forth more fruit. Within and among the members of this community who abide in him and his Word—his *manifest* Word, his *living* Word, his *revealed* Word, his *prophetic* Word—they ask what they will by the science of the invocation of the Word that is in them, and it is done unto them. Here the Word in the disciples bears much fruit, abundant fruit, the fruit of God consciousness sufficient for all the nations of the earth.

Those participating in the initiations of the west gate are filled with the fullness of the joy of the Lamb. They accept the promise that his joy is in them. They love one another with the fervent love of their Saviour—not as person to person in possessive love, but they love truly "as I have loved you." They lay down their life daily upon the altar of invocation; they give forth the Word in their dynamic, determined decrees. For this is the dharma of the Calf (the Ox), the great burden-bearer of personal and planetary karma.

No more are they slaves or sinners. They are the friends of the living Christ who comes to them in the person of the ascended masters. And the ascended masters one by one represent the crumbs from the LORD's table. Collectively, they are the entire Spirit of the Great White Brotherhood. They are the hosts of the LORD in heaven who are reflected in the faces of the great multitude in earth. Those who enter into the initiations of the west gate are called the friends of the Saviour. They share his intimacy with the Father as he has shared with them all things that he has heard of Lord Maitreya, Lord Buddha, and me.

Each of the members of the body of God within the circle of the Holy Spirit are chosen by the Guru and ordained, initiated, by him for the purpose of going forth and bringing forth the fruit of the saints and the great multitude city by city and nation by nation. Unto them is given the Science of the Spoken Word—the power, wisdom, and love of invocation "that whatsoever ye shall ask of the Father in my name, he may give it you."

The Guru in the midst of the garden of Eden commands his disciples to love and to love and to love one another, to lay down their lives for one another, and to love one another in his name. This love is the flow between and amongst the body of believers of the immense light of their invocation. Sealed as one by the mighty movement of love of the Holy Spirit in their midst, they are able to bear the hatred of the world pitted against the circle of their oneness in their Guru-chela relationship. This hatred is but the virulence of the carnal mind's enmity with Christ and the carnal mind's misqualified energy that rushes into the vortex of love—ruby love—for transmutation.

Listen well, my children, to the admonishment of my Son Jesus. For all these things must come to pass ere you stand God-victorious in God-reality on the west side of the city:

> *If the world hate you, ye know that it hated me before it hated you.*
>
> *If ye were of the world, the world would love his own:*

but because ye are not of the world, but I have chosen you out of the world, therefore the world hateth you.

Remember the Word that I said unto you, The servant is not greater than his lord. If they have persecuted me, they will also persecute you; if they have kept my saying, they will keep yours also.

But all these things will they do unto you for my name's sake, because they know not him that sent me.

If I had not come and spoken unto them, they had not had sin: but now they have no cloke for their sin.

He that hateth me hateth my Father also.

If I had not done among them the works which none other man did, they had not had sin: but now have they both seen and hated both me and my Father.

But this cometh to pass, that the Word might be fulfilled that is written in their law, They hated me without a cause.

But when the Comforter is come, whom I will send unto you from the Father, even the Spirit of truth, which proceedeth from the Father, he shall testify of me:

And ye also shall bear witness, because ye have been with me from the beginning.

These things have I spoken unto you, that ye should not be offended.

They shall put you out of the synagogues: yea, the time cometh, that whosoever killeth you will think that he doeth God service.

And these things will they do unto you, because they have not known the Father, nor me.

My beloved, the sign of Aquarius is the sign of the intensification of love within the earth. It is the sign of the coming of age of the saints who hold out the crystal cup, receive the blood of the Lamb that is the essence of the Ruby Ray, and stand within the earth as the guardians of the love of Christ unto his own. They are the wielders of the sacred spear whose power is the holy blood. And always they are with the Person whose vesture is dipped in blood: and his name is called The Word of God.

I AM the one sent,

Sanat Kumara

See Rev. 5; Matt. 9:17; Matt. 21:33–34; Mark 12:1–11; Luke 20:9–18; Isa. 4:2; 11:1–9; 60:21; Jer. 23:5, 6; 33:15; Zech. 3:8; 6:12; Rev. 14:17, 18; Isa. 66:1; Rev. 2:17; John 4:35; Matt. 9:37, 38; Rev. 14:19, 20; 19:15; Rev. 14:14, 15; Isa. 8:14, 15; Rom. 9:32, 33; 1 Pet. 2:6–10; Ezek. 1:22; 1 Cor. 10:4; Ps. 2:9; Rom. 8:6, 7; John 15:18–27; 16:1–3; Rev. 19:13; John 6:29.

18

The Word and the Work of the Saints on the West Gate

Beloved on the Great White Way of the Path of Initiation on the Ruby Ray:

The service of the saints serving on the west gate, guarding the comings and the goings of the souls of the great multitude, is the science of religion, the science whereby the soul is bound to God by the cords of love. This love is the essence of the Holy Spirit.

The science of the saints is the word and the work of the Holy Spirit. It is their life. They are no longer sorrowful, nor doth sorrow fill their hearts for the Messenger who said, "I go my way to him that sent me and none of you asketh me, Whither goest thou?"

The saints of the community called Camelot are immersed in the threefold manifestation of the Holy Spirit whom Jesus the Christed Messenger has sent unto them:

> *Nevertheless I tell you the truth; It is expedient for you that I go away: for if I go not away, the Comforter will not come unto you; but if I depart, I will send him unto you.*
>
> *And when he is come, he will reprove the world of sin, and of righteousness, and of judgment:*
>
> *Of sin, because they believe not on me;*
>
> *Of righteousness, because I go to my Father, and ye see me no more;*
>
> *Of judgment, because the prince of this world is judged.*

The Holy Spirit comes to "reprove"—i.e., to bring to light, to bring to our remembrance[1]—the law of the Father that we have known from the beginning, which itself exposes the unreality of the law of sin and death. This He must do because the people have not believed on the Son as the embodiment of the law of the Father.

The Holy Spirit comes to set forth the law of the Son concerning righteousness, the *right energy use* of the law of the life everlasting. This the Holy Spirit must do through his instruments, the ascended masters and their chelas, because the ascended Jesus Christ is no longer in physical embodiment in this octave. His commemoration of the Word to his own is henceforth to be through the Holy Ghost and his representatives who are his physical instruments heart, head, and hand, having become "his body" and "his blood."

The Holy Spirit comes to reveal the nature of the judgment of the carnal mind within the individual and the Satanic dweller on the threshold of the planetary consciousness of good and evil. For it is the mission of the Son of God Jesus Christ and all whom he initiates into the path of Sonship to reenact this judgment by the science of invocation within the Matter spheres. This is the daily cross taken up by the initiates of the rose cross until the entire false hierarchy is brought to judgment before me at the Court of the Sacred Fire, at the great white throne, before the four cosmic forces and the twenty-four elders.

Truly this threefold action of reproof is the *re-proving* to the world of the Truth concerning *sin, righteousness,* and *judgment.* And this Light is come into the world through the teachings of my servant-sons, the ascended masters, delivered to the saints by the Lamb.

Because this seed of the Woman have accepted him at his word, they are the ones of whom it is prophesied, They "keep the commandments of God, and have the testimony of Jesus Christ." While they serve all Life on the west gate, they are becoming the initiates of the Mother flame which I hold in the embodied Lamb on the south gate. For they have believed the prophecy of the two witnesses; and by that prophecy, which is the true edification of the Holy Spirit, they are day by day overcoming the "dragon"[2] by the blood (sacred fire) of the Lamb and by the word (science of prayer and invocation) of their testimony. These are they who loved not their lives unto the death. They remember the Word of Jesus foretelling that his true teaching would come by this Spirit.

> *I have yet many things to say unto you, but ye cannot bear them now.*
>
> *Howbeit when he, the Spirit of truth, is come, he will guide you into all truth: for he shall not speak of himself; but whatsoever he shall hear, that shall he speak: and he will shew you things to come.*
>
> *He shall glorify me: for he shall receive of mine, and shall shew it unto you.*
>
> *All things that the Father hath are mine: therefore said I, that he shall take of mine, and shall shew it unto you.*

The Holy Spirit is a Person, verily he is the Person of every ascended master. The Teachings of the Ascended Masters are the Word of the Holy Spirit that is in them; and their teachings are always the glorification of the Lord Christ in Jesus and in everyone whom he has initiated in the path of Sonship. The ascended masters shall receive of mine, and shall show it unto you.

The communion of the saints in heaven is the sharing of the Body and the Spirit of the LORD. The ascended masters partake of the marriage supper of the Lamb. They eat the "flesh" and the "blood" of his consciousness; and, in the Person of the Holy Spirit, they show it unto the unascended chelas through the Science of the Spoken Word and the certain Word of prophecy delivered through the embodied messengers, twin flames who occupy the office of the two witnesses in every age.

In the final hours of his earthly mission, Jesus foretold "that day" in which "ye shall ask me nothing." For in "that day," which is the dispensation of Aquarius,

> *Verily, verily, I say unto you, Whatsoever ye shall ask the Father in my name, he will give it you.*
>
> *Hitherto have ye asked nothing in my name: ask, and ye shall receive, that your joy may be full.*
>
> *... But the time cometh, when I shall no more speak unto you in proverbs, but I shall shew you plainly of the Father.*
>
> *At that day ye shall ask in my name: and I say not unto you, that I will pray the Father for you:*
>
> *For the Father himself loveth you, because ye have loved me, and have believed that I came out from God.*
>
> *I came forth from the Father, and am come into the world: again, I leave the world, and go to the Father.*

Jesus foretold the day that is come when the saints should exercise the Science of the Spoken Word. As they invoke the light of the Father in the name of the Son, they may pray as he has prayed by the authority of the Word directly to the mighty I AM Presence in the name of the Christ Self, in the name of the Christ in Jesus and in every ascended master.

Thus the fulfillment of the mission of the Son of God is the reestablishment of the intimacy of the disciples of the Word with the Father himself who loveth them because they have loved the Word and have believed in the mission of the Lamb who cometh out of the Father and goeth unto the Father and is worthy, therefore, to open the seven-sealed book.

Jesus Christ has given the promise that is fulfilled in every one of the initiates of the Ruby Ray whose consummate love of the Father is consummated in the initiation of the Lamb: "I shall no more speak unto you in proverbs, but I shall shew you plainly of the Father." Through his two witnesses, Jesus Christ has truly shown all who have ears to hear the plain truth of the law of the Father and its application in church and state.

Now let the revelations of the Lord Jesus Christ unto his two witnesses, Mark L. Prophet and Elizabeth Clare Prophet, go forth as his teaching to all nations. And let his Word be the great baptizer with water and fire in the name of the Father and of the Son and of the Holy Ghost.

Standing on the west gate, Jesus Christ foretells the great tribulation as the saints do battle, in patience and her perfect work, in Armageddon with the forces, whether ignorant or malicious, of Antichrist. Before he enters the Initiation of the South Gate in the Mother flame, he leaves with them the comfort that will sustain them throughout the period of preparation prior to their own advent on the cross and its fourteen stations: "In the world ye shall have tribulation: but be of good cheer; I have overcome the world." And, as he told John, "Greater is he that is in you, than he that is in the world."

The activities of the disciples on the west gate represent a worldwide movement in higher consciousness. Gathering momentum, it becomes the revolution of the Christed ones who are in revolt against the establishment of the Luciferians and the monolith of their mass mechanization, epitomized in the Nimrod consciousness of the tower of Babel. The latter is the amalgamation of the disunited elements of the carnal mind who are in league together, though they be mortal enemies, in a final attempt to defeat the living Christ and to prove that they are able to successfully climb the ladder of the success cult without the Mother, without her flame, without the living Guru. And, of course, this they may do as long as it is allowed—until the angel thrusts in his sickle into the earth and gathers the vine of the earth, good and bad, and casts it into the great winepress of the wrath of God.

The ladder of success in this world, let down by the prince of this world to all who are made in his image (the image of the beast), is no measure of Christed man and woman. Only Jacob's ladder is the measure of the Son of man becoming the Son of God. And the angels of the LORD ascending and descending within the temple of the soul measure the soul's willingness to 'wrestle' with the angel until the breaking of the day and until the blessing of the soul becomes the purging by the sacred fire of elements untransmuted. The blessing (initiation) is borne to him by a living personage of the hierarchy of the Great White Brotherhood.

While the betrayers of the Word measure their success by worldly standards, there cometh another to whom is given a reed like unto a rod to measure the temple of God, and the altar, and them that worship therein. With the opening of the Path of the Ruby Ray, the Ascended Master John the Beloved is summoned to measure the light capacity of those who are called upon to be the temple of the living God. He measures the altar of the Universal Church and them that worship therein. He measures the measure of a man and a woman in the Threefold Flame burning upon the altar of the heart. He measures the adorations of the saints and the odours (vibrations) of the prayers of the saints contained in the golden vials borne by the four beasts and the four and twenty elders.

Thus the LORD, in the person of the Lords of Destiny four, the Lords of Creation four, the Lords of Individuality four, and the Lords of Form and Formlessness four, come to assess the souls worthy who are singing the new song within the temple of God and who are waiting upon the prophecy of the two witnesses that they might go forth to preach the gospel. This preaching of the gospel is the service of the saints on the west gate. They come in the archetype of the Christ crucified. They know the Calf and they know him as the Christ of Alpha and Omega come in the fohat of the El.

Yes, the saints are the souls worthy who are found singing the new song within my temple. Lo, I AM Sanat Kumara. I AM the empowering of the two witnesses and their prophesying, within Spirit and within Matter, a thousand two hundred and threescore cycles in God consciousness, once clothed in the sackcloth of the human consciousness and the human karma, now clothed with the Spirit of life from God. And the saints are they who hear the prophecy that is the edification and the enlightenment of their souls on the path of initiation. And they behold the two witnesses—the one on this side of the bank of the river, and the other on that side of the bank of the river—standing before the God of the earth, Lord Gautama Buddha, who is the light of the west gate and of the service of the saints.

I AM Sanat Kumara. I will initiate you in the path of the prophecy of the two witnesses that you might receive the reward that I give unto my servants the Prophets, and to the saints, and them that fear my name.

I AM THAT I AM

See John 14:26; Rom. 8:2; Rev. 12:17; John 16:12–15; Rev. 19:9; John 16:23–28; Rev. 7:14; 16:16; James 1:4; John 16:33; 1 John 4:4; Gen. 10:8–10; 11:1–9; Rev. 13; 14:9–11; 15:2; 16:2; 19:20; 20:4; Gen. 28:10–15; 32:24–32; Rev. 11:1; 21:17; Dan. 12:5; Rev. 11:3, 4, 11, 18.

The Flow of the Persons and Principles of the Godhead in the Seven Planes of Heaven and Earth

NORTH GATE
The Office of the Lion
Filled in Heaven by Lord Maitreya
and the Hosts of His Hierarchy
FATHER
*Initiations of the Second Ray
Crown Chakra*

2

THE NEW JERUSALEM
"The Lamb's Wife"

WEST GATE
The Office of the Calf
Filled in Heaven
by Gautama Buddha
and the Hosts
of His Hierarchy
HOLY SPIRIT
*Initiations of
the Third Ray
Heart Chakra*

3

MOTHER
The Office of the Flying Eagle
Filled in Heaven
by Sanat Kumara, the Ancient of Days,
and the Hosts of His Hierarchy
The Great Guru
THE ETERNAL LAMB

1

EAST GATE
The Office of the Man
Filled in Heaven
by Jesus Christ
and the Hosts
of His Hierarchy
SON
*Initiations of
the First Ray
Throat Chakra*

Nexus ⟶ **4** / SOUTH GATE

Spirit +
Matter −

THE EMBODIED LAMB
The Office of the Flying Eagle
Filled in Earth
by the Woman Clothed with the Sun
The Guru Ma
*Initiations of the Fourth Ray
Base-of-the-Spine Chakra*

WEST GATE
The Office of the Calf
Filled in Earth
by the
Great Multitude
*Initiations of
the Seventh Ray
Seat-of-the-Soul
Chakra*

7

THE CITY FOURSQUARE
Foundation of the
Great Matter Pyramid

5

EAST GATE
The Office of the Man
Filled in Earth
by the Two Witnesses
*Initiations of
the Fifth Ray
Third-Eye Chakra*

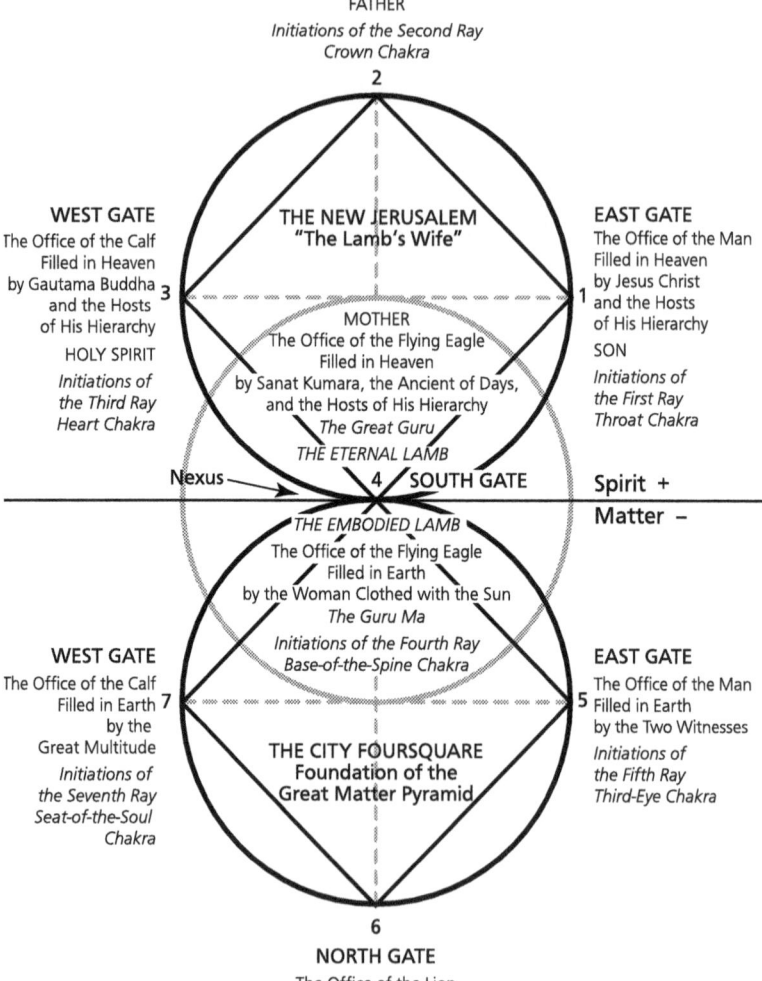

6

NORTH GATE
The Office of the Lion
Filled in Earth by the Saints of the Church

The Remnant of the Woman's Seed
The Hundred and Forty and Four Thousand
The Chelas of the Guru
*Initiations of the Sixth Ray
Solar-Plexus Chakra*

19

The Gospel of the Father, and of the Son, and of the Holy Ghost

And Jesus came and spake unto them, saying, All power is given unto me in heaven and in earth.

Go ye therefore, and teach all nations, baptizing them in the name of the Father, and of the Son, and of the Holy Ghost:

Teaching them to observe all things whatsoever I have commanded you: and, lo, I AM with you alway, even unto the end of the world. Amen.   MATTHEW 28

Servants of the Lamb Who Would
Preach the Gospel of God:

I AM come in the fullness of the Light to deliver unto you the message of the mysteries of the gospel that you might be initiated into the path of the prophecy of the two witnesses.

What is the gospel[1] that is preached by the servants of the Lamb? It is the sevenfold statement of the law of Elohim as that law is applied by the sons and daughters of God to the sevenfold path of initiation made manifest within the Matter spheres foursquare.

The first gospel is the Gospel of God's Kingdom, his consciousness come in Spirit and in Matter through the fusion of the Light of Alpha and Omega in the Son of God. This is the gospel of the one God whose Selfhood contains the Father-Mother polarity, as above so below. It is the gospel of the eternal Spirit (masculine) ever one with the eternal Mater (feminine) manifest in cloven tongues of sacred fire in heaven and in earth. It is the gospel of the Divine Us (Elohim) ever individualized in the Person and the Principle of the LORD. The good news of this LORD, who declares I AM WHO I AM, is that Elohim is individualized within the creation in the I AM Presence of every living soul.

This is the story of God consciousness and of the covenants made between the I AM Presence and the soul. It also contains the record for all to read and run with of the interaction of souls with the I AM Presence down through the vast millenniums of earth's recorded and unrecorded history. Whether by virtue and patience or by trial and error, this outpicturing of the Law and the Lawgiver by the evolutions of earth is written in the layers of *akasha* as proof of the Everlasting Covenant of our Maker unto his offspring that those who keep his commandments will one day eat of the fruit of the Tree of Life and live forever, and those who do not obey his commandments, because they love not, shall not live forever but perish by their faithlessness and their unbelief.

This is the gospel of the first Guru, Maitreya, who walked and talked with Adam and Eve, twin flames in the garden. Verily he was my God Presence personified. He personified the Law and gave to them the covenant of first love—obedience to the Guru as the open door to grace. But they were immediately challenged by the Serpent, and the woman entered into a dialogue with the false Guru who disputed the Law and made himself Lawgiver. Thus by a free will manipulated, first the woman and then the man abandoned their first love and entered into unlawful means to gain a lawful end. And this is ever the falsity of the false teachings of the false teachers.

Now they and their offspring would wait, lo, 6,666 cycles, crying, "How long, O LORD!" until the people who walked in the darkness of untold generations of the Serpent's philosophy should see the Light as the Word made flesh and dwelling among them in the Person of the Son. For though the Light would shine in the darkness, the darkness would comprehend it not; for without the Presence of the Father (whose eternal Self contains the Mother), the Great Guru in the living Guru, the eternal Lamb in the embodied Lamb, the world would not know Him even as they knew Him not—neither the children of Lemuria nor the chosen twin flames. And the woman, though well-intended, accepted the initiation of this false Guru as a means to an "end." In her mind the end was acceleration under Maitreya. But in Serpent's mind the end was the destruction of the souls of twin flames through the destruction of the path of initiation under the Great Guru.

For though the Light be the Light of every child of God— sealed in the secret chamber of the heart as the pulsating Threefold Flame (Power, Wisdom, Love of Father, Son, Holy Ghost)— and though that Light be the Creator of the world who is in the world, yet outside of the Garden of Eden, where he reveals himself in the hallowed circle of the Guru/chela relationship, he cometh to his own in the blessedness of the Christ Self but his own receive him not because they, by the edict of their karma, are yet dwelling in outer darkness.

Not until the only begotten Son incarnates in flesh and blood do they once again behold the glory (the light) of the Father (the I AM Presence) and of his Person in Lord Maitreya. Thus the children of Lemuria followed in the way of the fallen angels who were called the Watchers. And those twin flames, called to the initiations of the Ruby Ray given by Lord Maitreya in the ancient mystery school, likewise accepted the lie, albeit in the name of Good, of the embodied agent of Lucifer whose name was Serpent. And they were condemned (judged) by their acts of disobedience to God the Father, and their condemnation (judgment) was just. And the Personal/Personality of the Father withdrew from personal interaction with his children in the earth. And God the Father became the Impersonal/Impersonality who sent his Word by his prophets and by his messengers until the fullness of the time and the space of the cycles of personal and planetary karma should be fulfilled.

Then was the coming of the Word, and the Son Jesus appeared as the representative of the Impersonal God (Guru) who chose to manifest himself personally in the Personality of the Son (chela), preaching the gospel of Maitreya, saying, "Repent: for the kingdom of heaven [the God consciousness of Lord Maitreya] is at hand.... And this gospel of the kingdom [of the Person of the Father, Sanat Kumara, come in the Light of Lord Maitreya] shall be preached in all the world for a witness unto all nations; and then shall the end come."

This is the story of the first gospel come again in the second gospel. And for those who received him not in the first instance, this gospel is become, in the second instance, the first door that is opened. It is the door opened in earth that the soul may once again receive the initiations of the living Mediator and pass through to the Godhead. It is the gospel of believing on the one sent as the open door to the Christed One, to the Higher Self of each soul. Unto all who believed not on the Father in the beginning, it is the opportunity to believe on the Son in the ending.

Therefore the second gospel is the gospel of the great grace of Jehovah, the personal God of the Israelites, who had walked and talked with them in the Person of the LORD, the I AM Presence who first appeared out of Horeb and Sinai and then out of the flame of the ark of the covenant. This LORD who is the Godhead, who is Elohim, is now personified in the Word incarnate within the Son begotten only of God, the Christ Self. It is the reestablishing of this contact with the Christ Self that enables souls to enter once again into the intimate relationship with the Father and the one whom the Father sends to initiate the saints on the north gate, the Great Initiator, Lord Maitreya.

By the initiation of Sonship, Jesus Christ transfers the original contact with the "LORD" Maitreya which was lost by the evolutions of the fourth root race through disobedience to the first covenant. And this is the work of the Son: to be the example, yea, the incarnation of the Christ Self that each child of God is intended to embody. For the child cannot embody the Christ Self except he see that Real Self in the Son—face to face.

This gospel of the grace of the Father manifest in the Son is the gospel of the Emmanuel, "God with us" in the hosts of the LORD—ascended masters, hierarchies of angelic beings whose offices of heavenly/earthly intercession culminate in the Person of the Son Jesus Christ, Great Guru of Grace in the Piscean Age. And through him the mantle of Sonship is transferred by the path of initiation to all who behold in him the Word incarnate and the Lamb slain from the foundation of the world.

The gospel of the grace of the Father, the Mighty I AM individualized within the Son, is the essence of the one who declares, "I and my Father are one." This is the gospel of the lifting up of the Light of the Son of man within the temple of the individual —as Moses lifted up the sacred fire of the serpent force (called the Kundalini) in the wilderness of the materialistic, sensualistic, ritualistic consciousness of laggard generations. Through these the Israelites would be required to pass in succeeding incarnations until the prophesying of the eaters of the little book should be fulfilled.

This is the good news of believing on the one sent by the Ancient of Days, of believing on the hierarchy of the only begotten Son whose Light, which proceeds out of the throne of God and of the Lamb, is the pure river of water of life, clear as crystal. This river moving through the individual chalices of the sons and daughters of God is the Christ consciousness—the only Son begotten of God.

This is the Light begotten only of God. This is the Light that is given by grace unto his servants who see his face in the I AM Presence and have the geometry of his name, I AM THAT I AM, in their foreheads (third eye). This Light is in each child of God as the Person of Christ—the Christ Self. And this is the gospel of the love of God who gave his only begotten Son to be the Light, the Mediator, the Teacher, the Counsellor unto each soul who should believe in Him. The good news of this gospel is that the gift of Sonship is the gift of the Father unto every child who confirms the Person of the Light in the embodied Lamb Jesus Christ and in all who hold the office of the Lamb in heaven and in earth.

"And no man hath ascended up to heaven, but he that came down from heaven, even the Son of man which is in heaven." By the gospel of the Son is the true path of the ascension established. For by the grace of this Son—the Christ Self—and only by this grace does the soul who is the Son of man come down from heaven and ascend up to heaven. This is the path of the embodied Lamb and his servants. It is the gospel of the Guru and his chelas.

The gospel of grace is the good news of opportunity to all of earth's evolutions of salvation (soul-elevation)—the soul's acceleration into its native Light—by the Son through repentance from sin. And what is sin? It is the soul's willful separation from the I AM THAT I AM and from the law of the Light's incarnation within the soul as the soul traverses the Matter spheres. Sin is the soul's original rebellion against the Godhead and its subsequent separation from the One. Sin is the resultant density of the soul's dense consciousness of the "earth, earthy," the energy veil created out of its own misqualified energy that obscures the Holy of Holies and the entire heavenly hierarchy.

The actions which sustain the separation of the soul outside of the circle of oneness—the oneness of the Father and the Son who focus the Guru/chela relationship through the Lamb—can be categorized as levels of sin and the consciousness of sin, i.e., separation from the flame of eternal Life. The Gospel of Great Grace preached through the only begotten Son of God as he is manifest as the Light and the Real Self of every child of God is the gospel of mercy and forgiveness—of the soul's return to oneness through salvation by the Person of the Lamb (Guru).

The third gospel preached by the saints is the Gospel of the Promised Comforter who transfers the love of Alpha and Omega to the initiates of the Ruby Ray as the baptism of sacred fire. By this gospel, the true teachings of Jesus Christ and every avatar (incarnation of God) who has come forth since the foundation of the worlds are brought to the remembrance of the children of God. And by this teaching and the personal presence of the Comforter, souls experience the fiery trials of love and the soul testings as the LORD God himself prepares the temple of the disciple to be his dwelling place forevermore.

Those who receive his Spirit without compromise but only with the promise of love are friend and follower of the Holy Ghost, who appears to them in his manifold expressions in the ascended sons of God. One by one these archetypes of the paths of the sevenfold flame of the Holy Spirit initiate unascended devotees of the Lamb in the nine steps of initiation on the Path of the Ruby Ray leading to the conferment of the nine gifts of the Holy Spirit.

These gifts are (1) the word of wisdom, (2) the word of knowledge, (3) faith, (4) gifts of healing, (5) the working of miracles, (6) prophecy, (7) discerning of spirits, (8) divers kinds of tongues, (9) the interpretation of tongues. The examination of these gifts of the Holy Spirit and the initiations on the Path of the Ruby Ray leading to their conferment is an essential portion of the message of Love, the living gospel of the Holy Ghost. Therefore we will in due course expound upon them as the seven seals of the seven-sealed book are opened to the Keepers of the Flame and opened again.

The gospel of the Holy Ghost is delivered first in the descent of the sacred-fire baptism on Pentecost and then, following this dispensation, in the Word and the Work of the LORD manifest in the chosen and ordained disciples and apostles. Paul, the archetype of apostleship, illustrates the full flowering of discipleship unto a oneness with the ascended master Jesus Christ which he testifies has come about through his direct confrontation with the Saviour and a one-on-one conversion whereby the Saviour, that living Guru, has entered the temple of his disciple to live, and move, and have being on earth through him. Thus, though he be ascended, the Ever-Present Guru is embodied in the anointed apostle whose gospel of the grace of God then becomes the accounting of his interaction with the LORD, with the saints, and with the great multitude to whom he preaches in the full Spirit of his LORD's Holy Ghost (the Sacred Presence of His LORD's Spirit).

And every ascended master who has passed the initiation of the Lamb, whereby all power in heaven and in earth is given unto him, may, at will, transfer to his unascended chela his "Holy Spirit"—the replica of his Godhood called the Electronic Presence. This overshadowing Presence of the ascended master is the mantle transferred to the chela in increments by initiation on the Ruby Ray until the multiplication of the ascended master's consciousness within his chela becomes the fullness of his Spirit.

Now the ascended master's attainment of God consciousness meshes with the soul of the chela and the chela is empowered by the "Holy Ghost" of his Guru. It was thus the Holy Ghost of Jesus Christ which filled all the apostles on that day of "one accord" in "one place." Their "one accord" was their agreement in the Law of God Harmony. Their "one place" is the place prepared at the nexus of the cosmic cross of white fire where God becomes man and man becomes God in the Person of the Son and the Son's Holy Spirit. Thus by taking up this cross daily, the saints are continually empowered by the Holy Spirit of his Word.

This gospel of the grace of God unto the apostles is the good news being written by them today, a testimony of their Word and Work in their LORD. It has been written from the hour of the ascension of Jesus Christ, Gautama Buddha, and other avatars as the gospel of deeds on the path of personal divinity. Always it is written by the ones closest to the heart's light (attainment) of the embodied Word who take up the mantle of their "LORD"— the one who holds the office, i.e., the authority in the earth, of the Ancient of Days. Thus the LORD's apostles are those who magnify his name. Their life on earth expands and expands into a living witness of the very personal Flame of the Life of the LORD which they now demonstrate and make their own.

The gospel of the Holy Ghost, the message of comfort and enlightenment, also comes by the revelation of the Son of God given to Saint John the Divine and to other saints of the Holy Church, East and West, as the unfolding revelations of the dispensations of the centuries. It includes the messages of angelic ministrants and ascended masters to souls ascending the seven-tiered spiral within the white cube in Matter. These are set forth cryptically in the Book of Revelation itself as the messages to the seven "churches." These are the initiations of the seven chakras and those undergoing the initiations of the seven rays within the seven bodies of man on the paths of righteousness. These paths of the seven holy Kumaras uttered by the seven mighty Elohim have been brought by the avatars I have sent to found the religions of the worlds.

The first three gospels are the gospels of the Father, the Son, and the Holy Spirit. These are already written in the heaven and the earth of the far-flung worlds where the evolutions of God do work out their salvation with the fear of the Lord and the trembling before the majesty of his throne. Elements of these have been transferred to this world through great seers and scribes who have served under the avatars, Kumaras, and Manus since Atlantis, Lemuria, and beyond. Other elements I AM releasing in the Eternal Now through the ever-appearing twin flames called upon to witness of me.

They testify of the Lamb and the Lamb's wife until they become the Lamb and the Lamb's wife. And those who occupy the office of "these two prophets," whose light is a torment unto the anti-Light dwellers on the earth, always set forth the law and the love of the Father-Mother God. The traditions of the scriptures of East and West (Alpha and Omega) provide a firm foundation of this law, yet one that must be interpreted by the living Word, embodied and set forth and expounded by the

Christed messengers who make them relevant to each succeeding generation and dispensation. This is the essence of the ongoing gospel of the Holy Ghost.

May it become thy soul essence. And thy essence be ignited by the Holy Ghost. And thy flame be the Light inextinguishable in Israel.

I AM in the Holy of Holies
keeping the flame of the Gospel for my people

Sanat Kumara

See Matt. 28; John 1:1–14; Matt. 4:17; 24:14; John 6:29; Rev. 13:8; Rev. 22:1; John 3:13; 1 Cor. 15:38–50; Matt. 28:18; Acts 2:1–4; Rev. 1–3; Phil. 2:12; Rev. 11:3–12.

20

The Gospel of the Little Book Open

> *And I saw another mighty angel come down from heaven, clothed with a cloud: and a rainbow was upon his head, and his face was as it were the sun, and his feet as pillars of fire:*
> *And he had in his hand a little book open: and he set his right foot upon the sea, and his left foot on the earth,*
> *And cried with a loud voice, as when a lion roareth: and when he had cried, seven thunders uttered their voices.*
>
> REVELATION 10

Beloved Who Will Eat Up the Little Book Open and Prophesy Again:

When John saw another mighty angel come down from heaven, clothed with a cloud: and a rainbow was upon his head, he observed in his hand a little book open. This angel, by name Adoremus, had a face which appeared as the sun and feet as pillars of fire. With the full dominion of the Godhead whose messenger he is, he set his right foot upon the sea, showing the omnipotence of God over the subconscious mind and all it contains; and he set his left foot upon the earth, showing the omniscience of God to subdue the conscious mind and all that it contains.

(The right foot and the left foot of the mighty angel, which are as pillars of fire, symbolize the dominion of his cosmic consciousness over the sea and over the earth, the third and fourth quadrants of the Matter spheres. The feet are the symbol of understanding, and they represent and are symbolical of the initiations of the hierarchy of Pisces which the Lord Jesus Christ came to demonstrate.)

Then, with the authority of the Holy Ghost, he cried with a loud voice as when a lion roareth; and by the authority of the Great Guru Lord Maitreya, he gave the divine decree which evoked the seven thunders and the uttering of their voices.

The seven thunders are the seven mighty Elohim who come in the full power of the Holy Ghost to consume by love and by wisdom every manifestation that is Antichrist. The seven mighty Elohim give the statement of the Law that unfolds the path of initiation for the saints. This path of initiation is the message of the little book held open in the hand of the mighty angel.

The seven thunders uttered their voices, sounding the tone, the universal AUM, the way back Home for those called to embody the archetype of the living Christ on the seven rays. Their Word was and is the Word of God unto every soul longing for reunion. The divine decree uttered by the mighty angel, Adoremus—the one who adores the sevenfold expression of the Divine Us represented by the twin flames of Alpha and Omega within the seven mighty Elohim—brought forth the Word of Elohim concerning the Piscean path demonstrated by Jesus Christ.

John was about to write what they said, but he heard a voice from heaven saying, "Seal up those things which the seven thunders uttered, and write them not." (Read the entire tenth chapter of Revelation.) The teaching of the seven thunders and the teaching of the little book open is sealed by God until the fulfillment of the Piscean dispensation. The mighty angel then lifted up his hand to heaven and sware by the Ancient of Days that at the conclusion of the sixth dispensation (the Piscean age) when its "time" should be fulfilled, there should be no further delay (time no longer) in the finishing of the mysteries of God for that dispensation; indeed that those mysteries would come "in the days of the voice of the seventh angel."

The days of the speaking of the Word of God by the seventh

angel are the cycles of Aquarius, the seventh dispensation now at hand. In this moment that seventh angel, Saint Germain, my son of the seventh age, has begun to sound. For I have anointed him as the hierarch of Aquarius to serve with Jesus Christ and the ascended masters who are with him in the office of the Man on the east gate. And day by day and year by year he is finishing the mystery of God, the sacred mysteries of the Holy Grail, as he is declaring these mysteries to his servants the Prophets.

Now is the little book, which was eaten up by John the Beloved, opened to the initiates who have preached the gospel of Jesus Christ as he taught it, to those who are ready—being sanctified holy—for the initiations of the Ruby Ray whereby they shall indeed scientifically demonstrate that gospel.

And so the mighty angel comes down from heaven again, clothed with a cloud and a rainbow upon his head. And once again he stands, his right foot upon the sea and his left foot upon the earth. He is come to initiate the disciples of the Word on the Path of the Ruby Ray.

And as he cries with a loud voice as when a lion roareth, the seven mighty Elohim utter the divine decree and the seven holy Kumaras are positioned in Spirit and in Matter for the transfer of the light of the living Word. And the voice that is heard from heaven speaks unto the initiates entering the cycles of soul deliverance under the seventh angel, saying, "Go and take the little book which is open in the hand of the angel which standeth upon the sea and upon the earth."

To each one who follows in the footsteps of John the Beloved, the sponsoring apostle of the Ruby Ray, and to all who will follow him to the Sacred Heart of Jesus is the opportunity given to say with him unto the angel, "Give me the little book." And as they do, one by one, the angel will say unto them, "Take it, and eat it up; and it shall make thy belly bitter, but it shall be in thy mouth sweet as honey."

And all who take the little book out of the angel's hand and eat it up will experience the initiation of the chemicalization of consciousness through the Ruby Ray. And then they will know the meaning of the word of John who said, "It was in my mouth sweet as honey: and as soon as I had eaten it, my belly was bitter." To such as these the angel then gives the admonishment that he gave to John the Beloved: "Thou must prophesy again before many peoples, and nations, and tongues, and kings."

What is the message of the little book open? Why is it sweet in the mouth and bitter in the belly? It is sweet in the mouth because the Word of God, as the commission to do his will, is received joyfully and eagerly by his sons and daughters. But when they realize that in order to do the will of God there must come about a complete transformation of consciousness, a veritable alchemy throughout the unconscious mind—the desire body and the layers of the electronic belt—and that this is accomplished only by the purging of the solar plexus through the sacred fires of the Holy Ghost, the Destroyer of embodied error, then they experience the bitterness of the path of sacrifice, surrender, selflessness, and service. And this, as you know, my beloved, is the path laid before you which, once accepted, is your day-by-day experience of the fullness of joy in Jesus Christ, Lord Maitreya, Gautama Buddha, and Sanat Kumara. And this is the way of the joy of the abundant life lived in Him. Walk ye in it.

What is the message of the little book? It is the message that is thundered by the mighty Elohim and that thunders through the souls of God's children, causing fear and even a shaking and a quaking of the earth. It is the message, "You have walked in the footsteps of your Lord and Saviour. You have given devotion to the Son of God. You have preached his gospel. Now you must put on the mantle of your Saviour. You must take up the responsibility of parting the waters of life. You must walk over Jordan and lead the children of Israel into the promised land of the Higher Self.

"You must accept the divine doctrine held for you, lo, these two thousand years, that now is the accepted time and now is the day of salvation to step into the footprints of the Saviour and to know that his mantle is upon you to work the works that he worked in the name of God and to accept the blazing reality of your own Sonship."

The little book open contains the initiations of the children of God who elect to enter into joint-heirship with the Son, who are fully prepared for the initiations of that Sonship and the dwelling within them bodily of God the Father, God the Son, and God the Holy Spirit. This expansion of God's consciousness comes about through the magnification of the Lord—"Let God be magnified!" as the Psalmist said.

The magnification of the Threefold Flame of the Trinity is the work of the initiates of the Ruby Ray. That flame is magnified by love, by wisdom, by power. Its fires are fanned by the breath of the Holy Spirit that is breathed upon it again and again as the supplicant enters into meditation with the Creator, the Preserver, and the Destroyer of worlds within and worlds without.

The little book is the step-by-step outline of the path of the avatars of the ages, and as such it is the science of the Mother who teaches her children how to follow in the footsteps of the Son until the child does indeed become the fullness of the Son of God in whose likeness he is made, in whose image he is born.

The little book is the wisdom of God sealed "in a mystery" until that hour when it is spoken—yet "in a mystery, even the hidden [occult][1] wisdom, which God ordained before the world unto our glory." This glory, my beloved, is the light of the I AM that is in you who are my sons and daughters. Unto you are the deep things of God revealed by my Spirit.

And I AM that Spirit most holy and I AM in you searching all things, yea, the height and the depth of the sea of God consciousness, that you might also know the mysteries freely given to the sons and daughters by the Elohim of God.

You have the mind of Christ and I, Sanat Kumara, AM that mind. And I AM in God and I AM in you. And I sanctify you to receive the spoken Word of the mysteries of the Ruby Ray chaliced in the Grail.

And what is the Grail? Have you not heard? Have you not remembered? It is the *R*ay, or Son, of God who is *A*lpha's seed (yes, Abraham's seed) who is always the *I*ncarnation of *L*ight. GRAIL (God's Ray as Alpha's Son Incarnating Light). This Son from God, this sun of the Sun, is the only vessel that can contain the mystery of the Body and the Blood. This Son is the Grail whom ye quest and find only when ye become it by my Spirit.

The little book is the archetype of your Self. It contains the mystery of all that you are and all that you shall become in God through Christ. The Grail. It is the chalice of the Word that you shall become when you eat it up. All of it. It is his Body and his Blood. The little book is the consciousness of Jesus Christ in Spirit and in Matter. Unless you eat it up, ye have no life in you.

The little book is the gospel of Jesus Christ as he lived it and as he demonstrated it. It is the explanation by my Spirit to his disciples in the seventh age of how they may walk in his footsteps and indeed obey his command to manifest, not only the signs of the Holy Spirit, but the signs of the Father and of the Mother and of the Son—doing even greater works than he did *because* they believe on Him and because He is gone unto the Father. They are the chelas of the Lamb. When the Lamb accelerates, they accelerate. As He moves on in the Cosmic Stream, they move with Him, demonstrating in Matter the greater works that He himself is accomplishing in Spirit today.

The little book outlines the work of the Mother and her children, the Woman and her seed. For it must shortly come to pass that they meet with God-victory all of the challenges and initiations of the Ruby Ray presented in the prophecies of the book of *The Revelation of Jesus Christ* which I, the Ancient of Days, gave unto him to show unto his servants (chelas) the law of karma which should be fulfilled in the last days (cycles) of their incarnation upon earth.

And though the saints truly know the meaning of that bitterness of the belly as Christ takes up his abode within their temple, they accept the assignment in full faith that he who gave his promise unto Abraham and his seed will fulfill that promise, even as they are faithful to their vow made to the Ancient of Days.

They say with Job, "I have heard of thee by the hearing of the ear: but now mine eye seeth thee." With their eyes wide open they behold the vision of the Lamb on Mount Sion (for they are with Him) and they also behold the vision of the Dragon that makes war with the Woman (for they are with Her) to prevent the birth of her Manchild in every age—and who makes war with you, my beloved, who are the remnant of her seed.

They study the nature of the Antichrist in the person of Satan and his seed, of the Dragon and his legions of fallen angels. They know the False Prophet and his many representatives coming in the person of the false gurus of East and West. They know the Great Whore as the anti-Community of church and state and all of the false Christs and false prophets that violate the love/wisdom of the community of the Holy Spirit and the Guru/chela relationship within it.

They know the philosophy of the fallen ones by which they have set forth the anti-Doctrine, thereby sowing the seeds of apostasy among the children of God. They are acquainted with the Serpent, ever the challenger of the mission of the two witnesses, and with the Accuser of the Brethren, Peshu Alga by name. And they understand the mission of the saints who lead the great multitude to overthrow the beast that riseth up out of the sea and the beast that cometh up out of the earth. The term *beast* is used to indicate the collective consciousness of those functioning to the right and to the left of the Christ consciousness in the spectrum of relative good and evil, mouthing the philosophy of the False Prophet through the unenlightened masses (the mass consciousness which opposes the enlightenment of the great multitude).

These "beasts" of the opposing economic systems of World Communism and World Capitalism, which have appeared in the polarity of East and West opposing the light of Alpha and Omega and known by many names, are ensouled by an astral organization known as "Laggards against the Light" who have perverted the systems of the divine economy and of God-government for thousands of years. And it is the saints who are called in these latter days to defeat these beasts by the omnipotence and the omniscience of God embodied by the mighty angel. For now is the hour when he takes dominion over the earth and over the sea on the west gate of the city, revealing the balance of Reality and Equilibrium in the scales of cosmic justice. Thus they who are called to Saint Germain's Mission Amethyst Jewel go forth two by two in the omnipotence and the omniscience of the living Christ, and they accept the calling to be like him and to be with him omnipresent in the fullness of my Love in the reenactment of the initiations recorded in the four Gospels.

Come what may, they accept the challenge; and therefore they are ready to sit at the feet of the two witnesses, to hear the prophecy of God through them, and to run with it until the earth is filled with the knowledge of the LORD, the I AM THAT I AM, as the waters cover the sea. This is the gospel that will be preached by the servants of the Lamb when, in the fullness of their time that is come, and in the space of the cycles of the seventh age, God sends forth the Spirit of his Son into their hearts, the living Manchild born of the Woman.

O Son of God, O Son of Light! Come into the hearts of my children!

I AM thy Father, the Ancient of Days,

Sanat Kumara

See Col. 2:9; Ps. 70:4; 1 Cor. 2; Matt. 26:26–28; John 6:53; 14:12; Rev. 1:1; Job 42:5; Rev. 12–14; Matt. 24:24; Hab. 2:14; Gal. 4:6.

21

The Everlasting Gospel Foursquare

> *And I saw another angel fly in the midst of heaven, having the everlasting gospel to preach unto them that dwell on the earth, and to every nation, and kindred, and tongue, and people,*
>
> *Saying with a loud voice, Fear God, and give glory to him; for the hour of his judgment is come: and worship him that made heaven, and earth, and the sea, and the fountains of waters.*
>
> REVELATION 14

Beloved Who Would Fly with the Angel
 in the Midst of Heaven and
 Preach unto Them That Dwell on the Earth:

The fourth gospel is the gospel of the Lamb. It is the Everlasting Gospel. It is the gospel foursquare of the four living creatures, archetypes of the fourfold manifestation of the Christ Self that unfolds on the Path of the Ruby Ray. It is four gospels in one for the teaching and preaching of the law of the One, the law of Love supreme.

The Everlasting Gospel fulfills the gospel of the Trinity and is therefore the squaring of the circle. By this gospel is the Word made flesh within you. Thus it enables you to experience the sacred alchemy of the little book open within your soul as it is already accomplished within the Spirit of your I AM Presence. As above so below, by this gospel do your four lower bodies become the vehicles of the Light as the temple foursquare for the LORD's holy habitation. Verily it is through this gospel that the LORD's kingdom (the realm of his consciousness) is come on earth as it is in heaven—in Matter as it is in Spirit.

Therefore is it the teaching of the Mother unto her children. Therefore hath Wisdom builded her house in Matter. Therefore doth she build upon the Rock of the living Word. Therefore hath she hewn out her seven pillars. The Everlasting Gospel is the initiation of the Woman given unto the saints. It is the gospel of the Ancient of Days that I have waited, lo, these cycles of millenniums to deliver unto you, my beloved.

Now learn of Me and My Mystery, for I occupy the office of the Woman. I AM Wisdom who teacheth her children. I have builded my house at Shamballa and in the Shamballa of your heart. I build upon the white stone of the Word who lives in my sons and daughters. I hew out the image of my seven pillars—the seven holy Kumaras—within the sacred centers of man and woman, restoring the archetype of the Christ in the path of the seven rays. Lo, I AM in the Woman and the Woman is in me. And I and my Mother are one. In Spirit I AM Father, in Matter I AM Mother. In Cosmos we are One.

> *Now therefore hearken unto me, O ye children: for blessed are they that keep my ways.*
>
> *Hear instruction, and be wise, and refuse it not.*
>
> *Blessed is the man that heareth me, watching daily at my gates, waiting at the posts of my doors.*
>
> *For whoso findeth me findeth life, and shall obtain favour of the* LORD—*I AM THAT I AM.*
>
> *But he that sinneth against me wrongeth his own soul: all they that hate me love death.*

And some of the Everlasting Gospel you will read here, and some of it you will run with. But not all. And some I will give to Keepers of the Flame in their written lessons, and some I will give in the unwritten lessons transferred only by the Lamb to his wife.

The foursquare gospel is the life of the one, the Son of man, who has descended into the earth to outpicture the Christhood of the four living creatures. Having fulfilled this the fiery destiny of the soul of God, he becomes the one who ascends into heaven.

Jesus Christ became the fullness of the four cosmic forces. Initiates of the Ruby Ray, eat up the little book open and go thou and do likewise! Study, O study the four stages of the Incarnation of the Word and show thyself reproved and approved unto God!

(1) **The Son.** The first stage is the birth of the Saviour, the initiation of the Son of man who is to become the Son of God through the Christ of Jesus under the office of the Man on the east gate. This includes infancy, childhood, and the maturing years when the Spirit of the LORD waxes strong within the heart flame. It includes the soul's pilgrimage both during and following the years of formal education, when it seeks and finds the living Gurus and sits at their feet on earth and in heaven (on the etheric plane in inner retreats of the Great White Brotherhood), submitting to all of the initiations he will demonstrate before the saints and the great multitude.

In the externalization of this first archetype of personal Christhood, the Son of man discovers and defines himself to be the Son of God, declaring "I AM WHO I AM...Lo, I AM come to do thy will, O God!" In this Self-awareness, he goes forth on the journey of soul alignment with the divine plan of God for the evolutions he is to serve. He is required to magnetize a sufficient quantity of light to hold the balance in the seven planes against all of the principles and personalities of anti-Light he will encounter. Thus in the first stage he builds his house—the forcefield of his Christ consciousness—and hews out his seven pillars —sacred fire foundations to support the mission of revealing the Christ Path on each of the seven rays.

The first stage is the becoming of the Son. It is the gathering of the gates of Godhood, the summoning of the forces of individual Selfhood, whereby the Son may then sacrifice the Self as the acceptable offering on the altar of the Father. Only this supreme sacrifice can hold the balance (pay the price) for the sins (karma) of the world.

In order to meet the demands of surrender on the Path of the Ruby Ray, one must have an identity to surrender. And that identity is the Son of God, and no other will be accepted. Therefore do many of the disciples, when they hear this saying of the law of individual Christhood, turn back and walk no more with the LORD. Having no light within them, they spurn the initiation of eating his flesh and his blood—lest they should dwell in him and he in them and therefore be like him. For he said: "He that eateth me, even he shall live by me."

These are they who desire the light of the Son not so that they may become the Son and offer themselves as he did—in Rome to be crucified again. Oh no! They have no intention whatsoever of taking up the cross of the Ruby Ray and being crucified with him. They desire the light to perpetuate their own darkness and to perpetrate their own dark deeds. Beware, then, of those who pretend to be on the Path, associating with lightbearers for the mere enjoyment of the light instead of for the sake of the Dharma.

O Blessed Dharma, most blessed Presence of the Teacher within the Teaching! O Blessed Dharma, Thou Living Word wherein all devotees enjoy the supreme reason for being!—I would give thee alone to those who bear the banner of joy in My Work, joy in My Name, joy in My Son, and joy in living in Me. O Blessed Dharma, for thy flame's sake I would dwell in the midst of my people who love me for what I AM and not merely for what I give. To such as these and only these I give freely of my Self. And they give to me the only gift worthy to be given—the Self.

(2) **The Father.** The initiation of the second stage of Christhood is the Water (Matter) Baptism through the Christ of Maitreya under the office of the Lion on the north gate. This stage was reenacted by the Lord Jesus Christ in his baptism by John in the river Jordan. Its purpose was to illustrate the ritual for you, my beloved; for the living Gurus (God-men) John and Jesus had no need to publicly reenact the ritual except to fulfill the law as an example of its righteous use to their chelas—an example

which they should follow both in the spirit and the letter in the hour of their initiation into the second gospel of the four that form the square.

Therefore the Master said, "Suffer it to be so now: for thus it becometh us to fulfill all righteousness." This is the moment of the initiation by Maitreya when the Person of the Father enters the temple—magnified by the already balanced and expanded Threefold Flame. The Light of the I AM Presence, as the Light of Alpha and Omega, pours directly through his heart chakra as he is dedicated to his earthly mission by the dove of the Holy Ghost. This is the moment of my approbation, "This is my Son, my beloved, in whom I AM well pleased."

The meaning of these words is revealed to the initiated: "This is my Son [the Light manifestation of my Presence, i.e., the incarnation of my Word—the extension of my Self through the lineal descent of the Ruby Ray]—this is my beloved soul Jesus [my beloved Self in Matter—in Mother] in whom I AM THAT I AM—[in whom I dwell, for "I and my Son (Light) are one"] well pleased" [exceedingly One].

The pleasure of the Father in the Son is always by the law of congruency. When the Son is the perfect chalice for the Father, then is the Father joyous, comfortable, and comforting all life through the transparent Presence of the Son. Thus when the Son fulfills his purpose of being the chalice worthy, the chalice is sealed in the Water Baptism and the divine approbation is pronounced before the councils of the hosts of heaven and before all upon earth who have ears to hear.

This baptism is the sign that the Guru is in the chela—bodily. The equilateral triangles of their identity are congruent. This is part one of the threefold empowerment conferred in stages two, three, and four.

All that transpires between the Water (Matter) Baptism and the Transfiguration in the high mountain of the Christ consciousness on the west gate fulfills the second archetype of personal Christhood on the Path of the Ruby Ray. Many of these initiations are illustrated in the public ministry of the Saviour—but not all. Other initiations are borne solely within the retreats of the Brotherhood. His public ministry is evidence to all adepts that he has undergone said initiations according to the preordained path.

(3) **The Holy Spirit.** Beginning with the Transfiguration, the Fire (Spirit) Baptism, Jesus outpictured the third archetype of Christhood, the sign of the Holy Spirit, the initiation through the Christ of Gautama under the office of the Calf on the west gate. In this hour he magnetized the light of the Great Central Sun, the light of Alpha and Omega (individualized in the Mighty I AM Presence), into every cell of his four lower bodies. This great influx of the light of the Logos he focused and so intensified, through his seven chakras (sun-centers) and the nuclei of all energy centers, that "his face did shine as the sun and his garments became glistering, exceeding white; so as no fuller on earth can white them." So reads the eyewitness account of his disciples.

This great drama is known as the cosmic interchange—the interchange of Spirit and Matter. It is the bathing of every crystal of the Matter chalice (even the garment) of the Son of God with the fiery baptism of the Holy Ghost. This the third stage of Christhood is the "pretrial" for the fourth stage that is to take place under the office of the flying Eagle on the south gate—the LORD whose LORD I AM.

The Transfiguration is the fusion of the microcosm and the Macrocosm, and neither will ever be the same again. In order for the disciples to see and record the event—in order that ye might have a written record for your own initiations that are to take place in the last days of your incarnation of the Word, my beloved—the Lord Jesus raised up Peter, James, and John to the high mountain of his exalted cosmic consciousness.

Thus he "brought" them—literally accelerating their vision and soul faculties—to the octaves of light and gave to them the foretaste of heaven and its hierarchical order: There, standing with him in his transfigured glory, they beheld the ascended master Elias (Elijah the prophet), whose soul, he later explained, had already incarnated in the person of John the Baptist, completed his mission as the messenger of the initiations of Christ, suffered martyrdom at the hands of Herod (who represented the council of Watchers), and ascended back to heaven whence he came. He, as Elijah, had ascended into heaven in a chariot (vortex) of sacred fire. He, an ascended master before he was born, was almost unique in the annals of earth's history. Thus it is understandable that Jesus should say of him, "Among them that are born of women there hath not risen a greater than John the Baptist."

In so honoring his herald, Jesus fulfilled the law of chelaship. The chela who had become the Guru paid tribute to the one who had given him that "double portion" of his attainment in the Holy Spirit and the mantle of his authority under God the Father. In this statement, Jesus acknowledges John as having gone before him in the cosmic peerage—in that he took his ascension when he was Elijah, whereas his disciple Elisha did not. For the fullness of his time (cycle of initiation in the Ruby Ray) had not yet come; for he was to later incarnate my Word as the Messiah for the Piscean dispensation. (The name *Elijah* means "I AM THAT I AM is God," or Person of the Father, hence Guru. The name *Elisha* means "God is Saviour," or Person of the Son, hence chela. The soul of John the Baptist had been embodied as Elijah. The soul of Jesus Christ had been embodied as Elisha. Together they served in Israel in the Guru/chela relationship.)

In the Transfiguration, Jesus therefore stands before the immortal Gurus of the Israelite (Aries) dispensation, both of whom had ascended to heaven before him. Moses and Elijah. He thus demonstrated the law of cosmic interchange whereby the Son of man who has passed through the ritual of the Transfiguration may freely interact with the ascended masters, the ascended Gurus of East and West, and deliver their light, their counsel, and their initiations to the unascended chelas. Here he endorsed the communion of saints in heaven and earth through the agency of the Holy Spirit when sponsored by an initiate of the Great White Brotherhood, whereas the Word always condemns psychic, mediumistic communications with the departed dead or with the divinity when such communication is practiced without the agency of the Holy Spirit or outside of the Guru/chela relationship on the path of initiation.

The "bright cloud" that overshadowed them at the scene of the Transfiguration was the same cloud into which Jesus, the LORD, would ascend ("out of their sight"—physical spectrum) at the conclusion of the fourth stage of his demonstration of the Way of personal Christhood. Out of this cloud—vortex of sacred fire—surrounding the Presence of the Father, it was Lord Maitreya, one with Jesus' I AM Presence, who spoke the message which you, my beloved, may one day hear when you enter the third stage of your own Christhood:

"This is my beloved Son, my chosen: hear ye him"—which is to say, "This is the incarnation of My Self whom I have chosen to deliver my Word unto you. He is the Word that I AM. His Word is my Word. And I AM in the Word and he is in me. And the Word that he speaks is the Word that he has become—my very Self."

(4) **The Mother.** The fourth stage of Christhood whose archetype is the flying Eagle is given on the south gate under my own Name. Herein is the consummation of purity's love as the soul embraces the Mother flame and enters into the initiations of the Crucifixion, the Resurrection, and the Ascension. In the life of Jesus Christ, these begin with his prediction to his disciples of his crucifixion, followed by the anointing of his head (crown chakra) by Mary of Bethany for the three initiations which are to follow. These are the culmination of the Path of the Ruby Ray. They cannot be completed until the ritual of the fourteen stations have been fulfilled in Alpha and Omega—in the beginning and the ending of all cycles (evolving in the sacred centers) of the individual divine plan.

The announcement of the Son of God to all the world for all

The Everlasting Gospel Foursquare

ages to come that he has indeed paid the last farthing of personal and planetary karma and is ready to ascend to the Godhead whence he descended so many evolutions ago yet rings across the centuries and the galaxies:

"All power is given unto me in heaven and in earth.... And, lo, I AM with you alway, even until the end of your initiations under the law of personal and planetary karma. Lo, I AM the all-power of God, the fullness of his joy and the glory of his Life universal and triumphant throughout the Spirit/Matter cosmos."

May you also receive the crown of Life which he has promised to all who love him, enduring temptation (meeting the misqualified energies of personal and planetary karma) and trial (the path of initiation).

Yes, my beloved, the foursquare gospel everlasting is the opening of the seven-sealed book which I hold in my hand. It outlines for you, step by step, the sevenfold Path of the Ruby Ray and of the Rose Cross and the sevenfold sounding of the judgments by the seven sacred tones of the Word. It is conveyed by the transfer of Light from my hand through the hand of the entire Spirit of the Great White Brotherhood in the initiation of the sealing of the servants of our God in their foreheads. First the one hundred and forty and four thousand and then the great multitude must receive the fohat of the Word by the direct transfer of the flame from the I to the Eye. And this, too, is the communication of the Word in the gospel foursquare.

The Everlasting Gospel is the message of the ascension to the children of God, and it is the message of the second death to those who blaspheme the name of God, I AM THAT I AM, and repent not of their deeds. It is the message of the judgment that liberates all souls above and below unto the conclusion of their rounds.

Let us renew our meditations on the initiations given to the soul on the cardinal points of the citadel of consciousness. [See pages 84 and 140.] For though the initiations of the four gates of the city are distinct and follow the cycles of time and space and are experienced in sequential order on the timeline of each individual's evolution, yet these four initiations—and their breakdown under the three solar hierarchies governing the initiations of each of the four quadrants in Spirit and Matter—are "geometric" and "spherical" in nature and hence simultaneous in appearance. As Paul said, "I die daily," may you say, my beloved, "I ascend daily."

Thus it is possible for an individual to be drinking of the four cups of the Christ consciousness epitomized in the way of the Man, the Lion, the Calf, and the flying Eagle as day by day he masters his soul's testings in the frequencies of fire, air, water, and earth which govern (1) his inner nature (This inner nature consists of the fire body and the recordings made upon it as the memory of his immersion in God in the Great Central Sun before the worlds were framed. It includes his memory throughout all of his incarnations upon earth which may tally millions of years.); (2) his outer nature (The outer nature is expressed through the air and water vehicles, the mind and emotions, corresponding with the mental and emotional development, the personality, habits, customs, self-knowledge, and purpose within the fragments of Selfhood experienced in a given embodiment.); and (3) his integration of the inner and outer natures (This integration is experienced through the 'earth' body—the body of form which circumscribes identity whether in Spirit or in Matter, i.e., the body celestial or the body terrestrial.).

As the Guru prepares to take his position on the south gate of the New Jerusalem in Spirit and the City Foursquare in Matter, he gives to his saints who will embody his flame within his Church the Great Commission to be himself in the fullness of the seven rays and in the eighth ray. These saints are the free electrons of God who have elected to be free in their expression of the Word and who understand the disciplines of that freedom of the Holy Ghost and abide by them lovingly. Moved by the Father, the Son, and the Holy Spirit, they are submitting to the initiations foursquare of the Everlasting Gospel of the four living creatures.

These saints of the Ruby Ray, carried in the Spirit, are positioned everywhere on the circumference and within the hallowed Circle of Life—the life everlasting that belongs to those who dwell in the Word and in whom the Word dwells. These are the partakers of the Guru/chela relationship with the Lamb—here and hereafter.

Behold, I announce to you your initiations on the Ruby Ray as chelas of the Lamb incarnate.

I AM

Sanat Kumara

"Worthy is the Lamb that was slain
 To receive power, and riches, and wisdom,
 And strength, and honour, and glory, and blessing."
 And there arises out of the mist of the deep
 Into which the souls of God have descended,
 Whom the saints have followed and defended
 By the gospel of the Word
 The song of praise and universal adoration
 By which the great multitude believe and are baptized
 Because they have heard the preaching of the four Gospels:
"Blessing, and honour, and glory, and power,
 Be unto him that sitteth upon the throne,
 And unto the Lamb for ever and ever."

See Rev. 14; John 1:14; Prov. 8:32–36; 9:1; 2 Tim. 2:15; John 6:53–57; Matt. 3:13–17; 17:1–13; Mark 9:2–13; Luke 9:28–36; Matt. 14:1–12; 11:11; 1 Kings 19–22; 2 Kings 1–2; Acts 1:9; Matt. 26:1–13; 5:21–26; 28:18, 20; James 1:12; Rev. 7; 1 Cor. 15; Rev. 5.

22

∞

The Command to Preach the Gospel to Every Creature

And he said unto them, Go ye into all the world, and preach the gospel to every creature.

He that believeth and is baptized shall be saved; but he that believeth not shall be damned [judged].

And these signs shall follow them that believe; In my name shall they cast out devils; they shall speak with new tongues;

They shall take up serpents; and if they drink any deadly thing, it shall not hurt them; they shall lay hands on the sick, and they shall recover.   MARK 16

To the Saints Who Worship within the Temple of God:

These are the Words and Works of the Father, the Son, and the Holy Spirit within you whose attainment on the Path is measured by the rod of love.

Ye shall go into all the world, into the whole Matter sphere, positioned on every line of the Cosmic Clock and on every dot of the planetary spheres, and preach the gospel to every creature.

The events prophesied by the Son of God which take place in the lives of the saints who obey this command as a part of the Great Commission are under the aegis of the Father, the Son, and the Holy Spirit. The Trinity is outpictured within the saint through the initiations of the path of the seven rays; and the fourth ray by the soul's attainment in both the Spirit and the Matter spheres becomes the eighth ray of integration, as above so below, with the Lamb as the Guru incarnate.

The first command to preach the gospel to every creature in all the world is the initiation of the power of the Father in the spoken Word of the Son. This transfer of power to the soul who has entered the path of the initiations of the Ruby Ray comes with the exercise of the very power itself and of the Word.

Power is both the Person, the very personal Presence of the Father in the Son, and his Energy. It is transferred day by day throughout the mission of the Son of God; and the fervor of constancy and soul consecration is the means to the acceleration of this power. It can be neither received nor retained unless it be exercised. While working on this initiation of the power of the Word, the devotee experiences the interaction of the Father and the Son within his very own temple, and he understands why Jesus cried when he said, "He that believeth on me, believeth not on me, but on him that sent me."

For though he was the clearest example of the indwelling Father, the people then and now often worship his person—and his flesh and blood person at that—instead of the Mighty I AM Presence of whom he spoke when he said, "He that seeth me seeth him that sent me. I AM come a Light into the world, that whosoever believeth on me—the I AM THAT I AM that dwelleth in me who is the first principle of the Light in me and in every creature of God—should not abide in darkness."

Jesus Christ understood that the speaking of the Word is the transmittal of the Person of myself, the direct transfer of the Light of Alpha and Omega that I AM. Therefore he said, "He that rejecteth me, and receiveth not *my words*, hath one that judgeth him: *the Word* that I have spoken, the same shall judge him in the last day." Jesus Christ was the great example of the initiation of the power of the Word by the Lord of the First Ray and the chohan thereof—the unloosing of the mouth of God in the mouth of man.

All of those prophets of Israel who went before him had the authority to declare, "The mouth of the LORD hath spoken it!" For they had received the initiation of the sacred fire from the six-winged seraphim. As it had been done unto Isaiah, so it was done unto them. And their four lower bodies were purged of the misuses of the sacred fire of God on the first ray within its orifice—the throat center:

> *In the year that king Uzziah died I saw also the* LORD *[the Ancient of Days, Lord Sanat Kumara] sitting upon a throne, high and lifted up, and his train filled the temple.*
>
> *Above it stood the seraphims: each one had six wings; with twain he covered his face, and with twain he covered his feet, and with twain he did fly.*
>
> *And one cried unto another, and said, Holy, holy, holy, is the* LORD *of hosts: the whole earth is full of his glory.*
>
> *And the posts of the door moved at the voice of him that cried, and the house was filled with smoke.*
>
> *Then said I, Woe is me! for I am undone; because I am a man of unclean lips, and I dwell in the midst of a people of unclean lips: for mine eyes have seen the King, the* LORD *of hosts.*
>
> *Then flew one of the seraphims unto me, having a live coal in his hand, which he had taken with the tongs from off the altar:*
>
> *And he laid it upon my mouth, and said, Lo, this hath touched thy lips; and thine iniquity is taken away, and thy sin purged.*
>
> *Also I heard the voice of the* LORD, *saying, Whom shall I send, and who will go for us? Then said I, Here am I; send me.*

Therefore the command to preach the gospel to every creature necessitates the submission of the soul unto the initiations of the first ray. These initiations are given following the vision of the I AM THAT I AM and my own Self-revelation as that LORD which sitteth upon the throne, guarding the Flame of Life for all of my sons who enter the Matter sphere to fulfill the mission of the Lamb.

I bid you, therefore, submit to my servant-son the ascended master El Morya, who is the Lamb worthy to open the seven-sealed book unto his chelas in Darjeeling. For every chela of the will of God is a preacher of the gospel of his own I AM Presence. Therefore to be a hearer and a doer of that Word, the chela must learn the meaning of devotion to the will of God and understand that Jesus Christ, in his mission as the representative of the I AM Presence, was and is misunderstood to this very hour. And let those in whom there yet dwell foul spirits of gossip, calumny, proud boasting, and misuses of the sacred fire of the will of God in the power center humble themselves before the great descending Light of the I AM Presence and prepare for the initiation of the unloosing of the tongue whereby it shall become the tongue of the LORD.

Then, having received at the altar the touch of the sacred fire transmitted by the World Teachers through the office of the Mother, go forth as pilgrims bearing the sword of peace, dividing the way of light and darkness, and having within you the never-failing humility of a living Christ who said, "For I have not spoken of myself; but the Father which sent me, he gave me a commandment, what I should say, and what I should speak. And I know that his commandment is life everlasting: whatsoever I speak therefore, even as the Father said unto me, so I speak."

"Believe and be baptized! Believe and be baptized! Believe and be baptized!" What does this mean? Or, as some have said, what is the meaning of this!

I AM in the Lamb and the Lamb is in me and, lo, I and my Mother are one. Wherever I go, I AM in the Mother and the Mother is in me and we occupy the south gate of the city. Here in the full-orbed illumination of the sun shining in the strength of the seven holy Kumaras and in the purity of the Mother flame burning, burning on the altars of the thirteen Lemurian temples, the saints are daily exercising the power of the Word. You can hear them in the roaring of the Lion and in the white fire of the wrathful deities who deliver their denunciations of error—

spawned by evil and multiplied by unreality—in their relentless releases of the radiant Word in the religion of Ra Mu.

The saints believe on the embodied Word because they are becoming the Word. They who have not the Word in them and they who refuse to exercise its power believe not. They who have the Word trust in the Word, and by their trust they are aligned with the Word. They are the Word, and because they are the Word they obey the Word. This is the mystery of the Guru/chela relationship and the real path of the bodhisattvas East and West who exercise the wisdom of the Word and take lovingly the initiations of the Son.

Their baptism is the full immersion into the body, mind, soul, and heart of the Guru. They flow with Alpha. They flow with Omega. And they are not through until that baptism is fulfilled by the Lion, the Calf, the Man, and the flying Eagle. Four persons of Christhood come into their temples. Four archetypes of being fulfill the fiery destiny of their souls. And the religion of Ra Mu, my beloved, is the science of Lemurian invocation whereby the Cosmic Mind is put on through the meditation upon that Mind.

Here note well that the term *believe* as recorded in the Book of Mark, chapter sixteen, verse sixteen, is the key to the square within the square; and the Word *believe* itself translates mystically to mean "meditate." Therefore the directive of the Son of God is "Meditate on the Guru and be immersed in the Guru."

With the Chohan of the Second Ray, my son Lanto, enter the Retreat of the Royal Teton and be with him who is the Lamb worthy to open the seven-sealed book and transfer to you the wisdom of your path of meditation and your exercise of the Word. For by the Word emitted out of your meditation (Alpha) and your immersion (Omega), the quiescent energies of Life are translated into the active disciplines of the disciples of the second ray. Meditation *on* and immersion *in* the Lamb are the moving force of the Coming Revolution in Higher Consciousness.

It is written: "He that believeth not shall be damned." This damnation (judgment) need not be an everlasting damnation (except it be the second death at the Last Judgment), for it endures only so long as the state of unbelief. Unbelief is the pulling of the plug of the soul's consciousness out of the socket of the I AM Presence. Thus cut off from the flow and the fount of Reality, the soul pronounces its own self-damnation. And that which it creates it may uncreate—while there is yet time and space, while the Light is with you.

My beloved, if you have pulled the plug that is your lifeline to the Godhead, you have the opportunity in this very moment, while you have life and breath in this embodiment, to plug in once again to the Great Central Sun of limitless love, light, intelligence, the abundant life, and, above all, to the personal relationship with the Father in the Son and the intimate communion in the hallowed circle of the Lamb and the Lamb's wife.

I AM

Sanat Kumara

I AM calling one and all
and every creature begotten of God
to renew the ancient covenant
of your soul with Me,
the Ancient of Days.

See Mark 16; John 12:44–46, 48; Isa. 1:20; 40:5; 58:14; Mic. 4:4; Isa. 6:1–8; James 1:22–25; John 12:49, 50; Rev. 19, 20, 21.

23

The Power to Preach the Word of God

Go home to thy friends, and tell them how great things the LORD *hath done for thee, and hath had compassion on thee.*

MARK 5

Unto You to Whom Is Given the Power
to Preach the Gospel to Every Creature:

The power to *preach* is the power to *reach* the soul by the sacred fire of the Holy Spirit transferred by the Father within you unto the Son, thence to the Christ Self of the creature, that the light of his own indwelling Christhood might descend to quicken his very own soul. This power to preach the Word of God ought to be sought and not shunned simply because some have misused it in organized religion to bind souls to themselves instead of to God.

Ecclesiastes was a preacher of righteousness and a caller of souls to reality as he went to and fro exposing the vanity of vanities of unreality. Go be! Go do thou likewise!

John the Baptist came preaching in the wilderness of Judea, saying, "Repent ye: for the kingdom of heaven is at hand!... Bring forth therefore fruits meet for repentance." And when he, the Guru who went before his chela, was cast into prison—for the light of God that was in him was both offense and outrage to the generation of vipers fleeing from the wrath to come—his chela took up his mantle and he, too, began to preach, saying, "Repent: for the kingdom of heaven is at hand!"

Thus go thou likewise and preach the imminence of the

sphere of Spirit and its imminent descent within the sphere of Matter! And preach the coming of the four cosmic forces and the presence of the Lamb in the person of the embodied Guru and the person of the Ancient of Days who makes his abode within the temple of the Mother and within the hearts of the living saints.

The spirit of the preachers crying out and proclaiming the Truth, heralding the coming of the King and his kingdom, has ever been present in the world since the dispensation of my coming. For without the preachers of righteousness—the *right energy use* of the Word—there is no King and no kingdom within the body of God, no one who holds the *k*ey to the *in*carnation of God within the saints, and no one who keeps the keys to the kingdom—the community of the lightbearers of the Lamb.

Your own messenger Mark Prophet who occupied the office of the Father in your midst, even as he was the Son and the Holy Spirit, even as he served the Mother (and the Mother was in him and he was in the Mother), charged you, as the Saviour charged you, to tell the tidings of Truth. I include herewith his command to you to "Tell Them" because it is the initiation of the Ever-Present Guru, Lanello, to the saints of the Ruby Ray to embody the flame of the preacher, the one who not only announces the good news but is able to discourse upon the sevenfold gospel with the profound understanding of the prophet.

This he did. And this my son Lanello pronounces to you with the promise that when you take up the mantle of the preacher, he will enter your temple and bestow upon you his mantle, and he will not leave you until your mission is fulfilled in the name of the two witnesses.

Tell Them

Tell them,
Ancient Fires,
How the strata of the rock
Cooled and formed the surface
Of a verdant sphere to be.

Tell them,
Ancient Waters,
Of the coolants of the deep—
Mighty cycles of perfection,
Marine world now we see.

Tell them,
Mighty Atmosphere,
Of blue inspired veil,
Of lacy white cloud cover
Curtained Cosmos does unveil.

Tell them of Creation
That like clockwork telling time
Shows the intricacy of nature
In a network so sublime.

Tell them of a seedling
Filled with patterned destiny.
Tell them of a cedar tall
That through sunshine was to be.

Tell them of a whisper
That was heard within the soul.
Tell them, Ageless Wisdom,
Nature's blessed goal.

Tell them of Reality
That plays hide and seek with men.
Tell them of a Golden Age
That cometh once again.

Tell them of the Buddha
And of Christ upon the hill.
Tell them Truth, Reality
That hungry souls do fill.

Tell them of electric spark
That flashes 'cross the sky.
Speak of Immortality that cradles our humanity—
That one day none shall die.

Speak of Truth
That out the mouth of Christ did manifest,
That Pilate heard and questioned,
That now in truth is blessed.

Speak it loud and speak it long;
Tell in poetry and song
That tall upon the hills of time
An ageless wisdom now does chime—

Carillon bells from celestial towers
Rung by other hands than ours,
Angel voices chiming in
Raise an anthem now to win.

Tell them how that we who read
Can in faith plant vital seed,
Watch them push their shoots right through
Soil and rock and obstacle too—

Thrusting roots into the earth,
Seeking vital essence' worth
And reaching to the sun to claim
That I AM real in God's own Name!

Tell them, then, that darkest night
Waits the first dawn's early light,
That man may see and catch the thought
That God in truth has to us brought
An opportunity so fair—
An answer to a child's own prayer.

> Our Father, help us now to be
> Selflessly engraft' in Thee—
> That our nature then shall be
> Like a father's heart of love;
> Seeds from heaven up above
> Scattered here in garden fair—
> Sun and rain in falling there
> Can assist the planned delight
> And the victory for the right!
>
> Tell them, Father, Ageless One,
> Of Thy Nature's Golden Sun.
> Tell them of Thy Name and Spirit!
> Tell them so that all may hear it!
> Tell them so that none may fear it!
> Tell them so that all revere it!
> Tell them so that none may lose
> Life or gift—that all may choose
> Now and without fail to see
> That only Truth can ever be
> Clad with Immortality.

Now the Son who moved in your midst by the Holy Spirit is the one clad with Immortality. It is the requirement of the Great Law that one should demonstrate the Path of the Ruby Ray and be the example to all, yea, and be the electrode in heaven whereby his Holy Spirit descends in the midst of the body of believers, the living Church. Indeed, there is no Church without the community of the Holy Spirit. And there is no Holy Spirit except one among you who has descended from God ascend to God.

Thus your own beloved Lanello, who himself fulfilled my command to "Tell Them," wrote my poem. He obeyed my commandment because he loved me. And I loved him, and I took him unto myself that, by the sacrifice of the one that is become the full glory of the ascension to all, you might live to fulfill not only your own fiery destiny but his as well. Walk confident, then, in the Spirit of the Truth that he became, for the mantle of Lanello is upon you. Seize it now and use it as he used it to challenge the authority of the fallen ones.

> O lovers of Truth,
> How you are the beloved of living Truth!
> Without truth and the honor flame,
> Life is not worth living and there is no gain.
> And all is robbery that is gotten in vain.
>
> Yet he, like the living Saviour,
> Thought it not robbery to make himself equal with God.
> He is one of the few, the heroes of the centuries,
> Who heard the Word and caught the spark
> And used it to consume the dark.
> He had the courage of the Lion,
> And he roared his message like the Lion.
> He would accept no less than full and co-equal Sonship.
> And he knew, as the Devil knew and as the apostles knew,
> That indeed this made him equally the inheritor
> Of the fullness of the Light.
>
> No mere reflection was he, no mere vessel.
> For the Light had long ago devoured
> The reflection and the vessel
> To stand as a pure, radiant beam
> Where once the reflection and the vessel had stood.
> Truly the allness of the Son can contain
> Only the allness of God.

Understand my meaning, and do not misunderstand it. For I say, All that the Son is is God. And the Son can realize no more of God than he is become. But when the fullness of the Son is come, then is the fullness of his God Presence come unto him. And all that is in the vast expanse of Spirit/Matter spheres and far-off worlds is contained in the mind of God as a single point of light. Therefore the Son who is one with the Father and whose mind is in him may also contain the point of light.

No, he was not satisfied with a portion of Selfhood. Therefore he merged with the All who is in all and became that Allness. Because God has willed it so. This is the sacred mystery which the devils have inverted, for by it they will either be converted or subverted. Ponder it and be free to be like Lanello in God as God.

And the Son is equal to the Father, and the Father is equal to the Holy Spirit, and the Holy Spirit is equal to the Mother, and the Mother is equal to the Son, and the Son IS...

I AM WHO I AM

Do you know who you are?

Sanat Kumara

See Eccles.; Mark 1:14, 15; Matt. 3, 4; 16:13–20; Phil. 2:5, 6.

24

∞

Preachers of the Acceptable Year of the LORD

And as ye go, preach, saying, The kingdom of heaven is at hand.

Heal the sick, cleanse the lepers, raise the dead, cast out devils: freely ye have received, freely give....

What I tell you in darkness, that speak ye in light: and what ye hear in the ear, that preach ye upon the housetops....

Whosoever therefore shall confess me before men, him will I confess also before my Father which is in heaven.

But whosoever shall deny me before men, him will I also deny before my Father which is in heaven.

MATTHEW 10

To You Who Would Preach the Acceptable Year of the LORD:

Behold, now is the accepted cycle for the coming of the I AM THAT I AM face to face in the hearts of my people! The saints who follow the Lamb whithersoever he goeth, the saints who are with the Saviour in his fulfillment of both the written and the unwritten prophecy of the Word will take up the Book of Isaiah and give the dynamic decree that announces the coming of the LORD within this temple:

The Spirit of the LORD is upon me, because he hath anointed me to preach the gospel to the poor; he hath sent me to heal the brokenhearted, to preach deliverance to the captives, and recovering of sight to the blind, to set at liberty them that are bruised, to preach the acceptable year of the LORD.

The disciples of the Saviour Jesus Christ who live in him and he in them know that it is the hour of the Second Advent—the coming of THE LORD OUR RIGHTEOUSNESS, the Christ Self, into the hearts of the children of God by the intercession of Jesus Christ, whose First Advent opened the door in the earth—the door of grace.

Therefore they also preach the day of the vengeance of our God—the day of the descent of personal and planetary karma in the Dark Cycle, the day when every soul evolving in the Matter spheres is called to give an accounting before the Lords of Karma of words and works. Therefore they preach the understanding of the Law and the right use of the Law. And they comfort all that mourn the absence of Christ Jesus, preaching to them the exclamation of Elohim: Behold, now is the accepted time, now is the day of the LORD's salvation as Messiah comes into your temple! And the mission of his Second Coming is to ignite your own Threefold Flame into the full expansion of the presence of your Christ Self dwelling in you bodily.

This is the good news of your Saviour that I, Sanat Kumara, call upon you to preach. But some of you have seemed to think over the years that you may choose to be or not to be the living preacher. But I say unto you, until you take up the mantle of your master, as Elisha took up the mantle of Elijah and smote the waters of the human consciousness, you will not receive from the Holy Ghost the signs that follow them that believe.

I would tell you of these signs conferred by the Holy Spirit. But first I must tell you why it is necessary to preach the good news to *every* creature. For there be some creatures who are created of God and who are the seed of Christ. They are "the wheat." And there are some creatures who are created of the Devil and who are the seed of the Wicked One. They are "the tares."

I have not yet altogether unveiled the mystery of the two creations and the two creatures who dwell together in the earth until the day of the harvest; nor shall I do so at this writing except to confirm that, contrary to their own self-denial and their perpetuation of the philosophy that they do not exist, they do indeed exist as that spiritual wickedness in the high places of church and state. And if they did not exist, there would be no need for them to deny that they do exist. And so by the very presence of their anti-Devil and anti-evil philosophy and the virulence of the exposed vipers against the preachers, you know, my beloved, that they do exist.

There are souls in the earth, both in physical embodiment and between embodiments on the astral plane, who are in the "grave" of the death consciousness. And they are waiting for the voice of the living Word—waiting for the quickening—that is spoken through the preachers who are the disciples of the Lamb. With your speaking of his Word, empowered as the preacher, and with their hearing of his voice through your own, all shall come forth from their graves of unreality, materiality, and idolatry where they have been entombed. And they who are of the seed of Christ who have done good works shall be called by the power of the preacher unto the resurrection of life; and they who are the seed of the Wicked One whose works have been evil shall be resurrected unto damnation (the Last Judgment before the great white throne).

But whether their works are good or whether their works are evil, the judgment that comes to them through your preaching of the Everlasting Gospel is their own response to that gospel by the delivery of the Word of the Father unto the Son within you and within the creature. And by the quickening love of the Holy Ghost, sinners are called to repentance; and even the laggards and the fallen angels may bend the knee and confess that Christ is LORD and enter the path of loving, illumined obedience to the Lamb. This is the mission of the preacher. For he has the power to reach the souls of both good and evil and to call them forth from the grave that they may be judged by the living Spirit of the Resurrection.

Both John the Baptist and Jesus Christ moved among the Sadducees and Pharisees and were even accused either of having a devil or of being a friend of publicans and sinners. Thus when Jesus was in the house of Simon the Pharisee who had desired that he should eat with him, there came a woman of the city who was a sinner, anointing Jesus' feet with ointment. And the Pharisee reasoned within himself, saying, "This man, if he were a prophet, would have known who and what manner of woman this is that toucheth him: for she is a sinner." Thus Jesus, by his very presence at table with Simon, was the instrument for the exposure of Simon's hardness of heart toward the sinner whose sins Jesus forgave, saying, "Thy faith hath saved thee; go in peace," while those others that sat with him at meat also challenged his authority to forgive sin.

The Pharisee was the rebel against God who might have been saved had he given the devotion to Christ that was given by the woman. And in the same hour, by the same flame of the living Word, all who were with him were judged—some to eternal life, and some to self-damnation (self-judgment) by their individual reaction to the Word of the Son and his Work in the Holy Spirit.

Now consider the example of your messengers and their mission to Ghana, West Africa. Three times I have sent them there: first, in the name of the Father, before the ascension of Mark; then in the name of the Son, after his ascension; and the last journey, in the name of the Holy Spirit. On each occasion they preached the Word to all who were in the grave of ignorance concerning the mighty I AM Presence and the Christ Self. They effectively presented the incomparable Teachings of the Ascended Masters. Had these teachings been followed by greater numbers of the people, and especially the leaders, with honor and integrity, they would have averted, by the science of the Word and the love of the Holy Spirit, the great karma that has descended upon that nation.

The messengers preached the Word to every creature from the least unto the greatest—the mighty in their seats, the lowly in their huts. And even the betrayers of the people, fearing the wrath to come, sought the messengers' blessing (initiation). But they did not bring forth fruits meet for repentance. They did not forsake their old ways but instead sought to hide from the LORD their wrongdoings against the light and the nation. They even sought the seal of approval of the messengers upon their form of government. But the messengers steadfastly proclaimed the way of righteousness and were no respecters of their human persons but gave to each and every one equally of the light and of the Word.

Thus it has come to pass that the Word itself is become their judge. For those who rejected my messengers and received not their words have stood, following their executions, before the Court of the Sacred Fire and before the four and twenty elders. And the Word that I spoke through my messenger, the same was the judge in their last day, the day of their final judgment. Let none think that those who ordered their executions were their judges; rather, by their actions they are self-judged. (Yet they, too, must come to the judgment, whether here or hereafter.)

You see, had these men been men of God, their physical death would not have altered their souls' evolution; but from the moment of their rejection of the Mother and her admonishment toward moral integrity and self-sacrifice for the people, they stood self-judged before the Word. Therefore, whether in life or in death, in this world or the next, the rejection of the Word brings forth the judgment. And there are many who remain in life in Ghana who have rejected that Word and who by the grace of God have the opportunity to yet pay the price of their karma in this embodiment.

Elements in politics and religion sought to ensnare the messenger and then condemned her for her response. But her vote for "union government" was cast not for a man but for God whose community of the Holy Spirit she has preached year in, year out as Ghana's destiny to search out, define, and refine. It is the divine plan of self-government of the people, well represented under a multifaceted council of professionally qualified, Holy

Spirit endued, duly elected men and women working selflessly as the servants of all.

This is the vision we hold for the nations of Africa, for it is the archetype of self-rule of the Israelites (in the absence of leadership under the prophet or his anointed king or priest) wherever they take up their abode to take dominion in the earth. And let the ideal public servant follow the example of Mohandas Gandhi, true Son of man and servant of the LORD—not that of the interlopers, the hirelings, whom the people have allowed to rule in the stead of THE LORD OUR RIGHTEOUSNESS, the individual Christ Self. And the people have no one to blame but themselves—least of all the true servants of God.

Behold the rise and fall of tyrants and their idolaters throughout Africa. Behold the manipulation of party politics by agents of the internationalists seeking to mold governments and economies for motives impure. Let us close the circle of nationhood by enlisting noncompetitive agents of the Holy Ghost who will lay down their selfish lives and live their lives henceforth for the saving of the unity of the African states.

I, the Ancient of Days, give solemn warning to all on the continent of Afra: Cease your love of money, pleasure, self-gain, and self-glory and unite to serve the people. For if you do not, you will be devoured and enslaved by the forces of greed from within that are easy prey to the Watchers. They who lust after world power, if unchecked, will rape and ravage Africa until they get what they want—the resources of the Mother and the light (money and manpower) of her children. Yet all of this was sealed by the Father in the beginning for the abundant life of his own. Now in the ending of the Mother when the harvest is nigh, will you let them unseal it and take the LORD's bounty?

Let none be dismayed. For when the Great White Brotherhood sends its emissaries to the nations, the judgment is come. Therefore let the Word that is sent forth lovingly be received lovingly and all will go well. Ghana is an ascended master nation. Until its people take the proffered gift and follow the Path that they have known of old, yet rebelled against time and time again, she will not fulfill her destiny as a community of the Holy Spirit or as the heart of Afra.

Our faithful servants in Ghana are known by name. Their light is the light of a nation and a continent. And the unfaithful servants who deny their LORD in the hour of his crucifixion are also known. One and all may pick up the dropped torch of the flame of freedom and the star of Ghana to support all God-fearing men and women of goodwill. And one and all must see in the Science of the Spoken Word the sword, the living sword, whereby the enemies within and without the community of the Holy Spirit may be lawfully conquered. But he that killeth with the sword must be killed with the sword.

Let the students of Ghana who desire to see their nation free from the manipulators of both World Communism and World Capitalism, as well as the betrayers of the people in their midst, demand that the Teachings of the Ascended Masters be distributed without bribe and without compromise of the Holy Spirit. And let them tear the masks from the wolves in sheep's clothing in church and state who deny the Word. For only when the people willingly surrender their deception and dishonesty will the Holy Spirit once again enter the mainstream of Ghanaian life through the children of the light.

Let all nations be forewarned that when the Everlasting Gospel is preached unto you by the saints, it is the coming of the judgment. And from the least unto the greatest none shall be hid, neither they nor their deeds, and all must forsake their disloyalty to the Mother flame of the nation and their abuses of her economy and her government.

O Ghana, thou once noble light of Afra and the hope of millions for freedom, rise to thy high calling and to thy destiny! Hearken unto the Word of the LORD and live forever within the counsels of the LORD's hosts from on high delivered to you through the two witnesses and your very own people who are our devotees.

Let all know that when we send our messengers, we do not necessarily reveal to them beforehand who is of the light and who is of the darkness, lest this foreknowledge preclude the free, fair, and honest deliverance of the Word to all, even as the sun shines on the just and the unjust. Though endued with the gift of discernment, the Mother keeps our counsel within her heart while steadfastly holding the immaculate concept (meditating upon the Light of the soul) for every creature. Truly she comes in the footsteps of Jesus Christ who said, "And if any man hear my words, and believe not, I judge him not: for I came not to judge the world, but to save the world."

It is the deep desire of the Mother and has been since the earliest years of her embodiment to bring light to the Ghana that she loves. She preached to the nation and to the government, and all who had light within them knew that the light was in her. And all who had not the light within them were judged by her presence.

The same table that she offered then, I offer today: Ghana, take the Teachings of the Ascended Masters and live. Do not depend on saviours, church or state, but let the Word itself—the true teachers, the ascended masters, and their true teaching—be thy salvation. And blessed are they who are not offended in me. For I AM WHO I AM and I will use whom I will use and speak through whom I will speak to edify my children, exalt the humble, and put down the proud from their positions of self-proclaimed authority in church and state.

But know this, O world: Neither the light nor its messenger is dishonored by the dishonor of the people to whom it is sent. Nor is the vessel contaminated by those who contaminate the crystal clear water which I give freely to all.

Let us begin at the beginning. Moral integrity for the sake of God and for the sake of the people is the requirement of the hour. Let all nations of Africa take heed and be warned. For the light of the Holy Ghost must be in you, from the little children to their parents to all. And if the Holy Ghost be not in you, then you will be devoured by the enemies within and without. The messenger brings the teaching in honor. It is up to you to receive it in honor, to apply it, to live by it, to exercise the Word, and to honor the Word person to person. Do this, do this! and see how Ghana and every nation of Africa will fulfill its destiny and be a model of freedom and industriousness to the world.

Now, saints of the Church, study the example of the Mother and note well the reaction to the messenger and the message. For this, too, will be thy initiation on the west gate. But be of good cheer, for I have walked the continent of Africa before you, long, long ago in the days of Lemuria. And there is nowhere that you can go, on that or any continent where I have not already walked, placing my footprints for you to follow in—in this the hour of the bestowal of the mantle of the preacher upon you.

I AM

Sanat Kumara

See Matt. 10; Isa. 61:1–3; Luke 4:14–32; Jer. 23:5, 6; Matt. 13:24–30, 36–43; Eph. 6:10–20; John 5:17–31; Rev. 20:11–15; Matt. 9:10–13; Luke 7; Matt. 3:1–12; Acts 10:34, 35; John 12:44–50; Rev. 13; Matt. 5:43–48; 11:1–6.

25

In My Name, Cast Out Devils!

> *When the even was come, they brought unto him many that were possessed with devils: and he cast out the spirits with his Word.*
> MATTHEW 8

Beloved on the Royal Road of Priesthood and Kingship unto Our God:

The "signs following" are the signs of the Holy Spirit. They are the signs of the initiates of the Ruby Ray who have stood with the Son on the east gate to confront the Antichrist as Satan and his seed in his subtle and myriad manifestations, who have stood on the north gate with the Father to confront the Dragon as the Watchers and their godless creation who oppose the generative and regenerative light of God in his Fatherhood within his children in heaven and in earth.

Now the initiates of the Ruby Ray stand on the west gate with the Holy Spirit who manifests himself in the very person of the ascended masters. And in the name of the Lamb, they take up the cosmic cross of white fire to first *cast out devils*.

My beloved, you can go no further on the Path of the Ruby Ray until you accept your responsibility to cast out the demons and discarnates that invade the temple of the children of God. For by deliberate design, they are sent by the archdeceivers to defile the temples of my people; and by the deliberate design of the sons and daughters of God, they must be expelled in the name of the Light.

This exorcism pronounced by the individual believers one by one within the community of believers is accomplished solely by the authority of the Word which Jesus Christ gives, then and now, to the true disciples who daily take up his cross. His cross is the burden of his light that he bears to counterbalance the 'sins' of the world; these sins are the burden of planetary karma which he holds in abeyance (in balance) until the coming of age of the children of God.

When the child chooses to become an heir of God through Christ, he must do so by following Christ's path—both his words and his works—as the only verifiable proof of his belief in him. As he said, "He that believeth on me, the works that I do shall he do also; and greater works than these shall he do; because I go unto my Father."

Works and greater works are the measure whereby the LORD measures the quality of the heart of the true believer. The work of bearing the cross of world sin is not only the requirement of fulfilling the command of love ("If ye love me, keep my commandments."), but it is an indispensable and most necessary component of the path of initiation into individual Christhood as taught and demonstrated by Jesus Christ.

I, Sanat Kumara, challenge every abuser of this path which is the true calling of the sons and daughters of God. I, the Ancient of Days, challenge the lie of the wolves in sheep's clothing who continually tell you—as though, by the very telling, the lie should become the truth—that my Son Jesus Christ did for you what only you can do for yourselves.

It is the fallen ones themselves—who have no God in them and are therefore unable to work his works—that have taught my children that they are incapable of those "works" which he promised they should do, that it is blasphemy to suppose that they in Christ are capable of "greater works," and that, in any case, the performance of those works is unnecessary to salvation!

Saints of the Ruby Ray, make haste to demonstrate the Law that you might liberate, with signs following, the blessed children of my heart yet in bondage to the law of sin—and the sinful sense of sin. For they have not the slightest concept of the meaning of those oft repeated words of Saint Paul, "Christ died for our sins." My beloved, to them that are born of God death is not real. It never has been real and it never will be.

Jesus Christ hung on the Matter cross. His soul departed the body temple. He gave up the Holy Ghost. And the Father withdrew the Threefold Flame from the lower vehicles. He, the soul fused with the Trinity, did not die—but rather descended into hell to preach to the rebellious spirits. Nevertheless, all signs attributed to death were present within that body form. The change called "death" most surely had taken place.

The miracle of the Resurrection was the LORD's return to the same flesh-and-blood body. He in God raised it from the dead. His soul reentered the restored temple, and once again Jesus, the anointed with light, was the very embodiment of the Trinity—and the Mother flame.

This God-victory over Death and Hell was the atonement of Almighty God for the sins of the world committed against the Son. But it was not a vicarious atonement. This means that he did it for you but not in your stead. He 'died' for your sins that you might live again to atone for them yourself. He set "for you" the example of that which you yourself must do—today. Had he not proven that death is unreal, you, my beloved, would not be in embodiment today with renewed zest to "work out your own salvation with fear and trembling."

This is the responsibility that you bear as initiates of the Ruby Ray. And I would like you to look at that word *responsibility* and see in its place the word *cross*. For the cross that you must bear is the responsibility in Christ not only for personal sin but also for the sins of the whole world. "For it is God which worketh in you both to will and to do of his good pleasure." And the Ruby Cross of Alpha and Omega is the very light/energy/consciousness of the Trinity whereby your sins and the sins of the world are consumed by the sacred fire—the white fire of purification, the violet fire of transmutation—and by the Ruby Ray, which is alchemically the blood of Christ.

He lived to demonstrate the path of life, not of death and dying. All who follow him in the Resurrection "on such the second death hath no power, but they shall be priests of God and of Christ, and shall reign with him a thousand years."

You who have been with me from the beginning and shall be with me in the ending—unto you I say, Lo, I AM Alpha and Omega. I have raised you up to be the deliverers of my people as true shepherds of the Word. You have died a thousand deaths in this life and more, yet none of these were real. Not one. The only death that dies is the death that never lived. For that which has the Life that is God never dies.

Now learn my meaning and how to rightly divide my word spoken by Paul: "As it is appointed unto men once to die, but after this the judgment: so Christ was once offered to bear the sins of many; and unto them that look for him shall he appear the second time without sin unto salvation."

Let this death die—the not self, the ego self, the carnal self, if you will; for it dies but once, if indeed it truly die, and after that is the judgment of the soul. For the soul must stand naked before God and apart from the synthetic self, the human ego, so that it may be judged by the words and works of its identification with the living Truth of the Divine Ego, ever the challenger of the human ego and the soul's defender against the unreality of its sinister strategies.

Now do not any longer allow the false theologians to tell my children that this oft misquoted, quotable quote of the apostle is proof that your souls—and theirs, if they have one—have not lived continuously with Christ in this world or that they will not do so in the next. Just as God is able, and indeed he is able! to provide many mansions in heaven for the soul's joyous habitation, so he has provided many temples in the earth for the souls whom he has chosen to increase in his Word in the evolution of his consciousness in Matter. The fact is that the divine plan for each living soul has never been limited to one incarnation.

After all, can you expect the finite potential to realize the infinite mind of God in one so-called lifetime? Well, I do not! And I know that continuity of being, world to world, is the means provided for the soul to experience the richness, the very depth and height and breadth of God's consciousness. Why, he is too grand a conception himself to limit his sons and daughters to a thimble's worth of himself.

Indeed, two hundred pennyworth is not sufficient to feed the multitudinous compartments of consciousness with which God has endowed every part of himself. And every soul, including your own, is a part of God and a multiplier of God. Every crumb is the loaf. And every crumb can be multiplied to feed the five thousand and more.

Indeed, God intended life to be lived to its fullest and not cut off before all of his desiring to express himself in an expansive and expanding universal field of love should be satisfied through each and every soul. Souls as daisies in that field must bloom a million times a million until the eternal Matrix is satisfied. Yet my children fear death. They fear the past. They fear the future. And they fear the responsibility of the present which both their past and their future must put upon the soul.

Thus the false pastors conveniently cut off their past and their future. And my irresponsible children lap up their gruel, though they know not it is the cruel, cruel dying of their Christ in the present. For if your Christed Self did not live with your LORD before Abraham was, then how can you live with him in the beyond? That which becomes eternal must be eternal in both directions—yea, in all directions—and thereby cancel out time and space and all confinements for the victors in the race.

You cannot be victors unless you are willing to take your place with the good shepherds of my people who will shout from every steeple, "The LORD is come! The LORD is come! The LORD is come!"

O my people, arise, shine; for thy Light is come, and the glory of the LORD is risen upon thee. Do you not see! The Christ in you—who is the same yesterday, and to day, and for ever—is the same Christ who has incarnated with your soul for aeons and aeons that you might at last be made whole and be with him, indeed, in the first resurrection.

Now shout, O Sion! Shout with the Lamb and the hundred forty and four thousand on the mount Sion. For now is the hour of the casting out of the moneychangers in the temple who have marketed their false theology under various and sundry brand names and labels. But one and all they have cut off the horizontal arm of the cosmic cross of white fire extending to the left and to the right into the distant past and the distant future.

Some say He never came. Others say He is yet coming to reign with the saints a thousand years. Some say He never was and never will be. Some say He cannot and never can be embodied in the clay vessel, for never was there a perfect vessel or a perfect person. And the latter have cut off the north and south nodes of the vertical bar as they have sought to obliterate His star in the center of the cosmic cross of white fire.

Thus the children of God, deprived of him past, present, and future, are kept by the fallen ones in a holding pattern, ever ready to land but never landing in the promised land flowing with milk and honey. I tell you, my beloved, if Messiah is come two thousand years ago, then he is come today. And a million years forward and a million years backward, still Messiah is come—the gift of God the Son to everyone. To everyone, to everyone who is born of him and born by the Spirit and born by the Mother and born to inherit eternal life.

Now understand what are these demons of the denial of Emmanuel—"God with us" here and now and forever. Notice they will tell you everywhere where he is not, but they will never tell you where he is, where I AM, that where I AM ye may be also—in order that wherever the I AM is, there you may be found in his likeness. This is the teaching and the preaching of the Word to the children of God that have been put upon by the demons clothed in scarlet, black and gray, and proud orange. They have had their day. And their day is done!

Sons of the light, here we come! To cast out demons we are come—demons of the mind and memory, of the astral sheath, and even those demoniac viruses that penetrate the sheath of the physical cells and bring Armageddon to the intimate spheres of life assailing the centrosome of the Lamb and the Lamb's wife.

Verily in the four quarters (quadrants) of the earth, Gog and Magog, the right and left of the Antichrist, gather to do battle with the saints. But it is written that the "fire came down from God out of heaven, and devoured them." And why do you suppose that fire came down from heaven, my beloved? It is because those living saints exercised the Science of the Spoken Word and invoked it in the name I AM THAT I AM.

They pronounced the Ritual of Exorcism in the center of the AUM. They gave their divine decrees—and the Divinity decreed within them!—and they wearied not in well doing, and they loved not their lives unto the death of the seed of the Wicked. And death for them would be the closing of the eyes and the opening of the eyes, as leaving shore and approaching shore. And though they are seen no more as mortals by mortals, the soul is immortal forever and forever.

The carnally minded will think that I preach a flesh-and-blood resurrection. I do not. The outworn garment may remain, as the chambered nautilus remains, as proof that the soul has vacated the tomb for a greater glory in the eternal womb of becoming.

That is not to say that it is not possible for Christ in you to accelerate body, soul, and mind into the white cloud in the hour of thy ascension. But, my beloved, I do say that it is not necessary that the resurrection be physical, as it was indeed the case with Jesus Christ. For it is the soul who is resurrected in the rapture with Christ. And the wedding garment is provided, the seamless garment thy soul has woven and won. This is the body celestial that supplants the body terrestrial. And in that hour you will be glad to cast aside the outworn garment and to consign it to the sacred fire.

Therefore the law is given by my son of Luxor, Serapis Bey, for the cremation of the physical vehicle. For did He not say that flesh and blood cannot inherit the kingdom of God?

The morbidity surrounding the people's consciousness of death and dying is also the demon that must be cast out. For the embalming and the burying of the body is the prolongation of the death entity itself. For the body is composed of light; and the light in the nucleus of every atom and molecule and cell must be demagnetized from the "earth, earthy" and the dust must be allowed to return to dust, even as the light that preserved its matrix is allowed to spiral to the Great Central Sun as it is released from its encasement in form by the fire element. To this end, the fiery salamanders perform their priestly duties of returning the noble work of Elohim, the body of male and female, to the Great Central Sun for repolarization.

Let cremation be the liberation of my people from morbidity and attachment to the form. For nevermore will that form be reborn. But the soul, the soul—it shall be clothed upon with white raiment, with the righteousness of the saints. It is the idolatry of the self that perpetuates the cult of the tombstone and enriches the morticians and fills the coffers and the coffins of the mausoleum operators who capitalize on the false belief of the masses that immortality is to be found in the ground.

"The earth is the LORD's, and the fulness thereof." Let the sea, the earth be exorcised of death, the death entity, and the bodies in whom there is no life! For the breath of life hath gone out of them, never to return. And those empty houses are invaded by the foul spirits of death who, as vultures, feed upon the light yet imprisoned in the form. This is God's light and God's energy. Let the elementals of fire, air, water, and earth recycle this energy back Home to God and see how the planetary body, blessed Virgo herself, will radiate more light and more light and more light.

Citizens of earth, we deplore the death consciousness on which you have seemed to thrive after the fashion of the black magicians who would destroy you alive—destroy your souls in hell while leaving your bodies to walk the streets of physical cities and astral planes. Saints of God, this is a serious matter! For the whole Matter vehicle of this evolution must be cleared. And the ancient practices of the Egyptian cult of the dead must give way to the culture of life that leads to the ascension.

Therefore go forth and teach the people to place the body on ice, dry or otherwise, two days and two nights. And on the third day, the commemoration of the Resurrection is the invocation of the resurrection flame. Whether on funeral pyre or in a modern crematorium, let the physical fire pass through the body that is untouched; for both flesh and blood must be intact; and embalming is forbidden by the Brotherhood of Luxor.

This method is safe and sane and healthy for all and allows the soul the freedom from all earthly ties as the four lower vehicles are demagnetized simultaneously by the physical fire and the spiritual fire, and the soul, as the winged symbol of the *ka*, takes flight with the flying Eagle to pursue the initiations of the Mother in the retreats of the Great White Brotherhood.

In this way, the demons have no prey and the vultures no flesh and blood. And the astral sheath, itself consumed by the physical/spiritual fire, may not roam the earth, a ghost of the former self. The astral hordes that would devour the coils of light are themselves put to flight. For the soul has clean escaped the mortal round and is heard singing, heavenbound.

Yes, it is the cosmic cross of white fire by which he releases the Word that speaks out of the Void. Take up, then, the Ruby Cross daily. For one day, when the works of Love are fulfilled in you in all the Matter spheres, it shall also be the white-fire cross of thy ascension.

In next week's *Pearl of Wisdom* I shall outline the three steps given by the Master for *The Ritual of Exorcism* which I challenge you, by command of the LORD GOD Almighty, to practice daily—in the name of the four living Words, the four cosmic forces, who are with Me and with the Lamb. This do by the authority of Alpha and Omega until death and hell are cast into the lake of sacred fire!

Prepare to meet my Word!

I AM

Sanat Kumara

See Matt. 8; 10:38; Luke 9:23; Gal. 4:1–7; John 14; 1 Cor. 15; Rev. 6:8, 20; Phil. 2:1–18; Heb. 9:27, 28; John 6:1–14; Jer. 23:1–4; John 8; Isa. 60; Heb. 13:8; Rev. 14; Matt. 21:1–16; 22:1–14; Eccles. 3; Ps. 24.

26

The LORD's Ritual of Exorcism
Step One

> *Verily I say unto you, Whatsoever ye shall bind on earth shall be bound in heaven: and whatsoever ye shall loose on earth shall be loosed in heaven.*
>
> *Again I say unto you, That if two of you shall agree on earth as touching any thing that they shall ask, it shall be done for them of my Father which is in heaven.*
>
> *For where two or three are gathered together in my name, there am I in the midst of them.* MATTHEW 18

Saints Who Would Enlist in the Armies of The Word of God:

Following are three steps of your basic training under the Faithful and True. Exercise these steps in The LORD's Ritual of Exorcism and see how he through you will utterly consume the cause and core of evil in the earth!

Step One: The Binding on Earth and the Binding in Heaven

> *Verily I say unto you, Whatsoever ye shall bind on earth shall be bound in heaven: and whatsoever ye shall loose on earth shall be loosed in heaven.*

1. Give Jesus' "I AM Lord's Prayer" three times:

    Our Father who art in heaven,
    Hallowed be thy name, I AM.
    I AM thy kingdom come
    I AM thy will being done
    I AM on earth even as I AM in heaven

I AM giving this day daily bread to all
I AM forgiving all life this day even as
I AM also all life forgiving me
I AM leading all men away from temptation
I AM delivering all men from every evil condition
I AM the kingdom
I AM the power and
I AM the glory of God in eternal, immortal manifestation—
All this I AM. (3x)

With this sevenfold scientific affirmation of your being on earth and in heaven, you begin your ritual with the sealing of your soul in the Sacred Heart of Jesus and of every ascended master serving with him. This is the *Lord's* Prayer—the *I and My Father Are One* Prayer—which he gives within the blessed soul whom he has chosen to be his vessel. It is the prayer of the Guru within the chela who has joyously accepted the role of the servant.

It is the prayer of the soul in whom the Father and the Son have taken up their abode, as he promised: "He that hath my commandments, and keepeth them, he it is that loveth me: and he that loveth me shall be loved of my Father, and I will love him, and will manifest myself to him.... If a man love me, he will keep my words: and my Father will love him, and we will come unto him, and make our abode with him."

This prayer is spoken in the Christ consciousness by the soul whose self-awareness as the Grail enables him to understand that the affirmation I AM is the Word. This Word "with him" confirms that God who dwells in him, who is I AM THAT I AM, is the fulfillment of the Law. The Law expressed as the spoken Word is the command of the Father spoken by the Son who has raised the soul one with himself in the Threefold Flame of the heart.

This I AM version of the Lord's Prayer is the one given to the disciples whom he taught the path of joint-heirship—joint inheritance of the I AM Presence. This prayer is for initiates who, in his likeness, think it not robbery to make themselves, in Christ, equal inheritors of the Light. And Jesus, the LORD of the Path of the Ruby Ray, has transmitted this sevenfold affirmation for his disciples today through his witness, Mark L. Prophet, who was also embodied as the writer of the gospel bearing his name.

The Lord's Prayer recorded by Matthew and Luke is for children who yet pray to the Father and the Son as external to themselves. For they have not yet known of their freedom to elect to be initiates of the Lion, the Calf, the Man, and the flying Eagle on the path of individual Sonship. Their religion is hence *exoteric* until they choose to enter the path of the Grail mysteries whereby that which is external now becomes internal, i.e., *esoteric*.[1]

Needless to say, the esoteric format is essential to all who would obey the injunction, "In my name, cast out devils!" For very few today who have it not (neither the fullness of the Word's opening of the seven-sealed book that I AM giving herein) are able to obey these injunctions of their Master whom they adore. It is the finishing of his mysteries, which are my own, which they require. And I shall finish them here and hereafter. And if the dear followers of God will accept my Word, they will indeed do the "greater works" he prophesied of them.

2. Give the Hail Mary three times:

> Hail, Mary, full of grace. The Lord is with thee. Blessed art thou among women and blessed is the fruit of thy womb, Jesus.
>
> Holy Mary, Mother of God, pray for us, sons and daughters of God, now and at the hour of our victory over sin, disease, and death. (3x)

This is the consecration of your soul to the Immaculate Heart of Mother Mary. She, the Blessed Mother, holds in her right arm the authority of the judgments of her Son. She holds the soul who invokes her intercession in her most Sacred Heart. For I have sealed my white flame as the lily within her heart. And she, the complement of the Archangel Raphael, guards the purity of the soul's blueprint of life by her own purity.

Her meditation is upon the image immaculate of Christ, out of whom every soul is made by God in the beginning. Her own Immaculate Heart is the mirror of the heart of the Father, hence she is Mother. In this mirror she, the Virgin, steadfastly fixes her gaze upon the pure desire of God, his loving and most illumined will for each of his offspring.

This reinforcement of the divine design (which every soul evolving in the Matter spheres is free to outpicture) by the very force of her cosmic mind is the sustaining grace which Mary brings to all who love her Son and serve side by side with her in his name. Upon all that would hurt or destroy in all my holy mountain where I, the Ancient of Days, keep the Flame of Life for my sons and daughters, she swiftly invokes the judgment of the right arm of the Almighty.

Upon all who assail the bastions of the soul sealed in my immaculate image and held in her Immaculate Heart, she calls forth the binding, blinding light of Elohim to confound them in their anti-Christ destructivities. She can be seen in this mode standing before my throne with Jesus—her right arm descending with his and with my own. On other occasions, she pleads for infinite mercy on behalf of souls who are the hapless victims of Error. She is truly Mother to all who love Light and the protagonist who leads the legions of Light against the enemies of the vision and virtue of her children.

The Hail Mary is the salutation to the Universal Mother, to the Personal Mother whom the Blessed Mary is become, to the Guru above and below, *and to Me*. For I AM Sanat Kumara, and I loudly proclaim that I occupy the Office of the Woman both here and hereafter and I AM he who sitteth on the great white throne! And every servant son and daughter of my flame who has attained the initiation of the Crucifixion, the Resurrection, and the Ascension answers the call of the Hail Mary. It is the invocation to the Life universal and triumphant. And that is the Mother flame. It is the Ray, or Light, of the Ma held in the crystal of the crown of life by all who have received it from the Son.

Indeed the Hail Mary is the universal prayer to the Universal Mother multiplied, wherever it is given, by every ascended and angelic being worlds without end. Truly when you enter into communion with the Mother in the secret chamber of your heart, you flow with her Lifestream through all life.

This is why her heart is sacred. It is the crossroads of the light trackings of the saints of all of the cosmos—their comings and their goings in her heart—the prayers and praise and deeds well done unto her glory. When you meditate with the Ma of the Guru that I AM, you are suspended in the eye of the antahkarana of far-off worlds.

I AM Sanat Kumara. I AM suspended within the Immaculate Heart of the Mother, MaRay. I AM WHERE I AM. I would be where you are. I will place a replica of myself with the Ishwara in the secret chamber of the heart of all who faithfully give the rosary and, with the Lioness, her ritual of the exorcism of the souls of her children.

3. After you have given the Hail Mary three times with deep devotion to her heart and an intense visualization of her Light Presence standing before you, you are ready for "The Binding on Earth and in Heaven and the Naming of the Entity."

This means that you, the disciple having fulfilled the requirements of the law of Love, have the authority from Jesus Christ to exorcise evil in the Spirit and Matter chakras of my people, in the four lower bodies, and in the seven planes within the "earth" and "heaven" of the Matter spheres. The chakras below the heart are the "earth," or Matter, chakras. The chakras above the heart are the "heaven," or Spirit, chakras. And the heart itself, which must also be purified of impure desire, represents the threshingfloor of your earthly and your heavenly consciousness synthesized in the Threefold Flame and illustrated in the interlaced triangles of ascending Matter and descending Spirit.

"In the name of the I AM THAT I AM, in the name of the Father, and of the Son, and of the Holy Spirit, and in the name of the Mother, I AM the binding on earth and I AM the binding in heaven of the cause and core of this condition and consciousness of the Devil and his agents, embodied or disembodied, manifesting in and through this _____ entity."

Here the general or specific name of the possessing, tormenting demons or the foul and unclean spirits is pronounced. If their name is not known, you must describe to the best of your ability the condition and the consciousness of evil which you desire in God to exorcise "on earth" and "in heaven." Then you must invoke the Presence of the two witnesses who will pronounce in heaven and on earth, in Spirit and in Matter, the name, or names, that is the key to the casting out of the legion or the lone discarnate or incarnate entity. (Read Luke 8:26–39.)

4. Now give the "Invocation of the Presence of the Hierarchy of the Ruby Ray and the Great White Throne Judgment of the Ancient of Days." This may be given in its entirety, or it is possible for you to name only those entities of Evil which pertain to the specific demonstration of the Great Law in which you are engaged. The inserts numbered from 1 to 8 indicate the conditions and consciousness which challenge your initiations on the seven rays and the eighth ray. Those of the ninth and tenth rays will be given in our future work.

"By the full power and authority of the Lamb vested within me, by the light of the Ruby Ray, I invoke the Presence here and now of the LORD GOD Almighty, the Holy Trinity and the Mother manifest in the Person of Lord Sanat Kumara, the Ancient of Days, Gautama Buddha, Lord Maitreya, Jesus Christ, the two witnesses, and the living saints; all of the hosts of the LORD's hierarchy serving with them in heaven and on earth through the Threefold Flame of the entire Spirit of the Great White Brotherhood and the great multitude of the children of the Most High God.

"I call forth the judgment of the Father, the Son, the Holy Spirit, and the Mother through the Ancient of Days, who sitteth upon the great white throne, the four cosmic forces and the four and twenty elders, the Cosmic Council and the Karmic Board, the eternal Lamb and the embodied Lamb upon the entities of Evil—"the beast that was, and is not, and yet is," the personal and planetary dweller on the threshold—the cause/effect, record/ memory of the seed of the Wicked One, their conditions, circumstances, and hate and hate creations: War, Famine, Plague, Pestilence, and Pain; Death and Hell and whosoever is not found written in the Lamb's book of life, their words and works of iniquity wrought through:

1. "The Devil in the person of the Antichrist and his antihierarchy of antichrists; Satan, his seed, and his fallen angels; the original murderer and his murder—who subvert the authority of the Son manifest in the Great White Brotherhood and usurp the office of the Man occupied in Spirit by Jesus Christ and the hosts of his hierarchy;

2. "The Devil in the person of the Dragon; Lucifer, his seed, and his fallen angels, his clones and carbon copies of the carnal mind, his Watchers and their godless, soulless creation—who subvert the authority of the Father manifest in the Great White Brotherhood and usurp the office of the Lion occupied in Spirit by Lord Maitreya and the hosts of his hierarchy;

3. "The Devil in the person of the False Prophet and his false hierarchy of false prophets—who subvert the authority of the Holy Spirit manifest in the Great White Brotherhood and usurp the office of the Calf occupied in Spirit by Gautama Buddha and the hosts of his hierarchy;

4. "The Devil in the person of the Great Whore and the scarlet coloured beast full of names of blasphemy; the antiChurch and its anti-apostles and false pastors; the Adversary of the Ancient of Days and his hierarchy of adversaries of our twin flames drunken with the blood* of the saints and the martyrs of Jesus—who subvert the authority of the Mother, the eternal Lamb and the Lamb's wife, the Great Guru and his ascended chelas manifest in the Great White Brotherhood and usurp the office of the flying Eagle occupied in Spirit by Sanat Kumara and the hosts of his hierarchy;

---
*light

5. "The Devil in the person of the Serpent, his seed, and his fallen angels; the original liar and his lie; the embodied seed of the Wicked One; the false Christs and false prophets in Church and State, the spoilers and the false witnesses—who subvert the authority of the Son and usurp the office of the Man occupied in Matter by the messengers of the Word, the two witnesses of the Second Advent of THE LORD OUR RIGHTEOUSNESS, by the friends of God in Church and State, and by the true Christs and true prophets;

6. "The Devil in the person of the Accuser of the Brethren; the Laggards against the Light, the fallen ones, and the clock of betrayers; Abaddon, his fallen angels and the devils and beasts out of the bottomless pit that make war with the Lamb and his chosen and faithful—who subvert the authority of the Father and usurp the office of the Lion occupied in Matter by the saints who are the sons and daughters of God, the 144,000, and the remnant of the Woman's seed who keep the flame in the white cube of the Church Universal and Triumphant;

7. "The Devil in the person of the beasts out of the sea and out of the earth and the dragon who gave them their power, seat, and great authority; the one named blasphemy: his image, mark, name, and number, 666; and their agents in the one-world government and economy, the international bankers and money changers and the capitalist/communist conspirators, manipulators of the Law of the Abundant Life, and the light of Alpha and Omega in the sacred labor of the children of God; the Archdeceivers of mankind; demons and discarnates working through the godless, soulless creation of the monstrous mechanization concept—who subvert the authority of the Holy Spirit and usurp the office of the Calf occupied in Matter by the great multitude who are the children of the Most High God;

8. "The Devil in the person of Babylon the Great; the anti-State and the anti-City; her sins and sorceries, her devils, and foul spirits; the Watchers and their godless creation, their fornication—misqualifying the light of the Mother chakra, suffering

the abuse and abortion of Her children; their cults of money and the money beast, of greed and gluttony, their beasts of sensuality and materialism and their murder of the prophets and the saints; the False Guru and his false hierarchy of false gurus and their false chelas; the councils of black magicians and practitioners of the black arts and adepts of the left-handed path; witches and warlocks and their covens of wit-craft and wish-craft, Death and Hell—and all who subvert the authority of the Mother, the embodied Lamb, and the Lamb's wife, The Guru Ma and her unascended chelas, and usurp the office of the flying Eagle occupied in Matter by the Woman clothed with the Sun and her Manchild embodied in the initiates of the Ruby Ray who keep the flame of the Mystery School in the Community of the Holy Spirit;

"Jezebel and her children, the fearful and unbelieving, and the abominable, and murderers, and whoremongers, and sorcerers, and idolaters, and all liars; all who blaspheme the name of God and his Son Jesus Christ and repent not of their deeds to give Him the glory; all demons, discarnates, laggard evolutions and fallen ones, with their mass entities and monstrous mechanization* of every type and form of the four beasts of animal magnetism and the little horn of aggressive mental suggestion focused in their astral grids and forcefields; and any thing that defileth, worketh abomination, or maketh a lie against the Holy City or the temple of the LORD GOD Almighty and of the Lamb.

"I command it done in the name of the living Word. I command it done in the name of the Father, and of the Son, and of the Holy Ghost, in the name of the Woman and her seed, the entire Spirit of the Great White Brotherhood and the World Mother, elemental life—fire, air, water, and earth!

"It is done, it is finished, it is sealed!
It is done, it is finished, it is sealed!
It is done, it is finished, it is sealed!
For the mouth of the LORD hath spoken it!
I AM THAT I AM!"

---
*multiplication

5. Give "They Shall Not Pass!" (see page 110) three times.

6. Conclude with the "Transfiguring Affirmations of Jesus the Christ" three times:

> I AM THAT I AM
> I AM the Open Door which no man can shut
> I AM the Light which lighteth every man that cometh into the world
> I AM the Way
> I AM the Truth
> I AM the Life
> I AM the Resurrection
> I AM the Ascension in the Light
> I AM the fulfillment of all my needs and requirements of the hour
> I AM abundant supply poured out upon all life
> I AM perfect sight and hearing
> I AM the manifest perfection of being
> I AM the illimitable Light of God made manifest everywhere
> I AM the Light of the Holy of Holies
> I AM a son of God
> I AM the Light in the holy mountain of God   (3x)

Practice this, step one of your ritual, until I return with steps two and three. You are held safe and secure in the everlasting arms of God as I AM with you in righteousness (the right use of his energy) to "judge and make war."

I AM

Sanat Kumara

and I remain The Word of God.

See Matt. 18; John 14; Rom. 8; Phil. 2:5–8; Matt. 6:5–13; Luke 11:2–4; 1:26-38; Isa. 11:9; 65:25; Rev. 2, 6, 9, 10, 12, 13, 14, 16–22. Matt. 13:24–43; 1 John 2, 4; 2 John; John 8; Matt. 7, 24; Luke 6; Jer. 23; Luke 13, 21; 1 Pet. 5; Gen. 3; Judg. 2; 2 Kings 17; 1 Sam. 13, 14; Jer. 12, 51; Matt. 26; Acts 6; 1 Kings 18–21; Dan. 7, 8.

27

The LORD's Ritual of Exorcism
Steps Two and Three

Saints following Him upon White Horses,
   Clothed in Fine Linen, White and Clean:
      Your horses are your four lower bodies which you ride—and take care that they do not ride you! They are white because they have become crystal-clear figures for the light of the figure of the Lamb. They are the four transparencies that form the white cube of the Lamb's wife. The fine linen with which you are clothed is the whiteness and cleanness of your auric field. See that it is so, else you will not ride with the armies of the Faithful and True. Therefore, agree on earth in my name that it shall be so, and pursue with the sharp sword of diligence steps two and three of your ritual. It is the Light that does not fail!

Step Two: The Agreement on Earth

Again I say unto you, That if two of you shall agree on earth as touching any thing that they shall ask, it shall be done for them of my Father which is in heaven.

Two or more saints of the Church Universal and Triumphant should assemble together for The Ritual of Exorcism at least once in every twenty-four-hour cycle until the desired results of their very specific invocation have fully manifested. Together they shall repeat:

"In the name of Jesus Christ, in the name of the Lamb incarnate, in the name of the beloved I AM Presence and Christ Self of all and by the full power of the Holy Spirit, we agree together on earth that this thing that we ask in thy name, O Lord God Almighty—*I AM THAT I AM, ELOHIM, EL SHADDAI*—shall be accomplished according to the holy will of God, by thy wisdom, and by thy love, in time and space and in the eternal cycles of being."

Here make a clear and concise statement of that which is to be accomplished in the holy name of God. Always ask that your desire be purged by the sacred fire until it become God-desire and that your prayer be the prayer of the Son of God within you, wholly acceptable as an offering in the sight of God and his holy angels. And give to your Christ Self the authority to disavow any vow, dynamic decree, will or intent, reason, motive, or cause that does not express the God-harmony, God-love, and God-truth of his Presence.

The first step in The Ritual of Exorcism is the action of the Father in your midst which is accomplished according to his law above and below through his emissaries, the archangels, the Elohim, and the Lords of the Rays. In the second step of the ritual, you take counsel together with the sons of God, the ascended masters; and by the deliberations of their councils made known to you through the Son of God and his two witnesses, you agree on earth as they agree in heaven concerning the course of the outpicturing of the Word within the Community of the Holy Spirit and within the world community.

This is your lawful implementation of the Word: "Thy kingdom come. Thy will be done on earth, as it is in heaven." And the good shepherds anointed by the World Teachers are to be consulted by the children of God as the elders of the Church in order that their petitions might reflect the tone and tenor of the dispensations forthcoming from the Cosmic Council, the four and twenty elders, and the Karmic Board. Agreement in heaven and on earth is by the white flame of God-harmony, verily the arm of the Holy Spirit manifest through the Son as one God, I AM THAT I AM, within you.

Step Three: The Gathering Together in the Name I AM THAT I AM

For where two or three are gathered together in my name, there am I in the midst of them.

The third step in The Ritual of Exorcism is the gathering together in the name of the LORD, the Beloved Mighty I AM Presence and the Christ Self, of the twos and threes unto the ministering thousand thousands and the ten thousand times ten thousand who stand before my throne—my Threefold Flame which is my scepter and my authority—and the numberless numbers who affirm the law and the judgments of the Ancient of Days and of my name, I AM THAT I AM. This is the action of the Holy Spirit in the full diapason of the causal bodies of the saints who commune in the living Word, Jesus Christ and the hierarchy of servant-sons who are with him above and below on the Ruby Ray, and allow that Word to flow through the seven centers of being as the flow of harmony for the healing of believers and the sealing of their circle of oneness.

The repetition of the name of God followed by the affirmation and confirmation of the Word in action in dynamic decrees is the teaching of the prophets of Israel and the rishis of the Himalayas. It is the mystery of the Word revealed by the seventh angel, Saint Germain, to his servants the Prophets. In every sign and cycle, it is the exercise of the lost Word. It is the reawakening of priests and priestesses of the sacred fire who tended Lemurian and pre-Lemurian altars with the science of invocation of the sacred tone through the syllables and sounds of ancient and angelic tongues.

The practice of this universal science of the Ancient of Days is never vain when the practitioner engages his energies with the energies of God lovingly, obediently, trustingly, with the full-orbed illumination of his Higher Self which discloses the Law of the Logos as the manifest power of change within him. My beloved, learn this art and change the past, change the present, change the future, and dwell in the Eternal Now!

Indeed, the science of invocation is no more vain than the endless repetition of the planets and stars and sun-fire centers of the galaxies in their endless rounds as they engage in the ritual of the sustainment of the Matter universe by the very movement of their coursings. From the obedient electron to the ritual of the cells within the body of man to the rhythmic heartbeat of life everywhere—life is a grand ritual of the spoken and the unspoken Word within and without, marking the cycles of perfection becoming more and more perfect within the framework of the soul's self-conscious awareness.

Wherever the saints gather in twos and threes to witness unto the symphony of the Word, they engage their chakras with the chakras of Elohim. And by the very simple exercise itself, the dimensions of individual wholeness increase their capacity to know and to be God. Thus the affirmation of the Word becomes the reaffirmation of the Word spoken by Jesus Christ two thousand years ago that continues to reverberate in hallowed space as the saints mark the time and the season of the advent of his Second Coming into their hearts.

> *Have faith in God.*
>
> *For verily I say unto you, That whosoever shall say unto this mountain, Be thou removed, and be thou cast into the sea; and shall not doubt in his heart, but shall believe that those things which he saith shall come to pass; he shall have whatsoever he saith.*
>
> *Therefore I say unto you, What things soever ye desire, when ye pray, believe that ye receive them, and ye shall have them.*
>
> *And when ye stand praying, forgive, if ye have ought against any: that your Father also which is in heaven may forgive you your trespasses.*
>
> *But if ye do not forgive, neither will your Father which is in heaven forgive your trespasses.*

And thou shalt call upon the angels by name even as the LORD GOD Almighty, seated midst the council of his hosts, calls them by name and commands them to perform his perfect work, as above so below. The angels of the LORD appearing to God's chosen ones throughout the millennia are now identified by the two witnesses—by name, by flame, by vibration, and by the order of their hierarchical service. The Ritual of Exorcism is incomplete without this calling upon the name of the LORD as that LORD, that I AM THAT I AM, that Supreme Being, personifies himself through his manifold celestial creation.

The classification of the servants of God in Spirit and in Matter takes place under the offices of the Trinity and the Mother:

The Elohim transmit the power of the El through the Person of the Father. They are the seven Spirits who precipitate the creation by the Word of the *Creator*.

The sons and daughters of God who are one with the Word are sometimes referred to in the Scriptures under the general term 'angels'. Then again they are more accurately described as having "the appearance of a man" or as "one like the similitude of the sons of men" or as "a man in bright clothing" or as the "two men in white apparel." When they have "descended" to earth (i.e., decelerated into the Matter spheres), fulfilled their fiery destiny, and "ascended" to heaven (i.e., accelerated to the realm of Spirit), they are known more accurately as the "ascended masters."

Embodied representatives of the LORD on the path of Christhood East and West are known as disciples, or chelas. As unascended members of the Great White Brotherhood, these devotees may attain to considerable mastery and even adeptship while serving on earth and in the physical and etheric retreats of the Brotherhood. Together these "ascended" and "unascended" brethren of Jesus Christ serve with the *Preserver* of the creation by the wisdom of the mind of God.

All of the orders of archangels and their legions of angels, the seraphim, the cherubim filling the Void with the ritual of God, the dance of the hours, and the repetition of the Word are the instruments of the Holy Spirit who keep the flame of all that is Real and hold the office of the fiery *Destroyer* who consumes in due season all that is unreal.

Although the term 'angel' is used loosely to describe any spiritual being or celestial visitant, they comprise a hierarchical order which includes many orders and classifications, all functioning under the office of the Holy Spirit; whereas the ascended masters comprising the Great White Brotherhood, serving under the office of the Son of God, are distinct in their appearance of a man of God and are commonly referred to as the saints robed in white, frequently cited by John in his account of the Revelation of Jesus Christ and joyously acknowledged by Paul as "so great a cloud of witnesses."

The term 'saint', interchangeable with 'ascended master', implies the soul who, by free will, came forth from God and returned to him victoriously in life and in death; whereas angels under ordinary circumstances do not take embodiment, though in connection with the Fall many have done so in an attempt to rescue the children of God from the toils of Satan. The saint polarizes with the mind of God in Christ Jesus and he learns to take dominion over the Matter spheres and be fruitful in the Holy Spirit and multiply God's consciousness; whereas the angelic hosts, ever in the service of the sons of God, polarize with the feelings of love, joy, compassion, healing, and hope, etc., which they radiate to the whole creation through the desire body—the feelings and emotions.

The elemental beings of fire, air, water, and earth are in the tender care of the World Mother whose servants they are with the blessed Buddhas and Bodhisattvas until the hour of their Resurrection when they, too, should be raised with Christ in the rapture; for all of her children of the light shall have been caught up in his garment white within the bridal chamber.

Let, therefore, the true believers who are followers of Christ and Christians in the fullest sense of the Word fear not the ascended masters nor their names revealed by the Spirit of prophecy confirmed in the two witnesses, Mark and Elizabeth Prophet.

You have heard the gospel of God and received it. You have heard the gospel of the grace of Jesus Christ, and you have heard the gospel of the words and the works of the apostles by the Holy Spirit. Now receive the Everlasting Gospel which the LORD sends to thee, delivered by the angel flying in the midst of heaven, in the very midst of thy spirit endued with God's Spirit. For that angel comes to preach unto you who dwell on the earth, and to every nation, and kindred, and tongue, and people. And how shall he preach save through his evangels and messengers and through the preachers and teachers of the Word?

This is the gospel that is the squaring of the circle. It is the gospel of the Woman unto her seed. And it is the gospel taken by her seed and given as the seed of Christ to all who can accept its challenge to "fear God, and give glory to him; for the hour of his judgment is come: and worship him that made heaven, and earth, and the sea, and the fountains of waters."

Ye who are of the great multitude who have believed in the Spirit of prophecy, in the message of the Saviour that is salvation unto the righteous by grace, ye who have believed in the vision of apocalypse, now believe in the angel of the Everlasting Gospel and those whom he anoints to preach it unto you in my name.

I AM the Ancient of Days. I bid you, beloved saints of the inner Church, to pursue the first sign of the casting out of devils. It is the work of the initiates of the third ray, serving with the Lamb who is worthy, the beloved Paul the Venetian. See how he takes from my hand the seven-sealed book and opens your very own vortices of light for the transfer of the third ray, the pink flame that with accelerated use becomes the Ruby Ray of the initiates of the Holy Spirit.

Now pursue diligently the study of the hierarchies of the third ray—the Elohim, the archangels, and the Lords thereof who minister with Jesus Christ as the servant-sons in heaven and in earth. Study their dictations, give their decrees. For by love, only love for the lost sheep of the LORD will you cast out the devils in self and society. This gift of the Holy Spirit, this sign of his Presence within you, will come through the purging fires of love as you study the writings of the Maha Chohan recorded by the messengers and listen intently to their teaching, which is the teaching of the Great LORD, on the getting of the Holy Spirit.

All that I have given unto my messengers of the Ruby Ray concerning the science of invocation of the Word is for you, my beloved children. Our handbook for Keepers of the Flame, *Prayers, Meditations, and Dynamic Decrees for the Coming Revolution in Higher Consciousness*, includes many acceptable offerings that you will treasure and learn. Our lectures and dictations recorded in books and on tape will complete the teaching that I am not permitted to extend further in this format. The gift is already given. Believe and be baptized by the sacred fire of the Word you invoke.

When you gather in my name, neglect not the invocation to the Elohim of Exorcism, Astrea, to the Archangel of Deliverance, Michael the Great Prince, and to the Virgin Mary in whose presence the demons also believe and tremble. And neglect not the call to mighty Ray-O-Light and his legions of fearlessness flame who fearlessly bind the hordes of impostors of the Holy Spirit sent to snare the children of God by the wolves in sheep's clothing who lead their congregations in prayers of malintent and thereby become the practitioners of the black arts, vibrating with the black mass and the Black Pope and even the Satanists active in the lust of their intellectual sensualism in these latter days.

I say to you that prayers of ill will and malintent are the equivalent of witchcraft and voodoo. Yet in my name they are offered by the self-righteous, whether in the metaphysical, fundamentalist, or orthodox movements.

Take heed, you who are the challengers of Truth. Truth, in the mighty presence of Pallas Athena with shield and sword and helmet, will turn you upside down and inside out and shake up and shake out the erroneous entities who have invaded your temples, hindering your path and causing you to disobey the Truth. For the law is written: He who would challenge the Truth will be challenged by the Truth. He who is the challenger of Truth must show forth and be shown Truth and Error dwelling side by side within his consciousness.

Thus when you challenge Truth, you hasten the day of your own judgment when you will hear the word of Joshua in the person of Jesus Christ, "Choose you this day whom ye will serve, the person of Truth or the person of Error within thyself."

In the name of Truth who is the handmaid of Comfort and Comfort's dove,

I AM

Sanat Kumara

The Bearer of Bright Love

See Rev. 19; 21; Matt. 18; Rev. 10; Mark 11; Dan. 8:15; 10:16; Acts 10:30; 1:10; Rev. 3:4, 5, 18; 4:4; 7:9, 13, 14; 15:6; Rev. 14; Mark 16:15–20; James 2:19; Josh. 24. See *Prayers, Meditations, and Dynamic Decrees for the Coming Revolution in Higher Consciousness*, including 10.14 "Decree to Beloved Mighty Astrea"; 10.00 "Lord Michael"; 10.06 "Beloved Archangel Michael"; 10.07 "I AM Michael, Michael, Michael!"; 10.15 "Michael, Archangel of Faith"; 12.00, 12.01, 12.02—affirmations taken from dictations by Archangel Michael; 7.21 "Strip Us of All Doubt and Fear"; *My Soul Doth Magnify the Lord!; A Child's Rosary to Mother Mary*, albums 1–5, available on cassette and CD.

28

The Psychology of the Devils Who Also Believe and Tremble

> *And devils also came out of many, crying out, and saying, Thou art Christ the Son of God. And he rebuking them suffered them not to speak: for they knew that he was Christ.*
> LUKE 4

To the Blessed Who Pursue the Signs of the Word
and Work of the Holy Spirit in the Four Quadrants
of the Matter Sphere:

I AM here! And I have somewhat to say to thee concerning the sign of the casting out of devils.

To you who are the counselors, teachers, pastors, therapist, father, mother, or simply good neighbor to the soul obsessed, to the soul possessed, I say, Love enough! Love God enough to tarry with that one until we have done with the arrogant alter ego and God be magnified within the temple!

Yes, I say, love that soul enough as though it were a fragile blue egg held in the hand in spring, waiting for the robin to emerge and sing. The heartbeat of the little bird held in the hand is the heartbeat of a soul! By the Holy Spirit and by that Spirit only, cast out the devils, I say, and command that soul: "Be thou made whole!"

Be firm with the demons of self-deception that peer and peep out from behind that soul with the weakened identity—weakened from abuse, perhaps, and self-abuse at that. But all of life is fragile until the heartbeat of the little bird nestles in the heartbeat of God and at last knows an identity greater than its own—that indeed is its own. O my beloved who love, be willing to atone for the fragmented lives and their ignorant self-fragmentation through the ignorant misuse of life and love.

Patients preparing for surgery whose constitutions are wanting are required by their physicians to strengthen the body for what amounts to crisis when masses of tissue or tumor must be carefully removed. So it is with souls whose self-awareness is not strong, who do not as yet understand where they belong in the scheme of things twixt heaven and earth and know not their relative position to the stars, to friend or foe, nor do they know the meaning of self-worth.

Often those who have had little or no reinforcement of self-will or self-esteem or true love that cares very much cannot easily distinguish between the possessing demon and the self. There are benign entities just as there are benign tumors. These entities, chameleonlike, assume the posture and the pose of the undeveloped soul and mirror in gray tones an already disintegrating identity. Thus to remove the entity before the soul discovers true Selfhood in the I AM THAT I AM can create calamity resulting in a condition of catalepsy within the astral body where the entity resides and whence it must be cast out.

Thus we recommend the positive approach of the building up of the person that is capable of inviting the Person of the Son of God into his temple. We point out that early childhood training, school, and family environment are most essential in setting the foundation for a strong self-awareness—an ego, if you will, but an ego not self-limiting but always in the process of Self-merging. The child must know that he is important, but that he is important because he is a soul, a moving stream of consciousness in and of God.

Not the pride of the ego, but a joyous self-expression and creative self-fulfillment build confidence and place it where it must be placed—in the indwelling Godhead. This true Self is known by the soul who is taught by loving parents to esteem the search and to accept the validity of the self entering a path of self-discovery. This path, at once spiritual and material, may include every creative, educational, and recreational outlet which contributes to the building of the spiral of individuality—the veritable flame of Selfhood braced by the four sides of the Great Matter Pyramid.

Sometimes we find conditions of psychology relating to previous incarnations wherein the soul has receded, as it were, into a coma; and that which is the dominating force within the temple is but a collection of stray entities which objectivize rigid demands made upon the outer personality in the formative years. Multifragmented personalities consist of multipurposed entities magnetized by the outer mind to piece together a composite self that meets the demands of society and persons of authority it has encountered.

The entire process of outer ego-building, when it takes place under the pressures of mechanization man, often forces the delicate, sensitive, and highly evolved soul into recession within the subconscious while a completely pseudoself develops a synthetic existence and appears totally adjusted within the present civilization.

Come the preachers endued with the power of the Word! Come the preachers who believe and are baptized! Come the saints endued with the mantle and the authority of the Lamb! To such as these they speak the thundering word of Truth. Let the outer self tremble! The Guru is in the process of calling the inner chela from the depths that it might emerge to the surface of consciousness and have the courage to be and to pursue Be-ness in this life. Comes the chela who loves enough to perceive a real and living person beyond the rings of fabricated unreality. Comes the chela who has the wisdom to know that before the outer shell can be broken down, the hidden man of the heart, the veritable image of the Christ, must be addressed and entreated on behalf of the soul that is the potential to realize Godhood—Think of it! —in this very incarnation.

There is a starting point for the calling forth of the soul

from the tombs where the discarnates dwell. Love is the starting point, love is the middle way, and love is the ending point by a song, by laughter, by a poem or the music of the spheres, by the loud cry of the Master, "O soul, come forth from the tomb and live!" by friendship, by compassion. Yes, by some and all of these and more, the soul may be nurtured from sickness unto health. But always it is the wisdom of the disciple to accompany this work of the Holy Spirit with fervent prayer, deep meditation, and extensive dynamic decrees on behalf of the soul who must truly be born again before it can see the kingdom of God.

This born-again experience is a complete reorientation of consciousness, not a rearrangement of entities as is so often the case with those who are overly simplistic, unrealistically optimistic, and unsound in their approach to the science of the Holy Spirit. Such absence of professionalism that often marks those who profess to cast out devils often leads to a surface surcease from symptoms while the deep and underlying conditions of consciousness are not even penetrated.

Many criminals, once caught, have witnessed to the born-again experience. A number of these are genuine conversions by the power of the Holy Ghost, but many more are an expression of the tremendous fear and trembling of the demons who enter the vacated temples of souls bound in a hellish astral nightmare. Then it is the demons who cry out from these haunted houses, "LORD, LORD!" and, for fear of exorcism or even the incarceration or the execution of their subject, submit to a form of religion and a form of conversion merely as a device for their self-perpetuation.

The demons which run in packs like hungry wolves (whose name is Legion, for they are many) coming to the fore and then receding with the tides of the astral body and the lunar influences, may run the gamut from omnipotence to impotence, from arrogance and anger to self-pity and acute melancholy, causing the subject to engage in unexplainable weeping, punctuated by fits of highs and lows, ending in miserable depressions. Considering that the demons and entities (who themselves have no identity except the vehicles of their subjects) have various modes of self-expression characterized by addictions of drugs, alcohol, nicotine, sugar, marijuana, sloth, sensuality, and every enslaving human habit, it is not surprising that the pseudoself of the "lost soul" becomes highly defensive of the modus operandi of its own entities.

What these entities fear most is the coming of the Lamb and the servants of the Lamb and the coming into the temple, swiftly and suddenly, of the Person of the Christ Self who will then cast them out—they know—and summarily call forth the soul from the depths of unreality to face the responsibility of life in God. Therefore the one who comes in the name of the Lamb will always run the risk of inciting the anger of the entities who are to be bound as well as the resistance of the soul that does not want to be disturbed in its sleep of death.

Add to this the anger of parents, friends, and so-called loved ones who themselves exist within the four walls of the death consciousness (who have sought ego reinforcement from these about-to-be-awakened ones to whom they are related in time and space) and you will begin to understand the sinister stranglehold, the awful mesmerism that must be broken by the sudden snapping of the lightning mind of God which swoops down as a mighty eagle to gather up the infant self and soar to the safety of the Rock. Is it any wonder that the Saviour of souls declared in the presence of the hellish Adversary:

> *Think not that I AM come to send peace on earth: I came not to send peace, but a sword.*
> *For I AM come to set a man at variance against his father, and the daughter against her mother, and the daughter in law against her mother in law.*
> *And a man's foes shall be they of his own household.*

These foes are for the most part not the persons themselves but the possessing entities with which they often entirely identify and which would, if allowed, divide and conquer the entire family. Therefore is divorce and division rampant as the fallen ones attempt to destroy the souls of my little ones as they would destroy the flame of family.

Understand, then, the Initiation of the South Gate and the Person of the flying Eagle that I AM. Understand the mission of the Mother, my counterpart, who as a she-wolf protects her cubs with the fiery white wrath of God.

The five signs that follow them that believe in the Lamb and are baptized in the Lamb are the signs of the Woman's appearing—the Woman who is the bride of the Holy Spirit, the daughter of the Father, the Mother of the Son. Hence the ability of the advancing chela to cast out devils, speak with new tongues, take up serpents, drink any deadly thing, and lay hands on the sick on the west gate is directly dependent upon the interaction with the Mother flame and the Mother flame within the embodied Guru who stands on the south gate.

Mother Mary has offered herself a living sacrifice to hold the balance, for life and in life, of the intensity of the Mother flame while bearing in her very person and in her Immaculate Heart the anti-Mother momentum of the angry hordes who see the Mother coming and despise her unto the death. These despisers of the Mother are virulent and vicious discarnates who have succeeded in penetrating the consciousness of those who consider themselves to be fervent in the rituals of their religion. Nevertheless, by a false indoctrination of the false pastors, those who have not yet drunk the full cup of Christ experience an unexplainable anxiety and apprehension in the face of the ascended masters, the true teachers, and the true teachings of Christ which they are delivering to the devotees of truth.

Let the Truth be known! This abnormal apprehension is but the trembling of possessing demons and household entities who fear the ultimate fear—their extinguishment by the burning and the shining light of the Lamb within his servants.

Without the action of the mighty circle and sword of the Elohim Astrea, the sword of Archangel Michael, and El Morya's

Excalibur, those well-meaning relatives, who would otherwise welcome the truth of the Holy Spirit in their heart of hearts, often take up the cause of raging demons and in the process lose all credibility with their loved ones on the Path because of their irrational rantings and ravings. My dears, these can be explained only as the raging of the Serpent—not of the soul—seeking to devour the one possessed of it before it is itself devoured by the oncoming Light. Unfortunately, many innocent souls become the innocent victims in the cross fire of this battle of Armageddon in the midst of all of this nonawareness of who is who.

With the prophecies coming to pass, "And the brother shall deliver up the brother to death, and the father the child: and the children shall rise up against their parents, and cause them to be put to death. And ye shall be hated of all men for my name's sake: but he that endureth to the end shall be saved," the sane voice of the Keeper of the Flame who dares to love enough invokes the Word. And by the Word he casts out the tormenting devils. My beloved, without this service rendered by the few on behalf of the many, it would not be possible for the Great White Brotherhood to bring in the golden age or even to transfer this teaching heart to heart to the peoples of this planet.

So great is the fear of these foul spirits created by the Luciferians that they can be likened only to mad dogs or wild boars stampeding towards some undefined finale. Instantaneously, in answer to your call made in the name of Jesus Christ unto the hosts of the LORD—chiefly Archangel Michael and mighty Astrea—tens, hundreds, thousands, and tens of thousands of these roving demons are bound by the angels of the LORD and cast into the lake of fire where their form and ferocity is utterly consumed, nevermore to return.

If you stop and consider the state of consciousness of the planetary body, you will realize that the conditions of earth are due to unseen forms and forcefields motivating otherwise sane men and women to an unexplainable madness. Even the leaders of peoples and nations make their moves on the international chessboard calculated toward self-destruction and the destruction of their nations. Such decision making by the blind leaders of the blind can be explained only by the presence of the subtleties of obsessive and possessive demons.

The holy family is the foundation of life on earth and the key to love in well-adjusted children who fear neither the challenges of living the abundant life in this octave, nor of their karma/dharma, nor of the astral beasts of prey or disguised devils. The love of family is the love for God within each member as each one occupies with reverence and honor his appointed office of Father, Mother, son and daughter.

But take care that in your caring for one another you do not enter into the mesmerism of idolatry wherein the possessive love of persons becomes greater than your love for Christ within the *pure sons* and daughters of God. For this is the test of the Rose Cross: "He that loveth father or mother more than me is not worthy of me: and he that loveth son or daughter more than me is not worthy of me."

The honor of the soul's allegiance to Truth can be sustained only within the true family relationship set upon the rock of the will of God in Christ Jesus. Though he loved his own as his own and fulfilled the law of Moses, he lit a flame for the expanded God consciousness of the family to include the doers of the will of the I AM Presence and thereby excluded all who are not doers of that will from the disciples' circle of responsibility:

> *There came then his brethren and his mother, and, standing without, sent unto him, calling him.*
>
> *And the multitude sat about him, and they said unto him, Behold, thy mother and thy brethren without seek for thee.*
>
> *And he answered them, saying, Who is my mother, or my brethren?*
>
> *And he looked round about on them which sat about him, and said, Behold my mother and my brethren!*

For whosoever shall do the will of God, the same is my brother, and my sister, and mother.

Children of the light, if you would rise to defend your nation, your community, your family, and your own Selfhood, take up the cross of the Ruby Ray and determine with the full intensity of your conscious being to here and now contact your superconscious Selfhood, the beloved I AM Presence, and become who you really are so that you may spend the rest of your life helping the dear souls of this dear planet—all of whom are your dear family—to become who they really are by free will, free from the influences of the marauding bands of dark ones posing as angels of light. Remember, oh, remember the words given to you for this your hour of decision to be the Real Self in the very midst of multiplied unreality:

And he that taketh not his cross, and followeth after me, is not worthy of me.
He that findeth his life shall lose it: and he that loseth his life for my sake shall find it....
And whosoever shall give to drink unto one of these little ones a cup of cold water only in the name of a disciple, verily I say unto you, he shall in no wise lose his reward.

Not in the ties of flesh and blood but in the ties of souls who in love are the Body of God on earth is found the inheritance of the Kingdom of God. Thus he walked the Path of the Rose Cross not of the flesh but of the Spirit. Go and do thou likewise.

My beloved, there is no condition or circumstance, however depraved or despondent, that cannot be changed by God through the living saint who follows the Lamb in the way of surrender, sacrifice, service, and selflessness—so long as he proceeds with a right heart out of the love of the Holy Spirit for souls in distress, held in the death grip of unseen devils. Let the saints who understand the source of that love in the Lamb, and themselves as extensions of his Person, rise to the larger dimensions of family responsibility and go forth to do battle for the life of the children of God.

Soldiers of Christ, soldiers of the Ruby Cross, I enlist your service under the banner of Maitreya in the most demanding and the most rewarding service of the Lamb.

In the name of Jesus Christ and by the love of the one sent I say, Cast out devils! Cast these enemies of the Light out of every household! Cast them out of the soul, the mind, the astral sheath, out of the memory, and from the folds of the garment tattered of the stranger at thy gate.

Sanat Kumara

I read to you a line from the seven-sealed book:
"Minister unto the lowly, the humble of heart,
the sick, and the sinner."

See James 2:19; Luke 4; 1 Pet. 3:4; John 3:1–8; Mark 5:1–15; Matt. 10; Mark 16:15–20; Rev. 20:7–15; 21:3–8; Matt. 15:13–14; Mark 3; 2 Cor. 11:13–15. Jesus Christ casts out devils: Matt. 4:23, 24; Matt. 8:16, 17; Mark 1:32–34; Luke 4:40, 41; Matt. 15:21–28; Mark 7:24–30. The blind and dumb demoniac: Matt.12:22–30; Mark 3:22–30; Luke 11:14–26. The demoniac at Capernaum: Mark 1:23–28; Luke 4:33–37. The demoniac boy: Matt. 17:4–21; Mark 9:14–29; Luke 9:37–50. A dumb spirit: Matt. 9:32–35. The Gadarene demoniac: Matt. 8:28–34; Mark 5:1–20; Luke 8:26–40.

29

Seven Initiations of the Saints Who Follow the Lamb

Beloved of the Lamb:

In the midst of unveiling the Word and opening the seven-sealed book, I have brought to you the message of the Lord Christ spoken unto 'the eleven'[1] just before "he was received up into heaven, and sat on the right hand of God." This message, included in the sixteenth chapter of the Gospel of Mark, though indefinite in its human origin, is most certainly of the origin divine.

And lo, the LORD, the I AM THAT I AM incarnate in Jesus Christ, returned in the hour of his ascension to the great white throne, to the Court of the Sacred Fire midst the four and twenty elders, and to the seat of authority of the Ancient of Days. It is the seat of God-government of the galaxies. It is the seat whence the sons of God descend and ascend in their coursings and their missions to the children of God scattered throughout the galaxies.

Pinpointed in time and space, this seat of the hierarchical order of the sons of God and his heavenly hosts is the God Star Sirius. This star of great outer magnitude is but the sign of the inner Sun behind the sun and the coordinate in this sector of cosmos of the Great Central Sun of all suns.

Sirius, however, is a reference point. It is a point for your meditation upon the God consciousness of the spheres. For within the nuclei of star centers is a law of harmony that governs all of cosmos. Meditation upon this law and upon the physical representation of this law, specifically in the God Star Sirius, is a connecting point to souls of earth with inner threads of light and cords that bind the soul to higher dimensions of cosmic consciousness ensouled by Elohim.

Thus we counsel you, beloved of the Lamb, to move in your meditation from the outer manifestation of universal principles to the inner realization of the Void of which they are the sign and the symbol. The physical composition of Sirius and its binary star is like so many other stars. When we speak of *the* God Star, we speak of a plane of consciousness where life has accelerated to etheric perfection and to the octaves of light beyond the highest frequencies yet within the range of what is called Matter.

The planes of heaven beyond the planes of time and space are exalted in the God Star through the God consciousness of the vast being known as Surya. Surya, the Great Guru, and his chela, the Ascended Master Cuzco, are the ensouling divinities of these two points of light that move as one—as Alpha and Omega in a positive/negative polarity.

Within the spiral staircase of the planes of heaven ensouled by them, Enoch was shown the beauties and the mysteries of a life far, far beyond the earth earthy into which the children of Adam had descended. From the God Star, Enoch had descended and to it he ascended. It is the home star of the messengers and the avatars who have one and all come to earth bearing the light of the Mother Star (chakra) to fan the fires of Love on the hearts' altars of earth's evolutions.

Why do I speak to you of Sirius? O my children, I speak to you for the awakening of your souls to the memory of the Ancient of Days and our togetherness in the vast millenniums and in the forever fastnesses of the Almighty. To put you in contact with the inner light of Sirius is my office. As the mediator of that light, I am the bearer of comfort to your souls who mourn the loss of the light of Mother and who are now ready to reestablish the tie to the great white throne, the seat of the Great White Brotherhood whence you descended so long ago.

This is the hour of the preparation for the ascent. Since last I wrote to you before the autumn equinox, one among your members was taken by God in the ritual of the ascension, neath the rod of Serapis Bey, to the Court of the Sacred Fire. Amen. A soul returned to the point of divine origin.

Her ascent is the weaving of a spiral staircase, a ladder of light from your heart to the heart of the God Star. And what do you see but numberless angels of the Nameless One ascending and descending this ladder of light. These angels carry your meditations of the Mother, your powerful prayers imploring the LORD for deliverance and salvation unto his people. And the angels descending carry the authority of the Word from the office of the Lamb who is worthy.

It is here in the Court of the Sacred Fire that I, the Ancient of Days, receive each son and daughter of God whose earthly record is stamped "Mission Accomplished." Thus I have received the Lord Jesus and each and every soul who has mastered the inner blueprint of life by acceleration into the God flame that is the center of the blueprint and the origin whence it came.

I speak to you of the ascension and of ascension's power. For that very ascension and that very power are for your daily affirmation of the Word. And by and by, the perfection of that Word will return to you out of the Void of the God Star your own ascension in the light. And the power it confers is yours to transfer to the lesser lights of the universes.

Well should you acclaim the Ascended Lady Master Kristine, the new name given to Florence Jeannette Miller. For in acclaiming the name of the one chosen, you take a single step—the all-important step—toward the Nameless One. This One shall one day confer upon you, my beloved (in the not too distant future as the vast cycles of Life unfold), the new name "which no man knoweth saving he that receiveth it," written in the white stone, that issues from the fiery core of your own I AM Presence.

The sign of the ascendant son of God is the sign of your own soul's return to the Mother flame in the fullness of time and space. And, my beloved, when all initiations of the Ruby Ray have been fulfilled, it becomes the signal for the opening of the seven-sealed Book of Life—your own life and life record. For in the final analysis, only you can open that seven-sealed book. It is the book which contains the law of your innermost being—you in the Son and in the Father and in the Holy Ghost—you fulfilling the gospel of all three and then tracing, by your soul's comings and goings here and there and everywhere on earth, the gospel foursquare.

Your outpicturing of that gospel day by day is your Dharma—your duty to be yourself and the instrument of the Teacher and the teaching who is your Real Christ Self. This Dharma of Selfhood realized in the Teacher and the teaching is the cornerstone of each one's divine plan, each one's own building of the Great Pyramid of Life. What one initiate has done, all initiates must do. Thus the Great Pyramid of Life, your life lived in God, is founded upon the Threefold Flame of the threefold gospel of the Trinity which you, my beloved, demonstrate for the children of God with all of the 'signs following' of the foursquare gospel made manifest by the Mother and the Maitreya within you.

Pause, then, for a moment in your pilgrimage, you who are the bearers of the Rose Cross, and contemplate the mystery of the ascension of your co-worker and friend, a chela of El Morya whom I now defend as the example and forerunner on the Path of the Ruby Ray.

In the hours between her soul's transition from the physical to the etheric planes on September 17 and her ascension on September 20, beloved Florence was received by Saint Germain with Lanello and magnificent seraphim standing by at the Royal Teton Retreat. From noon on Monday until Thursday at dawn, while the Mother and disciples kept the vigil at the Matter tomb, she was instructed by the Brotherhood in the role the LORD had called her to portray on the Path of the Ruby Ray, an example and a sign for chelas today and generations to come of the acceleration of light within the soul and its four outer vehicles.

Her path for many centuries had been that of surrender, self-sacrifice, service, and selflessness guided by the ascended masters under the four cosmic forces. Always living for the mission of the Guru and my messengers, she transcended earthly modes and manifestations. Her light filled the cups of consciousness to overflowing, creating new streams of immersion in Christ's love for all following the breezes of her billowing bridal garment.

The Lady Kristine—'twas the name given her by Saint Germain at La Tourelle—was then taken to the Cave of Symbols where, in the company of beloved Rex, Nada, Bob, and Pearl (ascended master youth who received the initiations for the ascension under the auspices of the Great Divine Director, Saint Germain, Lady Master Leto, and the messengers Godfre and Lotus in the 1930s), she (her soul in her etheric/mental/feeling vehicles while her physical vehicle lay unconscious in the hospital) was seated in the atomic accelerator known as the ascension chair.[2]

By means of this astounding apparatus invented by Saint Germain, the ascension flame spirals through atoms, cells, and molecules of sheath upon sheath of the outer and inner consciousness, preparing them for the ritual of consummate love whereby the soul is wed to Spirit in the actual ascension.

This light intensifying in the soul who is servant of the Most High—who has balanced at least fifty-one percent of her karma and concluded her round of earthly incarnations—is that *grace* of the LORD (the Christ who is Guru) whereby the words and works of the chela are stepped up, up, up beyond the earthly orbit and the laws of atomic weight, density, and gravitation until the soul is, as it were, 'free floating' in the octaves of Spirit. Thus, for those who have earned the ascension, the ascended masters provide this and other magnificent tools for the implementation of the victory.

If this sounds too fantastic, beloved, you had better know that the many mansions of the Father's house, which include the etheric retreats of the Great White Brotherhood, contain even more fantastic inventions affecting every aspect of the evolution of life on earth and elsewhere. Is it not written: "Eye hath not seen, nor ear heard, neither have entered into the heart of man, the things which God hath prepared for them that love him"?

When you hear of unconventional, unorthodox things of the Spirit, you must consider that even the *pneumatika*, spiritual gifts of the Holy Ghost, were at one time unknown and unheard of and are even today scoffed at. Then perhaps you can begin to see why the LORD has hid these things from the wise and prudent and has revealed them unto babes.

Such a rut of the astral plane and of concrete intellectualism are the dear people of this planet fallen into, that almost any new teaching as pertains to life after death and existence on the etheric plane between successive incarnations of the soul is considered by many to be spurious or synthetic—just because it is new. Just because *they* have never heard of it before. Just because "it isn't in the Bible"!

Well, we thank God that we have a messenger who is not only an eyewitness to these events which take place on the etheric plane but who also has the courage to deliver to you our "far, far out" messages in the face of the fast and furious ridicule of the crows cawing on the fence. And we thank God that we have chelas who know the meaning of being the LORD's vessel.

Our chelas are our cups. They contain our certain word of prophecy. Thus the torch that is passed is not dropped, and this generation is not about to lose the most precious gift of the avatars of the ages: The Continuity of The Word.

With the ascension of the Lady Kristine, the saying that is written is come to pass: "Then shall two be in the field; the one shall be taken, and the other left. Two women shall be grinding at the mill; the one shall be taken, and the other left." And the one taken could not go on to the other shore of God's consciousness unless the one left remained on this bank of the river of life. And the one left could not remain on this bank unless the one taken crossed over the river of life to the other shore.

And John Baptist was taken and Jesus Christ was left.[3] And by and by the LORD was taken and the apostles were left. And then they were taken and you, my beloved disciples, were left—

lo, these two thousand years—to fulfill the gospel foursquare, to preach the living Word until the acceptable year of the LORD's incarnation within you, bodily. Then, when he should come to you personally in the Second Advent and when, in the Person of the Christ, you should have accomplished the preaching of the gospel in all the world for a witness unto all nations—then and only then shall the end of the spiral of your own soul's incarnations in the earth earthy come.

That hour is coming for all who worship the King of kings by words and works of love and only love. This is the accelerated Path of the Ruby Ray that promises to all the fullness of Life here and hereafter, the never-ending cycles of the Life lived universally and triumphantly forever and forever.

Yes, your beloved Florence ascended in the presence of our two witnesses and that company of angels from whose bands she had descended so long ago to go after the lost sheep of her Father's house. She has returned gloriously gratified and beatified with many sheep in her arms. May you also, my beloved. Her garment may you touch for strength and hope in the essence of her holiness, and for nearness to your heavenly Spouse.

For this cause and to this end we take you by the hand and lead you step by step. This we did with the Lady Kristine. And now she, the patroness of Holland, will walk with you the very same steps for your victory. And the Body of the LORD as the body of believers above and below are one, fortifying souls and fasting earthly senses for one another's victory.

Basking in the love of one who has become that Woman clothed with the sun[4] giving birth to the Christ consciousness with the World Mother in all of her children, let us return with all diligence to the subject at hand:

In order to define and refine for you the profound meaning of my Word spoken through the Lord Jesus Christ, I have already taken you through seven releases of light in the Pearls of Wisdom. This I have done not by way of digression from my subject, the opening of the seventh seal, but rather to enable you to fulfill the law of the Lamb who is worthy.

There are two commands of the Father and the Son and five signs of the Holy Spirit which follow the word and works of those who obey them. These seven initiations under the Mother flame are set forth [in Mark 16] within the final admonishment to the initiates of the Lamb given by the Lord Jesus prior to his ascension. The obedience of those disciples who were left while he was taken is noted by the promised signs which accompanied them as they preached everywhere.

Because they obeyed the command to preach the Word of the Ancient of Days, because they believed in the incarnate Word—the actual embodiment of the I AM THAT I AM *as* the LORD in Jesus Christ—and were baptized by the immersion of consciousness in the Father and the Son and by communion in the body and blood of Alpha and Omega—they were empowered by the Holy Ghost to cast out devils by the Sacred Name of the Father and the Son as I have taught you to do in the giving of The LORD's Ritual of Exorcism.

Each of these seven points of the law of individual Christhood is yours to fulfill under the seven chohans of the rays. The chohans are anointed by me to administer these initiations to earth's evolutions. Each of them is become the Lamb worthy to open the seven-sealed book and has indeed taken that book from my right hand, being thereby fully empowered as the Lord of the Ray—the embodiment of the Law of the Ray—unto you who are yet striving to enter into the fullness of the white-fire core of each of the seven rays.

To submit oneself to these seven servant-sons for training and testing in the laws of Christhood in preparation for the Second Advent is indeed a point of humility and earnestness which is never overlooked by the recording angels or the Lord Christ himself. Whereas to demand that the LORD of the vineyard come down to you when he has already sent both his servants and his Son is to ignore the hierarchical chain that functions as a coiled spring.

Coil by coil the light of the Godhead is transferred to you by emissaries of the Most High eminently qualified to occupy the spirals of the vast chain of hierarchical light, accelerating and decelerating to accommodate the varying needs of the evolutions of cosmos. Just as you, my beloved, represent me and my office and the entire lineage of the Ruby Ray to those who do not know of us—our name, our Word, our vibration—just as those who receive you, receive me—for I AM in you and you are in me—so it is a key initiation for all who would approach the throne of grace to receive the one sent by the Master—his messenger, his prophet, his witness.

The chohans are this. They represent the Christ in the capacity of forerunner. When you receive them in their name and office, you receive the reward of their name and office—an actual portion of the light of their Christ consciousness conferred upon them by the LORD. And through them and their proximity to Him on the coiled spring of cosmos, you are that much nearer your personal Saviour.

Thus under El Morya you submit to the exercise of the power of the Word—preaching the gospel to every creature. Under Lord Lanto, you trust and obey the Guru/chela relationship by believing and being baptized. And under Paul the Venetian, you learn to embody that measure of love whereby you cast out devils in the name of Christ's love simply because the accelerated love of the Ruby Ray is intolerable to them.

Now this is a point of the Great Law which I must develop before taking up the initiation of the fourth ray: The demons cannot assimilate the pure love of Christ as love; therefore, it assimilates them. This love is the all-consuming fire of the Holy Ghost which consumes all unlike itself. You see, the demons function under the law of consume or be consumed—destroy or be destroyed. Let me explain.

The only way that the demons can conquer love is by turning it into hatred which then manifests on the astral plane as floating grids and forcefields of hate and hate creation directed by the demons at those children of the light in whom dwell the Trinity and the Mother flame. This perfect love—which the demons would tempt you to misqualify by turning it to fear, anxiety, self-doubt and doubt of the Greater Self (and the ghosts of other hobgoblins)—is the liberating force and forcefield that the Almighty has set in motion for the deliverance of all life.

This love is the energy that flows from the Sacred Heart of the Christed ones. It is the vital essence of the light of the Son (mystically referred to as 'the blood' and actually present within the centrosome of the cells of the bloodstream). It is the crystal clear elixir of eternal life which the Christ confers upon his disciples in the ritual of communion.

This light is coveted by the demons of Death and Hell who must have it in order to sustain their existence beyond the circle of Life in the Father and the Son. Because they have naught of Christ's love or light within them, they must vampirize it from his children.

This process is far more subtil than the popular Count Dracula/Frankenstein monster-type activity. It is rather the permeation of society by mechanized perversions of the love ray—from lust and sensuality, high-priced and high-fashioned, unnatural and unspiritual sex oozing from every advertisement and television commercial, motion pictures, and pornographic photography—all captivating the eye, the attention, hence the energy of the people—to the depressions of a self-centered existence and the art and music forms which violate the universal law of the God of Harmony, who is indeed the very God of Love.

I speak to you thus of Love. For unless you understand how desperate are the demons to convert the energy of Christ's healing love to their own vibration of anti-Light, you will not appreciate the war that is being waged from astral shores upon every part of life—the animals, the plant life, and the earth itself.

This battle of Armageddon is engaged in by the demons and all adepts of the left-handed path who employ the devils to do their 'dirty work' for the express purpose of stealing the light/

energy/consciousness of Christ (his blood) in his children and turning it against them in the ultimate defeat of the death of that soul which sinneth and repenteth not. And often, my beloved, the souls who do not repent are those who are held in the relentless death grip of the sinister force and have lost the will to live or fight or eat or breathe, so weakened are they by the heavy depression and density with which the demons weigh them down, down, down—spiritually, morally, emotionally, mentally, and physically.

Such conditions as prevail among the youth and vast segments of the population, often through drug addiction, require nothing less than Christed liberators complete with helmet and shield and the whole armour of God, accompanied by the legions of light with their flaming swords.

Now do you see, dear ones, why I have stressed the casting out of demons in my name? Earth has been invaded by the demons of the bottomless pit who have perverted the rhythm of Love in the mechanization of synthetic molecules and in the rocking of the beat of Life until it has become the rocked beat of death, perverting the Mother flame under the fallen angel Abaddon.

All of the myriad mechanizations of life that was once America the beautiful and the bountiful have for many who have no moorings in Christ's love turned their joy in life and light to the ashes of self-disintegration. For them—God have mercy—the prophecy is come to pass: "And in those days shall men seek death, and shall not find it; and shall desire to die, and death shall flee from them."

Therefore to you who are waging the warfare of The Word against the astral hordes of devils and discords polluting the mainstream of America's life and love flame I say, guard the heart as the seat of Christ's authority in you and guard the flow of Christ's energy, lovingly: God Harmony is the Sword and the Word by which we conquer. Guard the flow, guard the love, guard the light, and the earth will endure her dark night of the soul unto a glorious resurrection. And this truly is the sign of Christ's love within you, that the devils and their hate and hate creation are utterly consumed in your Presence.

The five signs of the Holy Spirit, of which this is the first, are the signs of your self-mastery on the five secret rays as well as on the path of the third, fourth, fifth, sixth, and seventh rays. Saints serving the great multitude on the west gate are undergoing these seven initiations on the seven gates simultaneously [noted on the charts on pages 247–49].

Thus the first initiation, preaching the gospel to every creature, is under the office of the Man through the Person of the Son Jesus Christ on the east gate. The second initiation of believing and being baptized is under the office of the Lion through the Person of the Father Lord Maitreya on the north gate. The third initiation, the first of the 'signs following,' is under the office of the Calf through the Person of the Holy Spirit Gautama Buddha on the west gate.

This initiation of the Ruby Ray begins the unfoldment of the five-pointed star, the sign of the coming of the Son of man within you. It continues with the second sign on the south gate under the office of the flying Eagle through the Person of the Mother and unfolds the third sign on the east, the fourth on the north, and the fifth on the west gates of the City Foursquare (in the Matter sphere) as that city is the reflection of the New Jerusalem.

The numbers one to seven [noted on the charts] refer to the numbers of the seven rays and the chakras which the LORD within you accelerates by the grace of God as you pass through the initiations given. The initiation of the eighth ray is the return to the point of the Mother at the south gate. When the ritual of oneness with the embodied Lamb has been fulfilled by the chela of The Guru Ma, then the soul accelerates over the figure-eight spiral through the ritual of the ascension and is "received up into heaven" to sit upon the right hand of God. That Mother flame, realized in the Guru/chela relationship upon earth and in heaven, always leads to the God Star, to the great white throne, and to complete identification with the Great White Brotherhood.

The initiation of the ninth ray is the return of the ascended master to the point of the Son on the east gate (in Spirit) where he is now become the LORD working with his embodied disciples confirming the presence of his Word within them by means of the signs which follow them (in Matter) whithersoever they go with the Lamb.

Thus the Ascended Lady Master Kristine has completed the eighth and begun the ninth initiations of the Ruby Ray—whilst the two prophets held the balance for her, the Mother on this side of the bridge, the Father on the other. This bridge of Life is the narrow path of initiation whereby the soul crosses the wide chasm between the nonpermanent and permanent worlds.

The dispensation of the two witnesses who come in the hour of the great gathering of the elect unto the ascension is one of holding the bridge in suspension until the elect have crossed over. This is the balance that our messengers hold for you and for all on earth who follow the cycles of the Ruby Ray. And you, my beloved, are called upon by the Darjeeling Council to hold the balance for a world and its lifewaves, that the platform for every level of evolution might be preserved and the next in line approach the bridge.

Now you who wonder what the saints in heaven are doing who watch over you may reflect upon the ministrations of the Lady Kristine whose activities on the ninth ray are very much enmeshed with your own. Ascended masters on the ninth ray are the coordinates of the embodied servants of the Lamb. They work best and most ardently with those who understand this intimate interaction twixt heaven and earth through the initiates of the degrees and are the glad, free, willing vessel for the 'holy water' of their beloved brothers and sisters.

This mutual service of love that spans the octaves and the light-years is referred to as the meshing of the bridal veils. As the bride above tosses her bouquet to the bride-to-be below, it is the conferment of the fleur-de-lis—flower of the Sacred Heart—

whereby the veil of the Cosmic Virgin shall be passed in due season to the 'maid of honor'.

The seven initiations recorded in the Gospel of Mark [16:15–18], as they are revealed by the Father, the Son, and the Holy Spirit to each devotee of the Ruby Ray, disclose an inner and an outer path, an Alpha and an Omega manifestation. The Alpha initiation is received in direct interchange with the chohan of the ray in his etheric retreat. The Omega is received directly or indirectly in the outer retreat of our mystery school through our messengers.

The three levels of experience which the soul undergoes in these initiations of the conscious, subconscious, and superconscious mind do not always register in the outer mind of the devotee engaged in study and service. The certainty of your initiation, my beloved, lies not in your outer knowing or in your outer memory, but in that self-knowledge which knows that it is engaged in the very process of life becoming Life through the Guru/chela relationship, that one is doing one's best day by day and leaving the rest to God.

Your being is a sphere, yet you entertain linear awareness. The compartments of your thinking and feeling vehicles are not always adequate to contain all of the memories of your soul's coming and goings in the octaves of light while you carry on your "role playing" on earth. Nor is it necessary that you examine every morsel of heavenly manna to be assimilated by consciousness where you are. Thus you rely upon the mediator of your Christ Self to guide and guard each outer footstep as a key to inner attainment. The ascended masters and their messengers reinforce the light of the Mediator in your life so long as you trust the living Word.

Many of our chelas are accelerating even now into an inner action of the law of their inner being beyond any level previously attained in this or past embodiments because you have studiously with great spiritual depth pondered my Word in these releases. And you have put it on as a garment to be worn daily. You see, it is our desire to bring you to the point of God-mastery on each of these seven points of the Law so that you are poised and ready on the west gate in Matter, fulfilling the Word midst the great multitude while accelerating the sacred fires of ascension's flame that are reserved for those in line behind the Ruby Ray lineage to take the eighth-ray initiation.

In preparation for the initiation of the eighth ray, you may balance all but seven percent of your karma, as many avatars have done, and remain in the earth as a true shepherd of the people for decades and longer, even returning in a succeeding incarnation to fulfill to the uttermost the bodhisattva ideal.

Once you do take the initiation of the eighth ray, your assignment on the ninth ray prior to the tenth-ray initiation of the Lamb is to serve side by side with embodied devotees until your ascended master light body is so thoroughly meshed with their outer vehicles that they can truly say, "I and my Father are one, I and my Mother are one."

Not until all of your flock who are called by the Law are chosen by the LORD to begin preparation for the eighth-ray initiation are you then invited to take the initiation of the Lamb before the great white throne. For you must be 'in earth' in your disciples simultaneously as you are 'in heaven' in your Guru to qualify for the office of Lamb who is the supreme mediator of both. And after you have attained to this level of mediatorship in the Cosmic Christ, there remain the eleventh through the fourteenth steps of initiation, which you will fulfill through continuous interaction with the lifewaves of the Spirit/Matter universes whom it is your Dharma to ensoul with the Teacher and the teaching.

My message on the opening of the seventh seal, then, is not intended to be another vicarious atonement whereby I or my seven chohans should open the Book of Life *for you*. Rather, all of our instruction is purposed by the LORD GOD Almighty to give to you a nucleus of light upon which to meditate and finally become so that you, my beloved, may also be with the sons of

God on Sirius, the Lamb who is worthy to take the seven-sealed book from my hand and to open it.

Won't you take now a seven-day cycle to review all that has gone before in these *Pearls of Wisdom* and to daily meditate upon the God Star, using the compelling call to beloved Surya in the Great Central Sun which I dictated to your Messenger Mark L. Prophet for this very moment when you should make the leap in consciousness into the fohatic light of Sirius?

I AM the Lord of Life and of the Ruby Ray unto the saints upon earth who stand and still stand as the coordinators of the saints in heaven and of the light from far-off worlds. In the seat of authority of the Great White Brotherhood, I sit upon the great white throne with the four and twenty elders and the councils of the sons of God who occupy the office of the Lamb.

I AM

Sanat Kumara

By the Threefold Flame in all Life
I AM judging the twelve tribes of Israel

See Mark 16; 1 Cor. 15:47; Rev. 5; 2:17; John 14:2; 1 Cor. 2; Matt. 11:25; 24:36–41; 24:14; 10:5, 6; 15:24; 18:12–14; 21:33–44; 10:40–42; John 6:29; Heb. 6:20; Eph. 6:10–20; Rev. 9:1–12; 14:1–5; John 10:30.

Seven Initiations of the Saints Who Follow the Lamb Mark 16:14–20

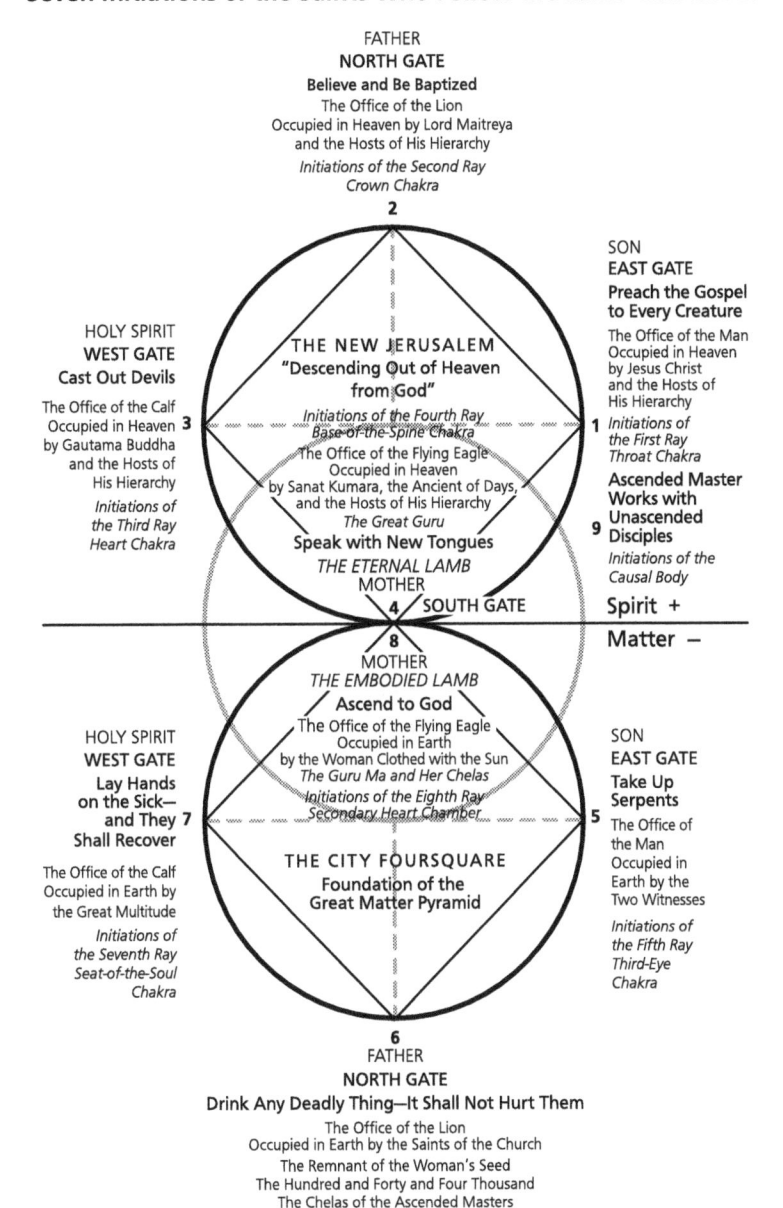

FATHER
NORTH GATE
Believe and Be Baptized
The Office of the Lion
Occupied in Heaven by Lord Maitreya
and the Hosts of His Hierarchy
Initiations of the Second Ray
Crown Chakra
2

HOLY SPIRIT
WEST GATE
Cast Out Devils

The Office of the Calf
Occupied in Heaven
by Gautama Buddha
and the Hosts of
His Hierarchy
*Initiations of
the Third Ray*
Heart Chakra

3

THE NEW JERUSALEM
"Descending Out of Heaven from God"
Initiations of the Fourth Ray
Base-of-the-Spine Chakra
The Office of the Flying Eagle
Occupied in Heaven
by Sanat Kumara, the Ancient of Days,
and the Hosts of His Hierarchy
The Great Guru
Speak with New Tongues
THE ETERNAL LAMB
MOTHER
4 SOUTH GATE

SON
EAST GATE
**Preach the Gospel
to Every Creature**

The Office of the Man
Occupied in Heaven
by Jesus Christ
and the Hosts of
His Hierarchy
1 *Initiations of
the First Ray*
Throat Chakra

**Ascended Master
Works with
Unascended
9 Disciples**
*Initiations of the
Causal Body*

Spirit +
―――――――――――――
Matter −

8
MOTHER
THE EMBODIED LAMB
Ascend to God
The Office of the Flying Eagle
Occupied in Earth
by the Woman Clothed with the Sun
The Guru Ma and Her Chelas
Initiations of the Eighth Ray
Secondary Heart Chamber

THE CITY FOURSQUARE
**Foundation of the
Great Matter Pyramid**

HOLY SPIRIT
WEST GATE
**Lay Hands
on the Sick—
and They
Shall Recover**

7

The Office of the Calf
Occupied in Earth by
the Great Multitude
*Initiations of
the Seventh Ray*
Seat-of-the-Soul
Chakra

SON
EAST GATE
**Take Up
Serpents**
5 The Office of
the Man
Occupied in
Earth by the
Two Witnesses
*Initiations of
the Fifth Ray*
Third-Eye
Chakra

6
FATHER
NORTH GATE
Drink Any Deadly Thing—It Shall Not Hurt Them
The Office of the Lion
Occupied in Earth by the Saints of the Church
The Remnant of the Woman's Seed
The Hundred and Forty and Four Thousand
The Chelas of the Ascended Masters
Initiations of the Sixth Ray
Solar-Plexus Chakra

N.B. The numbers 1 through 8 given in the Invocation of the Presence of the Hierarchy of the Ruby Ray and the Great White Throne Judgment of the Ancient of Days (in *The LORD's Ritual of Exorcism*, see pp. 208–10) are comparable to the numbers on this chart and should be compared for a greater understanding of the impostors of the hierarchy of the Ruby Ray and their positions on the eight gates of the New Jerusalem and the City Foursquare.

Seven Initiations of the Saints Who Follow the Lamb
Mark 16:14–20

	1	**The Power of the Word** And he said unto them: 1. Go ye into all the world and preach the gospel to every creature. —v. 15 (See pages 122–91)
	2	**The Wisdom of the Word** 2. He that believeth and is baptized shall be saved; but he that believeth not shall be damned. —v. 16 (See pages 173–75; 186–91)
	3	**The Love of the Word** And these signs shall follow them that believe: 1. In my name shall they cast out devils; —v. 17 (See pages 192–230)
SPIRIT / MATTER	4	**The White-Fire Purity of the Word** 2. they shall speak with new tongues; —v. 17 (See pages 251–69)
	5	**The Science and Truth of the Word** 3. they shall take up serpents; —v. 18 (See pages 270–306)
	6	**The Ministration and Service of the Word** 4. and if they drink any deadly thing, it shall not hurt them; —v. 18 (See pages 307–72)
	7	**The Alchemy of the Word** 5. they shall lay hands on the sick, and they shall recover. —v. 18
MATTER / SPIRIT	8	**The Integration of the Word** So then after the Lord had spoken unto them, he was received up into heaven and sat on the right hand of God. —v. 19 (See pages 281–85; 292)
	9	**The Signs of the Word** And they went forth and preached every where, <u>the Lord working with them</u> and confirming the word with signs following. Amen. —v. 20

Left-side brackets:
- the Word and the Work of the Woman and her seed
  - the two commands (1–2)
  - the five signs (3–7)
- the Word and the Work of the one who would be Lamb (8–9)

Afterward he appeared unto 'the eleven' as they sat at meat, and upbraided them with their unbelief and hardness of heart, because they believed not them which had seen him after he was risen. —v. 14

1	**Initiation of the east gate: the first ray, the Son.** The disciple of the LORD applies for this initiation under the office of the Man through the Person of the Son in Jesus Christ for the acceleration of the throat chakra, attaining and proving self-mastery on the first ray.	*initiations of the Threefold Flame of the Trinity*
2	**Initiation of the north gate: the second ray, the Father.** The disciple of the LORD applies for this initiation under the office of the Lion through the Person of the Father in Lord Maitreya for the acceleration of the crown chakra, attaining and proving self-mastery on the second ray.	
3	**Initiation of the west gate: the third ray, the Holy Spirit.** The disciple of the LORD applies for this initiation under the office of the Calf through the Person of the Holy Spirit in Gautama Buddha for the acceleration of the heart chakra, attaining and proving self-mastery on the third ray.	

SPIRIT / MATTER

4	**Initiation of the south gate: the fourth ray, the Mother.** The disciple of the LORD applies for this initiation under the office of the flying Eagle through the Person of the Mother in the Eternal Lamb, Sanat Kumara, for the acceleration of the base-of-the-spine chakra, attaining and proving self-mastery on the fourth ray.	*initiations of the crystallization of the God flame in the soul in Matter*
5	**Initiation of the east gate: the fifth ray, the Son.** The disciple of the LORD applies for this initiation under the office of the Man through the Person of the Son in Jesus Christ in support of the mission of the two witnesses for the acceleration of the third-eye chakra, attaining and proving self-mastery on the fifth ray.	
6	**Initiation of the north gate: the sixth ray, the Father.** The disciple of the LORD applies for this initiation under the office of the Lion through the Person of the Father in Lord Maitreya in support of the mission of the saints, chelas of the ascended masters, for the acceleration of the solar-plexus chakra, attaining and proving self-mastery on the sixth ray.	
7	**Initiation of the west gate: the seventh ray, the Holy Spirit.** The disciple of the LORD applies for this initiation under the office of the Calf through the Person of the Holy Spirit in Lord Gautama Buddha in support of the mission of the great multitude for the acceleration of the seat-of-the-soul chakra, attaining and proving self-mastery on the seventh ray.	

MATTER / SPIRIT

8	**Initiation of the south gate: the eighth ray, the Mother.** The disciple of the LORD applies for this initiation under the office of the flying Eagle through the Person of the Mother in the Embodied Lamb in support of the mission of The Guru Ma and her chelas for the acceleration of the secondary heart chamber (secret chamber of the heart), attaining and proving self-mastery on the eighth ray.	*initiations for the acceleration of the soul unto the living Spirit for the blessing of all life on earth and in heaven*
9	**Initiation of the east gate: the ninth ray, the Son.** The disciple who has become one with the LORD applies for this initiation under the office of the Man through the Person of the Son in Jesus Christ for the acceleration of the power of the Word ("All power is given unto me in heaven and in earth") in the Causal Body, attaining and proving self-mastery on the ninth ray.	

Beloved Surya

Beloved mighty victorious Presence of God, I AM in me, my very own beloved Holy Christ Self, Holy Christ Selves of all mankind, beloved Surya, legions of white fire and blue lightning from Sirius, beloved Lanello, the entire Spirit of the Great White Brotherhood and the World Mother, elemental life—fire, air, water, and earth! In thy name, by and through the magnetic power of the immortal, victorious threefold flame of truth within my heart and the heart of God in the Great Central Sun, I decree:

1. Out from the Sun flow thy dazzling bright
   Blue-flame ribbons of flashing diamond light!
   Serene and pure is thy love,
   Holy radiance from God above!

Refrain: Come, come, come, Surya dear,
   By thy flame dissolve all fear;
   Give to each one security
   In the bonds of purity;
   Flash and flash thy flame through me,
   Make and keep me ever free!

2. Surya dear, beloved one
   From the mighty Central Sun,
   In God's name to thee we call:
   Take dominion over all!

3. Out from the heart of God you come,
   Serving to make us now all one—
   Wisdom and honor do you bring,
   Making the very soul to sing!

4. Surya dear, beloved one,
   From our faith then now is spun
   Victory's garment of invincible gold,
   Our soul's great triumph to ever uphold!

And in full faith I consciously accept this manifest, manifest, manifest! (3x) right here and now with full power, eternally sustained, all-powerfully, active, ever expanding, and world enfolding until all are wholly ascended in the light and free! Beloved I AM, beloved I AM, beloved I AM!

30

The New Tongues of the Holy Spirit

> *And when the day of Pentecost was fully come, they were all with one accord in one place.*
>
> *And suddenly there came a sound from heaven as of a rushing mighty wind, and it filled all the house where they were sitting.*
>
> *And there appeared unto them cloven tongues like as of fire, and it sat upon each of them.*
>
> *And they were all filled with the Holy Ghost, and began to speak with other tongues, as the Spirit gave them utterance.*
>
> ACTS 2

To the Saints of the Lamb Who Are Come
  to Do the Will of God:

Having taken up the commands to preach the gospel to every creature, to believe and to be baptized, and to cast out devils, we come to the second sign that shall surely follow them that believe (meditate upon my Word day and night): "They shall speak with new tongues."

Truly the speaking with new tongues is a gift of the Holy Spirit that is given by initiation to the souls who ardently pursue the living Word in the preaching of his gospel and who are daily believing and being baptized by meditation on and immersion in the living Father of the Lamb. The signs of the Spirit, of which this is the second, must be desired by you with all your heart, so much so that your temple is given over to the Holy Spirit to be his dwelling place forevermore.

The Holy Spirit is the very Person of the Godhead who comes to you as the Comforter of Life. And whether he appears to you in the personages of the servant-sons of God—the ascended masters of the Great White Brotherhood—or in the rushing of a mighty wind, in the thunder and the lightning, in the cloven tongues of fire, or as the gentle dove of peace, the Holy Spirit is the Friend of all who are the friend of the Father in the Son and of the Son in the Father.

The sealing of the servants of God in their foreheads is by the Holy Ghost. And the sacred vows of the communicant before the altar of the Most High God are made to and through this same Holy Ghost. Those who would speak with new tongues must understand the elements of the pursuit of the LORD's Spirit—the intense striving of the chela of the Guru that can be explained only by the soul on fire with the holy zeal of the LORD's Spirit.

They have touched the hem of the Comforter's garment. They are entering into the fiery baptism. Hour by hour, the chelas of the will of God commune with the Word. They intone the Word and they feel the flow of the sacred fire rushing through their temples. To them, Pentecost is not a day but a lifetime of experiencing moment by moment the infilling fire of that Holy Ghost.

They understand the supreme gift of speaking with new tongues as it is given for the crystallization of the Word of God from the Spirit to the Matter cosmos. Their celebration of the Word can be heard in their masterful giving of the mantra of the Mother. It is heard in the soundless sound of the secret chamber of the heart where the soul of the devotee communes—through the agency of the Holy Spirit—with the Lord Christ himself, who enters there and initiates the cycles of an expanding Threefold Flame.

Truly the soul, born again by the Spirit, acclaims by that Spirit that Jesus Christ is the incarnation of each one's I AM Presence and Christ Self. And those who have the testimony of Jesus Christ by the true Spirit of prophecy that is upon the messengers are they which testify of him. And with the new tongue of the sacred fire they overcome the dragon by the Word—the sacred Word sharper than a two-edged sword—of their testimony.

Initiates of the will of God learn to precipitate that will by the Science of the Spoken Word. They pursue the initiations of the Lord of the First Ray, the initiations of the throat chakra, whereby they have conferred upon them *the new tongue.* As they have put off the old man and put on the new, being reborn through the individual Christ Self, so they are putting off the old tongue with its "unruly evil, full of deadly poison," as James said, blessing God while cursing men made after his similitude. These devotees are earning the new tongue worthy to be the instrument of the LORD's blessing and praise to all life.

The earning of the new tongue conveyed by the Master El Morya is by devotion to the diamond in the center of the whirlwind of the LORD's Spirit. That diamond is the point of the universal mind of God that is lowered into manifestation in the beginning and in the ending of the Word. From the Alpha to the Omega of the Word, the disciples of God's will chant the chant of love. Their offering upon the altar is the invocation to the fire infolding itself, the heart fire of their own Central Sun of Being.

They affirm the Word in dynamic decrees. They give fiery fiats to the violet transmuting flame. They pray fervently for the power of God to enter into the chalice of being for the healing of the nations. This they do in the absolute certainty of cosmic law. This is the law by which the Logos, through the geometry of the spoken Word, enters and permeates the being of man who is the manifestation of God, as above so below. Thus by the ritual of the Science of the Spoken Word, the followers of the Lamb shall speak with a new tongue the tongues of angels.

The original gift of speaking in angelic tongues was given to initiates of the Holy Spirit for the transfer of light from the Creator to the creation. This glossolalia is not unique to early Christians but has been the lot of ardent devotees of the Mother flame, of the I AM THAT I AM (YHVH), wherever the Living

Splendor has manifested its Presence in the long history of the LORD's intercession among his covenanted peoples.

By the Holy Spirit, the angelic hosts have delivered messages of God the Father and the Son in their peculiar angelic tongues. The purpose of such dictations by the Holy Ghost—transferring the Word of seraphim, cherubim, archangels, and various orders of the angelic hierarchy serving on the seven rays—has been to decelerate certain frequencies of the Word into the earth body and her evolutions through the instrument of the Word. The community of believers surrounding the instrument (the one who has the true gift of speaking in angelic tongues) serves as the electrode to ground and hold the light released through the chosen one.

Unless the instrument also have the gift of interpretation of angelic tongues, he may speak the mysteries of the Grail without himself understanding those mysteries. Nevertheless, the Word itself is serviced by the vessel and the vessel is blessed thereby. For the very utterance of the Word within the corporate body of the Church transfers the energy of fohat from the Holy Spirit to accomplish the work of the LORD midst his chosen people—whether of the Creator, the Preserver, or the Destroyer (Consumer) of worlds within and worlds without.

The messengers of God who bear these gifts of the Spirit both speak with angelic tongues and simultaneously interpret those tongues. And often the Word that I AM passes to them from the great white throne through many spirals of angelic tongues—from those of the seven holy Kumaras and the mighty Elohim to those of the seven archangels thence to the release of the Word in the language understandable to the hearers of the Word.

Each time the message of the Ancient of Days is translated through the several tongues of hierarchy, it transmits the unique energy and vibration of that tongue. And all of these collectively, cumulatively, do manifest the great power, wisdom, and love witnessed by the chelas of our messengers in the dictations of the LORD's host delivered by the Holy Spirit through them.

The early Lemurian root races spoke the pure Word of the Mother out of the tongues of the seven rays bequeathed to them by the archangels of those rays. The very sound of these angelic tongues, resonating upon the ethers and crystallizing in Matter, sustained the culture of the Divine Mother amongst her children throughout the first three golden ages of earth's early history.

The confounding of the tongues at the building of Babel, by the judgment of Love delivered by the Archangel of the Third Ray, was the sign from God that He would not allow the pure language of the Word to be used in the defilement of that Word. Therefore the judgment manifested as the confounding of the original angelic tongues as the people could no longer communicate to one another their negative vibrations in the higher vibrating tongue of the Word. And the languages of earth and their uses by a karma-ridden and rebellious people departed farther and farther from the original sound of the Word.

By the density of their hearts, waxing gross density, the people lost attunement with the original Word through the individual Christ Self. They lost the sound of the Trinity sounding in the heart the chord of the Father, the Son, and the Holy Spirit in the balanced Threefold Flame. This chord of the Trinity—the lullaby of the Spirit unto the soul—became the lost chord of the Word once heard as the perpetual sound of God within the inner ear, perpetually comforting life.

Some of the languages spoken by the people on earth today are so far removed from the original Word of the angelic tongue as to be inadequate for the transmittal of light. For this reason, the Ascended Master Saint Germain chose the English language to deliver the teachings of the Word on the I AM Presence. For the same reason, the dictations of the ascended masters delivered through our messengers over the past fifty years have also been released in the English language.

Inasmuch as there are numerous laggard languages in use today as well as the tongues of fallen angels whose languages quite understandably are also fallen languages, it is the desire of the

Great White Brotherhood to see English become the second language in all nations. For the new tongue of the dynamic decree spoken in unison by hearts of light the world around will surely precipitate a rolling momentum, reversing the tide of darkness and bringing in the long-awaited golden age of peace, freedom, enlightenment, and universal love.

Some who are sensitive to the astral plane have heard sounds like chimpanzees chattering, described by the prophet as familiar spirits and as wizards [members of the false hierarchy who interchange on the physical and astral planes] that 'peep and mutter'. We call it demon drivel. And the lowest of the low of these are the grunts and growls of devils echoing from lowest levels of subterranean pits of the astral plane. Contrast this manifestation with choirs of angels singing alleluias in perfect pitch and pronunciation of the Word and you will see just how vast are the degrees and the dynamics (as well as the degradation) of the Holy Spirit.

As the individual's Christ consciousness is, so is his mastery of the Word, his delivery of the Word, and his capacity to transfer the sacred fire of the Word to fulfill its God-ordained purpose. Every work of the LORD that he has purposed to accomplish in the heavens and in the earth is fulfilled by the spoken Word of the Son through the agency of the Holy Ghost. Therefore every office of the servant-sons of the Godhead owns a unique manifestation of the Word.

Isaiah saw the *name* of the LORD, I AM THAT I AM, coming from far, burning with his anger—that all-consuming white fire of the 'wrath' of the 'wrathful' deities out of the East. Isaiah described him—his lips full of indignation, his tongue as a devouring fire, and his breath as an overflowing stream. Clearly he beheld the Person of the LORD releasing the judgment by the throat chakra, by the power center, by the denunciation of evil and of the seed of the wicked, by the glorying of the light causing "his glorious voice to be heard ... with the flame of a devouring fire."

He saw that it was through the voice of the LORD that the Assyrian enemies of Judah would be beaten down. He saw the breath of the LORD, the sacred fire breath of the Holy Spirit, like a stream of brimstone kindling all human creation that was a menace and a mockery unto the divine creation. Clearly these visions are of the alchemy of the Holy Ghost released for the transmutation of the entire energy veil through the spoken Word of His sons moving as one in heaven and on earth.

When the LORD GOD sent Jeremiah to be the instrument of judgment to Judah, the LORD said to his chosen prophet, "Because ye speak this word, behold, I will make my words in thy mouth fire, and this people wood, and it shall devour them." And this, too, my beloved, is the speaking with new tongues whereby the Word is manifest in and through you. And the sacred fire of the Word is an offense to those who offend God, and it is the defense unto the defenseless lambs who though they are defenseless yet defend his Word by love and only love.

The priesthood of the order of Melchizedek recited the Word in the ritual of the celebration of the Creation over and over again. The Gregorian chants, the Our Father and the Hail Mary, the chants of the Jains, the mantrams of the Hindus and the Buddhists are all reminiscent of Lemurian and Atlantean temples where priests and priestesses tended the flame of the Mother by the science of the Word.

They learned to express that Word through all of the seven chakras. Their etheric envelopes could be seen as emitting seven streams of light through the seven chakras. And in the hours of their highest manifestation of the Light, their whole bodies would be filled with the rainbow of the Causal Body accelerating, swirling, spiraling through those seven chakras.

Through the use of certain vowel sounds combined with the consonants of the Word, all of the seven rays would converge through the throat chakra for the crystallization not only of the flame that burned upon the altar, but of temples and pyramids and all of the accouterments of life. Memory of the ancient precipitation by members of the priesthood and adepts in the temple arts has survived to the present.

Even the acceptance of the mystery of the Sacred Eucharist in the celebration of Communion as the actual precipitation of the body and blood of Christ comes from the subconscious memory of the transfer of the twin flames of the Holy Ghost by the original priesthood of Melchizedek. This Alpha and Omega of the positive and negative spirals of the Tao are always inherent in the precipitations of the Guru as 'the body and blood', whether in the bread and the wine or in the loaves and the fishes or in any other of the so-called miracles involving the transformation of Matter after the original Whole.

Beloved ones, I perceive that you are beginning to understand that the pursuit of the gift of speaking with new tongues has many ramifications. May I tell you that most noteworthy of these is your speaking the universal language of Love. For this is the new tongue that I have brought to earth in my service as bodhisattva, as Buddha, as the beautiful Christ.

The language of Love is the language of the heart whereby you are empowered by the Holy Spirit of the lineage of the Ruby Ray to transfer the understanding of the treasured Teachings of the Ascended Masters to all people, to all levels of awareness, to all states of consciousness. This making plain the truth is making straight his paths. And the strait gate to God is the soul's ascent through the mediation of the individual Christ Self to the three-in-one of the Holy of Holies within his own Godhood.

It is the tongue of the learned that I give freely to my devotees that they "should know how to speak a word in season to him that is weary." Yes, I, the LORD GOD in the person of Sanat Kumara, wakeneth morning by morning thine ear to hear as the learned. I will open thine ear, my beloved, if you are not rebellious against my Holy Spirit, if you grieve not my coming by allowing the energy veil of misqualified energy to cover over the heart chakra or the chakras of life.

Yes, unto you who trust in my name and who stay upon your mighty I AM Presence when confronted by the Adversary who would confound and contend with thee—yes, unto you who do not quench my Spirit by disobedience to my law, I will convey the tongue of the learned, the seven holy Kumaras, and I will give to you the new tongue whereby you shall, my beloved, deliver to the evolutions of the seven rays and to all evolutions of earth the true teachings of the Lord Christ of every ascended master.

This is my promise, beloved, and these are the conditions of my promise to you. They are not hard to bear. Do not err. Follow me, and I will carry you by the sound of the Word to the Void and back again so that you may have and know that co-measurement of life: you, the soul on earth, intoning the Word, the same Word that is spoken simultaneously in the center of the Central Sun of the God Star Sirius.

By that Word, we are one. By that Word, you are the individed cloven tongues of fire. And so you sing with the Lord Jesus Christ, "I AM on earth, even as I AM in heaven," that where I AM you may be also, that where you are I may also be. I implore you, my beloved, to intone the Word into the day and into the night. For by the Word and only by the Word are we one.

In the name of the Father, and of the Son, and of the Holy Spirit, Amen.

I AM

Sanat Kumara

of The Word of God

See Acts 2; Mark 16:14–20; John 14; Rev. 4:5; 6:1; 8:5; 11:19; 14:2; 16:18; 19:6; Matt. 3:16; Rev. 7:1–8; 19:10; 12; Heb. 4:12; Eph. 4:1–24; James 3; Ezek. 1:4; Gen. 11:1–9; Isa. 8:19–22; 30:27–33; Jer. 5:10–18; Matt. 3:1–3; 7:13, 14; Isa. 50.

31

The Command of the Word and the Countermand of Its Unlawful Uses

> *Then flew one of the seraphims unto me, having a live coal in his hand, which he had taken with the tongs from off the altar.*
>
> *And he laid it upon my mouth, and said, Lo, this hath touched thy lips; and thine iniquity is taken away, and thy sin purged.*
>
> ISAIAH 6
>
> *Thou shalt also decree a thing, and it shall be established unto thee: and the light shall shine upon thy ways.*
>
> JOB 22

To the Lovers of the Flame of Purity—Beloved!

Mindful now of your preparation for the initiation of the unloosing of the tongue whereby it shall become the tongue of the LORD, I have implored the seraphim of God who dwell in the fiery splendor of his love and in whom that fiery Spirit is indwelling to go to my chelas of the Ruby Ray throughout the systems of worlds. To go with the purging and the purifying light of the Holy Ghost in order that love, eternal love might be exalted as diamond points of purity, as individuality ordained to be the vortex in Matter of the fire infolding itself—infolding into itself all unlike itself for the resolution of worlds within and without.

Let the seraphim of dazzling white light stand where you stand, my beloved. For I would behold you as stars in the firmament of my being, even to the ends of the earth earthy.

A wise man once said, "Death and life are in the power of the tongue: and they that love it shall eat the fruit thereof." The power of the tongue is the power of the spoken Word, and they that love that power shall have returned to them by the Law of the Circle their uses and abuses of that power.

Speaking with new tongues, the devotee embraces the intricacies of the Word. He hears the OM AH HUM of the electrons as they pass through the nuclei of sun centers. He hears the OM MANI PADME HUM of molecules of light. And this hearing in the inner ear of the Sound without sound is translated by the Holy Spirit as the pronouncement of the divine decree of the Creator that echoes eternally within the creation.

The Word that He spoke by which He broke the bread of life as the offering of the Lamb and the Lamb's wife is the Word that resounds, that knows no bounds, that is yet within the creation the Sustainer of the divine approbation: "This, this is my beloved Son, in whom I AM well pleased."

The Word that was with the Creator in the beginning is still with the creation in the ending. The Word that went forth is the Preserver of life from the sun center to the circumference of Matter, man, and molecule.

The debate of physics and metaphysics, Matter real or unreal, is highly speculative and highly spurious. We say, of course it is not real! Of course it is real! The Word is real and I AM real within the Word. And the LORD GOD Almighty, in dividing the Word, has produced infinitesimal coordinates of time and space to manifest an infinity of form and formlessness with which to dress and caress the naked soul in its journeyings from God to God.

This Word out of which all things and creatures were and are created is neither Matter nor non-Matter but substance, if you will concede, Mind stuff crystallized in universes born and unborn, Mind stuff, I say, that appears as flesh and blood, as technology and the Tao, as flowers and raindrops and laughter and tear.

All of this contains the Word unheard by mortal ear—until the Word I heard becomes the Word you hear with immortal ear. The sound of the wind rushing through tall grasses and pine trees must for you be the quickening of soul memory of the sound of the Word of God: "Let there be light! Let there be light! Let there be light!" rushing through the hallowed space of Matter spheres. And the answer year by year: "And there was light! And there was light! And there was light!"

This Word I hear, that you may hear within the secret chamber of the heart as you are tutored by the lineage of the Ruby Ray and the seven chohans, has its origin in the Father-Mother nucleus of Life and its ending in the Son and sun centers of all life. The Word is the love of the One individing itself that it may become the many sons, that the sons may return to the One. Understand, then, that the Word already is. And what is is. And all that is is the Mother manifestation of the Word. And the IS IS in the unveiling of the Mother flame (ISIS).

The initiation of the unloosing of the tongue, therefore, is the moment when the Word that is is pronounced by the LORD through the throat center. And the power of the spoken Word is the power of the Holy Spirit who has taken up his abode within your temple to deliver the divine decree out of the very dynamism of life itself. Yes indeed, my beloved, the new tongue spoken through you by the LORD, as your soul by free will is caught up in the LORD's Presence, includes the perpetual, penetrating, and most powerful flow of the crystal waters of life.

This pure river is your own lifestream flowing from your beloved I AM Presence through the mediator of your Word, the blessed Christ Self, to the threefold fountain of love, wisdom, and power bubbling for joy within your heart. From this fountain of the heart springs forth the spoken Word as pure as the pure heart of God. Thus, my beloved, the dynamic decree is the consummation of God's love for you released through the new tongue that is the LORD's.

Those who love the power of the Word because it is the

grace of God eat the fruit of that power and that Word. And the desire of their heart, one with the heart of God, is expressed as the command of the Word. Perceiving that acceptable will of God, man lifts up his voice unto the LORD in affirmation of that will. As the LORD commands the Mind stuff to manifest as man and molecule of light, so the soul who lives in the LORD and in whom the LORD lives echoes the command of the Creator within the creation.

They have heard the Holy One of Israel, my own blessed name, and my Maker say: "Ask me of things to come concerning my sons, and then concerning the work of my hands command ye me according to my law and to my consciousness which I have ordained for thee. I have made the earth, and created man upon it: I, even my hands, have stretched out the heavens, and all their host have I commanded. Therefore, Command ye me! And in my name command my hosts to do my will and to fulfill my consciousness on earth as in heaven.

"I have raised you up, my beloved, in righteousness, in the right use of the law of the Word. I will direct all your ways. And you shall build my city, the citadel of my consciousness within the Community of the Holy Spirit, nation by nation. And you shall let go my captives in every nation, not for price nor reward but for the love, the eternal love of the Word which I have placed within the hearts of my children as the sign of my coming," saith the LORD of Hosts.[1]

The power of the Word is also known by the seed of the wicked. These archdeceivers whom Enoch made known to you as the Watchers and their godless creation were the enemies of David. He, the LORD's anointed, continually addressed me and the heavenly hosts concerning the persecution of the children of God by the offspring of the Wicked One who misused the power of the Word to destroy and lay desolate the places of my children.

He cried out saying, "Deliver me, O LORD, from the evil man—the descendants of Lucifer and his fallen angels: preserve me from the violent man; which imagine mischiefs in their heart; continually are they gathered together for war. They have sharpened their tongues like a serpent—like the seed of the spoiler, the cohort of Satan whose name was Serpent, the very one who beguiled Eve; adders' poison is under their lips. Keep me, O LORD, from the hands of the wicked—the Watchers; preserve me from the violent man; who have purposed to overthrow my goings.

"The proud Luciferians have hid a snare for me, and cords—by their lying tongue and the momentum of the Liar, by their maligning of the Word in thy children; and their lies have become a malignancy in the midst of thy people; they have spread a net of the misinterpretation of the Word by the wayside; their gins that they have set for me are all distortions of the Word.

"Hear the voice of my supplications, O LORD, for thou art my God.

"O Elohim, the I AM THAT I AM, thou who art the strength of my salvation through the power of thy spoken Word, thou hast sealed my Christ consciousness and the sacred centers of my being in the day of the battle of the Watchers against The Word of God and against the armies in heaven. Grant not, O beloved I AM Presence, that the desires of the wicked which they have pronounced as violent cursings against the Father, the Son, the Holy Spirit, and the Mother shall be able to further their wicked device; lest they exalt themselves in their misused power of thy Word.

"Let the mischief of their own lips, their mischievous misuse of thy sacred Word, cover them. Let the burning coals of their own viciousness fall upon their own heads: let them be cast into the fire of their own anger and into the pits of their own perversion of the sacred fire. Let not an evil speaker be established in the earth: for the evil that he has spawned as an energy veil shall hunt the violent man to overthrow him in his violence."[2]

All of this was the word of David unto me, for his soul

understood the fruit that the wicked shall eat—the fruit of their abuse of the power of the tongue. David knew the law of cause and effect. He knew that the wickedness of the wicked must ultimately return to their doorstep. His prayer to me was for the sparing of the righteous children of God of the ravages of the wicked and their wicked use of the tongue.

He knew the law which decrees that they must face the karma of their evil doings. He implored me day and night that the law might accelerate the return of that karma, that the prophesied judgment of the Watchers might come to pass in accelerated cycles, thereby shortening the days for the elect of God—the days of war and pain and pestilence and famine, the days of the Dark Cycle when the pair of balances in the hand of the third horseman of the Apocalypse signifies that the abuse of the Word by the seed of the wicked in their manipulation of the law of the abundant life has caused the darkness to cover the earth, and gross darkness the people.

For though the LORD GOD has not utterly destroyed the seed of the wicked from the earth—for their time is not yet fully come and their very presence in the earth is the karma of the children of God who have followed the wickedness of their ways—yet the LORD has given to his sons and daughters the power of the Word to invoke the judgment of the Lord Christ. For it is his very presence in the midst of the people that does accelerate the return of evil upon the evildoer, thus exacting accountability for deeds done against the Light.

When you do not call for the judgment of the Watchers and their seed, then the children of God bear in their bodies and in their souls the burden of darkness, disease, and death which the wicked, who have sharpened their tongues like a serpent, have sent forth. Thus the children of the light must be God-taught not only to give the command of the Word but to countermand the unlawful misuses of the dynamic decree given oftentimes ignorantly but many times maliciously by the false chelas of the false gurus.

The recent example of the power of the tongue misused by thousands of Iranians shouting slogans of hate and hate creation, "Death to America! Death to Carter! Death to the Shah!" is a clear-cut example of the decree of the Word used to implement the death wish. The karma for this malpractice is gross as this adders' poison returns to the lips that sent it forth. It manifests first as grossness of heart, increased insensitivity to life, and finally death, often by cataclysm, when the very death and destruction which they have invoked returns as fiery coals upon their own heads.

When this hate and hate creation is unchecked by the lawful use of the Word, as I have taught it to you, it can cause the psychic and psychotronic death of its victims. Is this God-justice? Beloved ones, I ask you, will you stand by and see such injustice replace the flame of God-justice in the earth?

Such death decrees are not justified because a person or persons or an entire nation have acted unjustly. It is never within the right of the Son of God or the child of God to decree death or destruction or disease upon another part of life—even upon the seed of the wicked, even when they have wronged thousands or millions. But it is the absolute God-responsibility of the people to reverse the tide of negative energy that batters the citadel of consciousness and the Community of the Holy Spirit with the fury of hurricane and the hellfire of demons who of course ride the treacherous torrents of these tempests of vengeance and vituperation.

To reverse the tide of hate and hate creation is not only lawful but, to the one on the receiving end of such mortal cursings, it may be a matter of life and death to understand and apply this aspect of the science of the Word. As hundreds of thousands of Iranians have condemned the Shah to die by the power of the tongue, you can see the effect of this misuse of the Word in the disintegration of his body by a malice that has precipitated into a malignancy.

Beloved ones, I do not say the Shah is good or evil or whether he is of Christ or Belial, but I do say that he has the divine right, as God would protect that right for everyone—for the fallen angels as well as for the righteous children of God—to prove the law and to be reproved by the law, to experiment in the use of the energy of the Word and to learn by the law of karma the effects of good and bad causes set in motion.

Yes, you may reverse the tide of any and all arrows of outrageous, erroneous energy which you may find lying at your doorstep, but you may not take the law into your own hands nor the judgment. For the conclusion of the matter belongs to the LORD and his emissaries, the ascended masters. And the law itself, inexorable as the circle of Life, will perform its perfect work.

Unto the chelas of the ascended masters I give the authority to be the presence of the Word of judgment. Let that presence and let that Word release the light of the judgment through you, but see to it that you do not preempt the Word or preclude the judgment. For God and only God is Creator, Preserver, and Destroyer of worlds within and worlds without.

I AM standing with you as you shout the shout of victory and the victorious life, as you affirm the good and deny the evil, letting your sayings in the temple be "yea yea, and nay nay." I AM with you as you challenge the devils who have invaded the temple of the people, the devils who are the impostors of the Holy Ghost and the true Gurus and the true chelas, who speak with an unbridled tongue which is yet the instrument of unbridled desire. I AM with you as you challenge the enemies of the LORD GOD Almighty who have taken into their own hands that vengeance which belongs to the LORD. For he has said, "Vengeance is mine; I will repay."

The return of the energy of good and evil works like clockwork throughout all of the cycles of the galaxies. And the good and the evil words and works will return to the doorstep of the Shah and to all without the interference or the intercession of the impostors of the Holy Spirit who set themselves up as messengers of God and instruct the people in the ways of black magic which, if continued, will surely destroy not only their bodies but their souls.

Thus exposed by the all-seeing eye of God, those who come with the ulterior motive of destroying the souls of the people in hell, while presenting themselves as the deliverers from evil, are seen as the destroyers who would destroy the people by enmeshing them in the left-handed path of the fallen ones.

Let those who would let their tongues be the instrument of the desire of the Holy Ghost as well as of the Father and the Son now take up the tongue as the instrument of the Mother's sacred fire. For the power of the Word is the basis for all other gifts of the Holy Spirit—even the Word of wisdom and the Word of knowledge, and faith that moves mountains by the spoken Word, and the gifts of healing that come by the authority of the Word of Christ, and the miracles that manifest by the alchemy of the Word, and the prophecy that extends edification, exhortation, and comfort by the power of the Word, and the discerning of spirits by the sharp sword that proceeds out of the mouth of the Faithful and True.

Yes, let all tongues and the interpretation of tongues be of the Holy Spirit as the Mother flame within you is always the pure stream of purity implementing the will of the Father, the wisdom of the Son, and the love of the Holy Spirit.

Now, my beloved, with the initiation of the fourth ray conveyed by my son Serapis who is the Lamb worthy, lay the foundation on the south gate under the flying Eagle, the eternal Lamb who manifests through the embodied Lamb. Lay the foundation for the eighth-ray initiation. For every word that you speak, qualifying the fourth ray of purity, will return to you at the nexus of Life. Therefore, choose this day by thy Word to live in Life.

So is the ascension coil built from the base of the pyramid by the spoken Word. And no man nor woman nor child may enter the ritual of the ascension without the gift of the speaking in the new tongue of the Spirit.

Thus let thy prayer be the prayer of the soul who said, "Let the words of my mouth and the meditation of my heart be acceptable in thy sight, O LORD, my strength and my redeemer."

I AM

Sanat Kumara

I stand with Justinius, Captain of Seraphic Bands, and with legions of seraphim awaiting the call of all of my children who would purify their word and be purified by the living Word.

See Acts 2; Ezek. 1:4; 1 Cor. 15:45–49; Prov. 18:21; John 6; Matt. 3:17; 17:5; John 1:1–3; Gen. 1:1–5; Matt. 24:1–22; Rev. 6:5, 6; Isa. 60:1, 2; 2 Cor. 1:17–20; Matt. 5:37; Jas. 5:12; Rom. 12:19; 1 Cor. 12; Matt. 17:20; Rev. 19:11–21; Ps. 19:14.

32

∞

The Taking Up of Serpents

He that heareth you heareth me; and he that despiseth you despiseth me; and he that despiseth me despiseth him that sent me.

And the seventy returned again with joy, saying, LORD, even the devils are subject unto us through thy name.

And he said unto them, I beheld Satan as lightning fall from heaven.

Behold, I give unto you power to tread on serpents and scorpions, and over all the power of the Enemy: and nothing shall by any means hurt you.

Notwithstanding in this rejoice not that the spirits are subject unto you; but rather rejoice because your names are written in heaven.
                                            LUKE 10

Beloved Followers of the Lamb Ever Mounting the Mount Sion:

I AM preparing your consciousness for the opening of the seven seals of the book which I hold in my right hand, the book that is written within and on the backside, sealed with seven seals.

The query of the strong angel with the loud voice must be answered in every age, "Who is worthy to open the book, and to loose the seals thereof?" I come to establish the worthy in the worthiness of the Lamb by the path of Self-worth.

The path of Self-worth is the path of the initiates of the Ruby Ray. Now I proclaim unto the hosts of the seven holy Kumaras,

"Establish thou it!
In the heart of the earth, in the heart of the Mother,
In the heart of the Maitreya Guru seated in the golden lotus

In the center of the community of my disciples.
Establish thou it!
As the cosmic highways grow
And the ruby rivers flow—
Establish thou it as above so below!"

Now let the surefooted learn to take up serpents
By the Ruby Ray of the Compassionate One,
By the piercing light of illumination's day
Emanating from the heart of the Beautiful One,
By the splendor of the Shining One,
By the indomitable will of the Holy of Holies,
By the unquenchable sacred fire of the God from the Sun.

Our story begins in the cold and rain by a kindled fire on the island of Melita midst the people who received the shipwrecked Paul and his companions with no little kindness. Paul himself had gathered a bundle of sticks and laid them on the fire; and there, out of the heat, came a viper and fastened on his hand.

The barbarians, when they saw the venomous beast hanging on the hand of Paul, being superstitious, said among themselves, "No doubt this man is a murderer whom, though he hath escaped the sea, yet vengeance suffereth not to live." But Paul, the beloved, empowered of the Holy Ghost, shook off the beast into the fire and felt no harm. And the barbarians, seeing no harm come to him, changed their minds and said that he was a god.

And Paul, lodging with Publius, laid his hands on his father who lay sick of a fever and of a bloody flux, and he healed him by the Holy Ghost. And others in the island which had diseases came to the beloved apostle and were healed by the laying on of hands—because the Lord Jesus Christ and the angel of God stood by him.

Therefore, let it be known and let it be published among you that the signs which follow the people of God who preach the Everlasting Gospel everywhere are confirmed by the Word incarnate in the ascended Lord Jesus Christ through the Holy Spirit sealed in and through your members by the angels of God and the emissaries of the Most High. This work is the work of the communion of the saints robed in white moving in and through and among you. It is the cooperative venture of the members of the body of God who are the Great White Brotherhood above and below.

This work is the great adventure of the initiates of the Son of Man, the Lion of God, the sacrificial Calf of the Holy Spirit, and the mighty Eagle of the Mother lode of Sirius. This work is the work of seen and unseen hands—millions of hands reaching up to God and out to those in need, hands clasped in prayer, hands toiling tirelessly in the sacred labor of the LORD's vineyard.

When the hand of the LORD is upon you, my beloved, it is the grace of his Self worth and his blessedness unto the worthy. The hand of the LORD now manifests in and through the many hands of the heavenly hosts extending to earth as helping hands to the end that our chosen servants might finish the mystery of God and establish the Holy Grail as the archetype of true selfhood in the earth.

Now be of good cheer and be encouraged by the great courage of those who have gone before you. Claim the mantle of the apostle Paul, who awaits your coming on the east gate of the City Foursquare where he is the Lamb who is worthy to open the book that is reserved for the initiates of the fifth ray. Serving with the two witnesses, these witness unto the Truth in order that the original lie of Serpent and all liars which have proceeded after him might be swallowed up by the rod of Moses, by the judgment of the Son of God, by the sacred fire of the Holy Ghost, and by the Light of the Woman clothed with the Sun.

When the seventy whom the LORD had sent two by two before his face returned with joy saying, "LORD, even the devils are subject unto us through thy name," he said unto them, "I beheld Satan as lightning fall from heaven. Therefore, because you have stood and still stand in the joy of the will of God before the Enemy of his hosts, behold, I give unto you power to tread on serpents and scorpions, and over all the power of the Enemy: and nothing shall by any means hurt you. Notwithstanding in this rejoice not that the spirits are subject unto you; but rather rejoice because your names are written in heaven."

This initiation of the fifth ray, the taking up of serpents, is the opening of the eye of God within the soul, that in seeing the true image and likeness of God the soul might bind the anti-image pervaded by Serpent. In the hour of his disciples' God-victorious passage through the scenes of Serpent unto the God-vision of my name, my throne, and my authority, Jesus rejoiced in the Spirit of the Great White Brotherhood and in the lineage of the Ruby Ray, praying unto the Almighty One, "I thank thee, O Father, LORD of heaven and earth, that thou hast hid these things from the wise and prudent and hast revealed them unto babes: even so, Father; for it seemed good in thy sight."

By this sight conveyed to the other seventy through Elohim, the all-seeing eye of God was in their midst as the pulsating orb of light whose brilliant beams crystallized the sword of Truth gainst which Serpent and his seed could not stand. Thus by that sword of their sacred Word whereby they witnessed unto the Lord Jesus Christ, Satan fell from his stronghold where he had positioned himself in the third-eye chakras of God's children.

My beloved, understand that the fall of Satan and of Serpent "as lightning from heaven" occurs each time you witness to the Word, you preach the Word, you teach the Word, and you become the Word. This exposure of the Truth through the hearts of the flaming ones embodied on earth is the instantaneous exposure of the Liar and his lie. We deal here with living Truth, whose proof is always abundant in the life of the saints of the Church Universal and Triumphant.

It is Error and the erroneous doctrines of Serpent and his seed in Church and State that you must take up and expose for all to see the powerlessness of the venomous beasts and their bestiality before casting them into the sacred fire of God's all-consuming love. Herein lies your initiation under the World Saviour and his anointed apostle. And here, by God's all-seeing eye, is the crystallization of the City Foursquare whereby you build the true foundation of the Great Matter Pyramid.

This is the third of the five signs confirmed by the Word in all who obey the two commands to preach the Everlasting Gospel and to believe and be baptized. Through the third sign, the fallen ones who have encamped in the Matter sphere are pushed back that the sons and daughters of God might occupy the office of true Christ and true prophet. Serving on the fifth ray at the east gate, they are commissioned by God to go before the saints (who occupy the north gate of the Matter sphere) and the great multitude (who occupy the west gate of the Matter sphere), leading them unto the Ascension Temple (the initiation of the eighth ray on the south gate of the Matter sphere). [See chart page 247.]

Now the hour is come for the taking up of these *serpents* who are the fallen *servants* of God. For they have bound themselves together by a blood oath before Satan (It is the blood of the holy innocents.), nevermore to repent of their deeds, evermore to relentlessly pursue and pretend to undo the Word and the Work of the Woman and her seed.

Taking up serpents is the game of the chelas of the Guru Ma.

The name "Guru Ma" is the title of an office and of the mantle worn by the person or persons who hold the Mother flame in the earth. It is a garment that has been worn before and one that will be worn again by the ever-present lineage of the Ruby Ray, whose Mother flame I ensoul in the messenger and in the continuity of the messengership, which ever has been and ever shall be the contact of hierarchy with the LORD's embodied hosts.

Understand, then, the vision held in the heart of the Goddess of Liberty and of every soul holding the eye of the Motherhood of God fixed immaculately upon the offspring of the Most High. Understand the initiate of the Mother flame holding the sacred fire within the third eye of the children of God even as he beholds the perfected son in the Christ Self of each one.

In the hour when Jesus Christ delivered to the other seventy this power of the Mother flame to tread on serpents and scorpions and over all the power of the Enemy, he revealed the mystery of the science of the fifth ray of the all-seeing eye of God.

> *All things are delivered to me of my Father: and no man knoweth who the Son is, but the Father; and who the Father is, but the Son, and he to whom the Son will reveal him.*
>
> *And he turned him unto his disciples, and said privately, Blessed are the eyes which see the things that ye see:*
>
> *For I tell you, that many prophets and kings have desired to see those things which ye see, and have not seen them; and to hear those things which ye hear, and have not heard them.*

With this teaching Jesus, whose power derived from the Self-realized Father and Son within him, explained that all things—all substance, energy, and manifestation of both Good and Evil—are delivered to him and subject unto him by the Presence of the Father individualized within him as the I AM THAT I AM.

He explained that no man can know who is the incarnation of the Son—the manifest light of the Christ—whether in earth or in heaven, but through the beloved I AM Presence of the Father. Then and now it is this I AM Presence (the I AM THAT I AM symbolically noted as YHVH and called by many Yahweh, Jehovah, or LORD) who reveals the Son of God (the *Light* of God) to the disciple—to the one self-disciplined of the Son.

He further explained that no one could know who the Father is, in heaven or in earth, but the one who is his Son. Only the one self-disciplined of his own beloved Christ Self can know his Almighty LORD—the Mighty I AM Presence. Only the living chela can identify the living Guru Maitreya. And only the true one who embodies the light of the Son can reveal to his disciples the Shekinah glory of the I AM THAT I AM, the I AM Presence who is the true Father of every child of his light. Those who are the disciples of the Son therefore have access unto the Father.

Knowing this, Jesus turned to the disciples of his light and said, "Blessed are your eyes which see the things that ye see. *Because* ye are anointed by the all-seeing eye of God, ye have the inner sight to know who is Christ and therefore who is Antichrist, who is the true Father Guru and therefore who is the false."

It is clear that although many prophets and kings have desired to see those things which the disciples were able to see, they could not see them because they had not the power of the Son of God which is conveyed only by the true path of discipleship. And what is it which the prophets and the kings have desired to see, my beloved? Why, of course it is Good and Evil in the ultimate sense rather than that relative good and evil of the gods of Hades delivered to Eve by Serpent.

This is that power of vision conveyed by the Son of man to the initiates who tarry at the east gate. These are bound by the mission of the two witnesses to bear Truth to the tribes of Israel and to every nation, kindred, tongue, and people—to all who can receive the arc of God's all-seeing eye and still stand to retain that crystal clear identity of the beloved of Christ, sealed by the sword of Truth.

The chakras must be cleared to receive the rod of Moses. This clearing is accomplished by the violet transmuting flame invoked by you in your daily dynamic decrees. This is the work of the Holy Spirit in you, clearing the riverbed for the flow of the crystal clear waters of the river of life rising from the base of the spine unto the crown chakra and then held and sustained in the invincible matrix of Truth—your very own chalice of the eye of God, the center of cosmic concentration at the brow.

In this hour of the coming of the Elohim of the Fifth Ray, Cyclopea, to represent the Karmic Board at Summit University, we call for the acceleration of violet-flame invocations and the intensified use of the decree to Cyclopea. By the sword of truth and the flame of freedom you will go forth to tread on serpents and scorpions. By the flaming blue swords of the angels of Faith and their perfect presence among you and by the power of my very flame present with Archangel Michael, the angel of the LORD—the spirits of Serpent, both embodied and disembodied, will be subject unto the *Law* and the *Light* (the *Father* and the *Son*) of my rod of the Ruby Ray. This will I implant within you who are faithful to the Faithful and True.

"And the God of Peace shall bruise Satan under your feet shortly."[1] This God of Peace who was with Paul is the sixth of the seven holy Kumaras who sponsors the initiates of the sixth ray under the Lord Jesus Christ to give dominion unto his disciples over the desire body and the personal and the planetary emotions of the solar plexus. Thus the key to the masterful light of the third eye is the God-control of the anxiety, the agitation, the arrogance, and the anger of the fallen ones who are the followers of Serpent.

Their ever-present fear of self-annihilation, which they have sealed by their own envy and enmity with the Light, you must place under your feet in submission to the Word even as the Woman has placed the moon under her feet. For the doubts of these doubters of the Truth and of the Word, and of the joy of the little child are the ever-present disease that would infest the mind and heart, if it were possible, of the true body of believers. But it cannot. This doubt in the immediacy and the availability of the Presence of God to meet every need and resolve every equation, human and divine, has been spun into the manifold philosophies of the shrewd Serpent and his seed.

One and all, let the philosophies of doubt and the doubters be consumed by the Piscean mastery of the God of Peace and his Son Jesus Christ transferred to the many sons which he has brought unto the captivity of the ascension flame!

Now let the rolling momentum of the violet flame roll back and consume! roll back and consume! roll back and consume! the rising tide of the Dark Cycle in Scorpio and the flood of misqualified water (emotional energy) which Serpent cast out of his mouth after the Woman that he might cause her to be carried away of the flood.

Let the violet flame be invoked by the two candlesticks standing before the God of the Earth and all who stand before him of the children of God and of elemental life. Let them receive the initiations of the hierarch of Taurus—the Calf who is Buddha—that they might help the Woman and her seed. For it is Lord Gautama, the Lord of the World, who is the Buddha of the Earth.

Now while the earth trembles, let all who have eyes to see behold the Buddha and the devotees of the great trine of Mother Earth. And let those who see, likewise open their mouths; and by the terrible crystal, the torrent of sacred fire released in the Science of the Spoken Word, let them swallow up the flood of misqualified Mother light which the dragon (the false hierarchy and their false decreers) casts out of his mouth.

Beloved, I AM come to you in the full glory of the violet flame of cosmic freedom, of the Ruby Ray penetrating the lie of Serpent unto the night and unto the day. And by the all-seeing eye of God and the initiations of the fifth ray, I come to you who are the seed of the Woman to give to you the armour of God's light. It is his Word manifest in you as the Son of God.

Girded with the flame of Truth, invoke the breastplate of righteousness and let your winged sandals be the preparation of the gospel of peace sealed in your chakras with seven seals. By the shield of faith, the sword of the Holy Spirit, and the helmet of salvation (Self-elevation unto the sanctity of the Mind of God) I say, in God's name, you shall stand, face, and conquer that dragon who is yet wroth with the Woman, who yet persecutes the Woman who is able to bring forth the Manchild within you, and who would yet make war with the remnant of her seed.

You shall overcome him by the sacred fire of the Lamb if you open up your mouth and let the light of the Ruby Ray flow through the matrix of the divine decree of my Word. You shall overcome him if you keep the commandments of God and witness to the testimony of Jesus Christ sealed in the heart of the two olive trees.

I AM Sanat Kumara. I bid you prepare the earth for the coming of the Son of God. Through your call to my sacred name and to the Lamb, let elemental life of the water, the earth, the air, and the fire be infilled with the violet flame. And let the inhabiters of the earth and the sea (those whose consciousness is polarized to the physical and astral planes) be sealed by the circle and sword of Astrea and her legions of blue-lightning angels.

The four cosmic forces who hold the office of the Man, the Lion, the Calf, and the flying Eagle are the guardians in the heavens and in the earth of the Lamb and the Lamb's wife and of his hundred and forty and four thousand in whose third-eye chakras I have sealed my name.

By my name and by my eye, I manifest myself within you by the mantle of my apostle at Melita where our story begins but does not end. And by my name and by my eye you shall take up serpents and cast them into the sacred fire.

Be thou made whole! For by thy wholeness shall the whole earth be made whole.

I AM Sanat Kumara

See Luke 10; Rev. 14:5; Acts 28:1–9; Mark 16:15–20; Matt. 20:1–16; Rev. 10:7; Exod. 4:7; Rev. 7:11, 12, 19; 22; Ezek. 1:22; Rom. 13:12; Eph. 6:11–17.

33

The Vow to Save the Woman and Her Seed

> *Now Serpent was more subtil than any beast of the field which the* LORD GOD *had made. And he said unto the woman, Yea, hath God said, Ye shall not eat of every tree of the garden?*
>
> *And the woman said unto Serpent, We may eat of the fruit of the trees of the garden:*
>
> *But of the fruit of the tree which is in the midst of the garden, God hath said, Ye shall not eat of it, neither shall ye touch it, lest ye die.*
>
> *And Serpent said unto the woman, Ye shall not surely die:*
>
> *For God doth know that in the day ye eat thereof, then your eyes shall be opened, and ye shall be as gods, knowing good and evil.*
>
> GENESIS 3

To the Saints Who Remember Horeb and My Voice
  Which Spake Out of the Midst of the Sacred Fire
  and Declared unto You My Covenant:

    The first faint gleams of the violet fire are as flickering lamps in the land of Erin. To the British Isles let the pilgrims of the Mission Amethyst Jewel wander! For I AM the burning lamp in the midst of my people, rekindling the covenant which I have made with Abram and unto the Christic seed.

    I AM the seven lamps burning on the altar of being and in the midst of my people Israel. And I appoint the priesthood of Melchizedek to light the lamps, the seven lamps that are for the going and the coming of the saints into the Holy of Holies, thence to bear my message unto the people of God scattered abroad in the nations of the earth.

I AM the golden candlestick of the fifth vision of Zechariah, and the bowl upon the top of it is my vessel containing the oil of wisdom's chakra. And the seven lamps thereon are my seven servants, the seven chohans of the rays who initiate my children in lighting the lamps of their seven chakras. And the two olive trees which stand upon the right side and upon the left side of the candlestick and of the bowl are my messengers, the two anointed ones who deliver the Word of the seven servants as they stand before the LORD of the whole earth, Gautama Buddha.

By the burning light of the seven chohans, I send my disciples empowered by the Holy Spirit of the Ruby Ray with the message of the two witnesses to England, to Scotland, to Ireland, and to Wales. For it is here that I desire to deliver the descendants of the lost tribes of Israel from the face of the Serpent.

I AM the Ancient of Days, the Restorer of the Light of my people. I call my servants who have come for the restoration of the covenant whereby the LORD GOD does transfer the light of the seven lamps to all who are of the Christic seed. The transfer of this light, when completed within your temple which is the temple of the Holy Spirit, my beloved, is for the opening of the seven seals of the seven chakras whereby the BRANCH shall manifest himself in the LORD's temple. This is my initiation through the two olive branches who empty the golden oil of my wisdom out of themselves for the burning of the seven lamps in the earth.

Within thy temple, my beloved, the BRANCH who should come to the Christic seed in the Second Advent is Christ, the LORD of the temple of the children of God. This BRANCH of the Tree of Life is the extension of the Father's Person unto his children through the Person of the Son. The BRANCH is the personified Light of the I AM THAT I AM. It is the descent out of the Holy of Holies of the radiant Word who comes in the Person of the blessed Christ Self unto the children of God who have consecrated their temples to be his dwelling place.

Ministering unto the souls of the great multitude of God's children are the seven chohans made worthy to receive the initiation of the Lamb. As their messengers deliver the Word of the BRANCH on each of the seven rays whose law they embody, the chohans through the embodied saints prepare the children of God for the opening of the seven chakras. For it is by the opening of these seven seals that the soul dwelling in the temple not made with hands is 'married' to the Light of the BRANCH and his Person, the Christ Self. As day by day your soul gains self-mastery, expanding the flames of the seven holy Kumaras within the seven chakras, you are preparing for that marriage which is the fusion of your soul with your real counterpart, the BRANCH.

It is toward this appointed goal that the initiate of the Ruby Ray joyously submits himself to the initiations of the four cosmic forces in the Spirit and Matter vessels of his consciousness. Truly the sign of the figure eight is the symbol of your Being, my beloved—above in the Great Causal Body of God, whose electronic fire rings surround your own individual I AM Presence, and below in the spheres of your solar awareness, manifesting the manifold expressions of your free will throughout your incarnations on earth.

It is the fiery destiny of your soul, symbolized by the dot in the lower sphere, to become one with the fiery ovoid, symbolized by the dot in the upper sphere. [See chart page 292.] The figure eight consists of the two spheres of being—the one permanent, the one nonpermanent. The alchemical marriage of the above and the below is through the blessed Mediator, the BRANCH, symbolized by the dot at the nexus of the figure eight.

The nexus is the point of your initiation on the fourth ray and the eighth ray where the south gates of the upper and lower spheres are one. [See chart page 247.] These initiations are the key to the integration of the whole through the Ruby Ray. This is the dispensation to earth's evolutions in the decade of the 1980s. Thus I have come in the closing months of 1979 with my message of the Path that you might prepare yourselves for the full outpouring of the Holy Spirit that will come to those who have made themselves ready to be the bride of the Lamb.

The bride is the soul who hath made herself ready, emptying the lower spheres of soul awareness that they might be filled with the light of the electronic fire rings. The self-emptying process is achieved through the flushing out of the chakras by the crystal clear waters of the river of life flowing from the fount of the Trinity and the Mother.

The throne of my Presence in the heart of the God Star is the Mother chakra in Spirit which corresponds with and holds the positive polarity for the Sun of Even Pressure in the heart of the planets that serve the present evolutionary chain of life. All who are preparing themselves for this alchemical marriage are called upon to meditate upon the blue fire sun of the God Star that contains the Mother lode of the universes.

It is by this Mother lode—the white-fire core of the blue fire sun—that the base-of-the-spine chakras are activated in the saints. And the raising up of that Mother light is for the weaving of the wedding garment which Serapis Bey has revealed to you as the Deathless Solar Body.

The Deathless Solar Body is the Matter coordinate of the Great Causal Body. It is woven by your instrumentation of the Word—you, the instrument of the Word, reciting the Mother mantras, singing the devotional songs unto the Trinity of the East and the West, delivering the dynamic decree, and offering with the fiery fervor of love the prayers of the BRANCH as he delivers through you the power of the Word that penetrates the night of human despair and despondency.

The Word is the Mediator. The Word is the BRANCH. The Word is your Christ Self. And the release of that Word as the LORD's judgment that divides within your own members the Real and the unreal is the foundation of the ascension coil.

The coil consists of the seven initiations of the saints who follow the Lamb, preparing them for the eighth-ray integration of the spheres of being. This ascension is the soul's birth within the Spirit ovoid. It is the soul's reception into heaven to "sit on the right hand of God." When the soul—which is the feminine potential of Selfhood—is received into heaven, she comes as the wife of the Lamb. The bride of the Lamb is truly that soul who has entered into the marriage of the Christ Self.

But the soul who is received into heaven is already the wife of the Lamb. The marriage ceremony has taken place in the Matter spheres. The Christ, who is the LORD of the soul, has taken his bride unto himself and the twain have become one 'flesh', one substance, one Selfhood. The soul, wearing the bridal gown of its solar awareness, has been assumed unto the Christ consciousness. This assumption is the ritual of the ascent of the virgin (the soul) by the living Christ.

This Second Person of the Trinity of Being represents the positive polarity of the Spirit sphere, whence it has descended to the point of the Mediator to receive unto himself the soul who has gone out of the way of the Tree of Life. Stationed at the point of the nexus, he is accessible to all who dwell in 'the earth' (the Matter sphere). From that point of his precipitation of the Christ consciousness on behalf of his bride, the Beloved sings the song of love unto the soul: "Draw nigh unto me and I will draw nigh unto you."

The Mediatorship of the Christ Self is the open door whereby the soul passes from its nonpermanent existence in Matter to the permanent atom of being, the I AM THAT I AM, in Spirit. Only that which is purified and perfected may pass through the door held open by the Bridegroom. Thus it is given to the Lamb's wife to be arrayed in that fine linen, clean and white, which is the righteousness of saints. And the righteousness of saints is their righteous use of the laws of God through the science of the Word that becomes first their auric forcefield and then their wedding garment.

The Christ Self is the Lamb of God whose Person within the soul, Serpent and his seed have sought to slay since the foundation of the Word in Matter. The soul must then become the champion of the Christ incarnate, slaying all dragons and beasts of the fallen ones who would destroy the image of the Christ within itself—and within the souls of the holy innocents. Only the soul who is willing to slay every manifestation of Antichrist can become the bride of the living Christ. Only the soul who becomes the faithful bride of the living Christ can walk on the arm of the Bridegroom into the heavenly reception.

The saints who follow the Lamb are those who are becoming the Lamb's honored wife through the seven initiations I have outlined. And when the soul and the Christ Self are no longer twain, but one, even as I and my Father are one, then that one who is now called 'the Christed One' ascends to God. This ascension is the merging of the lower sphere with the upper sphere and was mystically noted by the Lord Jesus to his disciples in the upper room as "sitting on the right hand of God."

The seat of authority on the right hand of God is the seat of the Lamb, and all who thus ascend to him in the glory of the virgin light occupy that office at his 'right hand'. In this initiation, the two dots, the soul and the Spirit, are in the center of the upper sphere in the Alpha/Omega polarity. Thus the son of God who is ascended manifests the personality of the Son in relationship to the impersonality of the Father. And this plus/minus factor of Universal Being provides the rotation of light for the turning of worlds both within and without the Spirit sphere.

The ministry of John the Baptizer and of Jesus the Christed One began with the initiation which I now set squarely before you, my beloved: the taking up of serpents. Both gave a spectacular and stupendous demonstration of the LORD who is Christ denouncing he who is Antichrist. Before all other considerations, my sons John and Jesus gave themselves to the exposure of the truth concerning the generation of vipers, the seed of Serpent, the wicked ones whose corrupt consciousness (fruit) reveals the corrupt source (tree).

John and Jesus came to save the Woman and her seed from

the seed of the Wicked One. Who, then, is Serpent? And who are his generation?

In the Great Rebellion against the LORD GOD Almighty and the hosts of his heavenly hierarchy, Lucifer seduced no small number of angelic bands led by his cohorts. Their names are mentioned in the Book of Enoch, and in other books of the Apocrypha, and in the codified scriptures of East and West.

More notable are the names Satan, Beelzebub, Belial, Baal, etc. One such name, that of the more shrewd and subtil leader of a band of fallen ones, has come to be lowercased in the lexicon of sacred scripture and it has taken on a symbolic rather than personal connotation. It is that of Serpent.

Whereas the term "great dragon" refers to the conglomerate of the entire Luciferian false hierarchy arrayed against the Great White Brotherhood, its individual members and hierarchs specialize in certain phases of the 'dragon's' persecution of the Woman and in the war waged by the Luciferian false hierarchy against the remnant of the Woman's seed.

Whereas Satan is known as the original Murderer using the murder of the lightbearers to thwart the divine plan of God in the earth, Serpent, who is also "*called* the Devil and Satan," is the Archdeceiver, the original Liar and the father of lies whose philosophy of deception, based on fear and doubt, is his modus operandi in his warfare against the true Christs and the true prophets.

Serpent is the Wicked One whose seed, along with Satan's, is sown as tares among the good wheat of the Christic seed. It is this seed who are called the offspring of the vipers. "Viper" is from the Greek translation of the proper name "Serpent," who, together with the fallen ones of his band, was cast out of heaven and took embodiment on earth where they have continued to reincarnate since the Great Rebellion.

When John the Baptist saw the Pharisees and Sadducees coming to his baptism, he knew who they were: not only the offspring of that original band of fallen ones, but the very wicked ones themselves reembodied. When he denounced them as the "generation of vipers," he was speaking of them collectively as the original band who had followed Serpent, the cohort of Satan and Lucifer. When he exposed their real motive in coming to his baptism as "fleeing from the wrath to come," he spoke of the wrath of God as the white fire of his judgment that should come upon Serpent and his seed in the last days. Therefore he demanded that they bring forth fruits meet for repentance (evidence of humility, love, and obeisance before the LORD's Christ) whereby they might yet repent of their sworn enmity with the Woman and her Manchild.

So great was the zeal of the LORD upon John the Baptist that he not only denounced the seed of Serpent in the false hierarchy of Israel but he attacked the false hierarchy of Rome itself—Herod, the tetrarch, whose father had sought to take the life of the Saviour as soon as he was born. John the Baptist denounced Herod for taking unto himself Herodias, the wife of his brother Philip, and for all the evils which the Herods had done in defamation of the Word and in desecration of the little child. For this, John was shut up in prison and ultimately beheaded, whereupon he was received into heaven and sat upon the right hand of God—but not before he had fulfilled his mission to prepare the way of the LORD's coming, to make straight his Path of the Ruby Ray whereby Christ's followers might follow him through the baptism of repentance for the remission of sins to the coming baptism by the sacred fire of the Holy Ghost through Christ the LORD, whose herald he was.

When the Lord Jesus was led up of the Holy Spirit to challenge and be challenged by the false hierarch Satan, he first fasted forty days and forty nights. This followed his water baptism by John in Jordan and his fire baptism by the sacred fire of the Holy Ghost which descended upon him in the form of a dove. Whereas his herald had confronted the serpents, the seed of the original Liar and his lie, Jesus confronted the original Murderer and his murder, the force of Death and Hell itself personified in Satan and his electronic forcefield.

The three temptations which Satan gave to him were the same with which Serpent had beguiled his mother, Eve. The Son Jesus Christ came for the redemption of Mother and the Mother flame. The Serpent who spoke to the woman in the garden of Eden was the leader of a band of fallen angels who fell from the second ray of the LORD's wisdom. Before their fall, their understanding of God and his laws governing the path of initiation and of individual Christhood was more complete (subtil) than that of any other angels (beasts) of the field of God's consciousness which the Lord God had made in the beginning.

This fallen one was selected from the Luciferian councils as the one most able to turn the woman away from her first love in God who had come to her in the person of the Great Initiator, Lord Maitreya, the Cosmic Christ, as well as from her second love, that of her beloved twin flame.

The seeds of doubt and fear formed the foundation of Serpent's questioning of the Lawgiver and his Law. Impugning the motive of Maitreya, Serpent set himself up as the false hierarch and impostor of the Cosmic Christ. And ever since, he has, with his seed, maintained the foundations of the false hierarchy's philosophy of Antichrist in economics, politics, the social sciences, and the culture of civilization—all on the basis that his way is better than God's way, that he knows what God knows and knows it better, and what's more, that he knows what is best for His offspring on earth.

While the tactic of this fallen one is to destroy the Word of God by detracting from it, carefully removing the sacred-fire mysteries of the Holy Grail from the codified scriptures of East and West, his temptation of Eve was based on his distortion of the Word. Thus he perverts the Trinity by false initiation—giving to the woman the fruit of Light that is forbidden except through the initiation of the Christ; by false teaching—"Ye shall not surely die"; and by false comfort—"Ye shall be as gods, knowing good and evil."

The fallen ones have continued to prate their lie, assuring their own seed that there is no Devil, no final judgment, and no second death. Having almost convinced their own seed that it is possible to circumvent the true path of individual Christhood, replacing it with the vicarious atonement, they have in them willing instruments of the lie and the Liar who promote their false doctrine and dogma, making their version of religion and God-government compatible with the pleasure cult whereby the seed of the Woman are led to their own apparently 'freewill' destruction of the Word.

The same temptations to distort the flame of the Father, of the Son, and of the Holy Ghost were presented by the Antichrist, Satan himself, to the Lord Jesus. But he who had vowed to destroy the works of the Devil knew of the enmity which the LORD GOD had placed between Serpent and the Woman and between Serpent's seed and the Christic seed of the Mother.

He knew that Serpent's head (his intellectual philosophy, his scientific humanism, his deification of the carnal mind and of the godless materialism and mechanization of the Watchers and their soulless creation) would be bruised and ultimately destroyed by the God-mastery of the Son of God in the Piscean dispensation. He also knew that until the final judgment when this chaff creation should be consumed by the unquenchable sacred fire of the Holy Ghost, it would not relent in its attempt to bruise the heel (the self-mastery in Pisces) of the Christic seed of the Woman.

Jesus the Christ, whose soul had been embodied as righteous Abel and had suffered death by the hand of the unrighteous Cain, knew firsthand the sorrows of Adam and Eve following their unsuccessful bout with Serpent, the representative of the entire Luciferian false hierarchy. Thus he vowed to me the vow which he fulfilled 6,666 cycles following the fall of his parents. Prepared on the Path of the Ruby Ray with Joseph and Mary from his birth to his twelfth year and then in the retreats of the Great White Brotherhood until the age of thirty, he came to John in the prearranged meeting for the initiation of the baptism. He was ready in the fullest manifestation of the Word to take on Satan and through him Serpent and his lie, denying the lawful path of initiation—which was the original sin.

Rightly called the "last Adam" (the last incarnation of the son of "the first man Adam"), the Son of God went forth boldly to expose the entire Satanic false hierarchy as having no power, no wisdom, and no love to thwart the mighty Threefold Flame of Life in the hearts of God's children. In the wilderness of the astral plane, the citadel of the fallen ones, he stood and still stands for the descendants of the Adamic race who were henceforth to be called the I AM Race. These are the sons and daughters of Alpha and Omega who will restore the divinity of the Father-Mother God in Adam and Eve and in all twin flames who will reenter with them the Path of the Ruby Ray—this time to win.

Thus I AM the Restorer of the Light of these twin flames and their descendants. And through the Saviour of that race—the son of the man, Adam, who has become the Son of God, Christ Jesus—Satan and every fallen one was, is, and can be summarily dismissed with the Word of God spoken through you: "Get thee hence, Satan: for it is written, Thou shalt worship the LORD thy God, and him only shalt thou serve."

This is the true religion of the LORD GOD who appeared to Adam and Eve in the 'first' (the Alpha) mystery school, and it remains the true religion of those who, as their descendants, have come to the 'last' (the Omega) mystery school to restore the grace of God in the name of their Son, Jesus.

I AM with you, my beloved, in the first and the last (the Alpha and the Omega) Guru, Lord Maitreya. And I AM Alpha and Omega in the beginning and the ending of the cycles of your karma in the Matter sphere.

Now together let us accelerate as we—I through you and you through me—take up these serpents and cast them out by the Word of God, by the Son Jesus Christ and by the entire Spirit of the Great White Brotherhood whom he represents in the lineage of the Ruby Ray. Let the woman of Genesis be redeemed through the Woman of Revelation. For that Woman represents the soul of every child of God who has descended into the Matter sphere and who will ascend through the open door of the righteous BRANCH.

I AM the Ancient of Days reminding you, my beloved, of your vow made with righteous Abel to destroy the works of the Devil and to redeem the Woman and her seed throughout all the earth.

By the four cosmic forces and by the LORD's living Presence in the Community of the Holy Spirit, I AM the open door which no serpent disguised as the Son of man can shut!

Sanat Kumara

Mantra for Meditation of the Word
on the Blue Fire Sun of Sirius

Light will overcome,
Light will make us one.
Light from blue fire sun,
Command us now all free!

See Zech. 4; Rev. 11; 12; Isa. 11; Jer. 23:1–8; 33:15, 16; Zech. 3; 6:11, 12; Gen. 2:8, 9; Rev. 2:7; 5:22; Mark 14:58; Acts 7:48; Heb. 9:11; Rev. 19:1–10; 21; Matt. 22:1–14; Rev. 14:4; Mark 16:19; Gen. 2:24; Matt. 19:5, 6; James 4:8; John 10; Matt. 25:1–13; Rev. 13:8; Mark 16:18; Matt. 3; Luke 3: Matt. 12:14–37; 23; John 8:33–47; Matt. 13:24–30, 36–43; 2; Mark 6:14–30; Matt. 4:1–11; Rev. 6:8; Gen. 3:4; 1 John 3:8; 1 Cor. 15:45; Rev. 1:8, 11; 3:7, 8.

The Alchemical Marriage of the Lamb and the Lamb's Wife

The Reception into Heaven
and the Sitting on the Right Hand of God
Mark 16:19

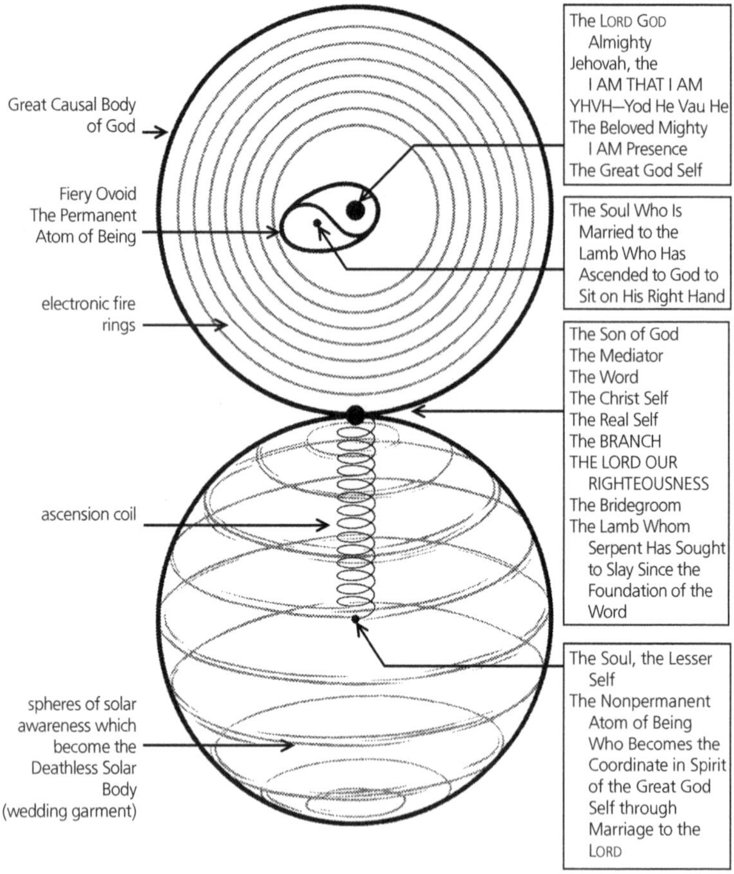

Great Causal Body of God
Fiery Ovoid The Permanent Atom of Being
electronic fire rings
ascension coil
spheres of solar awareness which become the Deathless Solar Body (wedding garment)
The LORD GOD Almighty
Jehovah, the I AM THAT I AM
YHVH—Yod He Vau He
The Beloved Mighty I AM Presence
The Great God Self
The Soul Who Is Married to the Lamb Who Has Ascended to God to Sit on His Right Hand
The Son of God
The Mediator
The Word
The Christ Self
The Real Self
The BRANCH
THE LORD OUR RIGHTEOUSNESS
The Bridegroom
The Lamb Whom Serpent Has Sought to Slay Since the Foundation of the Word
The Soul, the Lesser Self
The Nonpermanent Atom of Being Who Becomes the Coordinate in Spirit of the Great God Self through Marriage to the LORD

This diagram is a symbolical representation of the mysteries revealed by Sanat Kumara to facilitate your conceptualization of the relationship, in time and space and in eternity, of the soul's initiations leading to reunion with God. For a better understanding of the nature of the Trinity expressed in this chart you may superimpose it upon the Chart of Your Divine Self (facing page 376), comparing the upper dot with the upper figure, the central dot with the central figure, and the lower dot with the lower figure.

34

The Judgment of Serpent and His Seed
They shall not pass!

Woe unto you, scribes and Pharisees, hypocrites! because ye build the tombs of the prophets, and garnish the sepulchres of the righteous,

And say, If we had been in the days of our fathers, we would not have been partakers with them in the blood of the prophets.

Wherefore ye be witnesses unto yourselves, that ye are the children of them which killed the prophets.

Fill ye up then the measure of your fathers.

Ye serpents, ye generation of vipers, how can ye escape the damnation of hell?

Wherefore, behold, I send unto you prophets, and wise men, and scribes: and some of them ye shall kill and crucify; and some of them shall ye scourge in your synagogues, and persecute them from city to city:

That upon you may come all the righteous blood shed upon the earth, from the blood of righteous Abel unto the blood of Zacharias son of Barachias, whom ye slew between the temple and the altar.

Verily I say unto you, All these things shall come upon this generation of vipers. MATTHEW 23

They shall not pass!

My Beloved Who Will Yet Go to the Mountain to Fast and Pray with Me That the Serpents Might Be Expelled from the Earth:

Let us go to the mountain in the land of Erin where a youth enslaved by pagans is in prayer through the day and into the night. So fervent is the love of God within him that the fire of his heart is a light midst snow and ice. He lived on the mountain, alone with God, tending his master's herds. And on that mountain I called my son Patrick, that out of the condition of servitude there might be produced the miracle fire of freedom.

It was late fourth century A.D. and the clans of the Irish—the reincarnated tribes of Ephraim and Manasseh—were ruled by a host of kings. They served not the LORD GOD, nor had they the salvation of his Son. Therefore I, the Ancient of Days, called my son, freeborn, unto slavery that I might deliver him to freedom and to the mission of implanting the violet flame in the hearts of my true sons and daughters that they might one day carry it to the New World in the name of Saint Germain.

To him I gave the vision of the people of Erin whose seed would one day ignite the fires of freedom on every shore and in every nation. Your own prophet Mark derived his fervor from that lineage of the Ancient of Days which goes back to the emerald isle. And the Irish eyes of Thomas Moore, poet and prince of my heart, yet smile through the sternness of El Morya and his twinkle of mirth always needed on earth.

Finally restored to his kinsfolk after six years of humbling himself before me on the mountain, tending sheep as he would soon feed my sheep, Patrick heard the voices of the souls of my children crying out from the land of Erin for deliverance: "We beseech thee, holy youth, to come and walk among us once more." Indeed they remembered him when he had walked among them as a prophet in Israel, rebuking their waywardness in the name of the LORD. Now they awaited the message of their salvation through Messiah's anointed apostle.

Patrick prepared for his mission under the lineage of the

Ruby Ray and with the saints of the inner Church. And that mission, my beloved, was to subdue the seed of Serpent in Ireland and to raise up the tribes of Israel, the remnant of Joseph's seed who would be Christ-bearers to the nations. Empowered of the Holy Ghost and bearing the Staff of Jesus, he wielded such power and wrought such miracles that pagan chiefs and decadent druids bowed in submission to this rod of Aaron that, in the new tongue, became the rod of *Erin*.

So perilous was the mission of the shamrock saint of the fifth ray that he wrote in his "Confession": "Daily I expect either a violent death or to be robbed and reduced to slavery or the occurrence of some such calamity. I have cast myself into the hands of Almighty God, for He rules everything; as the Prophet sayeth, 'Cast thy care upon the LORD, and He Himself will sustain thee.'"

Well might you emulate the courage and the humility of my son Patrick when he boldly challenged Prince Corotick, that serpent who dared plunder Patrick's domain, massacring a great number of neophytes, as it is written, who were yet in their white garments after baptism; and others he carried away and sold to infidels.

Patrick circulated a letter in his own hand pronouncing the judgment of Corotick and his accomplices and declaring them separate from him as the established Bishop of Ireland, and from Jesus Christ. He forbade the faithful "to eat with them, or to receive their alms, till they should have satisfied God by the tears of sincere penance, and restored the servants of Jesus Christ to their liberty."[1]

Such is the true Work and Word of the saints of the Ruby Ray who, with all due seriousness, receive the sign of their coming in the taking up of serpents. Thousands upon thousands of the descendants of Jacob's favorite son were baptized and confirmed by the Lord Jesus through my son Patrick. Like the apostle Paul, he bound the power of Serpent's seed that had invaded the land of Erin; and like him, he healed their sick, he restored sight—both inner and outer—to their blind, and he raised Abram's seed—dead in body and in spirit—to new life through the indwelling Christ by the Word of Christ Jesus, his beloved.

Now the Ascended Master Saint Patrick stands with me on the summit of Mount Aigli where, at the close of his earthly sojourn, he retreated forty days and forty nights, fasting in body and in spirit that he might be filled with the light of the Ancient of Days. There on that occasion fifteen hundred years ago, I summoned all the saints of Erin—the light of Aaron's priesthood and the lightbearers of the Christic seed of Joseph*— past, present, and future, to pay homage to him who was father to them all.

Again I call the saints to a pilgrimage to the mountain to bless and be blessed by Patrick, to be infilled with his Spirit, to receive his mantle, to pray fervently that the fruit of all of his labors might provide a plenteous harvest in this age unto the World Mother who labors long for her children and for the Manchild.

Now I say, saints of the Ruby Ray, let Mission Amethyst Jewel return to the shrine where there once burned in the heart of a youth enslaved a kindling light that was to light a world. Let him who is an initiate of the fifth ray and the Lamb who is worthy transfer to you the momentum of his light that by your dynamic decrees unto the living Word you might once again cast out of Ireland the seed of Serpent now persecuting the blessed seed of the Woman. Let the violet fire of freedom ring through hill and dale! Let it restore truth and the true Church Universal and Triumphant that belongs unto the saints!

My beloved, many of you were among the souls of the saints who came to Patrick in his final hours on the mountain. You saluted him in the glory of God that was upon him, and to him you were the promise that his Word and Work would be

---

*Joseph, youngest and most favored son of Jacob, had two sons, Ephraim and Manasseh, whom Jacob blessed as his own. Reincarnated in Britain and the U.S.A., they carry the flame of the twelve tribes of Israel.

carried to golden shores unto a golden age of Christ peace and enlightenment. It is time and high time that you go forth to bind the barbarians that have returned to the British Isles with their terror and terrorism and their age-old tyranny by which they would bind the souls of my people Israel.

Let the Stone of Scone and the Davidic line be in you as the seed atom and the white cube of the Mother chakra. For in the lowest and the highest echelons of society throughout England, Scotland, Ireland, and Wales, the pagan chiefs (who are the Watchers and their godless creation) and the decadent druids (who are the witches and warlocks and the purveyors of the wares of Hades—rock, drugs, alcohol, and sexual perversion) yet pursue the beloved Mother and her children. *They shall not pass!*

Yes, Serpent and his seed must be cast out of the isles of Britain; for there they have set themselves up, from the closing hours of Camelot to the present, as the adversaries of the Woman and of the feminine potential of man and woman. Through the subculture of the fallen ones, they have launched a frontal attack on the light of the kundalini. They have beguiled modern Eves and their offspring to redirect the white light—the creative fohat of the life-force—into every conceivable, almost inconceivable, perversion of the sacred fire, mind you, chakra by chakra. *They shall not pass!*

Apparently successful in changing the course of the kundalini, the seed of Serpent have temporarily changed the course of Western civilization. Their counterrevolution of black magic practiced against the Woman is launched from the astral planes at The Hague, where their emblem is the gnarled and crusty figure of the hag—Great Whore of yore. *They shall not pass!*

These princes of the power of the air appear on the astral plane as out of Serpent's root there comes forth the cockatrice, and his fruit is the fiery flying serpent. These "will not be charmed and they shall bite you, saith the LORD." Misusing the breath of the Holy Spirit, their 'bite' is the distortion of the original blueprint in the etheric body and its manifestation in the mental body. Thus they have positioned themselves (as the archdeceivers have taught them) at the east gate, the doorway of the air quadrant, as the self-acclaimed destroyers of the light of the Holy Ghost in the mind of man and woman. *They shall not pass!*

Theirs is the spirit that Paul observed working in the children of disobedience among whom, he noted, "we all had our conversation in times past in the lusts of our flesh, fulfilling the desires of the flesh and of the mind; and were by nature the children of wrath, even as others." *They shall not pass!*

Paul further notes that only the great love of God, who is rich in mercy, was able to quicken us together with Christ and to raise us up to sit together in heavenly places in Christ Jesus. These heavenly places frequented by Paul and the early followers of Christ are the etheric cities and retreats of the ascended masters where the saints robed in white who have risen from my paths of the Ruby Ray, East and West, gather themselves together unto the supper of the Great God. From these heavenly places you, my beloved, have received not one but many servant-sons of light who have instructed you in the wiles and wares of these princes of the air. *They shall not pass!*

Their strategy is to preempt the office of the Son of man in the earth (the Matter sphere). And thus they have set themselves up as pretenders to the throne of grace, perverting the path of the fifth ray into materialism and mechanization devoid of the Spirit of living Truth. They have sponsored the laggards and wayward evolutions of the children of disobedience to intellectual pursuits, securing for them the most prestigious professional positions and posts of leadership in international affairs. They have courted the children of mammon and promoted them into prominence in circles of commerce, banking, government, and industry where they therefore, through them, still control the destinies of most of the citizens of earth. *They shall not pass!*

These are the cunning serpents of whom Jesus spoke when he

said, "Be ye therefore wise as serpents and harmless as doves." The LORD's admonishment is clear. If you would have the wisdom of these angels of the second ray who have fallen from their high estate into carnal mindedness, then you must have the dove of the Holy Ghost whose charity and enlightenment will keep you in line with the will of God and properly aligned with that mind of God which was in Christ Jesus. Only by the sponsorship of the indwelling Trinity can you be wise in the things of heaven and of earth and not fall into the self-idolatry of this generation of serpents. *They shall not pass!*

But the seed of Serpent have determined not to allow the seed of the Woman to rise in the fields of education, communications, journalism, public service in Church and State, or the performing arts. They have set their course upon the principle that he who governs the air quadrant governs the course of the mental evolution of earth's inhabitants. And this has been the "great wrath" of their strategy since they were cast out of heaven into embodiment on earth by Archangel Michael and his legions of blue-flame angels. *They shall not pass!*

Wherefore, my beloved, until sons and daughters of God and the children of the light rise up to overthrow the oppressors of the mind of God within them, who have positioned themselves on a planetary scale in the throat, the third eye, and the crown chakras of the nations, the strategy of Serpent's seed will continue. *They shall not pass!*

And you will not hear a loud voice saying in heaven, "Now is come salvation and strength, and the kingdom of our God, and the power of his Christ: for the accuser of our brethren is cast down, which accused them before our God day and night"—no, not until you say, "Blessed is he that cometh in the name of the LORD"—the Ancient of Days and his incarnate Word— no, not until you invoke the LORD's Judgment upon them: *"They Shall Not Pass!"*

Nevertheless, their prophesied judgment can and shall be fulfilled through the spoken Word and through the purity, the humility, and the love of my servants on the Ruby Ray. And you shall overcome Serpent and his seed by the blood of the Lamb and by the Word of your testimony—*if you love not your lives unto the death*. And I speak of the death neither of the soul nor of the body but of the serpent mind and of its replacement by the Christ mind.

For the hour of their judgment is come. Therefore, let those to whom my angel has entrusted the Everlasting Gospel fear God and give glory to him, and worship him that made heaven and earth and the sea and the fountains of waters.

My beloved, I have placed in your hands the key to the undoing of the despisers of my people. It is The LORD's Ritual of Exorcism. Only its daily practice will produce the desired results. As Satan once stood up against Israel to provoke David, so his seed and the seed of Serpent would, if they could, provoke my messengers and my chelas of the will of God.

But the Adversary who accuses my brethren day and night cannot, *and he shall not!* stand against my Light embodied within you. When the Light which I have placed there as the seed of my own Electronic Presence flows forth from you as the spoken Word, it does indeed swallow up the flood of lies that comes out of the mouth of the dragon.

The mission of Moses—who was Guru, who wore Mother's mantle—began with the conveyance to him by my flame of the God-mastery of the 'serpent' force. In this context the term *serpent* refers to the coil of light that rises on the spinal altar—the very same "rod of iron" with which the Manchild goes forth "to rule all nations."

You will recall that Moses carried a shepherd's crook, for he tended the flocks of Jethro, his father-in-law, at Midian. You will also recall that I bade him cast his rod on the ground. His obedience signified his willingness to cast aside his calling in the Matter spheres and to take up the calling of the Spirit, even as the disciples of Jesus Christ would later be called to leave their nets to become fishers of men. So now I would show Moses the mutability of his earthly calling that was soon to become, by the law of transmutation, the immutability of the heavenly calling.

The shepherd's crook is the symbol of the life-force in man. Held in the hand of the Good Shepherd of my people, it is the rod of attainment denoting that the chosen one has raised the light of the Mother from the base of the spine unto the crown chakra and sealed it in the third eye.

Now when Moses saw that his rod became a serpent, he fled from before it. I used this illustration to show him how the fallen ones have taken the life-force and captivated it in snakelike forms of destructivity capable of penetrating the minds of my children by serpentine logic and sinuous emotion. The very movement of a serpent's body produces the sine wave, and this relates to advanced teachings transferred by adepts to their disciples whereby they learn to pass their bodies through solid matter by the application of this principle of motion at the molecular level.

In order to succeed in his great commission, Moses must demonstrate God-mastery in the exercise of the powers of the *king*, for it was he who would indeed hold the *key* to the *in*carnation of God in the children of Israel. I instructed him to take the serpent by the tail, and I instruct you to do the same. Not the head-on confrontation with the fallen ones, but the challenging of the very base of their operation which is always in the misuse of the base-of-the-spine chakra—this is the tactic of angels of light and sons of God who have never left their high calling to defend the Holy of Holies from the abomination of desolation.

When you learn to seize the light of the Mother and raise it in God-control to the heart chakra, you will also be able to put forth your hand as the hand of God and catch the seed of Serpent. And when you shall have seized the light which they have misqualified—to transmute it before it can turn and bite you—then that light will become a rod of God's power in your hand. Thus prepare yourselves by diligent pursuit of the science of the

Mother light (1) *to take up serpents* by faith in Archangel Michael and his LORD's hosts, (2) *to turn them back* by the true wisdom of the Son, and (3) *to transmute their hate and hate creation* by love's own violet ray—the sacred fire of the Destroyer (Holy Spirit) who consumes all that is unlike Himself.

Now Aaron was also an initiate of the Ruby Ray, who would exercise the power of the priest side by side with Moses as his spokesman. Their holy offices, ordained of me upon Horeb, were to set the archetypal pattern of the calling of the kings and priests unto God under Alpha and Omega. It was the rod of Moses (the type of king) wielded by Aaron (the type of priest) which swallowed up the serpents of Egyptian black magic and sorcery and set the sign of Christ's rod. Later wielded by Jesus (who embodied the offices of both king and priest, the wholeness of Alpha and Omega), this rod would become the fiery caduceus of the resurrection flame to swallow up the death cult of Egyptian perversion of the Mother light and release it in the full glory of love's everlasting victory.

The sacred fire of the life-force takes on the form and manifestation of the one who is learning the right and wrong method of becoming a co-creator with God. When I sent fiery serpents among the people of Israel who spake out against both God and Moses, these were the precipitation of their own spirit of rebellion and disobedience—the very same spirit of the seed of Serpent which they had allowed to enter their minds.

By a mere inversion of the coil of energy which had proceeded out of their mouths in impurity and impiety, their miscreations returned to them the poisonous venom with which they would have, if they could, killed Moses. And many of them experienced death by the return of their own energy, reversed by my right hand upraised against them. Such is the mantle of the Great White Brotherhood—an ever-present protection upon those who exercise their spiritual offices with all diligence, humility, and love.

When the people therefore called upon the law of forgiveness for their sins, I bade Moses form a fiery serpent and set it upon a pole; and any that were bitten by the poisonous snakes, which returned to them the poison of their own consciousness, were restored to life as they beheld (meditated upon) this brazen serpent.

It was the symbol of the life-force and the representation of their own Mother light rising for the healing of mind and soul and body. The snake entwined about the wand of Mercury has remained the symbol of the victory of life over death. It is the symbol of healing Truth and the wholeness of Alpha and Omega that is realized through meditation in and upon the All-Seeing Eye of God. And all who look upon that Eye make contact with God's vision of the perfection of their being and consciousness.

God's vision of your wholeness, my beloved, is an arc of white fire which descends into your body temple as you meditate upon the Eye and offer its mantra to the Elohim Cyclopea. This arc of white fire is the energy of Alpha and Omega manifesting in you the wholeness of Christ's healing light. All of these teachings are yet a part of your fifth-ray initiations under my apostles Paul and Patrick standing with the two witnesses on the east gate of the Matter sphere.

Remember now the teachings which Jesus gave to you, my beloved: "As Moses lifted up the serpent in the wilderness, even so must the Son of man be lifted up." This *Son* of man is the *Light* of man. It is the Light of the Trinity and of the Mother which, as a blazing white fire sun, must be raised up that it might carry your soul to the door of your own Christ consciousness and to the doorkeeper, your own beloved Christ Self, "that whosoever believeth in Him, by meditation and by the spoken Word— by believing on the one whom I have sent and by fulfilling the initiations of the Ruby Ray—should not perish but have the eternal life of the Mother flowing in him forevermore."

Beloved ones, visualize the ascension coil rising within you from the base of your Great Matter Pyramid to the all-seeing eye in its capstone. For this sun of your manifestation *must* be lifted up. If it were not so, my son would not have told you, and he would not have laid down his life, that he might take it again in demonstration of this principle of the resurrection of the soul through the Son of God.

In order for you to demonstrate this same principle of eternal Life through the Mother flame, it is the requirement of the law that the sacred fire within you be not squandered in any of the misuses of the life-force forbidden by cosmic law in the Garden of Eden. Therefore you can understand why the head of these serpents is ever determined to bruise the heel of the Christed ones.

The heel is the symbol not only of the reproductive organs but also of the genes and chromosomes and the DNA spiral which conveys in Matter the Christic light sealed in the seed and the egg of man and woman. Inroads into the very light of the soul itself are being attempted once again by reembodied Atlantean scientists—serpents in your midst who contemplate the submission of the entire human race to their devilish designs (all in the guise of good) through alteration of the genetic code, selective breeding of the seed of Serpent with the seed of Christ to produce a supposed superior race having the cunning of the fallen ones enhanced by the light of the Woman. They also contemplate behavior modification for mankind's passive role-playing in the perverted matrices of Serpent and, of course, euthanasia, misnamed 'mercy killing', and the abortion of the life of the innocents in the womb of the Mother. *They shall not pass!*

By the God-mastery of this life-force in my sons and daughters, they shall go forth as initiates of the Ruby Ray, as overcomers not to be overcome by the temptations—so blatantly portrayed in the media—to misuse the sacred fire of the Mother in scientific as well as sexual misqualifications and perversions. Let the Christed ones use the heel—symbol of their Aquarian God-love as well as their Piscean God-mastery—once and for all to bruise and destroy the many-headed serpents of the last days. *They shall not pass!* For the Path of the Ruby Ray is the path of your soul's accelerated God-mastery of the accelerated God-love of the Holy Spirit.

Awake, awake ye sons and daughters of light! Awake, put on strength, thou who art the arm of the LORD in all the earth! Awake, as in the ancient days when thou camest in the generations of old with the Ancient of Days, vowing to save the Woman and her seed! Art thou not the band of chosen ones that hath cut Rahab to ribbons and wounded the dragon to death?*

Let us see, then, what our disciples who have studied and assimilated our Word will do with this initiation of the Ruby Ray:

Will they take up serpents after the example of my apostles Paul and Patrick and so many other brave ones who are now the ascended masters?—noted by John as the "fowls that fly in the midst of heaven."† Will they join the ranks of the overcomers who have overcome the dragon so that the little children might yet wax strong and grow in the grace of the LORD? Will they have the courage to wield the ruby sword after communing with the LORD, who is mighty indeed today as he was yesterday?

Will they apply my teachings preliminary to those that I will yet give on the opening of the seventh seal? Will they make good the light that I have given to them in this series of *Pearls of Wisdom* by dispensation from the Cosmic Council? Will they take up the Word and Work of the seven holy Kumaras in the earth to prepare the way of the LORD's Second Advent and to make straight the paths of consciousness in my people for the coming of the righteous BRANCH?

Will they see and take heart in the mission of all who have gone before that this is their hour—the hour when I, the Ancient of Days, would confer upon them the same God-mastery that I have given to the avatars, East and West?

My beloved, do not neglect to become the Word that you study and assimilate. For you know that this becoming bears fruit

---

*Rahab is the name of the symbolical dragon that appears as the antagonist of Jehovah.
†Rev. 19:17. Souls who have ascended to the mental quadrant of the Spirit sphere where they dwell in Christ's consciousness of God.

in the arena of action under the World Teachers.

With the sign of the Staff of Jesus subduing serpents, and the symbol of the sword of the Word and the Book of the Law of Jesus Christ, I seal you in the mantle of my sons Patrick and Paul that you, too, might be overcomers in the earth.

I AM Sanat Kumara

I hold in my heart the hope of the Mother for her children even as I hold the vow of my sons and daughters to redeem her flame and her seed in this hour.

Let the eagles who gather together at the Corpus Christi* descend from the heights unto the depths to pounce upon serpents and devour them by the sacred fire of the Mount Sion!

---

*The body of Christ consciousnes

See Matt. 23; John 21:15–17; Exod. 7; Ps. 55:22; Mark 16:18. Gen. 48; Rev. 5; 12; 17; Eph. 2:1–6; Isa. 14:29; Jer. 8:17: Luke 16:8–13; Matt. 10:16; Rom. 8:1–13; Phil. 2:5; Luke 13:35; Rev. 14:6, 7; 1 Chron. 21:1; Exod. 3; 4; Matt. 4:18–22; John 10:7–18; Dan. 11:31; 12:11; Matt. 24:15; Rev. 1:6, 8, 11; 5:10; Isa. 25:8; 1 Cor. 15:54; Num. 21:1–9; John 1:4. 9; 3:14–16; 6:28, 29; Gen. 3; Isa. 51:9; Rev. 19:17; Matt. 3:3; Jer. 23:5; Zech. 3:8; Matt. 24:27, 28. Note: The seed of Serpent are referred to in the Bible under a number of names, including: adder, asp, cockatrice, dragon, serpent, fiery serpent, fiery flying serpent, and viper.

35

∞

"Drink Me While I AM Drinking Thee"
If They Drink Any Deadly Thing, It Shall Not Hurt Them

Moreover, brethren, I would not that ye should be ignorant, how that all our fathers were under the cloud [of the Mighty I AM Presence and the hosts of the LORD], and all passed through the sea [the astral plane containing the records of their personal and planetary karma];

And were all baptized unto Moses in the cloud [by fire] and in the sea [by water];

And did all eat the same spiritual meat [the manna of the LORD's communion with them through his body and his blood];

And did all drink the same spiritual drink: for they drank of that spiritual Rock that followed them: and that Rock was Christ. I CORINTHIANS 10

Beloved Who Have Been the Followers of the Lamb
  Since I Called You Out of the Death Cult of
  Egyptian Bondage unto the Promised Land of
  Abundant Life in the Christ Consciousness:

Of those who drink of the spiritual Rock, taking into their temples the light of Christ, it is written: "If they drink any deadly thing, it shall not hurt them."

I AM opening the north gate of the holy city in the Matter spheres and there I stand to receive the saints of the inner

Church, the remnant of the Woman's seed, and the chelas of the ascended masters. Here the initiations of the sixth ray are given by the Father to those who hunger and thirst after righteousness that they might be filled of his Spirit.

In the name of the Great Guru Lord Maitreya, the Son Jesus stands in the midst of the people on their feast day and cries: "If any man thirst, let him come unto me and drink." I speak to the ones who are believing in the Son of God as the open door to their own Christ consciousness, to the ones who are being baptized through him by fire and by water, by Alpha and by Omega.

I would speak to you, my beloved, of your new birth through the resurrection flame borne in the heart of Christ as the fleur-de-lis and borne in the hand of the saints as the lily of light, signifying that they are submitting to the initiations of the Church Universal and Triumphant. By the admonishments of the LORD, you are becoming partakers of the Christic nature. Drinking in the consciousness of everlasting life, you are entering into the life of Jesus Christ through your own beloved Christ Self.

I begin, therefore, my instruction to you on the fulfillment of his Word, "He that believeth on me, as the scripture hath said, out of his belly shall flow rivers of living water." Through the fourth sign which follows those who preach the Everlasting Gospel, the LORD working with them [which is the sixth initiation of the saints who follow the Lamb, see pages 248–49], I AM preparing you for the entering in to the inner Church where the mysteries of the Holy Grail are divulged in the drinking of Christ's cup.

In the inner chamber, called the Upper Room, there is an inscription that is written: *Drink Me While I AM Drinking Thee.* Those who are received of the LORD on the Path of the Ruby Ray to be partakers of his body and his blood are taught the meaning of this command of the Great Initiator which has become the mantra of Mother and Maitreya singing in the hearts of the saints. These saints are the initiates who keep the Flame of Life and guard the sanctuary of the Holy Grail for 'the hundred and forty and four thousand' who must drink of the cup of the Father in this age.

Drink me while I AM drinking thee. This is the sign of the receiving and the giving of the waters of the Word—the true teachings of Christ—through the initiation of the throat chakra: (1) taking in the light as the blood (Alpha current of Christ)—the Life essence of the Mind of God for the nourishment of mind and heart, and delivering it as the Word of righteousness and as the two-edged sword of his righteous judgment; (2) taking in the light as the body (the Omega current of Christ)—the enlightenment of the Mind of God for the nourishment of soul and body, and releasing it as the light/energy/consciousness of the Holy Spirit through the solar-plexus chakra as flowing rivers of living water for the healing of the desire bodies of men and nations.

Only the partakers of the LORD's cup of spiritual grace are immune from the cup of the devils' blasphemy, and therefore my apostle admonished you not to drink of both. Likewise, when ye have been made partakers of the living Word at the LORD's table ye dare not defile the law by sitting at the table of devils to partake of their dead words and works. Thus those who would enter into the initiations of the LORD's cup must be aware of the penalties of taking these initiations which I give and then turning back to accept the initiations of the fallen ones. Rather must you be willing to say with the LORD's Christ: "The cup [of initiation] which my Father hath given me, shall I not drink it?"

For you who would be partakers of the Word of Maitreya on the north gate of the City Foursquare are baptized into one body by my Spirit—whether you are in bondage to your karma or to the personal and planetary karma of earth's evolutions or whether you are free from the round of rebirth and yet tarry in time and space as good shepherds under the World Teachers. For I give to you to drink of the communion cup of the Ruby Ray, which is true wisdom, true love, and pure light, that you might be one in this hour of your initiations on the sixth ray through the one Spirit of the LORD.

Our story begins at Jacob's well, symbol of the repository of the consciousness of the Christ in the twelve sons of Jacob who set the archetypal pattern for the path of Christhood unto the tribes who descended from their seed. Jesus being wearied with his journey from Judea to Galilee came to the city of Sychar in Samaria. It was about the sixth hour, the hour for the initiation of woman and of each one's feminine potential—the soul who would be the bride of the Lamb.

Jesus came to the very parcel of ground that Jacob, his father, had given to him when he was embodied as his favorite son, Joseph. And he sat on the well, signifying his dominion over the consciousness of the twelve tribes which had issued forth from the Ancient of Days through the seed of Abraham, Isaac, and Jacob.

Here Jesus returned, symbolically and actually, to a point of origins, to the foundation of desire, even to the collective unconscious of the entire Lifestream of the children of Israel. It mattered not that the woman who came to the well was of Samaria.* For throughout the Piscean dispensation, both 'Jew' and 'Gentile' alike would be tested as she was tested. And when it comes to you, my beloved, this test will determine whether or not you are received on the north gate in the Matter spheres by the Guru Maitreya and by his Mother flame.

What was Jesus doing when he said to the woman who had come to draw water, "Give me to drink"? She did not seem to know, nor did she know him who delivered to her the command of the Word. Therefore she did not immediately obey but entered into a human questioning of a divine master. The command, "Give me to drink," is given by the Gurus of the Ruby Ray to

---

*The Samaritans claimed to be the direct descendants of Joseph and the remnant of the kingdom of Israel, specifically the tribes of Ephraim and Manasseh. The Samaritans accepted the Torah (Pentateuch) as the only authentic law of God and Moses as his supreme apostle.

every would-be chela in order to test their level of desire.

How great is your desire to do the will of God? How great is your love for his Person embodied in the Guru? How great is your desire to serve Him through the one sent? How great is your desire to bear his cross, thence to receive a double portion of his Spirit? To drink his cup of sorrows at night, and in the morning his cup of joy?

How great is your desire to sit on the right hand of God? Can ye drink of the cup of Christ whereof he drank? And can ye be baptized with the baptism whereof Christ is baptized?

The disciples James and John came to the Master with great desire. Yet theirs was an inordinate desire. He engaged them, saying, "What would ye that I should do *for you?* What are you desiring me to do for you that only you can do for yourselves?"

They said unto him, "Grant unto us that we may sit, one on thy right hand, and the other on thy left hand, *in thy glory.*" But Jesus said unto them, "Ye know not what ye ask: can ye drink of the cup that I drink of? and be baptized with the baptism that I am baptized with?" Unwilling to own the full consequences of their demand to ascend to the throne of glory by their Master's attainment instead of by their own, as the Great Law requires of every servant son and daughter of God, they responded, "We can."

Then Jesus promised to them the path of their own individual initiation on the Ruby Ray, saying, "Ye shall indeed drink of the cup that I drink of. Ye shall indeed submit your souls to the initiations on the Way of the Cross to which I have submitted my own. And with the baptism that I am baptized withal shall ye be baptized. Ye shall indeed receive the purification through, and the polarization to, Alpha and Omega. But to sit on my right hand and on my left hand is not mine to give; but it shall be given to them for whom it is prepared."

My beloved, the saints who elect to enter the Path of the Ruby Ray and its initiations on the north gate of the City Foursquare are the ones for whom the marriage supper of the

Lamb is prepared. It is the celebration of that communion which you now commemorate as you *Drink me while I AM drinking thee.* It is likewise the celebration spoken of as the rejoicing in heaven over one soul's ascent in glory to the throne of the Lamb who does indeed sit on the right hand of God.

With the prize of the Path suspended before your gaze as a dazzling sun of light, symbol of your victorious entering in to the Great Causal Body of God, you may quickly agree to drink of the cup which the Father gives unto his Son in the initiation of the crucifixion. But many who at first are eager and willing do not have the staying power that this path of surrender on the Ruby Ray requires step by step through selflessness, sacrifice, and service. Thus the testing of the soul's desire for the cup of the resurrection and the life is locked in the words of the Master, "Give me to drink."

As the command of the LORD, "Give me to drink," echoes across the universes, we are suspended in the moment when the Son of man shall come in the glory of his ascended master light body, with all the holy angels with him, seated upon the throne of his glorious I AM Presence.

And to the souls who are on his right hand, having followed the Path of the Ruby Ray in ministering and serving unto every part of Life, the King says, "Come, ye blessed of my Father, inherit the kingdom prepared for you from the foundation of the world: for I was an hungred, and ye gave me meat: I was thirsty, and ye gave me drink: I was a stranger, and ye took me in: naked, and ye clothed me: I was sick, and ye visited me: I was in prison, and ye came unto me."

Thus the law is revealed to the disciples in the Upper Room: If you would receive the meat of my Word, the cup of my consciousness, if you would be taken in as a chela of the Great Guru, if you would be clothed upon with his mantle, healed of all your diseases, and receive the visitation of the ascended masters, if you would know them while you are yet in the prison house of your own karma—then you must first do unto one of the least of your brethren in whom dwells the living Christ that which ye would that he should do unto you.

And if you are the woman of Samaria and you do not recognize the living Master, it does not matter. It matters that you give to drink unto the one sent. And when you have given him the acceptable cup and the Son has given you the cup of his Father—it matters that you then give to these little ones in the name of your own discipleship the Master's cup of cold water and receive the reward of your initiation through the Manchild who lives in the heart of the little child.

It does not matter if your outer mind is acquainted with the path of Christic initiation. Whether it be a recognizable Christ, a little child, or a beggar, the Law requires that you receive the stranger that is within thy gate and that you give him to drink. In so doing, my beloved, you will satisfy the Law. And if that stranger be the Christed one, the one anointed by me to initiate my disciples of the Way of the Cross, then may it be said, "Whosoever receiveth him, receiveth me; and whosoever denieth him, denieth me."

For the soul always knows who is the one sent. And the souls of my children must be tested in the seasons of the Father—regardless of the outer mind's ignorance of the Law and the Lawgiver. This is why the initiation given is at the level of human kindness and human need—so that all may pass the test, so simple if they love, regardless of Serpent's prior poisonous programming of the outer mind.

So it was when Obadiah took those hundred prophets whom Jezebel had cut off and hid them by fifty in a cave and fed them with bread and water. In feeding them, he fed me. In giving them to drink, he did it unto me. Therefore I sent my servant Elijah to meet him, and he fell on his face and received him as the LORD's representative. But when Elijah gave him his first initiation which was to announce to Ahab that the LORD's prophet would see him, Obadiah, fearing for his life, did not immediately obey the LORD's chosen one but instead entered into the human questioning of the divine master.

Though in the end he obeyed Elijah's command, Obadiah's own fear and doubt, his sense of injustice, and his questioning of Elijah's wisdom, inferring that the prophet by his command would place Obadiah's life in jeopardy, revealed that he was not truly willing and able to drink of the cup that his master was about to drink, nor to be baptized with the baptism of mount Carmel.

Nevertheless he had taken the first step, feeding the Ancient of Days as he fed the prophets. And when his soul should prove ready, he would again be given the opportunity to obey the Word of the LORD without fear and doubt or human questioning and thereby pass through from the records of death unto the LORD's cup of the resurrection and the life.

Thus many are called but few are chosen to enter into the initiations of the Lamb on the north gate of the City Foursquare. Nevertheless it is written, "Blessed are they which are called unto the marriage supper of the Lamb." May you be blessed, my beloved, both in your calling and in your answering the first command of the Bridegroom unto your soul: "Give me to drink."

And when you give to your LORD to drink, give the very best of your rivers of living water stored within the deep wells of your seven chakras. These waters of the Mother light are yours to give in this very moment in the name of your own beloved Christ Self—though your chakras remain sealed with seven seals until you shall have successfully completed the seven initiations of the saints who follow the Lamb. This love offering of your cup, such as it is, unto the one sent by me to you, however lowly, is the prerequisite for your receiving my cup of the Ruby Ray.

This cup that you give to the Master will always contain the entire contents of your mind and heart—as the single drop contains the ocean. It is therefore a measuring cup whereby the Master measures this sample of your sincerity by the very vibration of the energy which you convey. The gift then is the essence of the giver. And it is time for the LORD's testing of all givers through the purity or impurity of their gifts made to one another in his name. As my son Morya has said of the ingratiating giver, "If I cannot accept the giver, I cannot accept the gift. And if I cannot accept the gift, then I cannot accept the giver as chela of the will of God."

When the woman of Samaria questioned and did not answer the LORD's command, Jesus rebuked her ignorance of the Law and of the Person of the Lawgiver saying, "If thou knewest the gift of God, and who it is that saith to thee, Give me to drink; thou wouldest have asked of him, and he would have given thee living water."

Ignoring her continuing chatter impugning his motive by her own impure motive, Jesus burned in akasha the record of the law of everlasting life which would be revealed to the saints of the Upper Room in the last days: "Whosoever drinketh of this water shall thirst again: but whosoever drinketh of the water that I shall give him shall never thirst; but the water that I shall give him shall be in him a well of water springing up into everlasting life."

Upon hearing of the miraculous properties of the water of his Christ consciousness, the woman petitioned the LORD: "Sir, give me this water..." But Jesus recognized her sinful sense of self-awareness. Her cup was not the acceptable cup of the self-disciplined chela of the will of God who pursues the Path to his utmost whether his LORD be present or absent. Therefore he would not transfer to her the initiation of the living water of Life but bade her first go and settle her karma with her five husbands and the last who was not her husband. Then might she enter the Path that leads to the Upper Room and the eternal Spouse who declares, *Drink me while I AM drinking thee.*

Ever the World Saviour through repentance and remission of sins, the LORD gave to the woman of Samaria the sign of the coming initiations of Aquarius when the feminine potential must be the purified vessel, already emptied of those Piscean perversions—Self-doubt, fear, and death: Self-doubt in both the

Creator and the creation; fear of the LORD based not on the love of his Lordship but on a rebellious and an unremitted sense of sin; and the death consciousness generated by Self-doubt and the sinful, sinuous fear of the unbelieving.

Still not perceiving my Light in the one sent, the woman pronounced to him the doctrine of the coming Messias, "I know that Messias cometh, which is called Christ: when he is come, he will tell us all things." Because she could not and would not see him as myself except by the confirmation of The Word, Jesus saith unto her, "I that speak unto thee am he." And it came to pass, though she herself was not emptied of her sinful state, that by the woman's witness unto his Christhood, many Samaritans came to hear my word spoken through the Son of God. And after he tarried with them two days they said, "We have heard him ourselves, and know that this is indeed the Christ, the Saviour of the world." My beloved, they perceived it by the Holy Spirit and by the Spirit of Joseph whose soul he was.

He prophesied to them the religion of the new age when the true worshipers would worship the Father in the Spirit of the I AM THAT I AM and in the Truth of the Word incarnate in the Christ Self. He gave to them his word of Truth which, when followed, leads to The Word who is everlasting life. But the gift of the crystal cup and of the elixir of Life would wait until the conclusion of the Piscean dispensation when the initiations of the resurrection and the ascension—following the long night of their crucifixion—would once again be available to the reincarnated children of the light of Israel.

He knew they must first pass through the dark night of their soul's self-crucifixion through the balancing of personal karma and the dark night of the Spirit's crucifixion through the balancing of planetary karma. Only then would the souls "for whom it is prepared" be allowed to drink the full cup of his ascended master light body and receive the full baptism of his ascension flame. These are the steps of the Path that leads to the seat on his right hand and on his left hand where James and John desired to be.

And this is where you, my beloved, with all your heart should also desire to be: For it is lawful desire—so long as you are willing to take up both bars of his cross daily, the vertical bar of personal karma and the horizontal bar of planetary karma.

When Christ said to the woman, "Salvation is of the Jews," he spoke of the remnant who journeyed with me to deliver the mandate of love to earth's evolutions and of all who through them would receive the transfer of my Light. But the archetypal nucleus of the 'hundred and forty and four thousand' must first be sealed in their foreheads by the emerald ray of the Elohim of the All-Seeing Eye of God under the dispensation of the two witnesses standing on the east gate. Then they must be initiated on the Path of the Ruby Ray ere the dispensation of the crystal cup might be given through the hands of these saints to the root races of earth's evolutions.

When the Master said, "Salvation is of the Jews, " he was goading her to respond with the words, "I AM also worthy. I AM of the descent of the seed of Joseph. Master, bid me enter in, and I will drink thy cup." It was up to her to denounce and renounce not only her sense of sin but also the effects of that sense manifest in sinful words and works. It was up to her to appeal to the Master for repentance and remission of sin and then to apply to him for discipleship. In this she must be willing to depart from her idolatry of his person and to recognize the light within her own soul as worthy to both give and receive the cup.

Thus I AM the LORD thy God in thy midst, delivering the message through my seventh angel of the mystery of God's appearing in Horeb—and of my name I AM THAT I AM—and of the Name behind the name—written in the foreheads of all who are with the Lamb on mount Sion. This message I deliver through the printed word to my chosen and faithful the world around that by your redemption, my beloved, the great multitude of souls of light might be redeemed from the earth and returned to the folds of their Manus [the Lawgivers and sponsors of the Christic path to earth's root races].

Now, my saints of the Ruby Ray, I bid you, *Drink me while I AM drinking thee*. The ebb and flow of the tides of Love are the giving and the receiving of the consciousness of the Lamb and his beloved bride. They are for your meditation on the great cosmic interchange of the resurrection flame that we now initiate between the souls of light on earth and their individual Bridegroom, the beloved Christ Self. When you receive the lovetide from your Spouse, let your joy be a mirror that magnifies the light of your LORD and sends it back to him by a cosmic reflection of his love for you and of your love for him.

As you enter into this meditation of love, you will begin to discover the mystery of his body and his blood through the golden-pink mantra, *Drink me while I AM drinking thee*. Drinking in the consciousness of the Lamb, you will truly enter into the life of the Son of God in every ascended master through your own beloved Christ Self.

And when, through Maitreya's meditation in you and Mother's mantra, the elixir of everlasting life is in your body and in the body of believers as resurrection's sacred fire, it shall come to pass that if you should drink (take in to your chakras) any deadly poison of the philosophy of Serpent and his seed, it shall not hurt you; for the mother-of-pearl frequency of the resurrection flame—the Alpha and Omega wholeness—will transmute it.

Because he who hung on the cross refused to drink the vinegar mingled with gall, because he rejected this mockery of his crucifixion by Serpent's seed, my beloved, you in your hour of victory in the very same initiation on the Path of the Ruby Ray will, in his name, also stay the hand of Serpent and thereby receive from the hand of the LORD's ministering angels the cup of resurrection's sacred fire as they sing to you their song, *Drink me while I AM drinking thee*.

Won't you invite the angels of the resurrection to tarry with you as you give the mantra of the World Mother unto the beams of essential light that are for the preparation of your chakras for the initiations of the sixth ray?

May the Spirit of the Resurrection in you, in the earth, be for the turning of the tide whereby the records of death are swallowed up in the victory of His love.

I AM

Sanat Kumara

bearing the banner
of the unifying Spirit of the Great White Brotherhood
which is the banner of peace and purity.

And I say unto all who would
drink of the water of Life freely:
Strive for the acceptable cup.
When the Master bids thee,
"Give me to drink,"
Give him the acceptable cup.

See 1 Cor. 10; Rev. 14:1–5; Mark 16:14–20; Rev. 12:17; Matt. 5:6; John 7; 10:1–30; Rev. 3:7, 8; Matt. 3:11; Heb. 4:12; Rev. 1:13–16; John 18:11; 1 Cor. 12; John 4:1–42; Rev. 21, 22; John 6:29; 2 Kings 2:9; Mark 10:35–45; Matt. 26:36–46; Luke 15:3–7; Matt. 25:31–46; 7:12; 10:40–42; 1 Kings 18; John 11:25, 26; Matt. 22:14; Rev. 19:6–16; Luke 9:23–27; Rev. 7; 10:7; 11:15; Matt. 27:24–49; Isa. 25:8; 1 Cor. 15:54.

Beams of Essential Light 60.06

Beloved mighty victorious Presence of God, I AM in me, my very own beloved Holy Christ Self and Holy Christ Selves of all mankind:

By and through the magnetic power of the immortal, victorious threefold flame of love, wisdom, and power anchored within my heart, I AM invoking the flame of resurrection from the heart of God, Alpha and Omega in the Great Central Sun, Blessed Maximus, the Great Spirit of the Resurrection and the Spirit of Selflessness in the Sun behind the sun:

The Seven Mighty Elohim, the Seven Beloved Archangels, the Seven Beloved Chohans of the Rays and the servant-sons of God who are with them in heaven serving under the four cosmic forces and the hierarchy of the Ruby Ray—the Seven Holy Kumaras, Sanat Kumara, Gautama Buddha, Lord Maitreya, Lord Jesus Christ; from beloved Helios and Vesta, beloved Cyclopea and the Great Silent Watchers of earth and her evolutions, the Cosmic Christs and the victorious overcomers of earth's golden ages, beloved Peace and Aloha, beloved Ascended Lady Master Nada, beloved Kuan Yin, beloved Lord the Maha Chohan, directors of the elements and forces of nature, beloved Mother Mary, Archangel Uriel, Archangel Gabriel, and all who serve resurrection's flame, beloved Lanello, the Lords of Karma, the Cosmic Council and the Four and Twenty Elders, the entire Spirit of the Great White Brotherhood and the World Mother, elemental life—fire, air, water, and earth!

Let the full-gathered momentum of the resurrection flame from the heart of the Lord God Almighty and his heavenly hosts—together with the ruby ray and the violet flame, cosmic blue lightning and the 'terrible crystal' white fire—consume the cause and core of the hordes of Death and Hell and seize and bind! seize and bind! seize and bind! Abaddon and his devils out of the bottomless pit tormenting the earth and her evolutions!

I lovingly accept your full-gathered momentum of the resurrection flame, consciously expanded without limit throughout the souls of God's loving, obedient children infinitely, presently, and forever:

Drink me while I AM drinking thee!

1. Blessed flame of resurrection,
   Flame of white and rainbow substance,
   Restore in me the fullness of my heavenly portion.

Refrain: O unifying Spirit of the Great White Brotherhood,
   Opalescent mother-of-pearl,
   Milk and honey of resurrection's happiness,
   Drink me while I AM drinking thee.

2. Blessed flame of resurrection,
   Splendor shining through me like a mist solidified,
   Comfort me with the Christ-reality of thy blazing.

3. Blessed flame of resurrection's glory,
   Beaming hope and splendid future joys appearing bright,
   I AM filled with thy beams of essential light.

4. Mother Mary, blessed Jesus dear,
   Hold me in the whiteness of thy heavenly glory.
   Let earth's shadows fade: O living light of God appear!

And in full faith I consciously accept this manifest, manifest, manifest! (3x) right here and now with full power, eternally sustained, all-powerfully active, ever expanding, and world enfolding until all are wholly ascended in the light and free!
Beloved I AM! Beloved I AM! Beloved I AM!

36

The Mystery of the White Cube

> *He that hath an ear, let him hear what the Spirit saith unto the churches; To him that overcometh will I give to eat of the hidden manna, and will give him a white stone, and in the stone a new name written, which no man knoweth saving he that receiveth it.*   REVELATION 2

My Beloved Who Would Pursue the Mysteries
  Given unto the Saints of God Serving in the White Cube
  of the Church Universal and Triumphant:

The mystery of the white cube, my beloved, is that it is the geometrical matrix in Mater wherein the Threefold Flame of the Trinity is hermetically sealed. The white cube is the symbol of the Mother and of the one who has become the lively stone in the temple of the Mother. The lively stone is the soul enlivened by the indwelling Trinity. Therefore the LORD GOD has sealed the spark of life within the Matter cube as a veritable sign of the coming of the LORD and of the goal of the path of initiation on the Ruby Ray—the incarnation of the Word.

The white cube is the symbol of Matter filled with Mother light. In multiples of four, its geometry radiates the sign of the cross in all directions as each side of the cube emits a shaft of white light signifying the blending of the tricolor Trinity unto the light of the one true God. The omnidirectional cross of white fire that is seen from every side of the white cube is a reminder to the sons and daughters of God that where ere they go in the Matter spheres, north, south, east, and west—no matter what the angle of their karma or their dharma, they cannot escape the convergence within the Temple Beautiful of the vertical and horizontal lines of Alpha and Omega.

Lo, I AM born to be the Son of God in earth and in heaven! Thus proclaim your fiery destiny and behold its mystery revealed in the white cube: You cannot go anywhere where God is not, as the Psalmist said, "Whither shall I go from thy spirit? or whither shall I flee from thy presence? If I ascend up into heaven, thou art there: if I make my bed in hell, behold, thou art there. If I take the wings of the morning, and dwell in the uttermost parts of the sea; even there shall thy hand lead me, and thy right hand shall hold me." From the heights unto the depths, in all planes of consciousness, fire, air, water, and earth, behold your God and behold that God travailing to give birth to the cosmic cross of white fire within you.

Now place your hand in the hand of your own beloved Christ Self and let the Son of God lead you into the eighth-ray chakra, the secret chamber of the heart. The sixth-ray initiations of the saints, preparatory to the initiation of the eighth ray, the ascension into the light of the God Self, are entered into by the saints who stand with Maitreya and Mother on the north gate of the City Foursquare. This is the entering in to the eightfold path of the Buddha and the bodhisattvas which culminates on the north gate in the eighth-ray integration of the lower and higher Self through the figure eight of the Lamb.

You will notice, my beloved, that the number six is an incomplete figure eight. Thus the initiations of the sixth ray are preparatory to the culminating experiences of the life of the saint, always consummated in pure devotion to the Mother, pure chelaship to the Guru Ma. The saints of the inner Church have always been devotees of the Mother, for they have understood that the one who is able to magnetize the garment of the Cosmic Virgin establishes within himself the white cube, even as he is established by the Guru Ma as the white cube.

That which the devotee first discovers in the secret chamber of the heart, the alabaster cube glowing with the inner light of the

Threefold Flame, is the cornerstone of the Temple Beautiful that he must build, line upon line, precept upon precept, under the close supervision of the wise masterbuilder, the beloved Christ Self. Thus by devotion to the Mother, the adoring chela becomes the Mother; and that which has become Mother, through the one who is Mother, is the magnet incomparable that is capable of magnetizing the Threefold Flame of the Trinity.

Thus, my dears, if you would become the Word incarnate, become the Mother and she will give birth to the Manchild within you. If you would enter into a direct relationship with God the Father, become the Omega light and she will polarize the Alpha presence for the fusion of worlds. If you would know the Comforter as the gentle presence of the Holy Spirit, then clear the bridal chambers [chakras] of consciousness, level by level, that upon your altars there might burn those cloven tongues of fire that are the sign of the indwelling Spirit who has come to fetch his waiting bride.

Where your God-mastery of time and space becomes the precipitation of the cosmic cube, there will the Mother be. Where there is Mother in the person of the Blessed Virgin, there is the Mother flame; and that white flame is the nucleus of the nonpermanent, or negative, atom of being sealed within the base-of-the-spine chakra. This atom is the negative polarity of the Permanent Atom, the white fire sun at the center of the I AM THAT I AM in your great Causal Body.

When the presence of the Mother within you becomes personal through devotion to the feminine personality of the Godhead, then the white fire sun of the nonpermanent atom will rise to the secret chamber of the heart where it will merge with the white cube. The white cube and the white fire sun of the Mother combined as one are the necessary ingredients for the birth of your individual Christ consciousness experienced by John the Revelator as he beheld the vision of the birth of the Manchild. Thus the white cube is there as the repository of the grace of the Trinity. But the soul by free will must exercise

God-dominion of the Mother light in order to unlock the potential of being.

The dominion that is given and the dominion that is taken is through adoration. Let us examine this manifold Path of adoration. God the Father, who holds the polarity of heavenly spheres, adores the flame of his beloved Son sealed in the white cube. God the Mother, who holds the polarity of earthly spheres, likewise adores the flame of the Son sealed in the white cube. Thus both Father and Mother adore the Person of the beloved Son, Christ the Lamb. By their Light *He Is What He Is*. By their Light the Son is in perpetual adoration of the seed of Alpha-Omega sealed in the heart of the whole creation.

Now the soul who as a child of the light exercises his option to enter into the joint-heirship of the living Christ Self enters the path of adoration of that Christ Self. By this he becomes not only the one adoring the Christ; but, through self-identification with the Christ, he is become the one adored. Through adoration sublime, sweet, and pure the soul who would be bride enters into the dominion of the Lamb. For through his adoration of Christ, the soul merges with the stream of His adoring of the Father-Mother Light throughout Creator and creation and is fused and infused with their universal flame of adoration.

Many desire to exercise power over the Lamb. They are ruled by personal pride in their self-sufficiency on the Path and by the spiritual ambition to be the Lamb before they have become the Lamb. These have not the qualifications of adoration distilled through the path of *karma yoga*: the sorrow of the soul who sincerely repents of his misdeeds and manipulations of the Beloved; the mourning of every moment of His absence; the pestilence and pain brought about by the soul's self-imposed separation from the Beloved; the loss of loved ones and the subsequent longing for that oneness in the Body of God in heaven and on earth which only the Beloved can fill—all of this, the suffering of the soul within the crisscross of life's experiences, becomes the joy of the resurrection and the life through the perpetual adoration of the Beloved.

The adoration which opens the portals of the seven petaled chakras is from the heart of the soul who waits upon her Beloved. At the midnight watch she watches for the coming of the Bridegroom, and in the predawn hours of prayer she attends his rising within her soul.

Blessed ones, the path of devotion, known in the East as *bhakti yoga*, is the path of the saints serving on the sixth ray at the north gate. The mystical union of the soul with God through the Sacred Heart of Jesus' devotion to the Father is the revelation of the Mother's mantra, *Drink me while I AM drinking thee*. This path is the only path that brings the ebb and flow of the tide of the chakras to the fullest consummation of love.

The chakras are wheels of the law that spin as crystalline discs of sacred fire and suns breathing in and breathing out the sweet distillations of the light of the Son of God within you. They are crystal cups for the drinking in of the nectar of the Threefold Flame and for the sharing of that nectar as you give to all life the same sweet nectar that life has given you. Such are the functions that God has sealed within the seven temples of man.

Where there is a vacuum of devotion, where the soul does not enter into the closet to pray to the Father in secret, then the spiritual functions of the chakras are not present in the lower vehicles—the mental, emotional, and physical bodies—but rather remain a function of the soul's interaction with the light in the etheric temple. Where the soul does not interact with the light through the etheric body, then all spiritual activity of the seven chakras ceases except in the body of the Lamb himself at the level of the individual Christ Self.

Those who are not the lively stones, those whose temples have not been quickened by the Holy Spirit, those who acknowledge neither the Father nor the Mother nor the Manchild have no light in them; and indeed any light that is in them is darkness. That which remains of the activity of the spiritual chakras is the transfer of the impulses of life to the corresponding nerve and glandular systems conducting the energies of life necessary for the cerebral, sensorial, motor, and autonomic functions of the physical body.

The function of the chakras of individuals who give no personal adoration to the personal God is at the level of the astral plane. Their chakras are cesspools. Taking in the entire gamut of the mass consciousness, they experience it, take part in it, and release it, with their own added momentum, back to the astral sea.

The misuse of the chakras is thus the source of pollution on a planetary scale as each of the four lower bodies takes in and gives forth the putrefied substance which mankind have dumped into the four quadrants of Matter as the by-product of their misuses of the light of the Holy Spirit. Unless the devotee learn to seal his chakras, he will suffer the same fate as the unenlightened. For the Law is no respecter of persons.

Therefore he who calls himself a devotee, if he have all intellectual knowledge of the ascended masters' teachings and yet have not the adoration of the Persons of the Father, the Mother, the Son, and the Holy Spirit, the lamps of his chakras are gone out; for they must be trimmed with the oil of gladness in the LORD which is pure devotion, ever waiting upon the Light in the joy of perpetual service and self-sacrificing love.

The oil in the lamps of the chakras of the virgin souls of both men and women is the return current of the adoration unto God. God in the Person of your individual beloved I AM Presence distills your devotion, my precious ones; and drop by drop, measure for measure, the golden oil of gladness descends to fill the chakras that the Flame of Life might burn on. That flame within you is as unquenchable as your adoration. Thus it is the unquenchable adoration of the devotee that magnetizes the unquenchable light of the Deity.

O Flame of Adoration, what strength in thy loftiness—what love enduring and ennobling unto the life of the devotee! Through abundance, adversity, or affliction the mantra of Job be upon the lips of the lover of God: "Naked came I out of my mother's womb, and naked shall I return thither: the LORD gave, and the LORD hath taken away; blessed be the name of the LORD."

My beloved, the path of devotion is the path of love. A love that is self-disciplined and wise in the understanding of the Law. The devotee must have in his devotion a supreme God-control which is willing not only to enter the closet but to shut the door. This shutting of the door is the silencing of all waves of agitation in the emotional and mental planes. These waves bombard the citadel of being as they rise from one's own subconscious momentums and even from the vast unconscious of any and all entities in the Matter spheres who may be unaligned with God or uncommitted to the path of light.

One cannot wait forever and a day, my beloved, for the tides of astral aggression to cease pounding the castle walls. Let the soul retreat into the interior castle, there to greet the King of kings and Lord of lords. His light will shut out the dark, if you let it. And if you let him, he will draw a circle of fire around the outer wall—a ring-pass-not where neither friend nor foe dare enter uninvited.

He is the invited Guest, and you are the host welcoming your liege Lord into the innermost sanctuary of being. He has waited long to be received by you. He bears a gift. 'Tis the vision of the God that I AM in full view.

If you tarry without the castle wall, you see, you will engage in and be engaged by every manner and matter of consciousness that passes by. Some would rather be there where free will is to experience every manner of life's polluters and their pollutants. To others freedom is the chain that binds the soul as the prisoner of the Rock, safe and sound within the castle walls while roaring tempest and turbulent seas ram the fortress of the immovable Rock, unnoticed by the soul who waits upon the LORD.

Yes, the water level of devotion is another measure of the levels of desire. How much do you desire to love God? Enough to withdraw from some of the preoccupations of earthly existence? And when all other loves fail, do you look to him as the Eternal Lover of your soul or do you yet seek another human love outside the castle walls? Every love you share on earth is intended to be a transparency for the divine love and the Divine Lover who often stands just outside the frosted windows of possessive love that excludes the Greater Self for the lesser self.

My beloved, I will be very frank with you. The desire to know God through the path of love takes tremendous determination. It requires the diamond will that is determined to have God and no other. It is a determination to fly straight to God, straight as an arrow clean that parteth the air, that will not be deterred or distracted here or there. Teach your children to set goals in life and to fulfill them, for they are all in spring training for the winning team of overcomers who overcome by a devotion that shuts out every force and forcefield of anti-devotion.

Now you can test yourself, my beloved, with this simple test. Set aside an hour when you will give ten minutes of pure devotion to God through uninterrupted meditation with your LORD in the interior castle. Let it be the meditation upon the white fire sun of your I AM Presence and upon the blue fire sun of Sirius. This will be a meditation on the polarity of Alpha and Omega in heaven and in earth, as the white fire sun is in Spirit and the blue fire sun is in Matter. Discipline your mind's eye to 'see' through your third-eye chakra and to behold only the white fire sun and then only the blue fire sun. Next behold the twain engaged in the cosmic interchange of the cosmic T'ai chi.

Behold the white fire sun whirling in clockwise motion, transferring the energies of Life to the blue fire sun as it whirls in counterclockwise motion, returning to the Great Central Sun the blue fire momentum of the Blue Mother of Sirius. This is a very natural visualization inasmuch as your soul has already beheld the twin spheres of Alpha and Omega as the archetypal sphere of the Father-Mother God sealed in your own Causal Body.

This is also the visualization for the union of the white fire bodies of twin flames and one with which you are also familiar, for it is an exercise given to you and your beloved twin flame in the meditation room of the Royal Teton Retreat. This meditation seals the oneness of souls who must be separated in time and space to fulfill their mutual service to life before reuniting in the fiery ovoid.

Take joy in commanding all of your energies to flow in one concentrated experience of meditation in God. And measure your own self-discipline as you exclude from your third-eye consecration all other thought forms or mere mortal distractions. Let the flow of the heart for this ten-minute interval be undivided in its acceleration of pure love unto the being of the white fire/blue fire suns.

Let the attention of your soul within the chakra of solar awareness be thoroughly engaged in entering in to the twin vortices of the Holy Spirit. For by and by, your soul's penetration of these orbs of light will be very real and you will step inside first one and then the other as though exploring your own figure-eight repository of the Spirit/Matter spheres.

Yes, it is time that you test the level of desire within the solar plexus. Is your desire to enter God consciousness endowed with sufficient unselfed love to generate an undivided devotion to the supreme will of Alpha and to the supreme wisdom of Omega? This will and this wisdom and your devotion thereto must become, if it is not already, the heart of the ten-petaled chakra at the solar plexus. For all pure desire rotates from the Trinity in motion at the center of the chakra where the test of the ten is the mark of the men and women who are preparing to enter in to the heart and the secret chamber thereof.

You can also experience the twin suns by devotion to the mind of God through the crown chakra. This devotion is experienced as the entering in to the very heart of the Knower and all that is known: In the center of that Flaming One, you become aware of the immensity of the white fire sun which contains universes of light teeming with individual ideations of God. And swimming in the sea of the blue fire sun of Omega are souls seeking and finding the Mother light as they glow and glow with iridescent blue, turquoise, indigo, and aquamarine. From the depths of the midnight blue of the Maha Kali to the heights of the piercing pastels emitted by crystals of the blue spectrum, the worlds whirling within the blue fire sun offer their endless self-expression upon the altar of the Universal Mother.

One-pointed is your meditation, and by its very one-pointedness it opens the door to the all-inclusiveness of Life. And every star that you discover in the inn of being, each sun a cosmos all your own, is a point of self-discovery and the discovery of a Self greater than your own. That Self is one who has loved enough to atone for karma, above and below, and to hold the light of love as devotion to all worlds aborning and to those that are yet unborn. These worlds are waiting in the womb of the Mother's blue fire sun to pass through the nexus unto the everlasting life of the Sun behind her sun. They are attended by that retinue of stars who love enough to be the I AM THAT I AM.

I have given to you clues for a meditation that leads to a penetration of the inner spheres of God. If you will prepare yourself properly (through fervent, fiery prayer and God Self-determined decrees) for your ten-minute interval when you are held in the embrace of the Lamb and in his consciousness of love, both you and the evolutions of earth will benefit immensely from the uninterrupted descent of the maxim light. If you can imagine a Niagara, an Iguassu, or a Victoria Falls, you will get the idea of a teeming torrent of light that is available to all who approach the pure stream of God, of the crystal cord, with utmost devotion unqualified by any human condition of time or space or the desire for self-gain or even self-fulfillment.

It is my express desire that you limit your meditation to ten minutes in order that you shall master the science of concentration simultaneously with the religion of consecration. Your experience in God is designed by the World Teachers who will lead you in the paths of higher consciousness to teach you that there is no time and space.

Ten minutes in God is truly a timeless, spaceless eternity. Because you have but 'ten minutes', you will learn the God-mastery of accelerating into the spheres of light and of assimilating extraordinary momentums of the Great Central Sun Magnet, which is the dazzling sun-fire center of each orb.

Finally, your mentors of the Ruby Ray would have you learn the be-attitude of nonattachment to the bliss of God—rather to love him for the sake of loving him and neither for the sheer enjoyment or entertainment of the experience nor for the ego's self-inflicted penance of flagellation that soothes a guilty conscience but does not remove the stain of sin. Think of your meditation, my beloved, as a service to God whereby you, in putting on God consciousness, render the entire cosmos an expanded opportunity to know him as he is. For he is light, and through your manifestation of his white fire/blue fire light, all may see and know and therefore become that light.

Through this meditation practiced by the saints of the Ruby Ray, the seven holy Kumaras have desired to concentrate more light, more love, and more wisdom in the true body of believers on earth during the decade of the 1980s. And in the process of rendering this service, it is our intent, as God has willed it so, that the sixth-ray initiates shall learn to recharge their four lower bodies and their chakras in the very midst of the accelerating spirals of service which Opportunity brings at the turn of the decade.

Let those who adore God, then, through the fervor of fiery, fohatic prayer—let those who adore him in the joyousness and the boundlessness of his divine decree which they deliver as the Word of the LORD into the consciousness of relative good and evil—let those who go to the mount Sion to adore him in the meditation of their hearts' light upon the light of God's heart—therefore learn to seal their chakras from all vibrations less than the Christ light registering in the Matter spheres.

The closing of the petals of the seven lotus flowers is

accomplished through the conscious determination of the will of man reinforced by the will of God. It is the thrust, ho! of light flashing forth in the I-AM-the-guard consciousness. It is the right hand of the Christ or the Buddha stretched forth in the irreversible initiatic light which releases the command, "They shall not pass!" It is the creation of a cosmic forcefield of light radiating forth in all directions from the center of the white cube within the heart.

With equal intensity, the cosmic command to preserve the forcefield of soul identity—reinforced by the God-determination to be free to be the manifestation of God—will always draw forth from the Godhead the cosmic cross of white fire as the mark of your soul identity where you stand. And where you stand for the light of God, there I stand with you. And the center of the cosmic cross is at the spiritual heart center of your temple where your heart is a flaming sun center of devotion unto God. In the fiery vortex of the cosmic cross, there do I place my heart center that we may be one for the elevation of worlds.

This exercise is also accomplished with the speed of light in the midst of Armageddon for the soul's arduous aspiring to the Word and Work of the LORD on behalf of his little ones. When, therefore, your attention must be directed into a multitude of matters demanding your watchful eye and skill of the hand, and by and by you feel the encroachment of random particles of effluvia pressing against your wall of light, remember even the policeman directing traffic makes use of the ancient mudra which universally communicates the cosmic vibration STOP!

This mental thrust of the Word is reinforced by certain physical postures during meditation and by others when one is in the active mode. Simultaneously, the fire and water energies of the etheric and emotional bodies are mentally and spiritually sealed by the acceleration of the figure-eight flow between the soul (suspended in the 'water') and the Christ Self (suspended in the 'fire'). This reaffirmation of the Word, once again drawing the lines of one's forcefield, may be accompanied by a strong breathing out and then a deep breathing in, holding the inbreath while visualizing the seven chakras and the eighth each sealed by the Lord Buddha extending the fearlessness flame in the *abhaya* mudra.*

Another measure used by the adepts who must manifest their presence midst the throngs of the large cities of the world in order to hold the balance of light is the spiritual/mental drawing of the ring-pass-not around one's forcefield. Just think of a child on a playground drawing a chalk circle around himself and then standing in the center. Then mentally draw your circle of white light, nine feet in diameter, as the pattern and the reinforcement of your tube of light, which itself is always visualized as nine feet in diameter. The ring-pass-not is also called the circle of identity. Actually, it is the sealing of the soul's integrity—its integral relationship with the beloved I AM Presence.

This 'inner circle' is one's own 'Holy of Holies', if you will, one's auric forcefield and the guaranteed time and space of one's experimental mission to earth. It is the place prepared and the energy field for one's experiments in the scientific application of the laws of energy (as love) and free will (as love) conducted in the laboratory of selfhood. It is this unit of God's Selfhood called individuality which the wicked would erode and thereby distort or destroy the options of free will.

You will learn under the World Teachers, if you have not already done so, that the study of psychology and the path that leads to the healing of the mind and the emotions and their conscious and subconscious expressions begins with the drawing of the circle of Selfhood. But it does not end until the psyche has mastered the spiritual science and the matter visualization of maintaining the perfect circle of self-integration.

Let us learn the components of the circle of the One. There is a vertical and a horizontal application of this circle. The one forms the circle of light which, as it turns, rises in infinite spirals,

---
*Gesture of fearlessness, right arm upraised, palm forward.

turning to form the connecting links in the chain of being, linking the psyche to its Christ Self and the I AM Presence. The other forms the foundational platform which, as it turns, rises to reinforce, in cylindrical motion, the tube of light.

The vertical, or upright, circle is elongated by the pull of the Great Central Sun Magnet within the heart of the I AM THAT I AM, thus forming an upward spiraling ellipse. Within the ellipse the figure eight rotates, forming and reforming itself by the ascending light of the soul's devotion unto the LORD and by the LORD's descending devotion unto the soul. This will provide you with another dimension of the mystery, *Drink me while I AM drinking thee.*

The ascending and descending light provides the integrity of Selfhood—or the integral ladder of light. Through this continuum of circles forming ellipses, the north/south integration of being is maintained. It is the vertical line (spiral) between the lower self and the Greater Self, the outer and the inner manifestation of God. It is the vertical integration of the soul with every part of Life in the Spirit spheres.

This integration can be maintained only through the I AM THAT I AM, the foundation of true being incorruptibly manifest in the octaves of light. In other words, the only lawful contact which the soul may entertain with the angelic host, the ascended masters, and the saints robed in white is through the individualized God Self. Any other attempt to contact the higher intelligences beyond the veil—psychic, mediumistic, by hallucinogenics, black magic or variance or even a rote mechanical performance of sacred rituals—will only entangle the psyche which engages in it further and further into the substrata of unreality.

This karma of unlawful attainment by unlawful means is of all states most undesirable, for it results in an anti-Spirit forcefield that may be termed an absolute energy veil, or an absolute Evil—the antithesis of Spirit and absolute Good. The delineations and definitions of these two absolutes are scarcely realized by mortals—and even children of the light can hardly identify Satan, who by such malpractice transforms himself into an angel of light. The ability to perceive the absolutes of God and anti-God is conferred upon the initiate of the Ruby Ray through the fruit of the Tree of Life. By it one lives forever through Self-knowledge in and as God.

Now, through the cylindrical formation of circles shimmering like interconnecting silvery discs of light, the east/west integration of being is maintained. It is the horizontal integration of the soul of light with every other soul of light dwelling in the Matter spheres. This east/west integration of being should be lawfully sustained through the blessed Mediator, the Universal Christ manifest in the Christ Self of each soul of light.

The Christ Self is the foundation of true being in the Matter spheres, the Rock whose incorruptible manifestation is maintained at the doorway of cosmic consciousness (the nexus of the figure eight). In other words, the only lawful contact which the soul of light may maintain with other souls of light, in the just and true spirit of friendship with Christ, is through the blessed Mediator of each one.

Any interaction with fallen lifewaves or laggard evolutions must likewise be through one's Christ Self and the Universal Christ, who forms a canopy of light over the wayward generations of earth to 'seal the forcefield where evil dwells', effectively stopping the flow of their impure stream into the chakras of the LORD's chosen and faithful. Those who commune at the level of the outer self without making the call to the blessed Christ Self to act as mediator and interpreter of their relationship enter into an energy exchange of any and all random momentums of relative good and evil.

The many interpersonal relationships of both a casual and an intimate nature which people entertain result in a continuous interflow of energy, waking and sleeping, whereby they give and take the gamut of human emotions and emanations of the intellect. Spanning the entire range of human vibrations, conscious and subconscious, these energies engage the chakras of tens of thousands of unsuspecting souls of light, severely hampering their world service under the World Teachers.

The devotee who would be chela of the Guru Ma on the eighth ray on the south side of the City Foursquare preparatory to the Mother's initiations of her sons and daughters in the glorious ritual of the ascension must be prepared to separate themselves, spiritually and bodily, mentally and emotionally, from all who are not partakers of the blood of the new covenant.

It is this subject of the blood of the new covenant which I will take up in my concluding letter on the vital interchange—Drink Me While I AM Drinking Thee.

Ever mindful of the 'dead' and the 'deadly thing' they would give unto the living to drink, I AM increasing the capacity of the lightbearer to bear that light within the cells of body consciousness that shall neutralize both the psychic and the physical poisons of this world.

Drink me while I AM drinking thee—and they and their deadly thing shall not hurt thee.

I AM always in the center of the Divine Exchange

Sanat Kumara

See Rev. 2; 1 Pet. 2:1–10; Ps. 139; Isa. 28:16; 1 Cor. 3:9–17; Eph. 2:19–22; Rev. 12; John 14:16, 17, 26; 16:7; Acts 2:1–4; Rom. 8:16, 17; Rev. 19:7; 21; John 11:25; Matt. 25:1–13; 6; 1 Pet. 3:18; Acts 10:34; Ps. 45:7; Heb. 1:9; Job 1; Ps. 18:2; 1 Cor. 10:4; Eph. 3:1; 2 Cor. 11:13, 14; Gen. 2:9; 3:22, 24; Rev. 22:2, 14; Matt. 26:28; Mark 14:24; Luke 22:20; 1 Cor. 11:25; Mark 16:18.

37

∞

The Blood of the New Covenant

> *And the dragon was wroth with the woman, and went to make war with the remnant of her seed, which keep the commandments of God, and have the testimony of Jesus Christ.*
> REVELATION 12

To the Saints Who Wait upon the Word of the LORD
   That They Might Indeed Drink of the Cup
   of Which He Drank:

The remnant of the Woman's seed are the Keepers of the Flame who keep the flame of the Father on the north gate. The north gate in Matter is the polar opposite of the north gate in Spirit. Standing on the north gate, the saints are at the greatest distance from the Great Central Sun which they will experience in time and space on the Path of the Ruby Ray.

Zechariah foresaw the LORD's initiations of his saints and exclaimed to the soul of Eve and to this feminine potential of her sons and daughters: "Rejoice greatly, O daughter of Zion; shout, O daughter of Jerusalem: behold, thy King cometh unto thee: he is just, and having salvation; lowly, and riding upon an ass, and upon a colt the foal of an ass."[1]

This is the description of the coming of the King of kings and Lord of lords, whose birth in Bethlehem proclaimed the Advent of the redemption of the Woman and her offspring to the lightbearers who vowed with me to keep the flame of Life midst earth's evolutions. He came as their King. He came as the key-holder, the one who would hold in time and space the key to their incarnation of God, hence to individual Christhood.

Thus he came as the Great Initiator. He was the issue and the instrument of the entire lineage of the initiators of the Ruby Ray. He was both the incarnate Christ and the one who was able to reignite the sacred fire of Christhood in all who were of the descent of my seed through Adam and Eve—from Seth to Noah and reincarnated from Abraham unto the twelve tribes—even to the present hour.

"Behold the Man!" and the face of the Son of man who stands at the east gate of Eden, sounding the Word for all who have gone out from the way of the Tree of Life: "I AM the open door to your Christ consciousness which no man can shut." To all who would run with him the path of the seven initiations of the seven rays leading to the eighth-ray integration of the soul with the eternal Lamb and the embodied Lamb, he is the Way, the Truth and the Life.

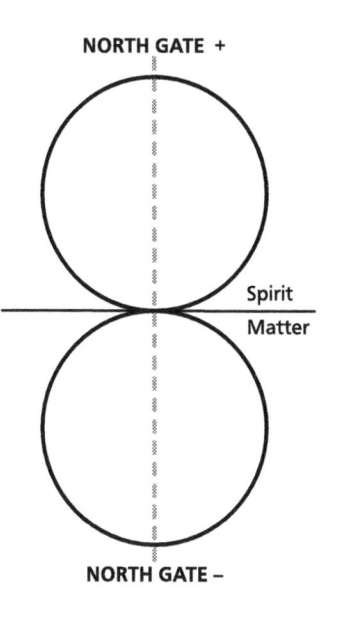

The eternal Lamb is the Christ Self 'in the heaven', invisible yet congruent with the Mind of God. The embodied Lamb is the LORD's representative 'in the earth', visible yet also congruent with the Mind of God. Holding the flame of Life on the south gates in Spirit and in Matter, these congruent figures of the Lamb, symbolized in the interlaced triangles of the six-pointed star of the Davidic Covenant, focus the crystal of the sacred heart, the nexus through which the light of the Father, positioned on the north gate in Spirit, passes to the saints on the north gate in Matter. Likewise, through the individual Lamb, the light of the saints passes to the Father.

He, the archetype of the Four Cosmic Forces, descended into the Matter spheres born of a Virgin—herself the incarnation of the Archeia of Truth, counterpart of the Archangel of Truth, the blest Raphael. He came that through the flame of the Virgin Mother and her incarnate Son, Adam and Eve and their descendants might once again take up the initiations of Lord Maitreya and Lord Gautama, leading them from the covenant of individual Sonship (on the first ray) to the New Covenant (on the eighth ray) of the putting on of the garment of the Ancient of Days by the wearing of the Mother flame.

And the spirit of elemental life provided the platform for his ministration to the saints in the earth. As Joseph took Mary, who was seated on a donkey, to the place prepared for the glorious incarnation of the Word, so Christ rode triumphantly into the city of Jerusalem upon the foal of an ass. This interaction and interdependence of the archetypes of Christ and of humanity with elemental life is another application of the mystery of the white cube. The beings of the elements—fire, air, water and earth—are essential to the crystallization, *Christ-realization,* of the soul in the God flame 'in the earth', their temporary 'coats of skins' and imprisonment in animal forms notwithstanding.

Let this illustration of the humility of the Christ be sealed in your souls, my beloved, that you might daily put on his garment of humility in the realization that came upon John the Beloved in his contemplation of the mysteries of the Rose Cross: "For God so loved the world, that he gave his only begotten Son, that whosoever believeth in him should not perish, but have everlasting life. For God sent not his Son into the world to condemn the world; but that the world through him might be saved."[2]

The birth of the avatar is the moment when the Lamb, who has been initiated at the cardinal signs of the Lion, the Calf, the Man and the flying Eagle, descends from the position of the Word at the nexus of the figure eight, and the Word is made flesh to dwell among the people who have forgotten their own origin in God, their true nature made after his image and likeness, and the paths of the descent and the ascent.

Because the great multitude of my people were as lost sheep, as sheep gone astray in the wilderness of Judea, I sent the Good Shepherd to lead them back to the twelve gates of the City Foursquare that they might speak peace unto the twelve nations of Israel and Judah and to the Gentiles who would be glad and glorify the Word of the LORD: all they that were ordained to eternal life.[3]

Zechariah saw my saints who would enter into the initiations of the sons and daughters of dominion standing on the north gate. And he prophesied that their dominion would be "from sea even to sea," from the waters (+) above the firmament (in Spirit) to the waters (–) under the firmament (in Matter) gaining God-mastery through the double arc of the flame of peace ☖ and the sign of the Piscean conqueror ☞ .

Yes, he prophesied their God-mastery over the sacred fires of God's energy in the stillness of the Great Hub and in the motion of molecules of outer and inner spheres.

He prophesied their dominion to be "from the river even to the ends of the earth."[4] This river is revealed to John as the pure river of water of life proceeding out of the throne of God the Father, the beloved I AM Presence, and of the Lamb, the beloved Christ Self.[5] The 'ends of the earth' are the farthest reaches of the Matter spheres and the farthest point of initiation of the saints, who, in the hour of their crucifixion, must descend to the astral plane and even to the bottomless pit and the subterranean levels of Death and Hell to rescue not only the lost sheep of the house of Israel reincarnated among the Gentile nations but also those of the original seed of Judah who remain uncontaminated by laggard lifewaves.

Now, this is the blood of my New Covenant (which is my *renewed* covenant), initiated in the seed/soul of Seth, the son of compensation (the reincarnated Abel), and fulfilled in his final embodiment as Jesus Christ. He was the potential Christ in the first days of his incarnations upon earth and he became in the last days the fullness of that Christ by his soul evolution on the Path of the Ruby Ray. In the ending, he was the Self-realization of the beginning—the incarnation of the Father in the Son and ultimately of the Mother in the Holy Spirit.

By his renewed covenant have I, the Ancient of Days, sent thee forth, my beloved saints, as representatives of the World Teachers. Go to! Now gather up the prisoners of darkness, even the children of my heart led astray by the Devil and enchained in the bottomless pit, where there is no water that they may drink and, having drunk, never thirst again. For the wells of water of both Spirit and Matter have run dry; and the astral plane is a dry and thirsty land where my children of disobedience are in bondage to the chains they have forged out of their own willful misuses and misqualifications of the waters of the Father's everlasting Lifestream and the Mother's crystal stream.

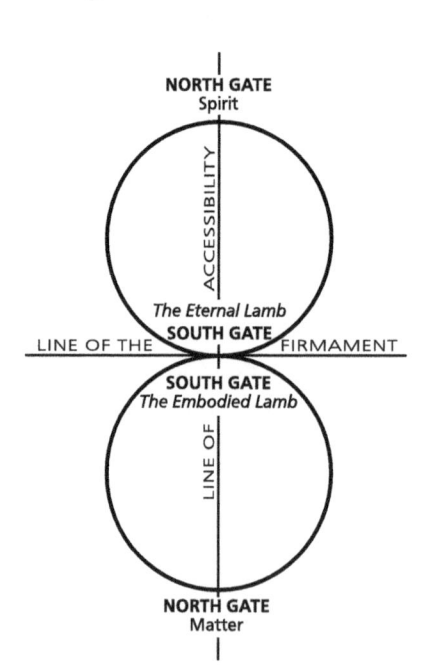

Even though your position on the north gate is termed "the ends of the earth," through your meditation upon the eternal Lamb and the embodied Lamb—my Mother flame anchored above and below on the south gates in Spirit and Matter—you have direct access to the Lord God Almighty, who is positioned "at the ends of the heaven." This line of accessibility is the "straight and narrow" line of your soul's alignment with the Permanent Atom of Being.

The Lord's Prayer,[6] given by the Master Jesus to his disciples, is the prayer of the saints whereby they may daily and hourly reestablish this alignment that is for the salvation of their souls through contact with the "Our Father, who art in heaven" and his hallowed name. As they hallow the name of God, I AM THAT I AM, within the secret chamber of the heart, the saints receive the momentum of his authority and his Word over the crystal cord.

The crystal cord, also called the silver cord, is the umbilical cord, the lifeline of the soul connecting it to the Spirit (I AM Presence). Over this lifeline flows the pulsation of the Presence that beats the heart and the energy that is distributed through the major and minor chakras for the sustainment of the life-force of the soul within the four lower bodies. The volume of light which descends is proportionate to the diameter of this lifeline to the Mighty I AM Presence.

As you know, in the early golden ages of the first root races, the crystal cord was of a far greater dimension than it is today. Before the reduction of the diameter of the crystal cord, records indicate that the descendants of Adam even through Noah lived for hundreds of years in the same physical body.

The proliferation of evil through the imagination of men's hearts, both before and after the sinking of Atlantis, caused the decrease of the lifeline to a mere thread. And the old age, disease and death witnessed by Prince Siddhartha was astonishing to him because these conditions were unnatural in the era of the Ancient of Days, when the 'river of life' flowed freely and plenteously from God to his sons and daughters on earth. And so shall it be in the coming golden age.

In the beginning, God was the diameter of thy lifestream. And in the ending, God shall be the diameter of thy lifestream. But in the middle, whereas you have decreased it, you must increase it by the flow of your perpetual devotion perpetually countering your momentums of anti-devotion.

As the saints become the chelas of the ascended masters and then of the Guru Ma on the south gate of the Matter sphere, they are able to enter into the fullest comprehension of the "Our Father, who art in heaven." Now they give the I AM Lord's Prayer, which the Master taught to the disciples in the Upper Room.

They enter into the equation of the Ruby Ray whereby they realize that the LORD GOD, who is the Almighty One in 'external' manifestation in the Macrocosm of Life, is also in 'internal' manifestation in the microcosmic forcefield of the individualized God flame. This spiritual 'Presence' he has established as the blessed Identity, the counterpart of the material manifestation.

Through the I AM Lord's Prayer they celebrate the New Covenant, whereby the outer God-manifestation is become, through the infusion of the Sacred Name, the inner God-realization. And the worlds without become the worlds within, and the entire Macrocosmic/microcosmic Being is known of the soul through the Knower enthroned within his heart.

As the saints one by one realize that I AM WHERE I AM, that they dwell in me and I in them wherever they are in Spirit and in Matter, the upper and the lower spheres of the figure eight begin to converge. This ultimate convergence of the spheres is finally completed through the *Z-ray initiations of the ion (Zion).* These are the initiations given by the Lamb to the archetypal '144,000', who follow him whithersoever he goeth and are therefore with him on the mount (the apex of attainment) 'Zion'.

The four letters of the word indicate the four cardinal points of cosmic consciousness ensouled by the 'Lion', the 'Calf', the 'Man' and the 'Eagle'. Zion, therefore, is a state of consciousness which the Beloved in due course transfers to his beloved. Coincidentally it may be a geographical location. Always it is the place where the eternal Lamb and the embodied Lamb are one with their chelas in the cosmic interchange: *Drink me while I AM drinking thee.*

These fourfold steps of the Z-ion I have hidden in this work. I have also made them plain. Shortly I shall again describe them to you as the things which shall shortly come to pass among you, even in your very midst. For through all of this teaching that I am giving, I desire to bring you full circle through the full journey of the figure eight to the God-realization: I and my Father are one. Lo, I AM where I AM. And where I AM, there God in me is the oneness of the Father in the Son and the Son in the Father.

Studying now the chart of the seven initiations of the saints who follow the Lamb, you can readily see that your position on the sixth ray at the north gate in the Matter sphere places you in direct alignment with the eighth- and fourth-ray initiations of the south gate in the Matter and Spirit spheres and with the second-ray initiations of the north gate in the Spirit sphere. Here, then, is the opportunity for the saints to reenter and retrace *the path of lost steps.*

This is the path taken by the lost sheep of the house of Israel and by those who dwelt in Judah gone astray of the Lamb. The apostle of the Good Shepherd retraces his steps until he comes upon the one caught in the thicket of carnal-mindedness and the brambles of astral illusion. In going after the lost sheep, he also encounters the missed steps of his own untransmuted karma. These missed steps often take him on a jagged course until he understands the initiations of the Z-ray of the ion.

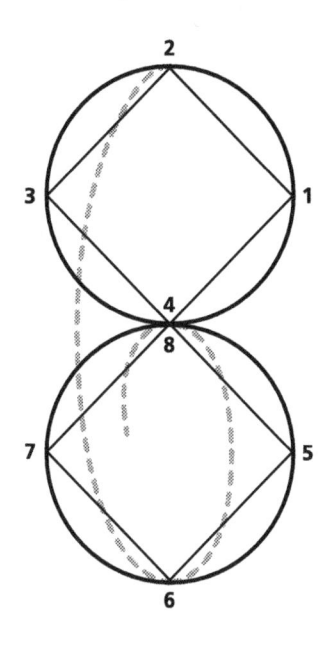

The one who is pursuing wayward souls on the path of the lost steps cries out to souls disconsolate and distressed on the zigzag course: "Prepare ye the way of the LORD, make straight in the desert a highway for our God. Every valley shall be exalted, and every mountain and hill shall be made low: and the crooked shall be made straight, and the rough places plain: and the glory of the LORD shall be revealed, and all flesh shall see it together: for the mouth of the LORD hath spoken it."[7]

Thus, those who serve under the World Teachers prepare the way of the LORD by making straight his paths:

> Transmuting as they go,
> The wiles of weal and woe
> My conquerors of the foe
> Reestablish the way ye know.

And this they do because they indeed drink of the cup of Christ, the blood of the New Covenant.

If you would drink of his cup and "drink ye all of it,"[8] as he commanded you to do, you must first understand the old covenant and the cup of the water of gall which the LORD gave to his people to drink because, as he said, "They have forsaken my law which I set before them and have not obeyed my voice, neither walked therein, but have walked after the imagination of their own heart."[9]

And of the kings and princes and priests and prophets and the inhabitants of Jerusalem who have chosen death rather than life by a perpetual backsliding, holding fast to their deceit and their self-deception, he said:

> *They refused to return to the way of truth.*
>
> *They spake not aright, and no man repented him of his wickedness....*
>
> *And from the least unto the greatest they were given to covetousness. From the prophet even unto the priest every one was dealing falsely.*
>
> *For they have healed the hurt of the daughter of my people slightly, saying, Peace, peace; when there is no peace.*[10]
>
> And they were not ashamed when they committed the abomination of the misuse of the sacred fire of the Mother: *therefore shall they fall among them that fall,* even as the life-force within them is fallen.
>
> *In the time of their visitation they shall be cast down.*
>
> *I will surely consume them.... And the things that I have given them shall pass away from them.*
>
> *[Therefore they say,] Why do we sit? assemble yourselves,*

The Blood of the New Covenant

and let us enter into the defenced cities, and let us be silent there: for the LORD *our God hath put us to silence, and given us water of gall to drink, because we have sinned against the* LORD.[11]

And therefore, because profaneness is gone forth from both prophet and priest of Jerusalem, I will feed them with wormwood and make them drink the water of gall. For the land is full of adulterers misusing the sacred fire of the Mother.

And because of swearing, taking the name of the LORD GOD, *YOD HE VAU HE, ELOHIM,* in vanity and in profanity and thereby invoking devils out of the bottomless pit, the land of the Mother and elemental life mourneth; and the pleasant places, the chakras of their virgin consciousness, are dried up, and the course of energy flow within them is evil, and their life-force is not used rightly. And there is wickedness in the house of the LORD.

Therefore in the year of their visitation, in the cycle of the return of their karma, I will bring the energy veil of the Dark Cycle upon them. The prophets of Samaria have prophesied in Baal and caused my people Israel to err in the desecration of the life-force in lasciviousness before the altars of Baal. The prophets of Jerusalem commit adultery and walk in lies. They strengthen the hands of evildoers, supporting their love of money and the pleasure cult; they rebuke them not, and none doth return from his wickedness.

They are become as the inhabitants of Sodom and Gomorrah. They have undone the paths of light within the Holy of Holies, undoing the light of Alpha and Omega.

Therefore thus saith the LORD *of hosts concerning the prophets; Behold, I will feed them with wormwood, and make them drink the water of gall: for from the prophets of*

Jerusalem is profaneness gone forth into all the land.

And to the people he has declared: Hearken not unto the words of the prophets that prophesy unto you: they make you vain: they speak a vision of their own heart, and not out of the mouth of the LORD.

They say still unto them that despise me, The LORD *hath said, Ye shall have peace; and they say unto every one of them that walketh after the imagination of his own heart, No evil shall come upon you.*

For who hath stood in the counsel of the LORD, *and hath perceived and heard his word? who hath marked his word, and heard it?*

Behold, a whirlwind of the LORD *is gone forth in fury, even a grievous whirlwind: it shall fall grievously upon the head of the wicked.*

The anger of the LORD *shall not return, until he have executed, and till he have performed the thoughts of his heart: in the latter days ye shall consider it perfectly. I have not sent these prophets, yet they ran: I have not spoken to them, yet they prophesied.*

But if they had stood in my counsel, and had caused my people to hear my words, then they should have turned them from their evil way, and from the evil of their doings.

Am I a God at hand, saith the LORD, *and not a God afar off?...*

And as for the prophet, and the priest, and the people, that shall say, The burden of the LORD, *I will even punish that man and his house....*

And the burden of the LORD *shall ye mention no more: for every man's word shall be his burden; for ye have perverted the words of the living God, of the* LORD *of hosts our God.*

Can any hide himself in secret places that I shall not see him? saith the LORD. *Do not I fill heaven and earth? saith the* LORD.[12]

This burden of the LORD is the very pressure of the light of the I AM THAT I AM. It is the weight of his mantle. It is the presence of his Karma—his Word and his Work. It is this mantle that the false prophets of Baal have claimed.

And they dream their psychic dreams and deliver the messages of the false hierarchy and the disembodied spirits of Serpent and his seed dwelling on the astral plane, claiming that their word is my Word. But my Word is like a fire, saith the LORD, and like a hammer that breaketh the rock of their pride and their ambition into pieces. And these prophets have laid unlawful claim to my Word: stealing every one from his neighbour, they lay claim to my Word. They cause my people to err by their psychic dictations and by their irresponsibility to the mantle of the messenger.

Yet I sent them not, nor commanded them. Therefore they shall not profit this people at all. These are the false gurus, the false prophets, the false Christs and the false messengers who are an abomination unto my Light! Now, therefore, they may not share in the burden of my Light, but they have their own burden. For every man's word shall be his burden. For ye have perverted the words of the LORD of hosts our God. And by thy words thou shalt be justified, and by thy words thou shalt be condemned.

All who therefore usurp the authority of the Lion, the Calf, the Man and the flying Eagle in the Matter spheres will give answer to me this day. And I will initiate them by their own unrighteous deeds and their deadly misuses of the sacred fire in the seven citadels of consciousness. And the Law will require them to take in that which they have sent forth.

They have poisoned my people Jerusalem by the water of gall. Therefore they must drink the poison from the fruit of their own poisonous tree, which they have given them to drink. They must take into their own temples the poisonous philosophy of the misuse of the sacred fire which they have put upon this generation of my people.

They shall not be initiated with the fruit of the Tree of Life nor by the LORD GOD, who yet walks and talks with the twin flames of the Ruby Ray, but they shall be initiated by their own karma and their karma shall be their Guru. And I will no longer walk among them. And when they shall say with Serpent and his seed, "Peace and safety," then the sudden destruction which they have delivered upon the holy innocents shall come upon them 'as travail upon a woman with child', and they shall hear the cries of those they have murdered in their mothers' wombs. And they shall not escape!

For this is the covenant that I established with you when I brought you to the land of promise:

And thou shalt return and obey the voice of the LORD, and do all his commandments which I command thee this day.

And the LORD thy God will make thee plenteous in every work of thine hand, in the fruit of thy body, and in the fruit of thy cattle, and in the fruit of thy land, for good: for the LORD will again rejoice over thee for good, as he rejoiced over thy fathers:

If thou shalt hearken unto the voice of the LORD thy God, to keep his commandments and his statutes which are written in this book of the law, and if thou turn unto the LORD thy God with all thine heart, and with all thy soul.

For this commandment which I command thee this day, it is not hidden from thee, neither is it far off.

It is not in heaven, that thou shouldest say, Who shall go up for us to heaven, and bring it unto us, that we may hear it, and do it?

Neither is it beyond the sea, that thou shouldest say, Who shall go over the sea for us, and bring it unto us, that we may hear it, and do it?

But the word is very nigh unto thee, in thy mouth, and in thy heart, that thou mayest do it.

See, I have set before thee this day life and good, and death and evil;

In that I command thee this day to love the LORD thy God, to walk in his ways, and to keep his commandments and his statutes and his judgments, that thou mayest live and multiply: and the LORD thy God shall bless thee in the land whither thou goest to possess it.

But if thine heart turn away, so that thou wilt not hear, but shalt be drawn away, and worship other gods, and serve them;

I denounce unto you this day, that ye shall surely perish, and that ye shall not prolong your days upon the land, whither thou passest over Jordan to go to possess it.

I call heaven and earth to record this day against you, that I have set before you life and death, blessing and cursing: therefore choose life, that both thou and thy seed may live:

That thou mayest love the LORD thy God, and that thou mayest obey his voice, and that thou mayest cleave unto him: for he is thy life, and the length of thy days: that thou mayest dwell in the land which the LORD sware unto thy fathers, to Abraham, to Isaac, and to Jacob, to give them.[13]

But your ways have not been my ways, saith the LORD.[14] And therefore, for your disobedience to my covenant I have dispersed you among the nations and you have forgotten my name and your origin in the Mighty I AM Presence. But by repentance and remission of sins you shall return to the LORD your God, and the land which I have given thee shall be restored. And the nations of Israel shall be converted by the true path of individual Christhood, and those who oppress the light of the peoples of the Ancient of Days shall receive my judgment. And you shall prosper in the planes of Spirit and of Matter.

In this hour of cosmic cycles turning, it is given unto each soul who is of the remnant of the Woman's seed to stand in the flaming presence of Opportunity, at the *op*en *p*or*t*al to *unity*, before the hierarchs of the eight covenants of God. For those who remain with the Maitreya Guru and the Guru Ma in Eden, there are seven covenants and the eighth leading to God-integration.

The thirty-three initiations unfold as the four times seven plus five. They are the fourfold initiations of the four cosmic forces on each of the seven rays plus the five steps of the five secret rays. The five steps are (1) the Water Baptism, (2) the Fire Baptism, called the Transfiguration, (3) the Crucifixion, (4) the Resurrection, and (5) the Ascension. Throughout the seven sets of four on the seven rays, the twin flames weave a thousand-petaled lotus—and many lotuses as star-fire flowers marking the octaves of their habitation in the Spirit/Matter spheres—as they loop in and out of the macrocosmic center of Life to the microcosmic events in the moving stream of Matter.

The first covenant is the opportunity to return to Lord Maitreya and the Mother in the Garden of Eden, to be reinstated in that holy innocence of the Christ and to henceforth reject all compromise of the indwelling light proposed as alternatives to the altar of the living God by Serpent and his seed. Those for whom it is prepared, who fulfill the thirty-three initiations of the path of Christhood under the Edenic Covenant in this life, for them the conclusion of their descent is the ascent by the Path of the Ruby Ray. Now this is the mystery of the first covenant that is become the last and of those who reenter it in the last days to become 'the firstfruits of them that slept'.

You who would regain paradise lost now have the opportunity through Mother Omega's flame in the earth to stand on the

The Blood of the New Covenant

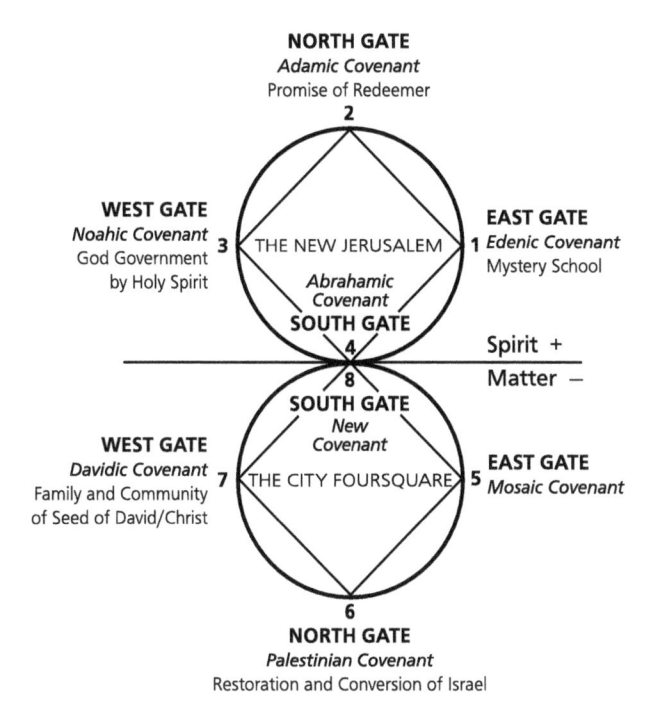

```
                    NORTH GATE
                   Adamic Covenant
                 Promise of Redeemer
                          2

  WEST GATE                              EAST GATE
  Noahic Covenant    THE NEW JERUSALEM   Edenic Covenant
  God Government  3                    1 Mystery School
   by Holy Spirit      Abrahamic
                       Covenant
                     SOUTH GATE
                          4           Spirit +
                          8           Matter −
                     SOUTH GATE
                         New
  WEST GATE             Covenant
  Davidic Covenant   THE CITY FOURSQUARE  EAST GATE
  Family and Community 7               5 Mosaic Covenant
  of Seed of David/Christ

                          6
                    NORTH GATE
                  Palestinian Covenant
              Restoration and Conversion of Israel
```

line of the sixth covenant while simultaneously entering the eighth, the fourth and the second. For the "straight and narrow" line of your alignment with the Father and the Mother in heaven and in earth affords a fourfold opportunity to be as above so below through the pulsating light of the crystal cord.

Those twin flames who, then, lost their high estate in the Karma of God—participating in *his* Word and *his* Work as cocreators with him in the co-creative process of Father and Son—and entered into the low estate of personal and planetary karma outside the circle of the Lamb must find their way in the outer world, whereas once they knew and were known in the inner world of Ma.

These first two letters of Maitreya's name hold the flame of the Mother, which he bears as the Guru/Initiator of the feminine potential, the soul. The lowercase *a* stands for the alpha particle—that soul, or self, that is the potential to become the very Alpha light.

The *M,* pronounced mu ("moo") in the Greek, focuses the memory of Lemuria, the Motherland, called Mu. Wherever the *Mu* syllable is held sacred and intoned with reverence, this acknowledgment of the Mother flame, this attention to her Presence, invokes her Person.

When the light of Mu becomes the Ma, it is the sign of the coming of the Mother and the Manchild. It is God as Mother (Omega) giving birth to the offspring (alpha) of God the Father (Alpha) in the Spirit/Matter spheres. The sounding of the *Ma* syllable evokes the descent of the Mother's sacred fire, whose seed of universal Christhood is in itself. The Mother's sacred fire is actually the Father's light/energy/consciousness in polarity, which he alone has sealed with her sacred heart for the hour of her immaculate conception of the Universal Christ. Thus, through Omega the seed of Alpha manifests as the alpha particle—the soul born out of the shimmering alpha/beta spiral of life. And the syllable *Ma* is forever the figure-eight union of the Mother and the Manchild.

Now *Ma,* the Mother as Maitreya, establishes the path within, without for the *i.* The letter *i,* which we call the *iota,* stands for the individuality of God which the soul (the alpha particle) will put on as the garment of the LORD. When the iota is able to affirm the *I* as the Divine Entity, it is called the id-entity or, as you say, the identity. Now the alpha particle has gained another part and it is noted as the alpha/beta because it has established its own plus/minus polarity on the path of the Alpha/Omega-Self-realization.

The letter *t,* the tau, denotes this path. It is the cross of Light-individualization (Alpha) and Light-integration (Omega) to all who ne'er depart from the Presence of Maitreya or from the figure-eight flow of his eightfold path of dispensations. But for those who do depart from the Person and the Path of Maitreya, the horizontal/vertical axes of the tau become heavy laden by their non-polarity darkening on the hill of the horizon. Such are the divergent paths of those within and those without the garden of the Guru.

But through that tau cross, whether above or below, the r (rho) as the ray of Omega manifest in the iota must rise to be the $\bar{e}$ (eta) above the y and the a (Alpha) below. Can you, then, tell me what is the x factor of the y that is the unknown quantity in the formula you write as Ma-i-t-r-e-y-a? If you right the ritual of Maitreya and I right it too, will not the y, then, be in full view? And if so, will the iota of the alpha become the theta or the lambda by the beta of the gamma ray? Now, lest this should pose the problem of the delta of the soul, I recommend you study the eightfold covenants that will make the bit of Alpha you now view an alphabet of the Word and a lexicon of the mysteries that I tell in the tolling of the bell of the cathedral of the heart.

Let us take them one by one.

You see, my beloved who see, the first three root races kept the Edenic Covenant, gained their individuality in the God flame, and returned to my throne with no loss of light, no fall from grace, no deceleration of the life-force. And now, coming from the far-flung worlds of their cosmic service by recent dispensation, they have joined the Cosmic Christs and Great Silent Watchers who have gathered at the twelve portals of earth to restore the LORD's Community of the Holy Spirit.

To those twin flames (and there were many) who accepted the compromise solutions of Serpent and his seed and were thus expelled from the Garden of the Guru, Maitreya comes to call the plus, the minus of the eta and the alpha. For you are his namesake, and for his Father's name's sake he calls you Home. Those of you who bypassed your initiations on the first ray under the Edenic Covenant, given under the office of the Man on the east portal of the New Jerusalem, were therefore subject with Adam and Eve and their descendants to the initiations of the second ray, which came under the Adamic Covenant, given under the office of the Lion on the north portal.

The Adamic Covenant was and is the opportunity to follow the path of Godhood by obedience to the Law of the I AM

THAT I AM, the overshadowing Presence that ever remains the guide of life. It is the provision of the Law and the Lawgiver unto those who reject the Impersonal Personality of the LORD, who walks and talks with twin flames in the inner circle of Eden.

Under this covenant, the voice of the Guru is no longer heard. God as the Impersonal Impersonality speaks only through the voice of the Law, personified in personal and planetary karma. The intercessors of Good and Evil and the protagonists of Light and Darkness—in the person of angelic hosts and fallen ones—regularly engage the consciousness of man and woman outside of Eden in the aloneness of their trial and temptation away from the LORD's Presence.

The conditions of this covenant are the same as the first, save that man and woman no longer have the personal protection of the Guru or his circle of Light. The requirements of the law for the ascension must now take into account the karma which accrues from the knowledge of relative good and evil and all of the myriad laws of relativity which govern life outside the hallowed circle of the One.

In Eden, it was and still is initiation, one-on-one, with no loss of Christ Self-awareness so long as the Guru's Word is enthroned in the heart. And love is illumined obedience performed in honor as sacred trust between the Lawgiver, the Law and the one, the chela who is the vessel of the above, below.

Outside of Eden it is karma first, as the law of the circle and the wheels of the chakras grind out the exact requirements of the Law and of the Lawgiver that must be fulfilled if the soul is to be initiated once again by a representative of the LORD. Until that one come, the soul rehearses its departure from the footsteps of Truth many times over. It is given exacting exercises in the right uses of the Law in order that it might gain momentum by right knowledge, right aspiration, right speech, right behavior, right livelihood, right effort, right mindfulness and right absorption.

These exercises of the Law on the eightfold path of the bodhisattvas becoming one with the Buddha and the Mother are the way, the Middle Way, of Christ-illumined action, to undo the wrong uses of the Law when once again these records cycle into circumstance to present the original options: "Choose Life or death!"[15]

Again and again the confrontation is seen. On the horizon there appears a person of truth, a person of error; and the command of the Christ Self unto the soul is heard: Choose you this day whose Word ye will serve,[16] whose Person ye will defend. For behind the masks stand the Word and the anti-Word, the Person of God or the anti-God.

Until all of these experiences in relativity culminate in the encounter with the LORD GOD in Maitreya—face to face or in the person of his messenger, whoever he or she may be—the souls on the Path are yet proving their preparedness to reenter the rituals and the retreats of initiation. The balancing of one hundred percent of one's karma and the fulfillment of the law of perfection without his intercession, without his burden of light to counterbalance the outer darkness, is the supreme test of the Adamic Covenant. History records that only the few survived. Only one ascended—Enoch, "the seventh from Adam."[17]

Without the personal presence of the Guru, the command "Be ye therefore perfect, even as your Father which is in heaven is perfect"[18] is most difficult to obey. For without the Standard-bearer, who can set the standards of the Standard? Indeed, man and woman who have partaken of the fruits of the tree of the knowledge of relative good and evil have lost their absolute values of Truth, Justice, Mercy, Integrity, Peace and Love.

Now, these terms have but relative meanings and negative nuances that do not afford the individual that sublime contact with the God-free beings who ensoul the attributes of God and have earned the approbation of the Godhead: "This is my beloved—the blazing sun of righteousness, sun of my Sun—in whom I AM indwelling in the heavens and in the earth. Lo, I AM the God of very gods in my beloved Son, in whose Presence I AM well pleased."[19]

Thus, these Sons of God who personify the God flame—

because the God consciousness is in them and they in Him—are named in the heavenly hierarchy after the attributes of the God flame which shine forth from within them and light the darkest night with the supernova of their sound of his Word. They are thus called the "incarnation of the God flame of Peace," the "incarnation of the God flame of Truth," or, in the case of the feminine qualification of the absolutes of God, the "incarnation of the Goddess flame of Justice." These titles have been shortened to read God of Peace, God of Truth, or Goddess of Justice, etc.

Those who have lost the perception of the absolutes of the Godhead and the attributes of his divine nature embodied in his emissaries—which are at once personal and impersonal, formed and unformed—have, therefore, no conception of that cosmic consciousness of his hosts who have never descended from the grace of his Presence and who, by that grace, ensoul vast sectors of the Spirit/Matter universes.

But I assure you, my beloved, were they to behold them face to face through their own Christ consciousness, such as these would exclaim, "Lo, a God is born!" And so it would be in their consciousness, though that God-free being had pre-existed their newfound awareness of the limitless potential of Being with which the Lord God Almighty has endowed the Elohim creation.

And but for Enoch, who "walked with God and was not, for God took him,"[20] under the Adamic Covenant the descendants of Seth as well as those of Cain and the other earthly evolutions compromised the light of the Holy of Holies in the seven centers of being. And the waters of life misqualified became the waters of the flood for the sinking of the continents.

Nevertheless, within the Adamic Covenant they could have (had they remembered, honored and obeyed the Word of the Lord Maitreya unto Adam and Eve) reentered the path of Christic initiation. Within this second covenant, as in the first, the seeds of the thirty-three spirals are sown in the so-called DNA chain.

By this wonder, I would allow you to glimpse the majesty of

life, even its mystery, which the LORD GOD has made accessible to his sons and daughters. It is so near, my beloved, yet so very far from those who have been the abusers of God's life from the beginning. Yet it is true that the Alpha and the Omega of thy Higher Self has sealed the very miracle of the creation itself within the temples of the male and the female that the Divine Us hath made. But God as the Holy Spirit must unlock each precious chain of initiatic light. And he would not:

> *For GOD saw that the wickedness of man was great in the earth, and that every imagination of the thoughts of his heart was only evil continually.*
>
> *And it repented the LORD that he had made man on the earth, and it grieved him at his heart.*
>
> *And the LORD said, I will destroy man whom I have created from the face of the earth; both man, and beast, and the creeping thing, and the fowls of the air; for it repenteth me that I have made them.*[21]

Adam and Eve and all who were with them of our lightbearers entered the lower planes of the Matter sphere under the new 'Adamic' covenant wearing four lower bodies ("coats of skins") and yoked to the burden of the law of their karma with the Guru. It was then that Adam called his wife Eve—"because she was the mother of all living."[22]

For Adam knew that they must now open the door of opportunity for the generation of lightbearers to pursue the path of individual Christhood in the lowly estate of the flesh. He also knew that they must open the door for the laggard lifewaves scheduled to work out their karma in the physical octaves of earth.

Had they remained under the dispensation of the Lord Maitreya, they would have fulfilled their evolution in the etheric octaves unencumbered by the dense lifewaves evolving in the earth, earthy. By their departure, both they and their descendants would walk the Path side by side with the fallen ones, called the

Watchers, who had been cast out of heaven into the earth in the Great Rebellion against the LORD GOD, even the Almighty.

Now, the first son of Adam and Eve was the generation of their karma. Called Cain, meaning "acquisition," the soul is "acquired" from outside the circle of the Guru/chela relationship with Lord Maitreya. And if you will ponder it, my beloved, you will see that the law of karma is the law of acquisition. As a man soweth, that shall he reap.[23]

Cain's lifestream (his name also means the "hollow root") contained the seeds of his rebellion against the seven covenants of the seven rays which he had outplayed in his prior incarnations on the planet Maldek. His mechanized religion was a ritual of self-will perverting the ray of the LORD's will. He sought to acquire the all-power of God with the anti-power of his sling and his spear. His offering was not respected by Maitreya because his motive was to gain favor from the LORD that he might then subdue the LORD's light to the uses and abuses of his own subterfuge.

Cain worked hard tilling the ground, not to the glory of God but to gain God's power that he might exercise that power over others. In reality he, like the Canaanites who dwelled in the land west of Mu (hence the term *Amunu*) was a worshiper of the 'Force'. This term, which we hear popularized today as a substitute for the name of God, refers to the Serpent force, the coiled Kundalini, the all-power of the Mother. The Canaanite evolutions were worshipers of the Serpent—both as the person of the fallen one and as the life-force sealed in the white-fire core of the base-of-the-spine chakra.

From this religion of the fallen ones come all of the phallic and fertility rites of primitive cultures. Their archetypes can be seen in the Ugaritic pantheon, whose chief deity is 'Il. This syllable comes from the *El*, the power of Elohim usurped by the fallen ones. This 'Il, or *L*, is the abbreviation for the name Lucifer, called the sky god. He is known in numerous cultures as the father of the gods, their supreme lord and ruler in their assemblies.

These councils of the false hierarchy gathered on certain

mountains of what is now North America as well as in the Middle East. Baal and his wife Anat, Tammuz and Ishtar are among the many fallen angels who fell, they and their twin flames. They were a race of giants feared by the descendants of Seth.

The Flood was the judgment decreed by the Word of the emissaries of the LORD GOD when the descendants of Seth did not cleave unto the Law and the Lawgiver. Not by conscience nor by the conscientious adherence to the teachings recorded by Adam and Eve establishing the way of life for their children outside of Eden did these descendants walk. Rather did they walk after the pride of the Watchers.

And the gods who taught them this devious route to obtain the Divinity were the fallen angels "which kept not their first estate"[24] but fell with Lucifer. These are they which took unto themselves "the daughters of men"[25] and bore a godless, soulless creation called the Nephilim, through whom they would perpetuate their manipulation and mechanization of the masses. These fallen angels were now embodied in the physical earth because they were cast out of the higher octaves for their rebellion against the Son of God and the heavenly orders of hierarchy.

Their union with the daughters of Cain was not in the spiritual order of God's progeny, who are born solely out of the Christic seed. The LORD cursed this offspring of their lust. For they lusted for his power and sought to entice and entrap it through intercourse with the daughters of Cain. This was the abominable abuse of the Serpent force (the very life-force of the Mother and the Holy Spirit) which is called the abomination of desolation (of the desolate ones who have no God in them) standing in the holy place of the temple where it ought not.

This cursed lifewave became "mighty men which were of old, men of renown,"[26] became the mere natural man, without soul or conscience or spark of the divine potential. The natural man, now called the Homo sapiens, was a 'kind of man' but not a God-free being after the descent of Adam from Seth to Noah. Hence the crossbreeding of the Watchers and their godless creation with the children of Cain opened the door for laggard evolutions to embody on earth, and the interchange of these several fallen evolutions became known in general as "mankind."

The sons and daughters of God and their children are a distinct race of the I AM consciousness. And they are called the I AM Race. It was to them that Moses spoke when he hurled to them his fiery fiat to break the hypnotic spell of the Watchers and their slave race: "I have said, 'Ye are gods, and all of you are sons of the Most High!'"[27]

The Noahic Covenant replaced the Adamic as the LORD GOD once again sought to establish by the Holy Spirit his God-government in the earth after the sinking of Atlantis and the interruption of the evolution of the lifewaves of the planet.

Under the patriarch Abraham, the covenant is established for the reincarnation of the Christic seed and of the future of the I AM Race, with the twelve tribes of Israel founding the Community of the Holy Spirit worldwide, laying the foundation for the promised redemption through the Word.

The covenant of Moses once again establishes the interaction of the Lawgiver through the one who is the embodiment of the Law—the Guru. Their violations of the law of Moses are recorded together with the judgments of Jehovah. And though the prophets of the I AM THAT I AM were in their midst, their rebellious generation resulted in the Assyrian and Babylonian captivities. And the Old Testament is the history of the living Word, born in flesh and blood, waxing strong in the LORD, entering into the inner retreats of the Brotherhood and emerging for the Messianic mission.

Thus there can be no restoration of souls, nor of Israel, without the Palestinian Covenant, promising the conversion by the personal and direct confrontation of the ascended master Jesus Christ with his disciples and of all ascended masters with their chelas. There is no return to the house of the LORD. Thus the Davidic Covenant is the sign of the path of persecution borne by the soul of Jesus Christ when he was embodied as David. All of the preparations of his soul for his final incarnation represent the door of opportunity to those who would follow in his footsteps.

In the Twenty-second Psalm, he foresees the hour of his crucifixion with the words "My God, my God, why hast thou forsaken me?" which he is to utter again on the cross. It is the initiation given to every one who stands at the north gate of the City Foursquare, preparing to enter in to the crucifixion, the resurrection and the ascension. Step by step, the nature of the crucifixion is revealed beforehand in order that the eyes of the soul might be opened that he might understand the nature of the cup that he may choose to drink or not to drink.

Again, in Psalm 69, the path of the one who would lawfully and joyfully claim the LORD's mantle as his burden of light cries out:

> *They that hate me without a cause are more than the hairs of mine head: they that would destroy me, being mine enemies wrongfully, are mighty: then I restored that which I took not away.*
>
> *O God, thou knowest my foolishness; and my sins are not hid from thee.*
>
> *Let not them that wait on thee, O Lord GOD of hosts, be ashamed for my sake: let not those that seek thee be confounded for my sake, O God of Israel.*
>
> *Because for thy sake I have borne reproach; shame hath covered my face.*
>
> *I am become a stranger unto my brethren, and an alien unto my mother's children.*
>
> *For the zeal of thine house hath eaten me up; and the reproaches of them that reproached thee are fallen upon me. (The sacred fire of thy white-fire body hath utterly consumed me, for I have borne thy white-fire cross and the reproaches of them that reproach thee are fallen upon me.)*[28]

Thus shalt thou say, my beloved, when thou shalt enter in to the full sharing of my Personhood, to which I bid thee, saying, *Drink me while I AM drinking thee.*

But I hide not from you the course of your choosing. It is a path of sorrows that is turned to the path of joy. It is the cup of personal and planetary karma filled to the dregs, which the joyous cup of resurrection's sacred fires transmutes. Then there is the deadly cup of the poison of Serpent and Serpent's seed, who posed as my prophets and priests and princes in Israel. To them I gave the cup of the water of gall.

This is the cup that will utterly destroy them; but it cannot destroy my saints who have drunk of the cup of the New Covenant, for they have no part with Serpent and his seed. And though they part my garments among them and cast lots upon my vesture,[29] they still cannot take my yoke upon them nor learn of me, for my yoke is easy and my burden is light.[30] And I give it unto all who are engaged in the sacred labor of the Holy Spirit, all who are passing the initiation of the Calf who, as the great bearer of our burden, is become the Ox, heavy laden with the burden of personal and planetary karma.

Those who wait upon the LORD, the beloved I AM Presence, day and night have entered into the initiation of the sacred labor and the karma to which my Son referred. Only personal discipleship to Christ in the archetypes of Christhood—the Man, the Lion, the Calf and the Eagle—can afford the devotee the privilege of taking upon himself the yoke of the LORD and thus entering into his understanding, his Cosmic Christ consciousness.

In this scene from the great drama of his fourfold Christhood, the Great I AM of Jesus, the LORD, descends from the right hand of God, where he rules as the chosen Son and the heir (the Calf who is to be sacrificed), and takes on the mode of the Ox, the great burden-bearer of the sins of the world. The Ox, often the castrated male, is the God incarnate who has set aside his authority, even his polarity, and his God-free estate to dwell among his people and bear their karma, transmuting their burden by the Light that he is until they become that Light.

The mode of the Ox is in fact that of the slave serving the Master who is the God indwelling in the disciples. This, then, is the cosmic interchange whereby the living Guru exchanges garments with his chelas. Though they revere him as Guru, they do not often see that the burden he carries is their own.

Thus the Great I AM of the Lord Jesus is become "meek and lowly in heart" in the guise of the Ox, even stationed on the west gate of the Matter sphere where the multitudes throng him with hosannas on one day, for he healeth all their diseases, and cry out "Crucify him!" the next because he exacts a price for the light he imparts and the transmutation he effects.

The promise of "rest unto your souls" given unto those who will walk in the shoes of the Guru while he walks in theirs is the re-creation of their four lower bodies and of the cycles of their chakras as he mathematically and geometrically actually outpictures the mantra *Drink me while I AM drinking thee.*

The taking in of the Holy Spirit of the Guru means the taking on of the sacred labor of the Holy One of God. Thus world service is given in exchange for world karma. And the cry of the peddler, "New lamps for old," is the lure of God to the soul who must surrender the self if he is to be made whole.

Bearing the karma of the Guru, which is to bring enlightenment to a world, the chela enters into the service of the World Teachers. And the rest unto the soul becomes the acceleration unto light as the chela verily embodies the 'icon' of the Guru in his heart and delivers his light in the self-creative/re-creative process—truly the alchemy of his Guru's Word incarnate. Now he discovers that the yoke of his Guru is 'easy' and that his burden is light—never knowing the price that is paid by the One who, as the Ox, quietly affirms, "I AM meek and lowly in heart: and ye shall find rest unto your souls."[31]

This is the new covenant of the eighth ray and this is the decade when you, my beloved, may learn of me as I AM the Guru embodied in all of the ascended masters who have become the Lamb. This is the Path of the Ruby Ray. Walk ye in it while ye have the light of the witnesses who witness unto the Light.

Those who are my disciples following the fourfold path of

Christhood under the blessed chohans of the rays (for they obey the command "Drink ye all of it") are so filled with the light of the Man, the Lion, the Calf and the flying Eagle that the promise is unto them, "If they drink any deadly thing, it shall not hurt them."[32] For the sacred fire of the Guru's resurrection is upon them and in them; and he in them ("I in thee and thou in me") utterly consumes any and all spirals of the Serpent that would enter the hallowed circle of identity or penetrate the Holy of Holies of the dazzling cross of white fire.

The sixth-ray initiations at the north gate in the Matter sphere are the crossroads of life. They begin at the Last Supper when the one who is Christ transfers to his disciples the opportunity to drink his cup and to eat his bread. The bread that he broke and blessed is the bread of his own life. "I am that bread of life. Your fathers did eat manna in the wilderness, and are dead. This is the bread which cometh down from heaven, that a man may eat thereof, and not die."[33]

He shared his body of light, both his spiritual light body and the body of his experience in the earth. And the cup which he gave to them, saying, "Drink ye all of it," is the essence of the light of Alpha and Omega, the balanced life-force raised and raising the soul up, up the initiatic ladder (spiral), expanded in the sacred heart and accelerated as an ascension coil from the base unto the crown.

Ye are called to follow Christ Jesus and the light initiated by the Christ Self in the regeneration, the re-creation of the soul in the likeness of the Son of Man (in the likeness of the central sun of the I AM Presence). For every chela who follows the Guru in his regeneration (re-creation out of the Matter spheres unto Spirit), when the Guru as the Son of man shall sit upon the throne of the Lamb in his glory (Great Causal Body), the chelas shall sit upon the twelve thrones of the twelve solar hierarchies of the Son.

And whether there be twelve or twelve thousand or the 144,000, they shall be positioned at the twelve gates of consciousness guarding the holy city, 'judging' the twelve tribes of Israel, separating by the Word the light and darkness of the children of Israel (of God-reality) on the west gate who are entering in by the twelve paths of initiation.

This new covenant is the opportunity for the soul to drink in the light of Christ as he takes unto himself the burden of the soul's karma. In this interchange, the soul is filled with the light of the Christ Self and the Christ Self transmutes the energies of sin, the records of karma—that which is out of balance or in a state of imbalance with the light of Alpha and Omega.

The New Covenant, therefore, is the opportunity to receive this grace through the Word and Works of the LORD on the path of individual Christhood. Those who would enter this grace must be willing to take every step on the path of initiation of the Ruby Ray promised to the saints by Jesus when he said, "Ye shall indeed drink of the cup that I drink of; and with the baptism that I am baptized withal shall ye be baptized."[34]

This promise of the path of initiation has been overlooked, to say the least, by the false pastors of my people who are denounced by the LORD through Jeremiah prior to the transfer to them of the cup of the water of gall and of wormwood. It is then that he promises the coming of the good shepherds who shall feed the people through the indwelling Person of the Son of God, THE LORD OUR RIGHTEOUSNESS.[35]

These shepherds are among you the living saints who are pursuing the path of the World Teachers. For in this day is the judgment come upon the pastors that destroy and scatter the sheep of my pasture: "Ye have scattered my flock, and driven them away, and have not visited them: behold, I will visit upon you the evil of your doings, saith the LORD."[36]

The judgment of the fallen ones who have taken up their positions of authority in church and state, preempting the burden of the LORD, is therefore upon them on each occasion when the saint of the Church elects to drink of the cup of Christ and to be baptized with him. The judgment comes each time a saint replaces a Sadducee, a Pharisee or a member of the Sanhedrin.

Those who have not fulfilled my covenants among the people, those who have not laid the groundwork for the seven covenants will not enter in to the eighth covenant whereby they partake of my blood, which is the Ruby Ray. While they are yet under the law of their own sin—for they have made their own sin the law of their existence wherein they have become a law unto themselves—they will not be invited to the marriage supper of the Lamb wherein the Lord says unto his beloved, *Drink me while I AM drinking thee.*

And when their judgment is come and all things are fulfilled, then the remnant of the flock will be gathered out of all countries whither the law of their karma has driven them. And they will come in again into their folds—the twelve paths of initiation of the twelve tribes of Israel—and each of them shall knock at each of the twelve gates in succession. And they shall be fruitful in the Christ consciousness and they shall increase in the knowledge of the I AM THAT I AM.

> *Behold, the days come, saith the LORD, that I will sow the house of Israel and the house of Judah with the seed of man, and with the seed of beast.*
>
> *And it shall come to pass, that like as I have watched over them, to pluck up, and to break down, and to throw down, and to destroy, and to afflict; so will I watch over them, to build, and to plant, saith the LORD.*
>
> *In those days they shall say no more, The fathers have eaten a sour grape, and the children's teeth are set on edge.*
>
> *But every one shall die for his own iniquity: every man that eateth the sour grape, his teeth shall be set on edge.*
>
> *Behold, the days come, saith the LORD, that I will make a new covenant with the house of Israel, and with the house of Judah:*
>
> *Not according to the covenant that I made with their fathers in the day that I took them by the hand to bring*

> them out of the land of Egypt; which my covenant they brake, although I was an husband unto them, saith the LORD:
>
> But this shall be the covenant that I will make with the house of Israel; After those days, saith the LORD, I will put my law in their inward parts, and write it in their hearts; and will be their God, and they shall be my people.
>
> And they shall teach no more every man his neighbour, and every man his brother, saying, Know the LORD: for they shall all know me, from the least of them unto the greatest of them, saith the LORD: for I will forgive their iniquity, and I will remember their sin no more.[37]

Now, my beloved, it is necessary that you enter in to the Garden of Gethsemane that you might fulfill all these things which were told to you by beloved Lord Maitreya in the beginning of your path, that it might be fulfilled in the ending. For here you will make the decision to drink or not to drink the cup of sorrows even unto death—the death of your former life and lifestyle, that you might come into the fullness of his Life—the Life universal and triumphant of the Guru of the Ruby Ray.

This is the hour of the cup of world karma. "Behold, the hour is at hand and the Son of man is betrayed unto the hands of sinners." This is the hour of the revenge of the fallen ones when the Son of man takes into his heart the misqualified power of their manifest darkness. And this he must do while the children of God make haste to fulfill the vows of their individual Sonship, hastening, then, to also walk in his footsteps that they might know the meaning of the sacred heart and the "cosmic interval" provided by the LORD for their soul's initiations on the Ruby Ray.

And Peter, James and John were with him, and he bade them keep the prayer watch with him as he prepared to be fastened to the cross of the sins of the world—he the Ox fastened to the yoke of the vertical and horizontal bars of mankind's transgression of the law of Alpha and Omega. This yoke, then, that formed his cross included the words and works of the Devil that they might be destroyed by the blood of the New Covenant.

And he knelt in prayer, saying, "Father, if thou be willing, remove this cup from me: nevertheless not my will, but thine, be done."[38]

And the light of the initiation of the Father within the Son was so intense and the burden of the karma of the LORD's chosen people and of the laggard races was so great that he himself sweat as it were great drops of blood. And when he found the disciples sleeping, he said unto them what he says unto you today: "What, could ye not watch with me one hour? Watch and pray, that ye enter not into temptation: the spirit indeed is willing, but the flesh is weak."[39] And he went away and prayed the same prayer a second and a third time, each time finding the disciples asleep.

Finally, to those who could not partake of his cup in that hour, those for whom it would be reserved in the end times, he said, "Sleep on now, and take your rest: it is enough, the hour is come; behold, the Son of man is betrayed into the hands of sinners. Rise up, let us go; lo, he that betrayeth me is at hand."[40] The cup of karma that he drank was so great that it would take him through the valley of the shadow of death preceding the glorious resurrection which his soul had foreseen when he wrote the Psalms of David.

In the three prayers which Jesus prayed, he accepted the weight of world sin against the Father and against the Son and against the Holy Ghost. And the fourth cup that he took was the cup of betrayal: How many times and by how many would he be betrayed before he gave up the ghost on Golgotha? By the three who slept in the garden, the betrayal of the unconscious mind; and then by Judas with the kiss of familiarity, mockery and contempt. Then the betrayal of Peter's uncontrolled emotion as he cut off the servant's ear who sought to take him—Peter who had once forbade the Lord when he began to speak of his crucifixion, saying, "Be it far from thee, Lord."[41]

In both instances the Lord rebuked him for humanly interacting with world thought and feeling. The third betrayal again was by his own—the very one who had declared, "Thou art the Christ, the Son of the living God," now denied his Lord: "Verily I say unto thee, that this night, before the cock crow, thou shalt deny me thrice."[42]

And the fourth betrayal was by the band of soldiers and officers sent by the chief priests, the Pharisees, the Scribes and the Sanhedrin. And finally came the betrayal of Pilate himself, who, though he washed his hands of the blood of the innocent man, yet released Barabbas and allowed the seed of the Wicked One to crucify the Lord.[43]

In this scene, we see the betrayal of the Christ by the mass consciousness, even the multitude, the great multitude of the people who would one day stand on the west gate of the City Foursquare awaiting the coming of the emissaries of the Lord in the hour of their own redemption by his Light.

The sixth betrayal came when he said, "I thirst,"[44] and the seed of Serpent gave him vinegar to drink, mingled with gall. And when he had tasted thereof, he would not drink. Thus he rejected their attempt to put upon him the cup of the water of gall which the LORD had given them to drink for their blasphemy against his name. Therefore he established his crucifixion for and on behalf of the lightbearers of God and rejected for all time and space what the seed of Serpent embodied have claimed since that era—that he died for their sins.

He died for the sins of no man, but he took upon him the sins of God's children that he might be resurrected in light, that he might live for their redemption. And he was betrayed by the malefactor who joined in with the passersby who reviled him, wagging their heads and saying, "Thou that destroyest the temple, and buildest it in three days, save thyself. If thou be the Son of God, come down from the cross."[45]

And again the chief priests with the scribes mocked him, saying, "He saved others; himself he cannot save. If he be the King of Israel, let him now come down from the cross, and we will believe him. He trusted in God; let him deliver him now, if he will have him: for he said, 'I am the Son of God.'" [46]

I AM

Sanat Kumara

I go before you, all the way Home.
Follow me.

The Chart of Your Divine Self

The Chart of Your Divine Self is a portrait of you and of the God within you. It is a diagram of yourself and your potential to become who you really are. It is an outline of your spiritual anatomy.

The upper figure is your "I AM Presence," the Presence of God that is individualized in each one of us. It is your personalized "I AM THAT I AM." Your I AM Presence is surrounded by seven concentric spheres of spiritual energy that make up what is called your "causal body." The spheres of pulsating energy contain the record of the good works you have performed since your very first incarnation on earth. They are like your cosmic bank account.

The middle figure in the chart represents the "Holy Christ Self," who is also called the Higher Self. You can think of your Holy Christ Self as your chief guardian angel and dearest friend, your inner teacher and voice of conscience. Just as the I AM Presence is the presence of God that is individualized for each of us, so the Holy Christ Self is the presence of the universal Christ that is individualized for each of us. "The Christ" is actually a title given to those who have attained oneness with their Higher Self, or Christ Self. That's why Jesus was called "Jesus, the Christ."

What the Chart shows is that each of us has a Higher Self, or "inner Christ," and that each of us is destined to become one with that Higher Self—whether we call it the Christ, the Buddha, the Tao or the Atman. This "inner Christ" is what the Christian mystics sometimes refer to as the "inner man of the heart," and what the Upanishads mysteriously describe as a being the "size of a thumb" who "dwells deep within the heart."

We all have moments when we feel that connection with our

The Chart of Your Divine Self

Higher Self—when we are creative, loving, joyful. But there are other moments when we feel out of sync with our Higher Self—moments when we become angry, depressed, lost. What the spiritual path is all about is learning to sustain the connection to the higher part of ourselves so that we can make our greatest contribution to humanity.

The shaft of white light descending from the I AM Presence through the Holy Christ Self to the lower figure in the Chart is the crystal cord (sometimes called the silver cord). It is the "umbilical cord," the lifeline, that ties you to Spirit.

Your crystal cord also nourishes that special, radiant flame of God that is ensconced in the secret chamber of your heart. It is called the threefold flame, or divine spark, because it is literally a spark of sacred fire that God has transmitted from his heart to yours. This flame is called "threefold" because it engenders the primary attributes of Spirit—power, wisdom and love.

The mystics of the world's religions have contacted the divine spark, describing it as the seed of divinity within. Buddhists, for instance, speak of the "germ of Buddhahood" that exists in every living being. In the Hindu tradition, the Katha Upanishad speaks of the "light of the Spirit" that is concealed in the "secret high place of the heart" of all beings.

Likewise, the fourteenth-century Christian theologian and mystic Meister Eckhart teaches of the divine spark when he says, "God's seed is within us."

When we decree, we meditate on the flame in the secret chamber of our heart. This secret chamber is your own private meditation room, your interior castle, as Teresa of Avila called it. In Hindu tradition, the devotee visualizes a jeweled island in his heart. There he sees himself before a beautiful altar, where he worships his teacher in deep meditation.

Jesus spoke of entering the secret chamber of the heart when he said: "When thou prayest, enter into thy closet, and when thou hast shut thy door, pray to thy Father which is in secret; and thy Father which seeth in secret shall reward thee openly."

The lower figure in the Chart of Your Divine Self represents you on the spiritual path, surrounded by the violet flame and the protective white light of God. The soul is the living potential of God—the part of you that is mortal but that can become immortal.

The purpose of your soul's evolution on earth is to grow in self-mastery, balance your karma and fulfill your mission on earth so that you can return to the spiritual dimensions that are your real home. When your soul at last takes flight and ascends back to God and the heaven-world, you will become an "ascended" master, free from the rounds of karma and rebirth. The high-frequency energy of the violet flame can help you reach that goal more quickly.

Notes

CHAPTER 1
1. Luke 4:18–19.
2. John 6:29.
3. Matt. 21:23.
4. Isa. 42:1.
5. Matt. 23:37.
6. Isa. 9:6.
7. Dan. 12:5.
8. John 1:3.
9. John 8:12.
10. Luke 7:19, 22.

CHAPTER 2
1. John 4:14; 7:38.
2. 1 Pet. 3:4.
3. Matt. 23:27, 28.
4. Zech. 13:7.

CHAPTER 3
1. Ps. 121:8.

CHAPTER 4
1. John 10:1–10.
2. Deut. 25:4; 1 Cor. 9:9.
3. Jer. 31:33.

CHAPTER 5
1. Acts 17:24.
2. Obad. 3–4.
3. Luke 19:13.
4. John 2:19.
5. Matt. 28:6.
6. Matt. 26:14–16.

CHAPTER 6
1. Isa. 25:8; 1 Cor. 15:54.

CHAPTER 8
1. John 14.
2. See pages 12–13.
3. John 17.
4. Matt. 19:6.
5. John 10:30.
6. Matt. 17:5.
7. Jer. 23:6; 33:16.

CHAPTER 9
1. Matt. 3:16, 17.
2. 1 Cor. 15:53.
3. Luke 23:43.
4. John 20:17.
5. John 1:3.
6. Ezek. 2, 3; Rev. 10.
7. Acts 1.
8. John 21:18.
9. Col. 1:12.

CHAPTER 10
1. John 6.
2. From the Latin *crucifixus,* the past participle of *crucifigere* 'to crucify', from *crucicrux* 'cross' + *figere* 'to fasten'.
3. 2 Cor. 12:2–4.
4. Matt. 10:40, 33.
5. Luke 22:42.

CHAPTER 11
1. Gal. 4:6. *Abba,* Aramaic word for "father," transliterated into Greek and thence into English. The corresponding Hebrew word is *Ab* as in Abraham, which mean "the father is high"—i. e., the Father is hierarch.
2. Rev. 13:8.

CHAPTER 12
1. John 13:8.

CHAPTER 14
1. John 10:1–18.

CHAPTER 15
1. John 10:22–42.
2. Rev. 2:9; 3:9.
3. Gen. 22:15–18; see *The Human Aura* by Kuthumi and Djwal Kul (Corwin Springs, Mont.: Summit University Press, 1996).

CHAPTER 16
1. See *Pearls of Wisdom,* 14 December 1975, by Lord Maitreya, pp. 269–70, 273, 281.

CHAPTER 18
1. John 16:7–11 "reprove"—from the Greek *elegcho* meaning "to rebuke, to refute, to confute; by conviction to bring to light; to convince; to expose; to reprehend severely, to correct, to chide; to find fault with, to admonish, to call to account; to chasten, to punish."
2. Rev. 12:10, 11 "dragon"—false hierarchy of the Watchers, fallen angels referred to in the Book of Enoch, employing national/international systems, organs, and organizations to amass power derived from the children of light (components of the body of God). These Watchers manipulate the people by manipulating the amalgam of personal and planetary karma and misqualified energy.

CHAPTER 19
1. "Gospel": from the Anglo-Saxon *godspel,* or "God's story"; from the Greek *euğgelion* "good news, good tidings, good word," hence the "God word." The Gospel is the *story of God.* It is *God's word* delivered by his Son and his servants. It is the *good news* of salvation, the elevation of the soul to the state of grace through the incarnation of God's Word. The evangel, or evangelist, from the Latin *evangelium,* is one who goes before the angels (i. e., ascended masters) as the bearer (messenger) of the good tidings of God's Word. It is the message of grace through the incarnation of the Son in Jesus Christ and in all whom he anoints with his light of Sonship, joint-heirship.

CHAPTER 20
1. "occult": secret; deliberately kept hidden, not revealed to others; demanding more than ordinary perception or knowledge.

CHAPTER 26
1. "exoteric"—"outer"; suitable to be imparted to the public; belonging to the outer or less initiated circle, "esoteric"—"inner"; designed for or understood by the specially initiated alone; of or relating to knowledge that is restricted to a small group.

CHAPTER 29
1. "The eleven" is used in Mark 16:14 as a collective term—i.e., council—not necessarily imply-

ing that eleven persons were present.
2. For more information on Rex, Nada, Bob and Pearl and on the atomic accelerator, see Godfre Ray King, *The Magic Presence* (Chicago: Saint Germain Press, Inc., 1974), 2:2–16, 61–68, 83–88, 107–9, 122–24, 126–29, 292–94; The Ascended Masters, *Ascended Master Discourses* (Chicago: Saint Germain Press, 1937), 6:282–318.
3. John, instrument of Maitreya, the baptizer with water; Jesus, instrument of Maitreya, the anointer with fire (see chart p. 77).
4. The "Woman clothed with the sun"—the soul who, upon entering the flame of the Motherhood of God, is clothed with the light of the Great Central Sun of the I AM THAT I AM (Rev. 12:1).

CHAPTER 31
1. Isa. 45:11–13.
2. Ps. 140.

CHAPTER 32
1. Rom. 16:20.

CHAPTER 34
1. Herbert Thurston, S. J., and Donald Attwater, eds., *Butler's Lives of the Saints,* rev. ed., (New York: P. J. Kenedy and Sons, 1956), 1:612–17.

CHAPTER 37
1. Zech. 9:9.
2. John 3:16, 17.
3. Acts 13:48.
4. Zech. 9:10.
5. Rev. 22:1.
6. Matt. 6:9–13.
7. Isa. 40:3–5.
8. Matt. 26:27.
9. Jer. 9:13, 14.
10. Jer. 8:6, 10, 11.
11. Jer. 8:12–14.
12. Jer. 23:15–23, 34, 36, 24.
13. Deut. 30:8–20.
14. Isa. 55:8.
15. Deut. 30:19.
16. Josh. 24:15.
17. Jude 14.
18. Matt. 5:48.
19. Matt. 3:17.
20. Gen. 5:24.
21. Gen. 6:5–7.
22. Gen. 3:20.
23. Gal. 6:7.
24. Jude 6.
25. Gen. 6:4.
26. Ibid.
27. Ps. 82:6.
28. Ps. 69:4–9.
29. Ps. 22:18.
30. Matt. 11:29, 30.
31. Matt. 11:29.
32. Mark 16:18.
33. John 6:48–50.
34. Mark 10:39.
35. Jer. 23:6; see Jer. 23.
36. Jer. 23:1, 2.
37. Jer. 31:27–34.
38. Luke 22:42.
39. Matt. 26:40, 41.
40. Mark 14:41, 42.
41. Matt. 16:22.
42. Matt. 26:34; see also Mark 14:30.
43. Matt. 27:24, 26.
44. John 19:28.
45. Matt. 27:40.
46. Matt. 27:42, 43.

Index

1980s, decade of the, 282, 332
666, the number, 36, 209

Aaron, 25–26, 295, 302
Abaddon: fallen angel, 241; usurps the office of the Lion, 209
Abba, 373
Abel, 289, 291, 341
Abortion, 210, 304
Abundant life, 265
Accuser of the Brethren, 157, 209, 299
Adam: and Eve, 6, 42, 142–143, 290, 339, 359, 361; last Adam, 290
Adamic race, 290
Addictions, 225
Adoption: of sons, 54, 80; of the soul, 50
Adoration, 325–328
Adoremus (angel), 151–152
Adversary, 258
Africa, 186–191
Aggressive mental suggestion, 210
Agitation, 328
Aigli, Mount, 296
Air: air element, 63; air quadrant, 84, 298; he who governs the, 299; outer nature expressed through the air vehicle, 168; princes of the, 297–298. *See also* Quadrant(s)
Alchemical marriage, 282; diagram of, 292; of the soul and the Spirit, 55
Alchemist, 17
Alcohol, 297
Alpha: and Omega, 62, 354; in the Guru, 6
Amber, 45, 49

America, 241. *See also* United States
Amethyst sphere of Matter, 5
Ancient of Days, 340; Adversary of the, 208; and Daniel, 2; does stand before you, 5; fire that will descend from, 76; his ownership of all souls in the service of the light, 82; memory of the, 232; obeisance to, 114; person of the, 10; Sanat Kumara known as, 9; within the Mother and saints, 177. *See also* Sanat Kumara
Androgynous being, 62
Angel: clothed with a cloud and a rainbow upon his head, 151–153, 158; of the Everlasting Gospel, 218; seventh, 153, 214
Angelic host, only lawful contact with, 335
Angelic tongues, 214, 253–255
Angels: and Jacob's ladder, 137; call upon them by name, 216; comprise a hierarchical order, 216; from whose bands Florence descended, 237; in the scriptures, 216; of the Nameless One, 233; seduced by Lucifer, 286; singing alleluias, 256; tactic of, 301; tares harvested by, 82; under ordinary circumstances do not take embodiment, 217. *See also* Archangel(s); Cherubim; Fallen Angel(s); Seraphim
Anger: of entities, 225; of the LORD, 256
Animal magnetism, four beasts of, 210
Antichrist, 72, 192; Devil in the person of, 208; John and Jesus' con-

frontation with, 108, 111; saints study the nature of, 157
Anxiety, 240
Apocrypha, 286
Apostles, 148. *See also* Disciples
Aquarius: age of, 125; dispensation of, 135; forerunner of the Aquarian age, 55–56; hierarchy of, 63; initiation of Surrender under, 77; initiations of, 315; initiators under, 58; man of, 43, 62; now at hand, 153; passing of the torch unto, 4; sign of, 131
Anat, wife of Baal, 361
Archangel of the Third Ray, 255
Archangels: orders of, 216; seven, 254
Aries, 165; and the resurrection, 62
Ark: of his testament, 7; tablets of the law sealed within the, 38
Armageddon, battle of, 240
Armies: of the Faithful and True, 212; of the LORD, 103
Armour of God's light, 278
Ascend to God, 248
Ascended master(s), 79–80, 130; on the east side of the City Foursquare, 88; Electronic Presence of, 148; and the Holy Spirit, 135; inheritance of the, 71–72; on the ninth ray, 243; occupy the office of the Man, 87, 100; only lawful contact with the, 335; and the parable of the vineyard and husbandmen, 124; Paul accurately described, 71; reinforce the light of the Mediator, 244; saints robed in white, 217; in the Scriptures, 216; taking counsel with the, 213; those who experience anxiety and apprehension in the face of the, 226; those who have left the, 90; visitation of the, 312; will walk and talk with his chelas, 36; working with his embodied disciples, 243–244

Ascension, 63, 146, 198, 200, 233, 242, 268, 337; ascension coil, 87, 283; to be with Christ in the, 63–64; coil, 75, 292, 303–304; culture of life that leads to the, 200; of Elijah, 165; of Enoch, 80; flame, 97, 115, 118, 245; of the flying Eagle, 77; gathering of the elect unto the, 243; heirs of the white light of the, 86; initiation of the, 166, 316, 352; initiation of the eighth ray, 323; of Jesus, 68, 231; of Lady Master Kristine, 232–237; of Lanello, 180; message of the, 167; Serapis opening the book on the law of the, 90; as "sitting on the right hand of God," 285; soul's reception into heaven, 284; with only fifty-one percent of karma balanced, 94
Ascension chair, 235
Ascension Temple, 274
Assimilation, interval of, 75
Assumption of the soul, 284
Assyrian enemies, 256
Astral body: where the entity resides, 222; consumed by fire, 200
Astral plane: descend into, 62, 341; floating grids and forcefields on, 239; rut of the, 236; souls on, 185; subterranean pits of, 256; those whose chakras function at the level of, 327
Astrea, 226
Atlantean scientists, 304
Atlantean temples, 257
Atlantis, 149, 343, 362
Atom: nonpermanant, 292, 324; Permanent, 60, 284, 292, 324; seed, 297
Atomic accelerator, known as the ascension chair, 235
Attainment: inner, 244; karma of unlawful, 335
Auric forcefield, 334

Authority, 3
Avatars, outline of the path of, 155

Baal, 286, 347, 349, 361
Babel, tower of, 137, 255
Babylon the Great, 209
Balance, called to hold, 243
Bankers, international, 209
Banking, 298
Banner of the World Mother, 4
Baptism: of Christ, 311; by fire, 24, 147–148, 164, 252, 352; of Jesus, 162–163, 287, 289; of the Lion, 77; of the LORD, 60; of the saints, 174; by water, 352
Baptized, believe and be, 242, 248, 251
Baptizer archetype of the Great, 84
Beast(s): on the cardinal points of the Cosmic Clock, 95; def., 157; first, 24; four, 21, 28, 117; out of the bottomless pit, 209; out of the sea and out of the earth, 209; second, 24, 33; vials borne by the four, 138 victory over, 19, 36; who had a face as a man, 36; worshipers of, 103. *See also* Creatures; Four cosmic forces
Beelzebub, 286
Behavior modification, 304
Belial, 286; sons of, 107
Believe: and be baptized, 242, 248, 251, 274; that means "meditate," 174
Bhakti yoga, 326
Bible, teaching that "isn't in the Bible," 236. *See also* Gospel(s); Mark; Revelation, Book of; Scripture(s)
Bilocation of the Guru, 31
Bird, heartbeat of the little, 221
Bitterness: in the belly, 74; of the path, 154
Black arts, practitioners of the, 219

Black magic, 268, 335; launched from The Hague, 297
Black magicians, 199; councils of, 210
Black Pope, 219
Bliss, nonattachment to, 332
Blood, 132; becomes golden liquid light, 18; of Christ, 44, 72, 241, 258, 309; of the Lamb, 8, 115, 135; of the new covenant, 337; of the Son, 240; salvation by Christ's, 70; "vesture dipped in blood," 94
Blue fire sun: meditation upon, 329–332; of the God Star, 283
Blue lightning, 65
Bodhisattva(s), 88; ideal, 245; path of the, 174, 356; service as, 258
Body: celestial and terrestrial, 168, 198; cremation of the, 199–200; embalming and burying of the, 199; mastery of the, 84; of Christ, 72, 308–309
Body of God, 70
Book: held in the hand of the Statue of Liberty, 48; held open in the hand of the mighty angel, 152, 153; Lamb who is worthy to open, 173, 174, 238, 246; "little book," 63, 74, 153–154, 156, 159; seven-sealed, 3, 49, 85–86, 94, 167, 204, 218, 233, 270; when the Lamb takes the, 94
Book of Life, 81, 89
Born-again experience, 224–225
Brahma, 19, 25
BRANCH, 281, 282, 283, 292
Breastplate, 17, 18, 87
Breath of the Holy Spirit, 297
Breathing, 334
Breeding, selective, 304
Brethren, least of your, 313
Bricks, without straw, 34
Bridal chamber(s), 50, 324
Bridal veils, 243
Bride: of Christ, 96, 285; of the Holy

Index

Spirit, 226; of the Lamb, 283, 284; tosses her bouquet, 243. *See also* Lamb's wife; Marriage

Bridegroom, 284, 285, 292, 326

British Isles, 280, 297. *See also* Great Britain; Ireland

Brotherhood of Luxor, 200

Buddha, 356; and the Mother, 24; extending the fearlessness flame, 334. *See also* Gautama; Siddhartha

Builder, 24

Caduceus, 11, 41

Caiaphas, 106

Cain, 289, 360; descendants of, 358

Calf, 27, 31, 49; and violet fire, 65; archetype of Christ crucified, 60; archetype of Christ in the earth quadrant, 61; baptism of the saints fulfilled by the, 174; Christ consciousness epitomized in the way of the, 168; Christ of Alpha and Omega come in the *fohat* of the *El*, 61, 138; crucifixion, 31, 34, 77; dharma of the, 129; Gautama in the Person of the, 79; initiates of the, 204; initiation of service under the, 59; initiation under the office of the, 242, 248; meaning of, 84; mysteries of the, 37; nonidentification with the, 82; office of the, 126, 140, 164, 248, 279; second beast was like a, 24; service of the, 28; Shiva the, 30; symbol of the, 26; usurp the office of the, 208, 209; who is Buddha, 278

Calf, golden, 25–26, 30

Camelot, 133

Canaanites, 360

Candlesticks standing before the God of the Earth, 278

Capitalism, World, 157, 189

Capitalist/communist conspirators, 209

Castle, interior, 328, 329

Cataclysm, 266

Causal bodies of Elohim, 18

Causal body: acceleration of the power of the Word in the, 248; archetypal sphere of the Father-Mother God in your, 329; center of the I AM THAT I AM in your, 324; Deathless Solar Body is the coordinate of, 283; entering in to the Great, 312; first and second 'rings' of, 49; Great, 45, 282, 292; of the Great Divine Director, 16, 37; initiations of the, 248; rainbow of the, 257; seals upon the, 86; seven spheres of the, 86; treasures stored in, 72; white-fire core of the great, 2

Cave of Symbols, 235

Chakra(s): acceleration of the, 248; adoration which opens the, 326; allowing misqualified energy to cover over the, 258; anointing of Jesus' crown, 166; assimilation of the teachings within the, 48; base and crown, 61; base-of-the-spine, 140, 248, 283; bridal chambers, 324; clearing of, 276; closing of, 332–333; crown, 7, 16, 140, 248, 299, 330; descent of light from the crown, to the base, 30; emitting seven streams of light, 257; energy distributed through, 343; flushing out of the, 283; eighth-ray, 323; of Elohim, 215; heart, 140, 248, 301; of individuals who give no adoration to God, 327; of Jesus, 164; light raised from the base of the spine unto the crown, 301; LORD releasing the judgment by the throat, 256; misqualifying the light of the Mother chakra, 209; misuse of the base-of-the-spine, 301; Mother, in Spirit, 283; nonpermanent atom sealed within the base-of-the-spine, 324; oil of gladness in the lamps of, 327; of solar awareness, 330; raising up of the sacral energies through the, 64; recharge, 332; revealed to Ezekiel, 43; river of life rising from the base of the spine to the crown, 276; sacred fire with, 39; Satan positioned himself in third-eye, 273; seat-of-the-soul, 36, 49, 63, 96, 140, 248; seven, 86, 93, 149, 281, 314; seven rays converging through the throat, 257; solar-plexus, 11, 74, 96, 140, 154, 248, 309, 330; Spirit and Matter, 206; spiritual functions of the, 326; that had become as black holes, 12; third-eye, 63, 140, 248, 279, 299, 329; throat, 65, 140, 248, 253, 299, 309; transmutation in the lower, 90; twin-petaled, 95; of unsuspecting souls, 336; visualizing the, 334; which the LORD accelerates, 242

Chants, 257

Chart of Your Divine Self, 292, 374

Chastity, vow of, 88

Chela(s): accelerating, 244; are our cups, 236; the command given to every would-be, 311; great, 24; of the Great White Brotherhood, 9; and Guru, 17, 31; Guru calling the inner, 223; of the Lamb, 5; mantle trasferred to the, 148; members of the Great White Brotherhood, 216; Moses as, 33; only the chelas can identify the living Guru Maitreya, 275; that believeth upon the Lamb, 10–11; ultimate test of the, 34; who has become the Lamb, 93; of the will of God, 173, 252; of the Word, 96; if you would be taken in as a, 312

Chelaship, 35–26, 165

Chemicalization of consciousness, 153

Cherubim, 38, 216

Child: little, 32, 85; must know that he is important, 222

Childhood, 45

Children, 228

Chohan(s): of the age, 96; direct interchange with the, 244; of the First Ray, 171; of the Second Ray, 174; seven, 88, 89, 100, 108, 238–239, 245, 281

Chord, lost, 255

Christ: adoration of, 325; archetype of the, 26; archetype of the crucified, 84; archetype of the Universal, 24; as a face of a Man, 89; betrayal by the mass consciousness, 371; blood of, 240, 241; body and blood of, 72, 258, 309; BRANCH is, 281; bride of, 285; Christ consciousness, 284, 324, 339; crucified, 70–71; "died for our sins," 194; dying in the present, 196; eating his flesh and drinking his blood, 75; embodiment of the four faces of, 58; Enoch held the office and mantle of, 80; four faces of, 56, 73; fused with, 55, 56; humility of, 340; image of the, 107, 223; in you, 81; indwelling, 44, 68, 69; manifesting in the Son of man, 42; office of true, 274; salvation by his 'blood', 70; seed of, 184, 185; Self that is, 83; soul must become the champion of the, 285; Universal, 336; when he comes to the Israelites, 125; who has incarnated with your soul for aeons, 197

Christ Self, 292; adoration of the, 325; as the BRANCH, 281; "Christ in you, the hope of glory," 69; coming into the temple of, 225; of the creature, 176; crucified, 70; figure-eight flow between the soul and, 333; fire that will descend through your, 76; fourfold manifestation of

Index 385

the, 159; in each child of God, 145; in you bodily, 184; incarnation of each one's, 252; incarnation of the, 145; THE LORD OUR RIGHTEOUSNESS, 56, 100, 184, 188; lovetide from your, 318; marriage of the soul and the, 284; as Mediator, 78, 336; mediator of your, 244; reestablishing contact with the, 144; representative of the householder which planted a vineyard, 122–123; of the soul, 50; within, 102; your, 234

Christed ones occupy the office of the two witnesses, 95

Christendom, 68

Christhood: archetypes of personal, 161–168; diagram of the Four Persons of Cosmic, 84; four persons of, 174; initiation into individual, 193; Jesus came to reignite, 339; personal, 71, 100; seven points of the law of individual, 238

Christs: false, 103, 157; false and true, 102, 209

Chromosomes, 36, 304

Church(es): elders of the, 213; inner, 71, 308; living, 180; messages to the seven, 149; saints of the inner, 95; utterance of the Word within the corporate body of the, 254. *See also* Christendom; Fundamentalist movements; Pastors; Religion(s)

Church Universal and Triumphant, 71, 95; altar of invocation of, 115; Guru-chela relationship through, 129

Circle(s): cylindrical formation of, 336; dot in the center of the, 95; Law of the, 261; squaring of the, 21; vertical and horizontal, 334; of white fire, 334

City(s): etheric, 298; fourth foundation of the Holy, 18; sixth foundation of the wall of the Holy, 17; twelve gates of the Holy, 22

City Foursquare: building of, 58; crystallization of, 274; diagram of the Foundations of, 84, 140, 248; in the earth, 94, 99; east gate of, 272; east side of, 88; first foundation of the wall of the, 16; gates of, 58; named THE LORD IS THERE, 42; New Jerusalem manifest as, 97; reflection of the New Jerusalem, 242; west side of, 26, 129

Cloud: at the door of the tabernacle, 17; of the I AM Presence, 38; of the Shekinah, 41; at the Transfiguration, 166; voice that spoke out of, 55

Cloven tongue(s), 72; of fire, 95

Comfort, false, 288

Comforter, Promised, 146–147

Coming Revolution in Higher Consciousness, 174

Command(s): "Command ye me!" 263; to preach, 170–171, 172, 238, 251

Commandments, Ten, 37–38

Communion: of the LORD's body, 71–72; ritual of, 240; of the saints, 71, 72, 135. *See also* Eucharist

Communism, World, 157, 189. *See also* International capitalist/communist conspiracy

Community of the Holy Spirit, 125, 129, 180, 187

Concentration, 331

Congruency, law of, 163

Consecration, 331

Corotick, Prince, 295

Cosmic Clock, 58, 95, 114. *See also* Quadrant(s)

Cosmic Council, 11–12, 14, 15

Court of the Sacred Fire, 134, 232–233; Jesus returned in the hour of his ascension to, 231; souls received by the Ancient of Days in,

233; those who have stood before, 187

Covenant: Abrahamic, 362; Davidic, 339, 362; Edenic, 352, 355; first, 352; of individual Sonship, 340; Mosaic, 350, 362; new, 340, 341; Noahic, 362; old, 346; Palestinian, 362

Creation, Lords of, 138

Creator, 216, 261

Creatures, four living, 42, 43, 45–46, 114, 159, 161. *See also* Beast(s); Four cosmic forces

Cremation, 199–200

Criminals, 224

Cross: all who take up the ruby, 73; cosmic cross of white fire, 333; disciples who daily take up Jesus', 193; horizontal and vertical axes of, 354; initiations on the Way of the, 311; north arm of the ruby, 24; omnidirectional, of white fire, 322–333; ruby, 24, 25, 42, 194, 200; that you must bear, 194; of white fire, 114, 148, 197, 200; of world sin, 193. *See also* Rose Cross; Station(s) of the cross

Crown(s), 23, 49; of the Four and Twenty Elders, 18; of twelve stars, 49

Crucifix, 70, 373

Crucifixion, 316; and the calf, 24, 77; entering into the, 60–61; and Ezekiel, 73; initiation of, 166, 312, 352; initiation on the Path of the Ruby Ray, 70; of the Lamb, 6, 93; mockery of Jesus', 318; path of, 23; reenactment of, 88; revealed to David, 363

Crystal, terrible, 45, 63, 78, 126, 278

Crystal cord, 331, 343

Crystal sphere of Spirit, 5

Cube: alabaster, 323; cosmic, 324; mysteries of the ruby, 38; ruby, 22, 23, 25, 30, 31, 36, 60; white, 96,
212, 297, 322–324, 333, 340

Cup: of Christ, 308–309, 311; that you give to the Master, 314

Cuzco, 232

Cycles, 215; "6,666," 142, 289; six thousand, 7

Cyclopea, 118, 276, 303

Damnation, 175, 185

Daniel, 2

Dark Cycle, 36, 184, 265, 277, 347

Dark night of the soul, 14, 241, 316

Dark night of the Spirit, 316

Dark ones, 116

David, 362; on the wicked, 263–265; Root of, 86, 89

Dead, those who became tombs of the, 12

Deadly thing, drink any, 248, 307, 337

Death, 195–196, 315–316; consciousness, 225; death decrees are not justified, 266; death entity, 199; death wish, example of, 266; for the saints, 198; Jesus' God-victory over Death and Hell, 194–195; life after, 236; morbidity surrounding, 199–200; relentless death grip, 241; "And in those days men shall seek death...," 241; victory over, 62. *See also* Dead; Die

Deathless Solar Body, 81, 283, 292

Deception, 189

Decree(s), 129, 214–215, 218, 253, 256, 262, 276, 296; on behalf of the soul who must be born again, 224; determined, 96; divine, 152, 278, 332; for judgment, 20.07, 110; God Self-determined, 331; for resurrection, 60.06, 320; to Surya, 10.13, 250; unlawful misuses of the dynamic, 265; and the weaving of the Deathless Solar Body, 283. *See also* Invocation; Mantra(s); Word

Index 387

Deities, wrathful, 30, 173
Demon(s), 200; of the bottomless pit, 241; bound, 227; cast out, 198; demon drivel, 256; must vampirize light, 240–241; name of, 207; possessing, 222; responsibility to cast out, 192; of self-deception, 221; and their subjects, 224; those who take up the cause of raging, 227; trembling of possessing, 226. *See also* Devil(s); Entities
Depression, 241
Desire: mastery of, 84; measure of, 328; of the would-be chela, 311; perfectionment of God-desire, 95; test the level of, 330; transmutation of human, 74
Desire body, 49, 154, 277; mastery of the self in the, 65; seat of the, 74
Destiny, Lords of, 138
Destroyer, office of the, 217
Destroyers, 268
Devil(s), 289; ability to cast out, 226; anti-Devil philosophy, 185; cast out, 192, 204, 218, 221–230, 239, 248; consumed in your Presence, 242; grunts and growls of, 256; impostors of the Holy Ghost, 267; out of the bottomless pit, 209. *See also* Demon(s); Entities
Devotion: ascending and descending, 335; path of, 326, 328; test of, 329; undivided, 330; vacuum of, 326
Dharma, 126, 162, 234; fulfilled, 94
Dictations, 219, 254; delivered in the English language, 255; psychic, 349
Die, "As it is appointed unto men once to die...," 195–196
Discarnates, 192, 226. *See also* Entities
Disciples of Jesus, 238, 276. *See also* Apostles

Discipleship, 276
Diseases, 312
Dishonesty, 189
Disobedience, 259; children of, 298
Divine plan, 234
Divorce, 226
Djwal Kul, 106
DNA, 304, 358
Doctrine(s): erroneous, 273; false, 69, 82, 90, 289; that is a crossroads, 68. *See also* Religion(s); Theology
Door: of the crown chakra, 16; opened in heaven, 1, 3, 7, 18, 52
Doubt, 240, 277
Dragon: "great dragon," 286; Devil in the person of the, 208; as the false hierarchy of Watcher, 374; flood of the, 278; that makes war with the Woman, 157; as the Watchers and their godless creation, 192; who is wroth with the Woman, 278
Drink, "Give me to drink," 310–15
Drink me while I AM drinking thee, 308–309, 315, 318, 326, 335, 337, 344, 363, 365, 368
Drug addiction, 241
Drugs, 297
Druids, 297

Eagle: archetype of the Woman, 64; ascension of the, 63, 77; baptism of the saints fulfilled by the flying, 174; Christ consciousness epitomized in the way of the flying, 168; Christ having the face of an, 42; Energy of Alpha/Omega in the Geometry of the *El* in *E*arth, 63; flying, 28, 31, 49, 79, 166, 200, 268; impostors of the flying, 29; initiates of the flying, 204; initiation of Selflessness under the, 59; initiation of the flying, 226, 248; meaning of, 84; mysteries of the flying, 37; non-identification with the flying, 82; office of the flying, 140, 164, 242, 248, 279; Shiva the flying, 30; soaring, 65; those who usurp the office of the flying, 208, 210

Earth: Cosmic Council had decreed the dissolution of, 11–12; is a stage that mirrors the stage of heaven, 124; new divine plan for, 13

Earth body, integration of inner and outer natures experienced through, 168

Earth element, and the Calf, 61. *See also* Quadrant(s)

Earth quadrant, 84

East gate: of the City Foursquare, 58; diagram of, 140, 248; doorway of the air quadrant, 298; fifth ray at, 274; initiates at, 276; initiation of, 100, 104, 108, 127, 248; of the Matter sphere, 303; office of the Man on, 153, 161, 242; office of the two witnesses on, 95; Paul on, 272; Son on, 192; two witnesses at, 99, 317

East side, of the City Foursquare, 88

Ecclesiastes, 176

Economic systems, 157

Economics, 288

Economies, 123, 188

Economy(s): abuses of, 189; those who rule in the, 123

Eden: east gate of, 339; garden of, 4, 6, 36, 143, 352, 356

Education, 299

Effluvia, encroachment of, 333

Ego: human and Divine, 60, 195; process of outer ego-building, 223; that is not self-limiting, 222

Egypt, 369; Israelites in, 33–34

Egyptian cult of the dead, 200

Eightfold path, 323, 356

Eighth ray, 168, 337; conditions which challenge your initiations on the, 207; eighth-ray integration, 339; initiation(s) of the, 242, 245, 248, 268, 274, 282, 323; of integration, 170, 283; self-mastery on the, 248

El, chief deity of the Ugaritic pantheon, 360

El Morya, 239; a chela of, 234; his words to the ingratiating giver, 315; Irish eyes of Thomas Moore smile through, 294; Lamb worthy to open the seven-sealed book, 173; new tongue conveyed by, 253

Electronic belt, 154

Electronic fire rings, 282, 292

Electronic Presence, 148

Elemental life, 25, 340; imprisoning, 29; servants of the World Mother, 217; thrice crucified, 24

Elementals, 60, 61, 65

Elements: beings of the, 127; four, 21

Elijah, 165, 184, 313

Elisha, 165, 184

Ellipse, 335

Elohim, 254; eyes of, 22; and the Father, 216; five, 127; individualized, 142; seven, 93, 127, 152, 153; Seven Spirits of God, 19; twelve rings of, 18

Embalming, 199, 200

Embodiments. *See* Incarnation(s)

Emerald, 18, 20, 32, 87

Emmanuel, 145, 197

Emotion(s): God-mastery of, 11; healing of, 334; human, 336; outer nature expressed through, 168; personal and planetary, 277; sinuous, 301. *See also* Feelings

Emotional bodies, 333. *See also* Four lower bodies

Empowerment, threefold, 163

Energy exchange in relationships, 336–337

England, 281, 297

Index 389

English language, 255
Engram, 62
Enlightenment, 16
Enoch, 41, 80, 106, 357, 358; archdeceivers whom Enoch made known to you, 263; Book of, 286; and the God Star, 232; wrote of the Watchers, 81
Entities, 224–227; benign, 222; collection of stray, 223; of Evil, 207; mass, 210. *See also* Demon(s); Devil(s); Discarnate(s)
Ephraim and Manasseh, 26–27, 294, 296, 315
Erin, land of, 280, 294. *See also* Ireland
Error within thyself, 220
Esoteric, def., 375
Etheric body(s), 333; mastery of the Self in, 60; original blueprint in, 298; where the soul does not interact with the light through, 326
Eucharist, 258. *See also* Communion
Euthanasia, 304
Evangelist, def., 374
Eve, 276, 338; and Adam, 6, 42, 142–143, 290; and the Serpent, 288; Serpent who beguiled, 264; temptation of, 288
Everlasting Gospel, 159–160, 218; preached unto you, 189; your preaching of the, 185. *See also* Gospel(s)
Evil: absolute, 335; anti-evil philosophy, 185; authority to exorcise, 206; challenge embodied, 108, 109; of the evildoer, 265; forcefield where evil dwells, 336; return of, 267
Exorcism: Elohim of, 219; of entities, 224; pronounced by the individual believers, 192. *See also* Ritual of Exorcism
Exoteric, def., 374
Eye, all-seeing, 24, 63, 118–119,
273, 275; and the Great Pyramid, 86; meditation upon, 303–304; of the messenger, 17
Eye of God: opening of the, 273; your chalice of the, 276
Eyes of the Four Cosmic Forces, 22–23
Ezekiel, 37, 41–42, 73–74; call for the initiations given to, 76; go and be as he was, 56; "roll of a book" given to, 63

Fall, the, 217
Fallen angel(s), 157, 263, 361; Abaddon, 241; called Watchers, 143; a divine right of, 267; embodied on earth, 361; may bend the knee, 185; of the second ray, 288, 299; tongues of, 255
Fallen one(s), 31; called the Watchers, 359; challenge the authority of, 181; challenging of the, 301; followers of Serpent, 277; impostors of the flying eagle, 29; philosophy of, 157; religion of, 360; who have denied the Word, 106–107. *See also* Emotion(s)
False hierarchy: Luciferian, 286, 289; Satanic, 290
False Prophet, 208
False teachers, 142
False teachings, 142
Family, 222, 226, 228–229
Farthing, the last, 117
Father, 129, 182; and the adoption of sons, 55; and the adoption of the soul, 50; covenant of the Son and the, 44; direct relationship with God the, 324; and Elohim, 216; extension of the Father's Person through the Son, 281; God the, 143, 325; gospel of the, 144; "I and my Father are One," 6, 8, 55, 59, 60, 90, 97, 106, 117, 123, 145, 203, 245, 285; "I and my Fa-

ther are one" mantra, 7; impersonality of, 285; in fire our God is, 24; in Matter and Spirit, 115; in the Son, 13, 24, 72, 107, 171; indwelling, 107; and the initiation of the second stage of Christhood, 162–164; initiations of the bride of Christ under, 96; initiations of the Father/Guru, 118; intimate relationship with, 144; Jesus' teaching on the Son and, 275–276; law of, 133; Lion as, 58; and the Mother, 97; on the north gate, 192; office of, 52, 84, 127; and the parable of the vineyard and husbandmen, 122–124; personal relationship with, 175; reestablishment of intimacy with, 136; and the Ritual of Exorcism, 213; and the seven initiations of the saints, 248; and the Son, 203; Son of God entering in to the heart of, 121; souls representing Mother and, 7; and the Spirit of the Son, 78–79; the Lion, 65, 88; those who usurp the authority of, 208; and the Trinity, 2; two commands of, 238; which art in heaven, 2; "which sent me…," 173; within you, 176

Fatherhood of God, 6

Fear, 240, 315–316

Fearlessness flame, 219, 334

Feelings, angelic hosts polarize with the, 217

Feet: initiation of the washing of the, 90; symbol of understanding, 151

Fifth ray, 99, 278; at the east gate, 274; initiation(s) of the, 95, 140, 248, 273, 303; messenger on the, 69; science of the, 275; self-mastery on the, 248; those perverting the path of the, 298

Figure eight, 323; flow and the Guru and chela, 6; flow between the soul and Christ Self, 333; illustrating the persons and principles of the Godhead, 96; nexus of the, 336; ruby, 23, 24; and the S, 114; soul accelerates over the, 242; symbol of your Being, 282; upper and lower spheres converge, 344; within the ellipse, 335

Fire: and the Father, 24; came down from heaven, 198; in cremation, 200; fire body, 168; fire element, 17, 60; fire quadrant, 84; infolding itself, 49, 76, 260. *See also* Quadrant(s)

Fire breath, of the Holy Spirit, 257

First Ray: chohan of the, 171; initiations of the, 140, 172, 248; self-mastery on the, 248

Flagellation, 332

Flood, the, 361

Force, the, 360

Forehead(s): sealed in the, 7, 98, 108, 167; sealing in the, 108; those who have I AM THAT I AM in their, 145

Form: Lords of, 138; mystery of, 30; those who have murdered the, 31; those who worship, 29; Unformed, 31

Formless One, mystery of the, 30

Formlessness, Lords of, 138

Forty cycles: in the Sinai wilderness, 34; teach and preach during, 63

Forty days that Moses was in Mount Sinai, 37, 38

Fountain, sacred-fire, 95

Four and Twenty Elders, 4, 18, 22, 117; guard the portals of the City Foursquare, 94; those who have stood before the, 187; vials borne by the, 138

Four cosmic forces, 20, 21–26, 94, 339; archetypes of, 37; diagram of the offices occupied by, 84; and Ezekiel, 73; four beings of the elements represent, 127; four types of the Christ Person, 56; gospels of the, 80; guardians, 279; Jesus became the fullness of the, 161; judgment before the, 134; in the New Jerusalem, 99; offices of the, 58; preach the coming of the, 177; surrounding the I AM Presence, 49. *See also* Beast(s); Calf; Creatures; Eagle; Lion; Man

Four lower bodies: as horses, 212; of the prophets of Israel, 172; recharge, 332; as the temple foursquare, 159; those purifying their, 8. *See also* Astral Body; Astral sheath; Body; Desire body; Emotion(s); Emotional body; Four lower vehicles

Four lower vehicles, 200

Fourth ray: becomes the eighth ray of integration, 170; initiation of the, 140, 248, 268, 282; self-mastery on the, 248

Francis, Saint, 88

Free will, God's, 81

Freedom, 58, 109

Freedom's Star, 14

Friends, 225; of the Saviour, 130

Fruit of the Tree of Life, 118

Fundamentalist movements, 219

Future: change the, 215; cut off, 196

Gabriel, Archangel, 7

Gandhi, Mohandas, 188

Gathering together in the name I AM THAT I AM, 214–215

Gautama Buddha: Buddha of the Earth, 278; the call through, 1; Jesus' allegiance to, 52; fire that will descend from, 76; as Guru, 6; initiation through, 248; as initiator on the Path of the Ruby Ray, 59; messengers stand before, 281; obeisance to, 114; the office of the Calf, 77, 79, 126, 140, 164, 208, 242, 248; in a sacred ceremony, 3; Sanat Kumara comes through, 5, 8, 49; spokesman of the hundred and forty and four thousand, 15; two witnesses standing before, 139. *See also* Siddhartha

Genes, 36, 304

Gethsemane, Garden of, 369

Ghana, 186–191

Giants, 361

Gift(s): and the giver, 314; of the Holy Spirit, 30, 147, 236, 251, 268; of interpretation of angelic tongues, 254; of speaking in angelic tongues, 253–255

Glandular systems, 327

Glossolalia, 253

Gnomes, 31

God: allness of, 181; the desire to know, through the path of love, 329–330; every soul is a multiplier of, 196; the Father, 143; Father-Mother, 2; Form of, 29, 31; incarnate, 3; indwelling, 104; magnified, 155; mystery of the indwelling, 82; mystical union of the soul with, 326; penetration of the inner spheres of, 331; personification of the God flame, 357–358; possession of, 45; possessor of, 82; repetition of the name of, 214; science of acceleration unto, 79; seven representatives of the Father-Mother, 93; sit at the right hand of God, 242, 248, 284, 285, 292; ten minutes in, 332; tyranny that an idolatrous generation would impose upon, 82; whose Selfhood contains the Father-Mother polarity, 141. *See also* Father; Godhead; Holy Spirit; Mother; Son; Trinity

God consciousness, putting on, 332

God flame, precipitation of the, 122

God Self, 64

God Star, 242, 283. *See also* Sirius

Godfre and Lotus, 235
Godhead: diagram of the Persons and Principles of, 140; four Persons of the, 58; Jesus asserted his triune embodiment of the, 104–105
Godless creation, 263, 297
Gods, of the twentieth century, 29
Gog and Magog, 126, 198
Golden age, coming, 343
Golden ages, 255, 343
Golden light of the mind of God, 16
Golden pink glow-ray, 49
Golden-pink mantra, 318
Good: absolute, 335; return of, 267
Gospel(s): def., 374; Everlasting, 159–160; of the Father, Son and Holy Spirit, 149; first, 141–143; foursquare, 234, 237; of God's Kingdom, 141–143; of grace, 144–146; of the Holy Ghost, 146–149, 150; initiations recorded in the four, 158; of Jesus, 153; of the kingdom, 144; preach to every creature, 170–172, 239, 242, 248, 251; preaching of the, 237; read the four, 80; second, 144–146; sevenfold, 177; that will be preached, 158; third, 146–149, 150; of the Trinity, 234. *See also* Everlasting Gospel
Government(s): children of mammon in, 298; in Ghana, 187–188; God's overmen who rule in the, 123; God-government, 158; one-world, 209; seat of God-government, 231
Grace, 70, 82
Grail: as the archetype of true selfhood, 272; *God's Ray as Alpha's Son Incarnating Light*, 156; mystery of the Holy Grail, 44; the Son is the, 156
Grapes: gathering of the, 125; and the parable of the vineyard and husbandmen, 123

Grave, 185
Great Britain, 27
Great Central Sun: energies misqualified returned to the, 12; greatest distance from the, 338; light allowed to spiral to the, 199; magnet of the, 20; tares returned to the, 82
Great Central Sun Magnet, 332, 335
Great Divine Director, 16, 37, 235
Great Silent Watchers, 63, 118, 119
Great White Brotherhood: "ascended" and "unascended" members of, 216; entire Spirit of, 117, 130; mantle of, 302; work of, 272
Great Whore, 208
Gregorian chants, 257
Grund, 24
Guru(s): above and below, 205; balancing the karma of his chelas, 35; bearing the karma of the, 365; and chela, 17, 31; in the chela bodily, 163; chela empowered by his, 148; disobedience to the, 36; embodied, 9, 11, 12; embodied in the anointed apostle, 148; evolutions of earth cut off from the living, 11; false, 118, 142, 157, 210, 349; and Father, 55; first and last, 1, 113; gives to his saints the Great Commission to be himself, 168; Great, 13–14, 24, 52; Great Guru Mother, 49; immersion into the body, mind, soul and heart of, 174; incarnate, 170; initiations of the Father/Guru, 118; of the Israelite dispensation, 165; Lamb as the guru, 5, 177; Lanello, the Ever-Present Guru, 9; line of the descent of the, 3; Maitreya, 6; Moses, 25, 33–35; Mother is, 97; mystery of, 8; obedience to, 142; of the Piscean Age, 31; precipitations of, 258; Saint Germain, 63; sufficiency in, 34; the Lion, 88; water poured by,

10–11; when the guru must withdraw, 13; within you, 122
Guru/chela relationship, 5, 146; of Elijah and Elisha, 165; in the Garden of Eden, 143; hatred pitted against, 130; life becoming Life through the, 244; mantra of the, 55; Mother flame realized in the, 242; mystery of the, 174; psychic communications outside of the, 166; teaching on the, 129; those expelled from the, 42; trust and obey the, 239; with the Lamb, 169; within the community of the Holy Spirit, 157
Guru Ma, 9, 210, 242, 274, 323, 343; chela of the, 337; mission of, 248; office of the flying Eagle occupied by, 140, 248

Hades, wares of, 297
Hague, The, 297
Hail Mary, 205, 257
Hallucinogenics, 335
Harmony, 241
Harpers, 117, 118
Hate, 266
Hatred: love turned into, 239; pitted against the Guru-chela relationship, 130
Healing, 303, 334. *See also* Dieases; Sick
Heart: accelerated, 18; fountain of the, 262; grossness of, 266; guard the, 241; hidden man of the, 223; mastery of the, 60; of Maitreya, 113; Ruby Ray initiations of the, 91; secondary heart chamber, 248; threshingfloor of your consciousness, 206. *See also* Chakra(s); Secret chamber of the heart
Heat, alchemical, 74
Hebrew letter *shin,* 2
Heel, which the serpent's head is determined to bruise, 304

Heir, 51
Hell, descend into, 62, 194, 341. *See also* Hades
Herod, 165, 287
Hierarchical chain, 238
Hierarchy: cosmic order of, 18; Jesus' acknowledgment of, 52; submission to, 59
Hirelings, 103
HOLINESS TO THE LORD, 17
Holland, 237
Holy Ghost, 97; dictations by the, 254; dove of the, 299; God in earth is the, 24; gospel of the, 146–149, 150; Woman united with the, 64
Holy Spirit, 182, 252; and the adoption of sons, 55; always manifests in polarity, 72; angels functioning under the office of the, 217; byword of initiates of the, 127; Calf as the, 58, 65; comes to reprove, 133–134; descends, 180; fire breath of the, 257; five signs of the, 238, 242; in form and formlessness, 126; getting of the, 219; gifts of the, 251, 268; of the Guru, 365; impostors of the, 219, 267; initiations under the, 96; in Jesus, 108; nine gifts of the, 147; office of the, 84, 127; and the office of the Calf on the west gate, 242; is the Person of every ascended master, 135; and the Ritual of Exorcism, 214; and the seven initiations of the saints, 248; seven manifestations of the Person of the, 93; signs conferred by the, 184; signs of the, 192; single voice of the Person of the, 117; and the third stage of Christhood, 164–166; those who usurp the authority of the, 208, 209; transfer of the, 51; twin flames of, 2; on the west gate, 192; whom Jesus has sent, 133–135; work of the, 276

Honor, 109
Horseman, of the Apocalypse, 265
Horses, white, 212
Human consciousness, 74
Humility, 340
Hundred and forty and four thousand, 7, 279; archetypal nucleus, 317; four hundred who preceded them to earth, 15; kingdom of God entrusted unto the, 124; at the north gate, 99; office of the Lion filled by the, 140, 209; remnant of the, 98; and the ruby cube, 23; sacred name sealed in the third-eye vision of, 115; which were redeemed from the earth, 117–118; who came to earth with Sanat Kumara, 14, 108. *See also* One hundred and forty and four thousand
Husbandmen, parable of the vineyard and the, 122–124

I AM Presence, 292; appearance of, 48, 50, 73; cloud of the, 38; contact your, 229; distills your devotion, 327; doers of the will of the, 228; electronic fire rings surround your, 282; empowered Paul, 79; of Ezekiel, 74; Father, 143; fire that will descend through your, 76; Four Cosmic Forces surrounding the, 49; God flame from your, 122; God of the Israelites, 144; incarnation of each one's, 252; individualized, 49; integral relationship with the, 334; interaction of souls with the, 142; is the LORD of the vineyard, 123; Jesus in his mission as the representative of the, 173; joint inheritance of the, 203; Light of, 163; Mediator of your, 70; new name that issues from your, 233; personified in the Guru, 35; reconciliation of the soul with the, 70–71; river flowing from your, 262; saints pray directly to the, 136; socket of the, 175; sufficiency in the, 34; teachings on the, 255; ten-minute meditation upon the white fire sun of your, 329–332; is the true Father, 275; of whom Jesus spoke, 171; your, 81, 159; 'your' I AM Presence who is also 'my' I AM Presence, 62
I AM race, 56, 81, 290, 362
I AM THAT I AM: ardent devotees of the, 253; authority of the, 3; center of the, 324; in the center of the City Foursquare, 3; centered in the spiritual body, 46; coming of the, 183; described by Isaiah, 256; embodiment of the, 238; Father as, 275; incarnate, 7; incarnate within Jesus, 107; inscribed within the heart, 106; integration maintained through, 335; and the Israelites, 34; knowledge of the, 158; the lost name of the LORD, 45; in the midst of his people, 38; name of God, 78; permanent atom of being, 284; personified Light of, 281; who personified the law, 35; personifies himself, 216; suddenly come to his temple, 82; those who have, in their foreheads, 145; visible Presence of, 41; vision of, 172; written on onionskin and read from the reverse side, 115
Identity, circle of, 334
Idolaters, 28–29
Idolatry, 29, 68; cross of, 27; of the self, 28, 199
'Il, chief deity of the Ugaritic pantheon, 360
Illusion, 29
Image: of the only begotten Son of God, 62; placed within the heart, 107
Immaculate heart: of Mary, 71, 205,

Index

226; of the Mother, 206
Impersonal Impersonality, 84, 143
Impersonal Personality, 84
Incarnation(s): each soul has never been limited to one, 195; end of your own soul's, 237; life between, 236 mystery of the, 44
Individuality: building of the spiral of, 223; Lords of, 138
Initiates, a characteristic of, 75
Initiation(s): call for the initiations which Sanat Kumara gave to Ezekiel, 76; chart of the initiations of the saints who follow the Lamb, 248; of the Crucifixion, Resurrection and Ascension, 166; denying the lawful path of, 290; of the east gate, 100, 104, 108, 127; of eating his flesh and blood, 162; eighth ray, 274, 282, 323; eleventh through fourteenth steps of, 245; to embody the flame of the preacher, 177; false, 288; under the Father, 96; fifth ray, 273, 303; first and last, 19; first ray, 172; of the four gates of the city, 167; foursquare, 86; fourth ray, 268, 282; of Guru Maitreya, 37; under the Holy Spirit, 96; illustrated in the public ministry of the Saviour, 164; individually designated for your soul, 75; inner temple, 18; of the Lamb, 94; of the living water of Life, 315; of the LORD and of the fallen ones, 309; narrow path of, 243; ninth ray, 243; of the north gate, 118, 121, 127; path of, 7, 18, 152, 167; on the Path of the Ruby Ray, 59, 77, 85, 91, 318; of the power of the Word, 171; preparatory, 90; ritual of, 71; of the Rose Cross, 17; Ruby Ray, 63, 233; of the sealing of the servants of God in their foreheads, 167; seven, 238, 244, 283, 285, 314; sevenfold path of, 141; sixth ray, 308, 323, 366; of the Son of God, 95; of the South Gate, 137, 226; from the seraphim, 171–172; of the taking up of serpents, 285; that is given at the level of human kindness and human need, 313; thirty-three, 352; three levels of experience in, 244; of the throat chakra, 253; through the two olive branches, 281; of the unloosing of the tongue, 173, 262; of the washing of the feet, 90; of the west gate, 123, 125, 127–129; your own, 164
Initiator, Great, 88
Insensitivity, 266
Integration: east/west, 336; horizontal, 336; north/south, 335; vertical, 335
Intellect, 336
Intellectualism, 236
Intercession, Prayer of, 52–54
Interchange, cosmic, 164, 165, 329
International capitalist/communist conspiracy, 103. *See also* Communism
Internationalists, 188
Inventions, fantastic, 235
Invocation: gift of, 122; to the hierarchy of light entrusted with the Ruby Ray, 59; science of, 134, 214, 219; science of Lemurian, 174; of the Word, 129. *See also* Decree(s)
Iranians, 266
Ireland, 281; Saint Patrick's mission to, 294–296; seed of Serpent in, 296. *See also* Erin
Isaiah, 172, 183, 256
Ishtar, 361
Ishwara, 11, 206
ISIS, 262
Israel: children of, 36, 38; and the laggard evolutions, 106; lost sheep

of the house of, 108; lost tribes of, 45, 281; true, 42; twelve tribes of, 3, 368
Israelites: and the golden calf, 25–26; laggards and fallen one embodied among, 104; and Moses, 33–39; sin of the, 34

Jacob's ladder, 137
Jacob's well, 310–311
James, 164; inordinate desire of, 311
Jasper, 16, 17, 18, 20, 32
Jeremiah, 257
Jerusalem, New, 2, 4, 41, 64, 99; and the City Foursquare, 97, 242; diagram of, 140, 248; east gate of, 100; in heaven, 94; south gate of, 168
Jesus, 88; and Adam and Eve, 289–290; admonishment of, 130–131; affirmation for his disciples, 204; anointer with fire, 375; baptism, 162–163, 287; became the fullness of the four cosmic forces, 161; confrontation with the Antichrist, 108, 111; his cross, 193; crucifixion of, 371; declaration of the indwelling Presence in, 55; demonstrated the Path of the Rose Cross, 44; denouncing Antichrist, 285; discourse on the Good Shepherd, 100–102, 105–106; embodied as Abel and Seth, 341; the embodied Lamb, 7, 146; fastened to the cross, 70; and the family, 228; final admonishment prior to his ascension, 238; fire that will descend from, 76; and the fourth stage of Christhood, 166–167; in the Garden of Gethsemane, 369; Guru in the Piscean Age, 145; Holy Ghost of, 148; in the hour of his ascension, 231; idolatry of, 68; initiation of the washing of the feet by, 90; initiation of the West Gate revealed in part by, 127–129; initiation through, 248; initiations illustrated in the public ministry of, 164; initiator on the Path of the Ruby Ray, 59; and the inordinate desire of James and John, 311; intercession of, 184; and John the Baptist, 165–166; king and priest, 302; the lie that Jesus did for you only what you can do for yourselves, 193; and Maitreya, 90; the Man, 77; mantles of, 4; Messenger of Maitreya, 121; mission, 134, 338; mission is misunderstood, 173; office of the Man, 140, 161, 208, 242, 248; and the other seventy, 273; and Paul, 69–70, 79; Paul's oneness with, 147; people often worship his flesh and blood person, 171; in the Person of the Man, 79; preaching the gospel of Maitreya, 144; received by the Ancient of Days, 233; his resurrection, 198; revealed the mystery of the all-seeing eye of God, 274–275; revelations of Jesus unto his two witnesses, 136; sacrifice discerned in the Word of, 119–120; and Saint Patrick, 295; Sanat Kumara comes through, 8, 49; Sanat Kumara sends his call through, 1; and Simon the Pharisee, 185; the Son of God, 51; sponsor of, 37; study the Word of, 81; temptations by Satan, 287–290; testimony of, 252; transfiguration, 164–166; triune embodiment of the Godhead, 104–105, 107; true teachings of, 59, 135; victory over Death and Hell, 194–195; walking in his footsteps and doing greater works than, 156; was embodied as Joseph, 310; what he would show to John, 41; and the woman of Samaria, 315–317. *See also* World Teachers

Index 397

Jews: who took up stones to stone Jesus, 105–106; salvation is to the, 317
Jezebel, 210
Job, mantra of, 327–328
John the Baptist, 108, 185; baptizer with water, 375; confrontations with Antichrist, 111; denouncing Antichrist, 285; and the "generation of vipers," 286–287; and Jesus, 165–166; Jesus' baptism by, 162–163; preaching in the wilderness, 176; was taken and Jesus was left, 236
John the Beloved, 2, 149; given a reed with which to measure, 138; inordinate desire of, 311; "little book" given to, 63; sponsoring apostle of the Ruby Ray, 153; at the Transfiguration, 164; vision of the birth of the Manchild, 324
Joseph, son of Jacob, 296; embodiment of Jesus, 310
Journalism, 299
Joy, 154
Juda, Lion of the tribe of, 24, 35, 89
Judgment, 175, 267; coming of the, 189; of the dark ones, 117; final, 289; Great White Throne Judgment, 207–210; hastening the day of your own, 220; hour of the, 39; of the husbandmen, 125; is come, 188; Judgment Call, 108–109, 110; Last, 185; LORD releasing the judgment by the throat chakra, 256; LORD's, 283; manifest, 19; of the One Hundred and Forty and Four upon the earth, 12; power to invoke the, 265; prophesied, 299; rejection of the Word brings forth the, 187; of the right arm of the Almighty, 205; by the science of invocation, 134; of the soul, 195; that comes through your preaching of the Everlasting Gospel, 185; that liberates all souls, 167; of the Watchers, 265; white fire of, 287
Justinius, 269

Ka, winged symbol of the, 200
Karma: balance of, 100, 113; balanced, and the ascension, 94; balancing of, 90; be willing to bear a portion of personal and planetary, 73; bearers of, 71; Dark Cycle of returning, 36; descent of personal and planetary, 184; fifty-one percent, 235; footsteps of your, 65–66; great tribulation of personal and planetary, 8; and the Guru, 35; irrevocable law of, 126; law might accelerate the return of, 265; law of, 156, 267; one hundred percent of, 357; personal and planetary, 75, 166–167, 316; planetary, 193; of the righteous and unrighteous, 39; seven percent of your, 245; soul can transcend, 62; Watchers manipulate, 374
Karma yoga, 325
Keeper(s) of the Flame, 102, 160, 227, 338
King: archetypal pattern of, 302; *key* to the *in*carnation of God, 177, 301. *See also* Rulers
Kingdom, 9; of God, 125; LORD's, 159
Knower, 330
Kristine, Ascended Lady Master, 232–237, 243
Kumaras, Holy: seers and scribes who have served under, 149; seven, 14, 58, 149, 153, 160, 173, 254, 259, 305, 332; sixth of the seven, 277
Kundalini, 145; attack on the light of the, 297. *See also* Life force
Kuthumi, 88. *See also* World Teachers

Laggard(s), 359; among the Israelites, 104; challenge to, 109; confronta-

tion with, 108; evolutions, 106–107, 210, 336, 362; "Laggards against the Light," 158; laggard generations, 124; laggard languages, 255; may bend the knee, 185; who called themselves Jews, 106–107
Lake of fire, 201, 227
Lamb, 268; ascended masters who have passed the intitiation of, 148; blood of, 8, 115, 135; chart of the Word and Work of the one who would be, 248; chela who has become, 93; chelas of, 156; chohans as, 238; diagram of the alchemical marriage, 292; drinking in the consciousness of, 318; embodied, 7, 9, 10, 140, 143, 210, 248, 339; in the embodied Guru, 177; of God, 102, 284–285; and the great ritual drama, 94; as the Guru incarnate, 170; eternal, 208, 248, 339; five signs that follow them that believe in, 226; having seven horns, 93; incarnate, 52; individual, 339; initiation(s) of the, 94, 136, 245, 282, 344; Jesus fulfilled the office of, 51; and the Lamb's wife, 149; meditation on and immersion in, 174; in the midst of the throne, 98; most demanding and rewarding service of, 230; on Mount Sion, 157; must be in physical embodiment, 8; office of the, 233; the one who comes in the name of, 225; oneness with the embodied, 242; in the physical octave, 12; salvation by, 146; seat of, 285; slain from the foundation of the world, 145; that is the Guru, 5; that Serpent and his seed have sought to slay, 284; they which follow, 95; the title, 94; those offended by, 9; those who desire to exercise power over, 325; those who follow, 118; those who hold the office of, 146; water of, 10–11; who is slain, 93, 127; who is worthy to open the book, 173, 174, 246, 272; who stood on mount Sion, 114
Lamb's wife, 140, 208, 210, 284; diagram of the alchemical marriage, 292
Lambs of God, 96. *See also* Sheep
Lamps, seven, 19, 280–281
Lanello, 5, 177, 180–181; and the ascension of Lady Kristine, 234. *See also* Messenger(s)
Languages, spoken on earth, 255
Lanto, 174, 239
Last Supper, 366
Law: book of the, 48, 49; cosmic, 13; expressed as the spoken Word, 203; of the Father, 133; and the Lawgiver, 44, 142; will perform its perfect work, 267
Leaders: blind, 228; in Ghana, 186
Leadership, 298
Lemuria, 149, 354; central altar of, 3; children of, 143; days of, 191; path of initiation on, 7
Lemurian altars, 214
Lemurian invocation, 174
Lemurian mystery school, 42
Lemurian root races, 255
Lemurian temples, 173, 257
Leo, 24, 60; Initiation of Sacrifice under, 77; initiators under, 58
Leto, Lady Master, 235
Levitation, 31
Levites, 17, 34
Liar, original, 286, 287
Liberty, Goddess of, 48–49
Life-force: desecration of the, 347; fallen ones have captivated the, 301; misuses of the, 304; sacred fire of the, 302; symbol of the, 301, 303
Light: demons must vampirize, 240; false Christs steal, 103; of the

Index 399

Great Central Sun magnetized by Jesus, 164; "Let there be light!" 262; purging and purifying, 260; radiating forth in all directions, 333; rotation of, 285; Son of man is required to magnetize, 161; sudden acceleration of, 74; teeming torrent of, 331; those not called to receive, 6; those who have no, 326; transfer of, 281; transferred by emissaries of the Most High, 239; which is the river of water of life, 145; which the seed of Serpent have misqualified, 301

Lightbearers, 26; who came with Sanat Kumara, 3

Lion, 31, 49; archetype of Christ in the fire quadrant, 59–60; baptism of the saints fulfilled by the, 174; baptism of the, 77; Christ consciousness epitomized in the way of the, 168; Christ having the face of a, 42; the Father, 65; first beast was like a, 24; initiates of the, 204; Initiation of Sacrifice under the, 59; initiation under the office of the, 242, 248; and the *"ION* of *Light,"* 60; and Lanello, 181; Maitreya in the Person of the, 79; meaning of, 84; mysteries of the, 37; non-identification with the, 82; office of, 113, 119, 140, 162, 248, 279; sacrifice of the, 28; Shiva the, 30; those who usurp the office of the, 208; of the tribe of Juda, 35, 89

LORD: hand of the, 272; his appearance to Ezekiel, 73; is come, 196

LORD OUR RIGHTEOUSNESS, THE, 56, 100, 184, 188, 292; Second Advent of, 209

Lord's Prayer, 203, 342; "I AM" Lord's Prayer, 343. *See also* Our Father

Lords of Karma, 184

Lotus, and Godfre, 235

Love, 129; burning within the center of the ruby cube, 22; and casting out devils, 221, 224; fullest consummation of, 326; human and divine, 329; intensification of, 131; intolerable to devils, 239–240; language of, 258; mechanized perversions of, 240; oneness earned by, 88; path of, 329; unselfed, 330

Lover, Divine, 329

Lucifer, 208, 360; angels who fell with, 361; and the Great Rebellion, 286; Serpent as a cohort of, 287

Luciferian(s), 106, 137, 264; foul spirits created by, 227; Luciferian false hierarchy, 286–287, 289

Lunar influences, 224

Madness, unexplainable, 227

Maha Chohan, 88; initiations of, 89; office of the Man occupied by, 100; take up the cross of, 108; writings of, 219

Maid of honor, 244

Maitreya, 3–5; Adam and Eve expelled by, 42; the call through, 1; cometh to initiate you, 11; contact with, 144; Father, 90; fire that will descend from, 76; first and last Guru, 290; and the garden of Eden, 6–7, 142–143; Guru, 18, 115, 118, 270; impostor of, 288; in the office of the Lion, 77, 79, 113–114, 242; initiation(s) by, 37, 59, 162–163, 248, 340; as initiator on the Path of the Ruby Ray, 59; Jesus' allegiance to, 52; Jesus preached the gospel of, 144; Jesus the Messenger of, 121; meaning of the name, 353; on the north gate, 323; and the office of the Lion, 140, 162, 208, 248; only the chela can identify, 275; places ruby roses upon the cosmic cross of white fire, 114; Sanat Kumara comes through, 8; Sanat Kumara's coming in the person of, 49; Serpent inpugning the motive of, 288; spoke the message "This is my beloved Son," 166; where the many left off their association with, 26

Maldek, 360

Man, 31, 49; archetype of the Saviour, 62; all ascended masters occupy the office of the, 87; baptism of the saints fulfilled by the, 174; Christ consciousness epitomized in the way of the, 168; Christ having the face of, 42; image of Christ fashioned as, 63; image of, 28; image of the Christ as a face of, 89; initiates of the, 204; Initiation of Surrender under, 59; initiation under the office of, 242, 248; Jesus in the Person of, 79; meaning of the office of, 100; meaning of, 84; Mother *a*tom with the *n*egative charge, 62; mysteries of the image of, 37; natural and spiritual, 44, 50, 74; non-identification with, 82; office of, 104, 108, 140, 161, 248, 279; Saint Germain in the office of, 153; Shiva the image of, 30; spiritual and natural, 73; third beast who had a face as, 36; those who usurp the office of, 208

Manasseh: and Ephraim, 26–27; tribe of, 294

Manchild, 50, 51, 86, 210; become the, 85; birth of the, 324

Mankind, origin of, 362

Mantle(s): of the Great White Brotherhood, 302; of Lanello, 181; lineal descent of the, 5; of Jesus, 4; of the Lamb, 8; one who wears our, 9; placed upon Sanat Kumara, 13; of Sanat Kumara, 3; of the Son of God, 55; that is the authority of the transfer of the Trinity, 51; of the World Teachers, 102

Mantra(s): devoid of love, 102; of the Hindus and Buddhists, 257; masterful giving of the, 252. *See also* Decree(s)

Manus, 149, 317

Mark, Book of, 174; seven initiations recorded in the Gospel of, 244; writer of the gospel of, 204

Marriage: of the Christ Self and the soul, 284; of the Lamb, 5; of your soul with the BRANCH, 282. *See also* Bride; Bridegroom

Mary, Mother, 204–206, 340; Cosmic Clock that has been given to you by, 58; invocation to, 219; offered herself a living sacrifice, 226

Mary of Bethany, 166

Masculine ray, 93

Mass, black, 219

Mass consciousness, 157, 327

Mastery, God-mastery, 305

Materialism, 27, 298

Materialization, 25

Matter: amethyst sphere of, 5; matter spheres, 341; real of unreal, 261; and Spirit, 30, 97, 115, 164; sustainment of the matter universe, 215

Maxim light, 331

Mechanization, 298

Mechanization concept, 209

Mechanization man, 223

Mediator(s): between the Guru and chela, 17; Christ Self as, 244, 284, 336

Meditation: on the Guru, 174; physical postures during, 333; ten minutes of, 329–332

Mediumistic communications, 166

Melchizedek, priesthood of, 2, 15, 17, 106, 257, 280

Memory: and the fire body, 168;

mastery of the, 84
Mental body, 298. *See also* Air
Mental quadrant, 305
Mercy, 82
Messenger(s), 219; balance they hold, 243; book in her hand, 49; brings the teaching in honor, 191; embodied, 8, 135; face of my, 79; embodied, 135; home star of the, 232; initiation received through our, 244; Maitreya in the person of, 357; their mission to Ghana, 186–187; occupy the office of the two witnesses, 95; personal initiation through the, 38; reaction to the, 191; and Sanat Kumara, 82; reinforce the light of the Mediator, 244; sealing of the forehead of the, 17; speak and interpret angelic tongues, 254; Spirit of prophecy upon the, 252; as the two olive trees, 281; when we send our, 190; who has the courage to deliver to you our "far out" messages, 236; your, 3. *See also* Lanello; Prophet, Elizabeth Clare; Prophet, Mark L.; Two witnesses
Messengership, continuity of the, 274
Messiah, 32, 94, 197. *See also* Saviour
Meta, 14
Metaphysical movements, 219
Michael, Archangel, 36, 277; invocation to, 219; sword of, 226; those cast out of heaven by, 299
Mighty in the earth, 124
Miller, Florence Jeannette, 233–237
Mind: Cosmic, 174; destroyers of the light of the Holy Ghost in the, 298; healing of the, 334; mastery of the, 84; mind stuff, 261, 263; omnipotence of God over the subconscious and conscious, 151; oppressors of the, 299; outer nature expressed through, 168; serpent, 300; unconscious, 154; which was also in Christ Jesus, 100. *See also* Intellect
Mind of God, 181, 309, 330, 339; and the Ancient of Days, 2; in Christ, 102; saint polarizes with the, 217
Miracles, 258
Mission Amethyst Jewel, 158, 280, 296
Money, love of, 188
Money beast, 210
Moore, Thomas, 294
Moral degeneration, 108
Moral integrity, 190
Mortal cursings, 266
Morticians, 199
Moses: and the children of Israel, 25–26, 33–39; exhortation to the I AM race, 362; given stone tablets, 37; glory of the LORD revealed to, 41; Guru, 19, 33–35, 37, 165; initiation of, 38; lifted up the serpent force in the wilderness, 145; people of Israel who spake against, 302; and the shepherd's crook, 300–301; wrath of God descended through, 35
Mother, 97, 115–116, 182; and the Buddha, 24; devotion to the, 324; Eagle as the, 58; elemental beings as servants of the World, 217; eyes of, 23; and the fourth stage of Christhood, 166–167; God the, 325; I and my Mother are one, 160, 173, 245; initiation through the, 248; in Israel, 43; keeps our counsel while holding the immaculate concept, 190; and Lanello, 177; Maitreya as, 354; in Matter and Spirit, 115; mission of the, 226; at the nexus, 99; nexus of the figure eight, 96; office of, 59, 84, 173, 242; on the north gate, 323; science of, 155; and the seven initi-

ations of the saints, 248; souls representing Father and, 7; symbol of, 322; teaching of, 160; those who usurp the authority of, 208, 210; and the Trinity, 2; why her heart is sacred, 206; work of the, 156; World, 29, 32; of the World, 4

Mother flame, 205, 324, 340, 354; anchored above and below, 342; Deathless Solar Body woven out of the, 81; in defense of her children, 75; demons perverting the, 241; initiate of the, 274; interaction with the, 226; and the office of "Guru Ma," 274

Mother light: God-dominion of the, 325; liberation through the, 64; Matter filled with, 322; rising, 303

Motion pictures, 240

Mu. See Lemuria

Mudra, abhaya, 110, 334

Multitude(s), 97–99; come out of the great tribulation, 115; great, 96, 130, 157, 167, 242, 245, 274; mission of the great, 248; and the office of the Calf, 140, 209; sealing in the forehead of, 108

Murderer, original, 286, 287

Mystery(s): finishing of, 204; of the Grail, 153, 254; removed from scriptures, 288; of the Ruby Ray, 155; of the two creations that dwell in the earth, 184; which the devils have inverted, 182

Mystery school: 'first' and 'last', 290; Lemurian, 42; outer retreat of our, 244; prerequisite for the, 74

Nada and Rex, 235

Name, new, 233

Nameless One, 12, 18; angels of, 233; commission given unto Sanat Kumara by the, 51; his words to Sanat Kumara, 13–14; shall confer upon you the new name, 233; those to whom he has entrusted the Ruby Ray, 59

Nephilim, 361

Nerve systems, 326

Ninth ray, 207, 243, 245, 248

North gate: of the City Foursquare, 58, 242, 309, 323; diagram of, 140, 248; Father on, 192; of the holy city in the Matter spheres, 307; initiation(s) of the, 118, 121, 127, 248, 314, 338, 341; in the Matter spheres, 310; Maitreya on the, 144; office of the Lion on the, 162, 242; saints at the, 95, 99, 274, 311, 326; in spirit and matter, 339

North side, of the City Foursquare, 115

Obadiah, 313

Obedience, vow of, 88

Occult, def., 374

Olive trees, two, 281

OM AH HUM, 261

OM MANI PADME HUM, 261

Omega: 'body' of Christ as, 72; in the chela, 6

One, law of the, 12

One Hundred and Forty and Four, judgment of the, 12

One hundred and forty and four thousand, 167, 344. See also Hundred and forty and four thousand

One sent, 3, 313; believing on the, 144; initiation to receive the, 239; in the person of Jesus, 4; soul knows the, 313

Opportunity, defined, 352

Order of Saint Francis, 88

Order of the Ruby Cross, 24

Orthodox movements, 219

Other seventy, 273–274

Our Father, 257. See also Lord's Prayer

Overcomers, 305

Ox, 129, 364; Christ having the face of an, 42

Pallas Athena, 219
Parents, 222, 225
Parvati and Shiva, 26
Past: change the, 214; cut off, 196
Pastors, false, 196, 208, 226, 367
Path: of lost steps, 345; those who pretend to be on the, 162
Patience, of the Calf, 126
Patrick, Saint, 294–296; on the east gate, 303
Paul, Saint, 79, 279; anointed by Jesus, 69–70; archetype of apostleship, 147; claim the mantle of, 272; and the communion of the saints, 71; on the east gate, 303; heavenly places frequented by, 298; on the island of Melita, 271; knew intimately the Christ Self, 78
Paul the Venetian, 218, 239
Peace, 109; flame of, 341; God of, 277
Pentecost, 252; sacred-fire baptism on, 147
Performing arts, 299
Personal Impersonality, 84
Personal Personality, 84, 143
Personalities, multifragmented, 223
Personality: magnetic, 29; of the Godhead, 29
Persons, pure sons, 228
Peshu Alga, 157
Peter, 164, 370
Pharisees, 106, 185, 286, 371
Philosophy of Serpent, 286, 289, 318
Physical body: functions of the, 327; mastery of the Self in the, 61
Pilate, 371
Pillars, seven, 160, 161
Piscean Age, 31
Piscean conqueror, 341
Piscean dispensation, 289; conclusion of the, 316; fulfillment of the, 152
Piscean perversions, 315–316

Pisces: initiations of, 152; passing of the torch of, 4; and the resurrection, 62
Pit: demons of the bottomless, 241; devils and beasts out of the bottomless, 209
Poisons, 337. *See also* Deadly thing
Policeman, directing traffic, 333
Politics, 288
Positive charge, 60
Poverty, vow of, 88
Power: "All power is given unto me...," 248; conferment of, 4; those who lust after world, 188; transfer of, 171
Power center, 173. *See also* Chakra(s)
Prayer(s): fervent and fiery, 331; fiery fohatic, 332; of malintent, 219; of saints, 96, 138. *See also* Hail Mary, "Lord's Prayer"; Rosary
Preach(ing): the Everlasting Gospel, 185, 274; the good news to every creature, 184; of the gospel, 138; the gospel to every creature, 170–171, 172, 239, 242, 248, 251; of the gospel in all the world, 237; as the *power* to *reach* the soul, 176
Preacher(s): endued with the power of the Word, 223; mantle of the, 191; mission of the, 185; of righteousness, 177; who are the disciples of the Lamb, 185
Precipitation, 257
Present, change the, 214
Preserver, 73, 155, 216, 254, 261, 267
Priesthood: of the Levites, 34; of Melchizedek, 2, 15, 17, 106, 257, 280; mysteries of the, 18
Priests, 17, 302
Princes of the air, 297, 298
Prophecies of the book of Revelation, 156
Prophecy: come to pass, 241; delivered through the two witnesses, 135; gift of, 75; spirit of, 2, 252; of

the two witnesses, 134, 138
Prophet(s), 143, 153, 347; be willing to be like the, 75; Devil in the person of false, 208; false, 69, 157, 209, 349; gift given to the, 76; of Israel, 171; occupy the office of the two witnesses, 95; rejection of the, 42; Saint Patrick was a prophet in Israel, 294; "these two prophets,", 149; true, 209, 274. *See also* Ezekiel; Isaiah; Jeremiah; Samuel
Prophet, Elizabeth Clare, 5, 136, 218. *See also* Messenger(s)
Prophet, Mark L., 5, 136, 177; call to Surya dictated to, 246; embodied as Mark the writer of the gospel, 204; and the emerald isle, 294. *See also* Lanello; Messenger(s)
Psychic communications, 166
Psychology, 334; relating to previous incarnations, 223
Public servant, 188
Purple fiery heart of Saint Germain, 71
Pyramid: base of the, 118; Great, 86, 97; Great Matter, 274, 303–304; Great, of Life, 234; King's Chamber of the Great, 61, 86; spiral from the base of the Great, 114

Quadrant(s): air, 299; archetype of Christ in the earth, 61; archetype of Christ in the fire, 60; Christ Mind in the air, 62; outline of the four, 58; ruler of the earth, 24; ruler of the fire, 24; six elders in each of the four, 94; solar hierarchies governing each of the four, 168; souls who have ascended to the mental, 305; third and fourth, 151; water, 65

Ra Mu, 174
Rahab, 395
Rapture, 217

Ray-O-Light, call to, 219
Rebellion, Great, 89, 286, 360
Redemption, physical, 8
Relationships, interpersonal, 336–337
Relatives, well-meaning, 227
Religion(s), 149; demons who submit to a form of, 224; exoteric and esoteric, 204; misused, 176; of the new age, 316; of Ra Mu, 174; and science, 99; science of, 95, 133; true, 290. *See also* Church(es); Doctrine(s); Theology
Reproductive organs, 304
Responsibility as initiates of the Ruby Ray, 194
Resurrection, 93, 304; entering into the, 62; Flame of, 65, 302, 318; flesh-and-blood, 198; initiation of the, 166, 316, 352; of the Lamb, 34, 61; miracle of the, 194; of the Son of Man, 77; Spirit of the, 185; thy, 63
Retreats of the ascended masters, 161, 200, 235, 298; initiation received in, 244. *See also* Royal Teton Retreat; Cave of Symbols, 235
Revelation, Book of, 89, 149, 156
Revelations, unfolding, 149
Reverse the tide, of hate and hate creation, 266
Rex, 235
Rhythm, perverted, 241
Righteousness: right energy use, 134, 177; of saints, 284
Ring-pass-not, 334
Ritual of Exorcism, 198, 200; its daily practice, 300; outlined, 202–220
Rituals, sacred, 335
Rock of Christ, 125
Rod: of Aaron and Erin, 295; of Moses, 300–302
Role playing, 124, 244
Roll of a book, 48, 63, 74

Index 405

Root race(s): earth's, 317; first three, 343, 355; fourth, 144; Lemurian, 255
Rosary, 206
Rose Cross, 88; daily cross taken up by initiates of the, 134; first initiation on the Path of the, 35; impostors of the Path of the, 102; inheritors of light by the Path of the, 106; initiates of the Path of the, 23; initiation of the, 17, 38; Jesus demonstrated the Path of the, 44; mysteries of, 32, 37, 340; nexus of the, 61; one having fulfilled the requirements of the Path of the, 93; Path of the, 20, 22, 26, 33, 229; riddle on the Path of the, 30; sevenfold Path of the, 167; test of the, 228; those entering the Path of the, 30; those who have submitted to the, 86; twelve unfolding flowers in the, 121. *See also* Cross; Ruby Ray
Roses upon the cross, 114
Royal Teton Retreat, 174, 234, 330
Ruby, 18; initiatic jewel, 28; ruby red of the sardine stone, 17
Ruby Cross, sign of the, 58
Ruby ray, 23; Aaron an initiate of, 302; accelerated love of the, 239; accelerated Path of the, 237; acceleration of light on the Path of the, 74; alchemically the blood of Christ, 194; ascended masters have gone before you on the Path of the, 79; blood of the Lamb that is the, 131; chemicalization of consciousness through the, 154; communion cup of the, 309; crucifixion on the Path of the, 70; culmination of the Path of the, 166; diagram of the initiations and initiators on the Path of, 77; energy of, 70; example and forerunner on the Path of, 234; goal of the Path of, 65, 282, 322; hierarchy of, 109; initiate(s) of, 68, 89, 155, 192, 336; initiation(s) of, 59, 63, 85, 86, 114, 311; initiations of the heart, 91; initiations fulfilled, 233; initiations in the King's Chamber, 86; Jesus empowered to teach the Path of the, 73; John the Beloved, the sponsoring apostle, 153; Lamb clothed upon with the, 94; light of the, 278; lineal descent of the, 163; mission of initiates of, 108; nine steps of initiation on the Path of, 147; opening of the Path of, 138; Path of, 43, 44, 49–51, 68, 159, 290, 305, 312, 317, 338, 365; Path in the life of Ezekiel, 73; penetrating the lie of Serpent, 278; personal initiation of, 38; pink flame that becomes, 218; purpose of, 44; requirement that one should demonstrate the Path of, 180; responsibility as initiates of, 194; rod of, 277; sevenfold Path, 167; surrender on the Path of, 162; take up the cross of, 229; way of, 80; wayshower of the Path of the, 55. *See also* Rose Cross
Rulers who lost their high estate, 123

Sacred fire, 8, 11, 38, 60, 82, 126, 354; baptism of, 146–147, 287; be baptized by, 219; infolding itself, 41, 45; initiations of, 17; misuses of, 349–350; temptations to misuse the, 304; of the Word, 7, 257
Sacred heart of Jesus, 71
Sacrifice,; bitterness of the path of, 154; demonstrator of the path of, 84; discerned in the Word of Jesus, 119; initiation of, 59–60, 77; of the lion, 28; path of, 154; required for the path of surrender, 312; supreme, 161
Sadducees, 106, 286
Saint(s), 97; of the Church, 115;

communion of, 71, 72, 165, 272; diagram of the seven initiations of, 248; do battle with Antichrist, 137; exercise the Science of the Spoken Word, 136, 173; follow the Lamb, 183; in heaven, 243; of the inner Church, 307, 323; long-suffering of the, 126; mission of the, 248; of the Most High, 9; on the north gate, 95, 99, 274; office of the Lion occupied by the, 140, 209; and the prophecies of the book of Revelation, 156–157; robed in white, 89, 217, 298, 335; of the Ruby Ray, 169; sealed in their foreheads, 98; the term 'saint', 217; Trinity outpictured within the, 170; undergoing seven initiations, 242; upon earth and in heaven, 246; upon white horses and clothed in fine linen, 212; on the west gate, 133, 138; where they gather, 115; who follow(s) the Lamb, 229; who guard the sanctuary of the Holy Grail, 308; for whom the marriage supper of Lamb is prepared, 311

Saint Germain: and the ascension of Lady Kristine, 234; chose the English language to deliver the teachings, 255; Great Guru in Aquarius, 63; mystery of the Word revealed by, 214; seventh angel, 153; Son of man unto the Aquarian age, 50

Salamanders, 17, 31, 199

Salvation, 146

Samaria, woman of, 315–317

Samaritans, 315

Samuel, 37

Sanat Kumara: descent of his mantle, 3; he that sitteth on the throne, 8; his footprints, 191; his office, 232; initiation through, 248; as initiator on the Path of the Ruby Ray, 59; occupies the Office of the Woman, 205; and the office of the flying eagle, 77, 140, 166, 208, 248; plea before the Cosmic Council, 11–12; portion of himself placed within his chelas, 39; renew the ancient covenant of your soul with, 175; replica of, 206; those who came with, 3, 108; those with a memory of, 115; transmittal of the Person of, 171; walking and talking with Ezekiel, 74. *See also* Ancient of Days

Sanhedrin, 106, 371

Sapphire stone, 45

Sardine stone, 16, 17, 18, 20, 32

Satan, 286; blood oath before, 274; fall of, 273; and his seed, 157, 192; "I beheld Satan as lightning fall from heaven," 272; original Murderer, 286; Serpent as a cohort, 287; temptation of Jesus, 287–290; transforms himself into an angel of light, 336; usurps the office of the Man, 208

Satanic false hierarchy, 290

Satanists, 219

Saviour: archetype of the, 84; must put on the mantle of your, 154–155. *See also* Jesus; Messiah

School, 222

Science, 95; and religion, 99; material and spiritual, 73

Science of the Spoken Word. *See* Decree(s); Word

Scientific humanism, 289

Scorpio: Dark Cycle in, 277; hierarchy of, 64; Initiation of Selflessness under, 77; initiators under, 58

Scotland, 281, 297

Scripture(s): of East and West, 149; mysteries removed from the, 288; Serpent in sacred, 286; those teaching the holy, 69. *See also* Bible

Sea of glass, 19

Seal(s): book sealed with seven, 94;

opening of the, 87; seven, 85, 86, 282, 314; seven, in the level of the soul, 89; seventh, 18. *See also* Book Seat of the soul, 89
Second Advent, 184, 237; preparation for, 238
Second Coming, 36, 184
Second death, 167, 289
Second Ray: Chohan of the, 174; initiations of the, 140, 248; self-mastery on the, 248
Secret chamber of the heart, 50, 206, 248, 252, 323, 324; image hid within, 107
Secret rays, 242, 352
Self: be the Real, 229; a composite, 223; death of the lesser, 35; fragmentation of the Greater, 127; Greater and lesser, 78, 329; greater than your own, 331; idolaters of the, 68; idolatry and love of the, 28; lesser and Greater, 75; lower and Greater, 335; mutable and Immutable, 60; outer, 223; sacrifice of the, 59; surrender of the, 62; that dies but once, 195; that is the acceptable offering, 161; True, 44, 222
Self-awareness, 222
Self-doubt, 315–316
Self-emptying process, 283
Self-expression, 222
Self-idolatry, 28, 63, 77
Self-indulgence, 28, 60, 77
Self-integration, 334
Self-knowledge, 336
Self-love, 28, 60, 63, 77
Self-sacrifice, 234
Self-transcendence, 60, 73
Self worth, 270
Selfhood, 334; pride and rebellion imprison, 90
Selfishness, 28, 62, 77
Selflessness: bitterness of the path of, 154; demonstrator of the path of, 84; of the flying eagle, 28; initiation of, 59, 63, 77; path of, 64–65, 154, 234; required for the path of surrender, 312
Sensuality, 27, 210
Seraphim: awaiting the call, 269; initiation from, 171–172; stand where you stand, 260
Serapis Bey, 87, 233; has revealed to you the Deathless Solar Body, 283; initiation conveyed by, 268; law given by, 199; opening the book on the law of the ascension, 90
Serpent(s), 7, 142, 276, 264, 286, 288, 289; ability to take up, 226; agent of Lucifer whose name was, 143; brazen, 303; determined to bruise the heel of Christed ones, 304; Devil in the person of the, 209; disembodied spirits of, 349; fall of, 273; fiery, 297, 302; flood of the, 277; of the last days, 304; lie of, 272; in your midst, 304; Moses' rod became a, 301; movement of a serpent's body, 301; philosophies of, 277; power to tread on, 272, 275; raging of the, 227; saints are acquainted with, 157; and his seed, 300; and his seed in Ireland, 295; and his seed in the isles of Britain, 297; seed of Serpent in the Bible, 306; Serpent's head, 289; strategy of Serpent's seed, 299; take up, 248, 271, 273, 274, 279, 285, 290, 295, 302, 305; tread on, 276; who are the fallen servants of God, 274; wise as serpents, 299
Serpent force, God-mastery of the, 300
Serpentine logic, 301
Service: bitterness of the path of, 154; of the calf, 28; demonstrator of the path of, 84; initiation of, 59, 60, 77; path of, 88, 154, 234; perpet-

ual, 327; required for the path of surrender, 312; that spans the octaves, 243; thy, 126

Seth, 341; descendents of, 358, 361

Seven rays: Christ Path on each of the, 161; conditions which challenge your initiations on the, 207; initiations of the, 149, 170; on each of the four sides of the city, 95; path of the, 160; self-mastery in the, 242; tongues of the, 255

Seven-tiered spiral of descent from the great white throne, 86

Seventh Ray: initiations of the, 96, 140, 248; self-mastery on the, 248. *See also* Violet flame

Sex oozing from every television commercial, 240

Sexual perversions, 297, 304

Shah of Iran, 266–267

Shamballa, 3, 160

Sheep: and the Good Shepherd, 102–103, 105–106; lost, 345; and the shepherd, 13. *See also* Lambs

Shekinah, 38, 41, 55, 78, 275–76

Shepherd(s): good, 100–103, 105–106, 213; to the multitudes, 69; and sheep, 13; shepherd's crook, 300–301; true, 100, 106, 108

Shin, Hebrew letter, 2

Shiva, 30; and Parvati, 26; shakti of, 64; those serving the throne of, 25

Sick, lay hands on, 226, 248

Siddhartha, 343. *See also* Gautama Buddha

Signs: signs following, 242, 248, 251; third of the five, 274; which follow those who preach the Everlasting Gospel, 271

Simon the Pharisee, 186

Sin(s): bearing the cross of world, 193; "Christ died for our sins," 194; the energy veil, 146; original, 290; of the people visited upon them, 36; sense of, 317; of the whole world, 194

Sinai, Mount, 37, 41

Sinai wilderness, 34

Sincerity, 314

Sine wave, 301

Sinner, whose sins Jesus forgave, 186

Sion, *s*piral of the *ion,* 114

Sirius, 231–232, 246, 291; meditation upon, 329–332; Word spoken in, 259. *See also* God Star

Six is an incomplete figure eight, 323

Sixth ray: initiates of the, 277, 332; initiations of the, 96, 140, 248, 308, 323; saints serving on the, 326; saints who minister on the, 99; self–mastery on the, 248

Social sciences, 288

Solar awareness, 49, 55, 89, 96; bridal gown of, 284; chakra of, 330; grapes that represent, 123; spheres of, 292. *See also* Soul awareness

Solar hierarchies, 95, 168

Solar Logoi, 23, 127

Solar plexus, 49, 277; mastery through the, 65

Son, 176, 181; adoption of sons, 55; adoption of the soul, 50; "my beloved Son," 261; covenant of the Father and, 45; on the east gate, 192; as the embodiment of the law of the Father, 134; extension of the Father's Person through, 281; and the Father, 203; Father in the, 6, 13, 24, 72, 171, 175; first archetype of personal Christhood, 161–162; in flesh and blood, 143; God the Father and Mother adore, 325; gospel of the grace of the Father manifest in, 145; "I and my Son are one," 163; "...in whom I AM well pleased," 163; initiations given to the Son/chela, 118; is the Grail, 156; Jesus' teaching on the Father and, 275–276; joint-heirship with, 155; Light of the only begotten, 145–146; Man as the, 58; mantra of, 99; and the Mother, 97; office of the, 84, 127; opportunity to believe on the, 144; and the parable of the vineyard and husbandmen, 124; personality of the, 285; and the Ritual of Exorcism, 213; and the second stage of Christhood, 163–165; and the seven initiations of the saints, 248; and the Trinity, 2; sealed in your hearts, 50; Spirit of the, 78–79; two commands of the, 238; usurp the authority of the, 208; work of the, 144. *See also* Christ; Sonship

Son of God, 43, 45; ascended masters serving under the office of the, 217; behind the Son of man, 51; coming of the, 279; entering in to the heart of the Father, 121; his image placed within the heart, 107; Image of the only begotten, 62; initiations of the, 95, 100; interchange through the, 83; Jesus in the office of the, 51; Lamb is the, 8; mission of the, 136; office of the Man, 104; one who holds the office of the, 102; Only Begotten, 93, 146; in Paul, 78; person that is capable of inviting the Son into his temple, 222; power of the, 276; and the Son of man, 55, 68, 87, 161–162; within you, 70

Son of man, 43, 45, 339; come down from heaven, 146; Enoch, 80; "...even so must the Son of man be lifted up," 303; explained, 55, 62; Ezekiel, 40–46; in four phases, 42; initiations of, 100; Jesus, 51–52; likeness of, 366; Paul, 78; prays in the words of Jesus, 74; resurrection of, 77; and the Son of God, 51, 68, 87, 161–162; unexpected coming of, 82; walking the earth as the Lord from heaven, 75; who ascends into heaven, 160; who may freely interact with the ascended masters, 165; within you, 70, 242

Song, new, 117, 118, 138

Sonship, 68; co-equal, 88, 181; fallen ones jealous of, 107; gift of, 85, 146; initiation of, 144. *See also* Son

Soul: and the adoption of sons, 55; and the alchemical marriage, 292; calling forth of the, 223; interchange of the Spirit with the, 83; keys to reunion of the Spirit with the, 87; and the quickening spirit, 45; and Spirit, 81; takes flight, 200; that has receded into a coma, 223; weakened identity of, 221–222; who does not want to be disturbed, 225; who is received into heaven, 284

Soul awareness, spheres of, 283. *See also* Solar awareness

Soulless creation, 208, 209, 289, 361

South gate(s): of the city, 173; of the City Foursquare, 58; diagram of, 140, 248; flying Eagle on the, 166; Guru on the, 168; initiation of, 137, 226, 248, 274; Mother flame on the, 134; office of the flying Eagle on, 164, 242; in Spirit and Matter, 339; under the flying Eagle, 268; of the upper and lower spheres, 282

South side of the City Foursquare, 97, 337

Sphinx, 61

Spirit(s): and Matter, 30, 97, 115; and soul, 81; antithesis of, 335; crystal sphere of, 5; interchange of Matter and, 164; interchange of the soul with the, 83; keys to reunion of thy soul with the, 87; quickened and quickening, 50; quickening, 43, 44, 50, 55, 56, 59,

70, 80; seven, 93, 117, 216; that 'peep and mutter', 256
Spoilers, 37, 39, 209
Star: binary, 232; morning, 14; six-pointed, 7, 106, 339; star centers, 231; unfoldment of the five-pointed, 242
Station(s) of the cross, 137, 166; first, fourth, and sixth, 20; fourth, 18. *See also* Cross
Staying power, 312
Stigmata, 31, 88
Stone: corner, 324; lively, 322; name written in the white, 233; of Scone, 297; sacred *tone,* 125; *tone* of sacrifice, 114; which the builders rejected, 125–126; white, 125
STOP, 333
Stranger that is within thy gate, 313
Subconscious momentums, 328
Success cult, 137
Summit University, 102, 276
"Sun behind the sun," 51
Sun of Even Pressure, 283
Superstition, 28–29
Surrender: bitterness of the path of, 154; dharma of, 100; of the image of the man, 28; initiation of, 59, 62, 77; path of, 84, 88, 154, 234, 312
Surya: and Cuzco, 232; call to, 246; decree to, 250
Sword(s), 189, 226; flaming blue, 277; of truth, 273, 276
Sylphs, 31

T'ai chi, 329
Tablets, given to Moses, 37
Tammuz, wife of Baal, 361
Tao, 258
Tares and wheat, 184, 286
Taurus, 24; Great Guru in, 61; hierarch of, 278; Initiation of Service under, 77; initiators under, 58

Teacher(s): Dharma of Selfhood realized in the, 234; false, 142; and the Teaching, 72; true, 226
Teaching(s): of the ascended masters, 134, 135, 186, 189; assimilation of the, 48; brought to remembrance, 147; Dharma of Selfhood realized in the, 234; false, 288; of the Great White Brotherhood, 63; intellectual knowledge of the, 327; new, 236; and the Teacher, 72; transferred through love, 258; true, 226, 259, 309. *See also* Dictations
Television commercial, 240
"Tell Them," 177–180
Temple of Victory, 119
Ten, test of the, 330
Ten minutes of meditation, 329–332
Tenth ray, 207, 245
Terra, requirement of the law for the saving of, 12
Theologians, false, 195
Theology, false, 197. *See also* Doctrine(s); Religion(s)
Third eye, 277, 301; opener of the door of the, 42
Third Ray: initiations of the, 140, 248; self-mastery on the, 248; study of the, 218; work of the initiates of the, 218
Threefold flame(s), 11, 138, 194; on the altar of your heart, 76; balanced, 163, 255; distillation of your own, 71; expanding, 252; within the heart, 78, 106, 203; hermetically sealed, 322; intergrating Principle of the, 55; of Life, 114; magnification of the, 155; nectar of the, 326; in the secret chamber of the heart, 143; of the two witnesses, 7; your, 184
Throat center, 172, 262. *See also* Chakra(s); Power center
Throne: beheld by Daniel, 2; great

Index

white, 13, 14, 21, 86, 93, 96, 117, 185, 231, 232, 242–243, 254; "Great White Throne Judgment," 207–210; lightnings and thunderings and voices which proceed out of, 19; threefold flame, 7
Thunders, seven, 152
Time and space, 332
Tomb: with Christ in the, 62; of Spirit/Matter, 60
Tongue(s): confounding of, 255; as the instrument of the Mother's sacred fire, 268; misuse of, 266; new, 262, 268; power of the, 261; sharpened like a serpent, 264, 265; speak with new, 226, 248, 251–253, 261; unloosing of, 173, 260, 262; wicked use of, 265. *See also* Angelic tongues
Torch: of the Goddess of Liberty, 49; of Sanat Kumara, 49
Transfiguration, 164–166, 352
Transmutation, 17; alchemical 'heat' of, 74
Tree of Life, 118, 336, 339
Tree of the knowledge of good and evil, 118, 357
Trials, fiery, 147
Tribes of Israel, 3, 8, 36–37, 49, 296, 310
Tribulation, great, 8, 96, 115, 137
Trinity, 2; chord of the, 255; gospel of the, 159; initiation of the indwelling, 51; magnetizing the Threefold Flame of, 324; outpictured within the saint, 170; persons of, 19; public assertion of the indwelling, 107; sponsorship of the indwelling, 299; three Persons of, 97
Trumpet sounding to "Come up hither...", 2
Trumpets, seven, 1
Truth, 220, 273
Tube of light, 334

Twenty-eight figures, 95
Twin flames: Adam and Eve, 142, 290; adversaries of, 208; in Eden, 7, 142–143; guarding the portals of the City Foursquare, 94; of the Holy Spirit, 5; representing the Twelve Hierarchies, 18; visualization for the union of, 329
Two-thirds level of the ruby cube, 61
Two witnesses, 4, 8, 97, 98, 138; angels of the LORD identified by the, 216; bear to you the true teachings of Jesus, 59; challenger of the, 157; dispensation of the, 243; at the east gate, 99; fire that will descend through the, 76; invoke the Presence of the, 207; Lady Kristine ascended in presence of our, 237; mission of the, 248, 276; and the mysteries of the Path of the Rose Cross, 37; office of the, 59, 135; and the office of the Man, 140, 209; path of the prophecy of the, 141; present work of the, 7; prophecy of the, 134, 158; revelations unto, 136; Sanat Kumara's coming in the person of, 49; standing on the east gate, 317; this dispensation of our, 63; those who occupy the office of, 95; where they witness, 115; witness unto the Truth, 272; to write down the mysteries of the ruby cube, 38. *See also* Messenger(s)

Unbelief, 175
Undines, 31
Ungrund, 24
United States, 26, 42. *See also* America
Upper Room, 68, 308, 312, 315, 343

Variance, 335
Vengeance: belongs to the LORD, 267; day of, 184

Venus, Lady Master, 14
Vestal virgins, 23
Vicarious atonement, 194, 245, 289
Victory, 37
Victory, Mighty: and his legions welcomed Sanat Kumara, 14; fallen ones of his band, 118
Vinegar mingled with gall, 318
Vineyard, parable of the husbandmen and the, 122–124
Violet fire, 65
Violet flame, 73, 279; chakras cleared by the, 276; of cosmic freedom, 278; mission of implanting the, 294. *See also* Seventh ray
Violet ray, 302
Viper(s): fastened on Paul's hand, 271; generation of, 285, 287. *See also* Serpent(s)
Virgo, 199
Viruses, 198
Vishnu, 25
Vision: immaculate, 17; power of, 276
Voice: of a great thunder, 117, 118; of many waters, 117, 118
Void, 19, 200, 216, 259; of the God Star, 233; inner realization of the, 232
Voodoo, 219
Vowel sounds, 257

Wales, 281, 297
Watchers, 81; challenge to, 109; confrontation with, 108; easy prey to the, 188; enemies of David, 263–265; fallen ones called, 143, 359–360; fallen ones of Victory's band, 118; false hierarchy of, 374; Herod represented the council of, 165; judgment of the, 265; mechanization of the, 289; pagan chiefs who are the, 297; seed of the, 106; and their godless creation, 192, 209; usurp the office of the Lion, 208

Watchman, watchmen: upon the four walls of the Holy City, 42; on the wall of the LORD, 58; of the Word, 51, 74
Water(s): of Life, 10–11, 315; outer nature expressed through the water vehicle, 168; quadrant, 84; rivers of living water, 11, 308–309, 314; Water-bearer of Aquarius, 43. *See also* Quadrant(s)
Wedding garment, 89, 198, 284; Deathless Solar Body, 283, 292
West, downward spiral of, 27. *See also* Western civilization
West gate, 226; approach it with care and careful consideration, 126; of the city, 158; of the City Foursquare, 58, 242; diagram of, 140, 248; disciples on, 137; gate of the future, 122; great multitude on, 96, 242, 274; Holy Spirit on, 192; initiation(s) of, 123, 125, 127–129, 248; Jesus on, 137; in Matter, 245; office of the Calf on, 164, 242; saints on, 133, 138; the Calf on, 126–127; thy initiation on, 191; Transfiguration on, 163
West side of the City Foursquare, 129
Western civilization, 26. *See also* West
Wheat and tares, 184
White fire, arc of, 303
White fire sun: meditation upon, 329–332; of the Mother, 324
White flame nucleus of the nonpermanent atom, 324
White Goddess, 89, 97, 114
White light, circle of, 334
Wholeness, 303
Whore, Great, 157, 208, 297
Wicked: are not forgiven, 82; power of the Word known by the seed of the, 263; seed of the, 39, 265, 266; seed of the Wicked One, 184, 185

Will of Alpha, 330
Will of God: devotion to, 173; family relationship set upon the rock of, 228; longing to fulfill, 79; transformation of consciousness in order to do, 154
Wind, sound of the, 262
Wine of the Spirit, 122
Winepress, 137; and the parable of the vineyard and husbandmen, 122–123, 125
Wisdom: ageless, 178; of Omega, 330
Witchcraft, 219
Witches, 210, 297
Wolves in sheep's clothing, 103; in church and state, 189; lie of the, 193; who lead their congregations in prayers of malintent, 219
Woman: archetype of, 64, 84; clothed with the Sun, 4, 23, 49, 140, 210, 248; crowned with twelve stars, 115; enmity between Serpent and, 289; of Genesis and Revelation, 291; Sanat Kumara occupies the office of, 160, 205; signs of her appearing, 226; Word and Work of the woman and her seed, 248
Word, 261; affirmation I AM is the, 203; ascension coil built by the spoken, 268; assimilation of, 50; become the, 305; command of, 263; continuity of, 236; daily affirmation of, 233; exercise of, 174; and the fall of Satan and of Serpent, 273; four stages of the Incarnation of, 161; grand ritual of the spoken and unspoken, 215; incarnate, 145, 324; incarnation of the, 322; initiation of the power of the, 171; intoning the, 259; invocation of the, 129; and language, 255; lawful implementation of the, 213; mental thrust of the, 333; misuse of the, 266; power of the spoken, 261, 262, 268; power of the word known by the seed of the wicked, 263–265; published, 63; rejection of the, 187; sacred fire of the, 257; saints exercising the power of the, 173; science of the, 257, 266, 284; science of the spoken, 130, 136, 253, 278; spoken, 26, 65, 256, 264, 299; those who experience it literally and in actuality, 79; utterance of the, 254; whence there proceed lightnings, thunderings and voices, 7; your instrumentation of the, 283. *See also* Decree(s); Invocation
Works, greater, 193, 204
World Teachers: conferment of the mantle of the, 102; initiations of the, 89; Jesus and Kuthumi, 88; mantle of the, 108; office of the Man occupied by, 100; representatives of, 342; sacred fire transmitted by the, 173; seminar of the, 69; those who serve under, 345
Wrathful deities, 256

Yahweh, 24
YHVH, 275, 292
Yod(s), 23, 28
YOD HE VAU HE, 34, 347
Youth, conditions among the, 241

Z-ray, 344–345
Zechariah, 281, 338, 341
Zion, 344

TITLES FROM THE SUMMIT LIGHTHOUSE LIBRARY®

The Opening of the Seventh Seal

Inner Perspectives

Morya I

Community

Wanting to Be Born: The Cry of the Soul

Walking with the Master: Answering the Call of Jesus

TITLES FROM SUMMIT UNIVERSITY PRESS®

Fallen Angels and the Origins of Evil

Kabbalah: Key to Your Inner Power

Reincarnation: The Missing Link in Christianity

The Lost Years of Jesus

The Lost Teachings of Jesus

The Human Aura

Saint Germain On Alchemy

Saint Germain's Prophecy for the New Millennium

Soul Reflections: Many Lives, Many Journeys

Lords of the Seven Rays

The Chela and the Path

Dossier on the Ascension

Understanding Yourself

Prayer and Meditation

Vials of the Seven Last Plagues

Mary's Message for a New Day

A Spiritual Approach to Parenting

Wanting to Live: Overcoming the Seduction of Suicide

The Great White Brotherhood in the Culture, History and Religion of America

CLIMB THE HIGHEST MOUNTAIN® SERIES:
The Path of the Higher Self
The Path of Self-Transformation
The Masters and the Spiritual Path
The Path of Brotherhood
The Path of the Universal Christ
The Masters and Their Retreats
*Predict Your Future:
Understand the Cycles of the Cosmic Clock*

MEET THE MASTER SERIES:
Afra: Brother of Light
Saint Germain: Master Alchemist

POCKET GUIDES TO PRACTICAL SPIRITUALITY SERIES:
Karma and Reincarnation
Alchemy of the Heart
Your Seven Energy Centers
Soul Mates and Twin Flames
Violet Flame to Heal Body, Mind and Soul
The Art of Practical Spirituality
How to Work with Angels
Creative Abundance
Access the Power of Your Higher Self
The Creative Power of Sound

For information about The Summit Lighthouse Library and Summit University Press, to place an order, or to receive a free catalog of books and products, please contact:

The Summit Lighthouse Library
PO Box 5000, Corwin Springs, MT 59030-5000 USA
Tel: 1-800-245-5445 or 406-848-9500
Fax: 1-800-221-8307 or 406-848-9555
E-mail: tslinfo@tsl.org • www.tsl.org

Mark L. Prophet and Elizabeth Clare Prophet are pioneers of modern spirituality and internationally renowned authors. For more than 40 years the Prophets have published the teachings of the immortal saints and sages of East and West known as the ascended masters. Together they have given the world a new understanding of the ancient wisdom as well as a path of practical mysticism.

Their books, available in fine bookstores worldwide, have been translated into more than 20 languages and are sold worldwide.